THE BEST AMERICAN NEWSPAPER NARRATIVES, VOLUME TWO

THE BEST AMERICAN NEWSPAPER NARRATIVES, VOLUME TWO

George Getschow, editor

Writer-in-Residence, The Mayborn Literary Nonfiction Conference

Number 2 in the Mayborn Best
American Newspaper Narrative Series

University of North Texas Press

Mayborn Graduate Institute of Journalism

Denton, Texas

10 9 8 7 6 5 4 3 2 1

Permissions:
University of North Texas Press
1155 Union Circle #311336
Denton, TX 76203-5017

The paper used in this book meets the minimum requirements of the
American National Standard for Permanence of Paper for Printed Library
Materials, z39.48.1984. Binding materials have been chosen for durability.

Cataloging-in-Publication Data is available from the Library of Congress
ISBN 978-1-57441-595-7 (pbk. : alk. paper) –
ISBN 978-1-57441-604-6 (ebook)

The Best American Newspaper Narratives, Volume Two is Number
2 in the Mayborn Best American Newspaper Narrative Series

The electronic edition of this book was made possible
by the support of the Vick Family Foundation.

TABLE OF CONTENTS

vi   BEST AMERICAN NEWSPAPER NARRATIVES, VOL. 2

Last Voyage of the *Bounty*: *Tampa Bay Times*
    By Michael Kruse 303

Alone on the Hill: The Arizona Republic Online
    By Shaun McKinnon 369

Almost Justice: The Beau Zabel Murder: *The Philadelphia Inquirer*
    By Mike Newall 443

Together Despite All: *The Boston Globe*
    By Sarah Schweitzer 487

The Best American Newspaper Narratives, Volume Two

The Best American Newspaper Narratives, Volume Two

George Getschow

Ten years ago, I stood in the back of a giant hotel ballroom in Boston craning to hear Tom Wolfe, the guru of a swashbuckling movement called "New Journalism," issue a dire warning. The occasion was the Nieman Conference on Narrative Journalism, and 1000 journalists and editors from around the world were present.

"It would be a shame to lose print journalism, which explains why and puts things in context, but it could easily happen," Wolfe said, because readers were already turning to the Internet for news that was instantly available, 24 hours a day, seven days a week.

Instead of giving readers the literary equivalent of white bread to satisfy their craving for nourishing stories, Wolfe called on his disciples— advocates of a bold and audacious literary form of nonfiction storytelling that uses dialogue, point of view, scene-by-scene construction and other dramatic techniques—to fulfill readers intellectually and emotionally, to move them, to make them feel more human. Narrative journalism, he said, is needed now more than ever to show the "emotional side" of a story.

"You are riding the wave of the most important writing done today," Wolfe proclaimed in his keynote address. "The future is yours. Go get 'em! The time is right."

I wondered then, and now, if Wolfe, heralded as one of the "pioneers" of New Journalism, might have forgot to set his watch. The term "new journalism," in fact, was originally coined in 1887 by Matthew Arnold, the assistant editor of Britain's *Pall Mall Gazette*, to describe the reform-minded paper's vivid, bold and dramatic way of telling stories of human exploitation—ways that connected emotionally with its readers. "The Victorian social reporters" —Arnold's generation—"and the American muckrakers who followed them, aimed at a factual literature of modern industrial life," writes Kevin Kerrane, in *The Art of Fact: A Historical Anthology of Literary Journalism.* "Their literary touches came less from artistic design than from the writers' sense of moral or political urgency: a determination to dramatize the reality of poverty, prostitution and prejudice."

A decade after Arnold coined the term "new journalism," Lincoln Steffens, the new city editor of the *New York Commercial Advertiser*, claimed literary journalism as his brand. Steffens "set out to create a paper that would have "literary charm as well as daily information"[1] and portray the news in a way that would connect to larger, universal truths about the human condition. Reporters learned from Steffens that context and empathy were a higher calling in telling true-crime stories than titillation and indignation.

> Here, Cahan, is a report that a man has murdered his wife, a rather bloody, hacked up crime. We don't care about that. But there's a story in it. That man loved that woman well enough to cut her all to pieces. If you can find out just what happened between

that wedding and this murder, you will have a novel for yourself and a short story for me. Go on now, take your time, and get his tragedy, as a tragedy.[2]

In taking this more artistic approach to nonfiction storytelling, Steffens realized he had to hire reporters at the *Commercial Advertiser* who weren't bound by journalistic convention. His aim was to hire reporters who possessed the sensibilities and imagination of fiction writers. As Steffens put it, he looked to hire "writers....not newspaper men but writers."[3]

To determine if his recruits were "writers" or "newspaper men," Steffens gave them a test: "go and see and write the difference between Fifth Avenue and Broadway or Thirty-sixth and Thirty-seventh Streets." Steffens claimed "the concentration of the staff on the technique in writing made them better reporters" and that readers benefitted from the results.[4]

But Steffens, like Tom Wolfe, was considered a maverick by other newspapermen of the era. At the same time that Steffens was counting on the publication of compelling narratives to capture readers, other major New York newspapers turned to the telegraph, or "wire," to grab them. To appeal to a much wider audience in the mid-19th century, many newspapers decided they had to deliver the news in a non-partisan, disengaged fashion. Some academics called this dispassionate approach to the news "objectification."

Objectification gave rise to the "inverted pyramid," a storytelling structure in which the who, what, when, where and why were summarized at the top of the story, followed by other "facts" in declining order of importance. The inverted pyramid fulfilled the industry's quest for "objectification" —the generic neutralization of news. The industry became convinced that shorter, nonpartisan and, for the most part, bland reports (leaving out all scene-setting, atmosphere, mood, color and meaning) that could be shared and printed in any newspaper or magazine, was their means to salvation.

Many journalists at the time lamented the telegraph's impact on storytelling, just as journalists today bemoan the impact of the Internet. Writing in the *Atlantic Monthly* in 1891, W.J. Stillman, a *New York Times* correspondent and critic of the telegraph, complained that "America has in fact transformed journalism from what it once was, the periodical expression of the thought of the time, the opportune record of the questions and answers of contemporary life, into an agency for collecting, condensing and assimilating the trivialities of the entire human existence...the effect is disastrous."[5]

The impact of the telegraph on the evolution of the inverted pyramid and other homogenized news is child's play compared to the revolutionary impact of technology on news generation today. Last year, for example, the Associated Press, announced that it was using "automation technology" in place of human reporters to generate thousands of sports and business stories.

At first, AP announced its automated system for churning out earnings reports and other business stories still required "a human touch." But now AP is fully automated, meaning that computers are generating stories and sending them out to the wire "without human intervention," according to a spokesman, making it possible for AP to greatly expand its business and sports coverage. "This will mean thousands of more stories on the AP wire, which will remain unmatched in the industry," Barry Bedlan, AP's deputy director of sports products said in a prepared statement. "Every college sports town will have some level of coverage."

AP's "robot reporters," of course, are a logical outcome of severing the news from the narrative. But many human reporters inside and outside AP worry that the wire service's full-speed-ahead march toward automating more of its coverage runs the risk of turning news into a commodity and AP itself, in W.J. Stillman's words, into an "agency for collecting, condensing and assimilating the trivialities of the entire human existence."

Some working journalists fear that as newspaper revenues continue to shrink, it's only a matter of time before "robot reporters" find their way into newsrooms across America. But if the robots show up, they'll likely face the wrath and resistance of writers and editors who remain ferocious guardians of the long tradition of storytelling in American newspapers.

No matter how many robots show up in the newsroom, it still takes an actual human being to tell a story that intrigues, delights, surprises, haunts and touches us at the deepest core of our being. "To reveal human emotion, readers still need story," says Bill Marvel, a Dallas-based author and literary journalist. "Facts don't give you goose bumps."

***

The great ideological divide between inverted pyramid-style journalism designed to be objective and literary journalism designed to give readers goose bumps has prevailed now among working journalists for more than a century. Scholars blame technology for creating the rift. Before the telegraph and before the Internet, there was very little distinction between literature and journalism. The "new journalists" of the 19th century — Mark Twain, writing for *Territorial Enterprise* in Nevada; Lafcadio Hearn for the *Cincinnati Commercial*, the *New Orleans Daily City Item* and the *Times-Democrat*; and Stephen Crane for *The New York Press* —achieved literary acclaim for their journalism and fiction, and most readers had a difficult time distinguishing one from the other.

Scholars have also had this difficulty. Some contend that literary journalists like Twain, Hearn and Crane paved the way for the New Journalists of the 20th century, writers like Tom Wolfe, Gay Talese, Joan Didion and Hunter S. Thompson. "Twain's wit, his style, his pithy observations and mordant insights, along with his frontier-honed skill at cutting through the sham, hypocrisy, pretense and show to get at the bare-boned reality of a thing, made his work sought after then and makes it readable and pertinent yet," writes Thomas Connery, the author of *A Sourcebook of American Literary Journalism*.

Lafcadio Hearn, a literary journalist and fiction writer, was so well versed in Poe that his friends in New Orleans called him "The Raven," says Christopher Benfrey, editor of *Lafcadio Hearn: America Writings.* "He knew his Baudelaire by heart. One thing he learned from Poe is that you've got to try to enter into the psyche of the criminal if you really want to make crime and criminality feel immediate to the reader."

In his narrative, "Gibbeted: Execution of a Youthful Murderer," published in the *Cincinnati Commercial* in August 26, 1876, Hearn makes his readers sympathetic to "a poor young criminal" convicted of killing a man during a drunken melee in Cincinnati. As it turns out, public executions, then and now, don't always go as planned:

> The next instant the Sheriff pressed the lever with his foot, the drop opened as though in electric response, the thin rope gave way at the crossbeam above, and the body of the prisoner fell downward and backward on the floor of the corridor, behind the scaffold screen. "My God. My God!" cried Freeman, with a subdued scream; "give me that other rope, quick." It had been laid away for use "in case the first rope should break," we were told.
>
> The poor young criminal had fallen on his back, apparently unconscious, with the broken rope around his neck, and the black cap vailing his eyes. The reporter knelt beside him and felt his pulse. It was beating slowly and regularly. Probably the miserable boy thought then, if he could think at all, that he was really dead— dead in darkness, for his eyes were vailed—dead and blind to this world, but about to open his eyes upon another. The awful hush immediately following his fall might have strengthened this dim idea. But then came gasps, and choked sobs from the spectators; the hurrying of feet, and the horrified voice of Deputy Freeman calling, "For God's sake, get me that other rope, quick!" Then a pitiful groan came from beneath the black cap.
>
> "My God! Oh, my God!"
> "Why, I ain't dead—I ain't dead!"

Is Hearn's account literature or journalism?

Perhaps no 19th century writer blurred the line between journalism and literature, between fact and fiction, more seamlessly than Stephen Crane, the author of *The Red Badge of Courage.* Surviving a shipwreck off the coast of Florida while traveling to Cuba to work as a newspaper correspondent, Crane and other crew members spent 30 harrowing hours in a 10-foot lifeboat tossed about the high seas.

"Stephen Crane's Own Story," was published in *The New York Press* shortly after the disaster. Though considered a work of journalism by most scholars, it employs many literary devices: first-person narration, dialogue, graphic detail, poetic language, haunting imagery, personification and the foreshadowing of death.

As the S.S. *Commodore* left the port of Jacksonville and turned her bow toward the distant sea, Crane wrote, the ship "gave three longs blasts of her whistle, which even to this time impressed me with their sadness. Somehow they sounded as wails."

Far out at sea, heading toward Cuba, the ship struck a sandbar and began swallowing water faster than a bucket brigade could scoop it out. Orders went out to lower the lifeboats. Crane wrote:

> Now the whistle of the Commodore had been turned loose, and if there ever was a voice of despair and death, it was in the voice of this whistle. It had gained a new tone. It was as if its throat was already choked by the water, and this cry on the sea at night, with a wind blowing the spray over the ship, and the waves roaring over the bow, and swirling white along the decks, was to each of us probably a song of man's end.

Crane penned another narrative of the *Commodore* disaster called "The Open Boat" that was published about five months later in *Scribner's Magazine.* Like Crane's newspaper account, the action tracks the author's experiences and events following the shipwreck—except this time the story is narrated by an anonymous "correspondent." None of the facts or the characters were invented. And both pieces explore the universal themes of survival, solidarity and man vs nature.

Yet "The Open Boat" is exalted by the academy as original and inventive literature, categorized as a short story in numerous collections of American fiction. So how is a reader to regard "The Open Boat" —as fact or fiction? More than 118 years after the *Commodore* sank, scholars are still deeply divided over the question. But at least one scholar maintains that if the Academy had a category for "literary nonfiction" in 1897 when "The Open Boat" was published, it would never have been classified as fiction.

"We must consider the possibility that, no matter the category in which it was published, Crane's story is entirely factual with no element of fiction whatsoever," concludes Stefanie Bates Eye, in an academic study of Crane's works. "In fact, had 'The Open Boat' been published in 1965 rather than in 1897, it would have certainly qualified as literary nonfiction." [6]

Richard Rhodes, a Pulitzer Prize-winning author who writes both fiction and nonfiction, believes that the worst thing that ever befell literary journalism and narrative nonfiction happened in 1867, when a Boston librarian designated the kind of writing we do with a negative: **non**-fiction, meaning "**Not** fiction.... Reminding us that we dwell in the swampy depths beneath poetry and fiction's golden-lit Olympus."

When "non-fiction" was split off from fiction, nonfiction was devalued in the eyes of the Academy —a terrible tragedy, Rhodes says. He considers narrative nonfiction—or "verity," as he likes to call it—a more challenging art form. "I've written fiction, and I've written verity, and I can say with confidence that verity is in no way fiction's fool," he told a group of narrative writers and editors at the Mayborn Literary Nonfiction Conference a few years ago. "It's actually more challenging to write than fiction, since it adds to all the challenges of writing fiction the further challenge of building it from elements of the real world, elements with external referents. Fiction you can just make up. Verity you have to verify. No, verity is the new workhorse. It carries all the freight of fiction but adds the density of fact. The density and the rigor... Verity, if you do it well, not only uses everything: it demands it."

Certainly no scholar or reader could claim that the prize-winning newspaper narratives gathered in this collection are "fiction's fool." Taken together, the Best American Newspaper Narratives showcase the same imagination, artistic design, characterization, intimate scenes, graphic detail and other literary devices employed in the best short stories produced in America today.

Shaun McKinnon's "Alone on the Hill" in the *Arizona Republic*, is a disquieting tale, one that will keep you up at night during a lightning storm. The opening scene is cinematic. A group of battle-hardened fire fighters dig in on Yarnell Hill and watch helplessly as a wall of fire, sparked by lightning, comes roaring down on them. Earlier in the day, the fire-fighting crew, known as the "Granite Mountain Hotshots," had hiked up the ridge to protect the small town of Yarnell from an advancing blaze. But then the wind whipped the fire back on them. Now, their escape route is cut off. No one could see the hotshots at the moment they faced the inferno on Yarnell Hill. But in this gripping man vs nature narrative, McKinnon muses that the "crew and the fire had not crossed paths by chance. They were driven by far greater forces: The human spirit, the fury of nature and the power of the past."

The dramatic saga of the sinking of the 53-year-old wooden ship, *The Bounty*, one hundred miles off the Outer Banks of North Carolina in October 2012 inspired two newspaper narratives—"The Last Voyage of the *Bounty*" by Michael Kruse of the *Tampa Bay Times* and "Taken Under" by Aaron Applegate of the *Virginian-Pilot*—and both, deservedly, earned a place in the Best American Newspaper Narrative anthology. Like Crane's two very different narratives of the sinking of the *SS Commodore*—both the *Tampa Bay Times* narrative and the *Virginian-Pilot* narrative track the dramatic action and harrowing events following the shipwreck. Large swaths of both stories could easily be mistaken for fiction, just as Crane's

"The Open Boat" was. And both pieces explore the universal themes of survival, solidarity and man vs nature.

Both narratives begin with *The Bounty* being torn apart as it sails directly into the path of Hurricane Sandy. The deckhands, realizing the ship is doomed, jump overboard into the frothing seas as the ship begins to implode. The writer, Michael Kruse, sets the scene as skillfully as any fiction writer.

> In the dark, in the wet, whirling roar of Hurricane Sandy, on a ship tipping so badly the deck felt like a steep, slick roof, the desperate, damaged sailor searched for a spot from which to jump. Close to the stern, he gripped the helm, now all but touching the water's high black churn. He let go and paddled and kicked in the buoyant but clumsy blood-orange suit he had wiggled into not long before. The ship spat up a heavy wooden grating, and it landed on his head. Crack. His adrenaline surged. He thrashed, straining to get away from the heaving ship, her three masts of tree trunk heft rearing up and slamming down like lethal mallets, her thinner, sharper spars piercing the surface like darts, the ropes of the rigging like tentacles, grabbing, yanking. Pffffft. The tip of a spar sliced down, catching the sailor, pushing him below. He gasped, choking on water, struggling back to where there was air.

In "Taken Under," Aaron Applegate of the *Virginian-Pilot* goes a step further. He puts us inside the head of Jessica Hewitt who just before *The Bounty* goes down jumped into the sea with her boyfriend. The weight of the heaving ship caught a rope tied to their harnesses that was keeping them afloat, dragging them under. Applegate mixes the deckhand's desperate actions and interior monologue, a fictional technique, to reveal what it's like to drown.

> *I don't have a chance*, Jess thought. A voice in her head pleaded: Not like this. Nobody is going to know.
>
> She clawed at the harness but couldn't rip it off.

She gnawed at the metal clip linking the rope to it, shearing off part of a tooth.

Underwater, her world slowed down. She thought about a comedian she liked who did a bit about terrible ways to die. Drowning was one of them.

Her body wanted her to breathe, breathe, breathe. The voice said: No, no, don't breathe! She couldn't help it. She inhaled the ocean.

In reading "Manhunt," a five-part narrative produced by a team of reporters for the *Los Angeles Times*, I was reminded of Lincoln Steffens telling his reporter at the *Commercial Appeal* covering a murder that context and empathy trump titillation and indignation. Christopher Dorner had been unceremoniously fired from the Los Angeles Police Department and was hell-bent for revenge—vowing to murder his former colleagues en masse.

Some writers might have refrained from offering the murderer's point of view. Not Christopher Goffard, who wrote "Manhunt." He knew, just as Steffens knew, that for readers to understand "the problem cop" they needed to get inside Dorner's head. An 11,000-word manifesto written by Dorner made that possible. "No one grows up and wants to be a cop killer," Dorner wrote. "It was against everything I've ever been...."

Another true-crime narrative, "Almost Justice" by Mike Newall of the *Philadelphia Inquirer*, is a taut, tightly-wound page turner, presented in 5 chapters that would be impossible for any reader to put down. The narrative opens as Beau Zabel, an aspiring teacher who has recently arrived in Philadelphia from Minnesota, immediately falls in love with the city.

Newall picks and chooses from a bag of details he's collected about the Minnesota transplant to illuminate Beau's character and personality. Beau had arrived on a Monday in a van with his mother, Lana. Beau unpacked his teaching supplies, a pocket Constitution, his childhood comforter, adorned with a red dinosaur wearing blue tennis shoes. Beau called his mother Momma. She called him Sunny Bunny. He grew up in a tidy, white-shingled house with red shutters and an American flag over the daisy garden. A wood-paneled bedroom with Grandpa's dusty hunting rifle encased on the wall. "The choking sweet smell" of the Hormel Plant, where Spam was made, Newall writes, wafted through his window.

In Philadelphia, Beau quickly landed a job at Starbucks, using his mother as a reference, and adopted a mangy orange Tabby named Jake, after Jake Chambers, a character in Stephen King's *Dark Tower* series. He walked the twelve blocks to Starbucks each day listening to tunes on his IPod. "Be careful," a coworker warned him. "It gets sketchy." But Beau wasn't worried, not at all. "He was brave and honest and principled," his cousin, Lauren Chaby said.

But walking home from work one night, just 42 days after he arrived in Philadelphia, some unknown assailant shot him from behind, the bullet entering below his left ear. He died instantly. His murderer took Beau's IPod, but left his wallet.

As any narrative writer will tell you, getting readers to care about our characters is the key to great storytelling. Our characters have to connect with them, emotionally. In Philadelphia, people did. Beau's death, and the hunt for his killer, became the talk of Philadelphia. The city would not rest until justice was done. Now, read Newall's narrative to find out if it was.

In nonfiction, how do you express the ineffable—a family facing the absence of their 7-year old boy gunned down by a madman? Eli Saslow, in his elegiac narrative, "Into the Lonely Quiet" in *The Washington Post*, shows us a father calling up photographs on his computer, desperately looking for "the right picture" of his son, Daniel, in the hope of inspiring politicians to change American gun laws.

When all the speeches, songs and homilies to the fallen children of Newtown, Conn. had faded away like green grass in winter, how does a family carry on without their child and with little hope that they'll ever find meaning in their loss? By asking the same question over and over again, the alliteration becomes a kind of wail.

> What was the meaning of the anger he felt lately while shopping at Costco, hoping one of the strangers in the aisles might be a gun nut who would recognize and approach him, so he had an excuse to shout back?

> What was the meaning of the endless tributes? A song performed in concert for Daniel because he liked music. A 5k race for Daniel because he liked to run. A mud festival for Daniel because he liked mud...

> And what was the meaning of their new nighttime routine? All four of them crammed into one room in a five-bedroom house, three on a queen bed and one on the futon so they could will one another through the night, Jackie up every few hours, Mark closing his eyes and thinking about Daniel, always hoping he might come to him in a dream, even though he never did.

What's it like to live with someone suffering from severe mental illness? To find out, another writer for *The Washington Post*, Stephanie McCrummen, went to Houston to hang out with a mother, Naomi Haskell, and her 19-year-old son, Spencer, suffering from early-stage schizophrenia. At a stoplight, the mother studies her son's demeanor: "how quiet he is, how stiffly he sits, hands in his lap, fingers fidgeting slightly, a tic that occasionally blooms into a full fluttering motion he makes with his hand, as if clearing invisible webs from his face."

She notices that her son's mouth is "not set in a smile or a frown but some line in between." She's worried that that "cloudy feeling" her son has spoken of before where his brain feels like it's "under a hair dryer," might return.

"How are you doing sweetie?" Naomi asks.

"Fine," Spencer says.

McCrummen's rendering of that scene reminds us of what the Russian biographer Henri Troyat, told us about telling details. "No detail must be neglected in art, for a button half undone may explain a whole side of a person's character... (their) inner life."

Spencer's mouth reveals more about the young man's "inner life" than interviewing a team of therapists ever could. With empathy and understanding, "Cloudy" takes us on a roller coaster ride through a world of hallucinations, paranoia, and depression, with frequent visits to the psychiatric hospital for electro convulsive therapy.

In Houston, at least Naomi can count on a network of psychiatric hospitals and therapists to treat her son's schizophrenia, and some apartment managers willing to rent rooms to the mentally ill. In Milwaukee, Debbie Sweeny isn't so lucky. Her son, Rob, diagnosed with schizoaffective disorder—a catch-all term for a brain disease that causes a combination of delusions, paranoia and mania—has spent the past six years tossed around in Milwaukee County's mental health system, "cycling week-to-week from house to hospital to homeless shelter."

Like thousands of other people in Milwaukee County, "Rob lives in a twilight zone—too sick to make it on his own, not getting the help he needs," writes Meg Kissinger of the Milwaukee Journal Sentinel Online.

In her emotionally-charged narrative, "Rob Sweeney," Kissinger uses an exchange of email correspondence between Rob's mother and Rob's caseworker, Steve Seidl, to reveal the depths of her frustrations with the caseworker assigned to her son.

> Seidl to Debbie: *"I don't think Rob should continue to be rewarded for his not cooperating with treatment."*

> Debbie to Seidl: *"I don't rescue him Steve... he shows up at my house, repeatedly, because you won't find him a place to stay. He can't be homeless!!"*

Seidl to Debbie: *"He tells you things to manipulate you, tug at your heart strings and make you feel sorry for him."*

Debbie to Seidl: *"This is ridiculous that he is mentally ill and has no place to sleep. He has no food, he doesn't even have his medicine!!! At the very, very least you should be driving out to him to give him his daily medication."*

In despair, Debbie sends Rob to California "hoping to find a better way for Rob to live." At first, Debbie's giddy. The Santa Clara County Mental Health Department told Debbie what she wants to hear—that they'll find Rob a place to stay and medicine to control his schizophrenia. Everything was looking up... until Rob stopped taking his anti-psychotic medication. Soon, Rob was back out on the street, leaving Debbie's dreams of providing her son a fresh start in ruins.

After a series of misadventures in California, Rob ends up back in Milwaukee, sleeping in hotels hear the airport, sometimes in his mother's garage and sometimes walking along the highway all night. Rob's case-worker eventually finds Rob temporary housing at a residential treatment center in Milwaukee. Shortly, however, the treatment center is named in a 2012 federal complaint as a hub for drug operations perpetuated by the owner, and is scheduled to close, leaving Rob's mother "at her wits end" once again.

Kissinger's tragic narrative teaches us how schizophrenia can, as Debbie says, "tear a mother away from her son." It also teaches us that in the lives of schizophrenics, there's seldom a neat and tidy ending to the story.

In the 1940s and 1950s, the U.S. Veterans Administration grappled with a perplexing question: How best to treat the psychological crises that afflict soldiers returning from war? Their remedy: lobotomies. In a story with shades of Ken Kesey's spellbinding novel, *One Flew Over the Cuckoo's Nest,* VA doctors lobotomized more than 1900 veterans at 50 hospitals authorized to perform the surgeries. In the mid-1950s, the development of the first antipsychotic drug ended the VA's lobotomy program. But in the "The Lobotomy Files," Michael M. Phillips narrative in *The Wall Street Journal* takes us on a shocking tour across the country to experience the lives of World War II veterans "gone terribly wrong."

Roman Tritz, a 90-year-old World War II bomber pilot from Wisconsin, remembers clearly his fight with the orderlies assigned to take him to a surgery room six decades ago to have a lobotomy. Phillips reconstructs the scene:

> The orderlies at the Veterans hospital pinned Mr. Tritz to the floor... He fought so hard that eventually they gave up. But the orderlies came back for him again on Wednesday, July 1, 1953, a few weeks before his 30th birthday. This time, the doctors got their way.

During eight years as a patient in the VA hospital in Tomah, Wis., Phillips reports that Tritz underwent 28 rounds of electroshock therapy, insulin-induced temporary comas and 66 treatments of high-pressure water sprays called the Scotch Douche and Needle Shower.

Tritz was formally discharged in 1957 after 2,272 days of being institutionalized. But Phillips tells us that his psychiatric symptoms—the voices, the delusions, the seizures—"ebbed and flowed" over the decades that followed. "He grew separated from his family and wary of friends, persecuted by thoughts of government conspiracies and the magnets he believes were placed in his head."

In the summer of 2012, VA doctors urged Tritz to undergo surgery to treat an intestinal condition. For months, he refused. Who could blame him? As Phillips writes, "He was reluctant to let VA doctors near him with a knife."

***

Mark Johnson of the Milwaukee Journal Sentinel had the challenge of striking just the right tone—and mood—for first year students at the Medical College of Wisconsin taking a human dissection course. It's the same challenge he would face if he were writing fiction. In Johnson's deft rendering of the students' first dissection, "The Course of Their Lives," readers would have an impossible time determining if it was fact or fiction. Thanks to Johnson's sensory details, we know the mood inside the room is almost suffocating.

> The steel table before them is actually a long, raised metallic box, almost a casket. Students open two doors on top, revealing a sunken interior. They step on bars at each end of the table, lifting the interior.

> Rising into view is a figure shrouded in white towels. A few pale toes jut out.

> The air thickens. An odorous wave of embalming fluid washes over the room.

> They unpack scalpels. They leave most of the towels draped over the cadaver, which lies face down. Only the back, where dissection begins, is uncovered. The skin is beige and wrinkly, more like a leather couch than someone's back.

> The students look at each other, then at the steel table.

> Who will make the first cut?

***

Eric Moskowitz's narrative in the *Boston Globe*, "Marathon Carjacking," about the nail-biting experience of a young Chinese entrepreneur carjacked and held hostage by the two Boston Marathon bombers offers so many lessons in narrative nonfiction that Roy Peter Clark, a senior scholar of the Poynter Institute, decided to "reverse engineer" the piece, deconstructing the story for writers, editors and readers "not just why it works, but how it works." Clark cites a dozen reasons why and how "Marathon Carjacking" works. But paramount to the success of the narrative is that it employs a non-linear structure for the sake of opening with a scene filled with action, drama and suspense—the stuff of good storytelling.

As Clark points out, the narrative "begins, like the ancient epics, *in medias res*—in the middle of things. There is no background information on where Danny was when the bombing took place. What we get instead is action, followed by more action:

> "The 26-year-old Chinese entrepreneur had just pulled his new Mercedes to the curb on Brighton Avenue to answer a text when an old sedan swerved behind him, slamming on the brakes. A man in dark clothes got out and approached the passenger window. It was nearly 11 p.m. last Thursday."

After the Boston Marathon Bombings, the city fathers and ordinary citizens spoke bravely about how the city wouldn't let terrorism defeat them. They appeared on television and were quoted in newspapers talking about their heroes, their strength and their resiliency. But inside the Sumner Redstone Burn Center, Sarah Schweitzer of the *Boston Globe* pulls back the curtain on another story out of sight of the cameras: doctors had to amputate Marc Fucarile's right leg above the knee and were contemplating cutting off his mangled foot on his other leg. There was no talk of heroes and resilience. Instead, Marc and his wife, Jen, were quarrelling. Jen "wants the old Marc back." But Marc can't give her his old self.

Schweitzer's narrative, "Together Despite All," exposes the great paradoxes and contradictions of one family's struggle to resume a "normal life" after the unthinkable happens. The bomb on Boylston Street had not only maimed Marc, it had "shattered their calibrated divisions of labor and love, the daily minuet of a life lived together," Schweitzer writes. "He was like so many of the Marathon day victims, transformed in an instant from a face in the crowd to the face of tragedy."

Months pass, but Marc's leg isn't getting any better. "Quite possibly, it's permanently mangled and unfixable," Schweitzer writes. And Marc and Jen's relationship isn't much better either, as they "funnel their anger and frustrations into one another." But they hang on and for their son's 6th birthday, they book a weekend at the Stoneham Elks Lodge, where Ninja Turtle party favor bags overflow on a folded table.

At the front of the room, Marc is DJing. For a minute, the arguing between Marc and Jen dissolves. From the speakers, Zac Brown croons:

> Gonna put the world away for a minute;
> Pretend I don't live in it;
> Sunshine gonna wash my blues away.

"Marc is playing the song for Jen. She stands still, tilts her head back, and hums."

Maybe, just maybe, the reader thinks, they'll survive the bombing afterall.

***

All the literary journalists in this collection recognize that they stand on the shoulders of the writers who came before them, giants like Mark Twain, Lafcadio Hearn, Stephen Crane. These early pioneers forged a new literary genre long before there was a name for it. Today, whatever you prefer to call it—new journalism, literary journalism, narrative nonfiction or even verity—the good news is that it's still growing, still evolving, still daring to be different.

As Tom Wolfe said, "The future is yours. Go get 'em! The time is right."

NOTES

1. Kaplan, Justin. *Lincoln Steffens: Portrait of a Great American Journalist.* Simon & Schuster, 2013. p 83
2. Steffens, Lincoln. The Autobiography of Lincoln Steffens, Volume 1 New York : Harcourt, Brace and World, 1931 p 317
3. ———, *The Autobiography of Lincoln Steffens,* Volume 1 New York : Harcourt, Brace and World, 1931 p 314
4. ———, *The Autobiography of Lincoln Steffens,* Volume 1 New York : Harcourt, Brace and World, 1931 p 321-322
5. Stead, William Thomas, editor, *The Review of Reviews, Volume 4* Office of the Review of Reviews, 1891 p 499
6. Eye, Stefanie Bates, "Fact, Not Fiction: Questioning Our Assumptions about Crane's 'The Open Boat'." Academic Journal, *Studies in Short Fiction* , Vol. 35, No. 1 , Winter 1998

ACKNOWLEDGMENTS

The Mayborn Literary Nonfiction Conference has become a kind of Mecca for narrative nonfiction writing in America.

Over the past eleven years, the Mayborn has conducted writing contests and workshops to encourage journalists and nonfiction authors across the country to produce "original" nonfiction literature in the form of reported narratives, personal essays and book manuscripts. The Mayborn's writing contests are now attracting writers from around the country in search of new literary plateaus—staff writers for *The New York Times*, *Village Voice*, the *Atlanta Journal/Constitution*, freelancers for *GQ* and *Outside* magazine, and other journalists and authors devoted to the narrative craft.

And we've awarded major cash awards and publishing opportunities in our literary anthology, *Ten Spurs*, for the ten "best of the best" submissions to the Mayborn. Now, you're holding in your hands our second anthology, aptly named *The Best American Newspaper Narratives, Volume Two*. It grew out of the vision of Jim Moroney, publisher of *The Dallas Morning News*, who urged us to launch a writing contest for narratives previously published in the nation's dailies. He even offered to fund it. How could we say no?

The contest was a smashing success during our first year, and our second year was even better. Nearly every major daily in America participated. For the second year in a row, our first-place winner was Eli Saslow, a national enterprise writer for *The Washington Post* for "Into the Lonely," about a family trying to find meaning in the loss of their 7-year-old son who died during the December 2012 mass shooting at

Sandy Hook Elementary in Newtown, Conn. "Into the Lonely" was also the 2014 winner of the Pulitzer Prize for Explanatory Journalism. Saslow, who lives in Portland, Oregon, is a speaker at the 2015 Mayborn Literary Nonfiction Conference.

Saslow received $5,000 and free registration to attend last year's conference. In 2013, Saslow won the inaugural Best American Newspaper Narrative Writing Contest for "Life of a Salesman."

Second place and $2,000 went to Eric Moskowitz, a reporter at the *Boston Globe*, for his gripping narrative, "Marathon Carjacking," about the nail-biting experience of a young Chinese entrepreneur carjacked and held hostage by the two Boston Marathon bombers.

Mark Johnson, a reporter for the Milwaukee Journal Sentinel Online, claimed the third place and $1,000 for "The Course of Their Lives," about the harrowing experiences of first year students at the Medical College of Wisconsin taking a human dissection course. His narrative, "I Boy," was selected a "notable narrative" by our judges in 2013.

Our judges selected three runners-up and six notable narratives for publication in our new anthology, *The Best American Newspaper Narratives, Volume Two*. The runners-up were Christopher Goffard of *The Los Angeles Times* for "Manhunt"; Stephanie McCrummen of *The Washington Post* for "A Cloudy Feeling"; and Michael M. Phillips of *The Wall Street Journal* for "The Lobotomy Files."

Six "notable narratives" were also selected by our judges: Aaron Applegate of *The Virginian-Pilot* for "Taken Under"; Meg Kissinger of the Milwaukee Journal Sentinel Online for "Rob Sweeney"; Michael Kruse of the *Tampa Bay Times*, for "The Last Voyage of the *Bounty*"; Shaun McKinnon of the *Arizona Republic* for "Alone on the Hill"; Mike Newall of the *Philadelphia Inquirer* for "Almost Justice"; and Sarah Schweitzer of the *Boston Globe* for "Together, Despite All."

"With the focus on narrative journalism that these awards represent," said Moroney, the *Dallas Morning News* publisher, "we hope they will encourage more compelling, important and interesting narrative stories that attract and retain subscribers."

Reading the dazzling prose and reportage represented inside *The Best American Newspaper Narratives, Volume Two,* should remove any doubt that Jim's hope will be realized. As you read the stories in this compendium, I hope you'll agree that our highly acclaimed narrative journalists and editors who spent weeks reading, evaluating and finally selecting the 12 best narrative submissions submitted from newspapers from East Coast to West Coast picked a collection of stories that rivals the best newspaper narratives produced in America today.

Our contest judges were Maria Carrillo, senior editor at *The Houston Chronicle*; Roy Peter Clark, a senior scholar at the Poynter Institute; Roger Thurow, a former foreign correspondent for *The Wall Street Journal*; Michele Weldon, assistant professor of journalism at Northwestern University; and Kelley Benham French, a former narrative writer for the *Tampa Bay Times,* who is now a member of the faculty at Indiana University. Their full bios appear nearby.

Publication of *The Best American Newspaper Narratives, Volume Two,* as well as an ebook version, was made possible by the Vick Family Foundation. Fran Vick and her family have been long-time friends and supporters of the Mayborn Conference and UNT Press, and we are deeply grateful to them. We also owe a debt of gratitude to Eric Nishimoto, an award-winning writer and illustrator who designed the eye-popping cover for this year's edition, and to Karen DeVinney, Assistant Director/ Managing Editor of UNT Press, who edited the collection with competency and patience with a writer-in-residence who kept missing deadlines. And finally, to Ron Chrisman, the director of UNT Press, who deserves our accolades for his commitment to publishing extraordinary "literary nonfiction" in all its forms to enrich the lives of readers.

Into the Lonely Quiet

The Washington Post

June 9, 2013

By Eli Saslow

In Newtown, Conn.

They had promised to try everything, so Mark Barden went down into the basement to begin another project in memory of Daniel. The families of Sandy Hook Elementary were collaborating on a Mother's Day card, which would be produced by a marketing firm and mailed to hundreds of politicians across the country. "A difference-maker," the organizers had called it. Maybe if Mark could find the most arresting photo of his 7-year-old son, people would be compelled to act.

It hardly mattered that what Mark and his wife, Jackie, really wanted was to ignore Mother's Day altogether, to stay in their pajamas with their two surviving children, turn off their phones and reward themselves for making it through another day with a glass of Irish whiskey neat.

"Our purpose now is to force people to remember," Mark said, so down he went into his office to sift through 1,700 photos of the family they had been.

The Bardens had already tried to change America's gun laws by studying the Second Amendment and meeting with President Obama in the Oval Office. They had spoken at tea party rallies, posed for People magazine and grieved on TV with Katie Couric. They had taken advice from a public relations firm, learning to say "magazine limits" and not "magazine bans," to say "gun responsibility" and never "gun control." When none of that worked, they had walked the halls of Congress with a bag of 200 glossy pictures and beseeched lawmakers to look at their son: his auburn hair curling at the ears, his front teeth sacrificed to a soccer collision, his arms wrapped around Ninja Cat, the stuffed animal that had traveled with him everywhere, including into the hearse and underground.

Almost six months now, and so little had gotten through. So maybe a Mother's Day card. Maybe that.

Mark turned on his computer and began looking for the right picture. "Something lighthearted," he said. "Something sweet." He had been sitting in the same chair Dec. 14, when he received an automated call about a Code Red Alert, and much of the basement had been preserved in that moment. Nobody had touched the foosball table, because Daniel had been the last to play. His books and toy trains sat in their familiar piles, gathering dust. The basement had always been Daniel's space, and some days Mark believed he could still smell him here, just in from playing outside, all grassy and muddy.

Now it was Daniel's face staring back at him on the computer screen, alit in an orange glow as he blew out seven candles on a birthday cake in September.

"Oh God. His last birthday," Mark said, rubbing his forehead, scanning to the next photo, knowing the chronology that came next.

Daniel dressed as an elf for Halloween. Daniel grinning after his hair was cut short on Dec. 4. Daniel in a video taken a week before his death, wearing reindeer horns and carrying cookies to the neighbor's house. "Bye, Dad," he was saying.

Next came a photo Mark had taken early that last morning. He and Daniel had been lying on the couch, half asleep, after the rest of the family had left for school. Daniel had noticed how the sunrise and the Christmas lights were reflecting on the window, like a red-and-orange kaleidoscope. "Wow," he had said. Mark had grabbed his camera and taken a picture of the window, and now he was searching that picture for a trace of Daniel's reflection in the glass, zooming in, running his fingers against the screen.

"He has to be in here," Mark said. Maybe he had taken another. He flipped to the next picture, but it was from four days later, of a police car parked in front of their house.

It sometimes felt to Mark in these moments like his grief was still deepening, like the worst was yet to come. After the gunfire, the funerals, the NRA protests and the congressional debates, they were finally coming into the lonely quiet. They were coming to the truth of what Newtown would become. Would it be the transformative moment in American gun policy that, in those first days, so many had promised? Or another Columbine, Virginia Tech, Gabby Giffords, Aurora — one more proper noun added to an ever-growing list? The FBI had closed its temporary Newtown office. Politicians in Washington were moving on to other issues. Scariest of all to Mark, he was starting to forget little things, too, losing pieces of Daniel to the recesses of his mind, so he had started a journal to log memories before they disappeared.

"I'm always one minute farther away from my life with Daniel," he had written one day. "The gulf keeps getting bigger."

He returned upstairs with four photos and brought them to Jackie in the living room. "For the Mother's Day card," he said. She looked at one that showed Daniel at 4, his freckled arms wrapped around her neck and his face buried into hers. She gasped. She touched her neck. "It physically hurts," she said, reaching for Mark. "Stomach, arms, legs, chest."

She had developed a habit in the last months of what her counselor called "defensive delusions," when she would imagine for a few hours that Daniel was away at a friend's house. Pretending helped her summon the energy to return a few e-mails or cook dinner, but the easiness of the mental game was starting to scare her. "Is it normal?" Jackie had asked the counselor at their last appointment. "Is this something other people do?"

"There is no normal," the counselor had said. "There are only hard days to get through."

So now, on this hard day, Jackie stared at the photo and considered whether to release another intimate moment to the world.

"Will it make a difference?" she asked Mark.

"I don't know," he said.

***

There were 26 of them in all — 26 victims, which meant 26 families left adrift, grasping for a way to continue on. Some found it in church, returning to the pews every Wednesday and Sunday with a Sandy Hook Bible group, lighting 26 candles each time they went. Others found it in the spiritual medium that contacted victims' families on Facebook, offering to facilitate a private seance and "connect them with the other side." Some started nonprofit foundations in their child's name or escaped back into jobs in Manhattan or ordered wine by the case or planted 26 trees or considered moving out of state or installed blackout curtains for privacy. One mother took a job sorting corporate donations to the Newtown community fund, organizing 26,000 bottles of "Sandy Hook Green" nail polish and 2,600 wool blankets, because the magnitude of the donations helped reaffirm the magnitude of her loss.

What the Bardens chose to believe in during those first days was cause and effect, order and logic. America's mental health system was broken, but they could fix it. Gun culture was extreme, but they could moderate it. This was the way they made sense of the world, which was why, less than a week after Daniel's death, Mark and Jackie met with a start-up advocacy organization called Sandy Hook Promise and offered to help.

They had never owned or fired a gun, so they took trips with Sandy Hook Promise and the parents of four other victims to California and New York, where they learned about the National Rifle Association and technological advances in gun safety. The governor of Connecticut sent them drafts of new legislation. Vice President Biden briefed them on congressional voting procedures. Four times this year, Mark and Jackie traveled to Washington with their photographs of Daniel and met with two dozen senators to discuss a bill requiring universal background checks on gun purchases. When the measure came up for a vote in April, all four of the Bardens watched from the gallery: the father, a professional jazz guitarist who rarely had the desire to play anymore; the wife, an elementary school reading teacher who couldn't imagine stepping back into a classroom; the eldest son, 13, fiddling with a Rubik's Cube to quiet his anxiety; the daughter, 11, suddenly afraid of big cities, and loud noises, and darkness, and strangers.

When the Senate vote failed, Mark was asked to introduce President Obama for a speech in the Rose Garden. "Let's go rip some bark off it," Obama told him. And yes, Mark was angry, too — angry enough that his hands balled into fists and trembled at the podium — but mostly he was unmoored. "So what does all of this add up to now?" he had asked a White House employee later that day, when the speeches ended.

Because if it amounted to nothing at all, what was the logic, the order, the meaning of their broken lives?

What was the meaning of the anger he felt lately while shopping at Costco, hoping one of the strangers in the aisles might be a gun nut who would recognize and approach him, so he had an excuse to shout back?

What was the meaning of the endless tributes? A song performed in concert for Daniel because he liked music. A 5K race for Daniel because he liked to run. A mud festival for Daniel because he liked mud. A Play Day for Daniel because he liked to play. Then there were the boxes of mementos that filled a room in their house, gifts created and mailed by strangers: magnets bearing Daniel's picture, paintings of him, wood carvings, wind chimes, T-shirts, pins and blankets stitched with a 10-foot image of his face. "To Our Angel," the packages read — or to "Dan," "Danny" or, weirdest of all, "Daniel Barden," so formal and unfamiliar, like the etching on a headstone.

And what was the meaning of their new nighttime routine? All four of them crammed into one room in a five-bedroom house, three on a queen bed and one on the futon so they could will one another through the night, Jackie up every few hours, Mark closing his eyes and thinking about Daniel, always hoping he might come to him in a dream, even though he never did.

* * *

And then it was morning.

Down the stairs into the kitchen came the son, James, carrying his backpack and soccer cleats, ready for the 6:20 bus to junior high. "How are you today?" Jackie asked him, as she did every morning. "Pretty good," he said, which was mostly true. He was starring on a competitive soccer team, working as a referee, playing bass in the school orchestra. "Can you believe these Barden kids?" one of Biden's aides had said a few months earlier, after spending a morning with James. So polite. So resilient. But sometimes Jackie watched him from the window while he played soccer alone in the yard, where he had always played with Daniel. She thought he looked lost. "Want to talk about it with someone?" she had asked him. "I guess," he had said, so now he was seeing a counselor who let him lie down in her office and work his Rubik's Cube.

Next down the stairs came the daughter, Natalie, Newtown's fifth-grade student of the month — a pianist and a violin player, a master of grade school hand-clapping games, a performer in the school musical. "Natalie is a social and academic marvel in my class," one teacher had written in Natalie's spring evaluation, not knowing that just getting her to class each morning had become a battle, because her newfound fear made her reluctant to leave home.

"I'm sick," she said now, rubbing her eyes. "I don't think I should go to school."

"Probably just allergies," Mark said. "You'll be fine."

"I should stay home," she said.

"How many times do we have to have this conversation?" Jackie said.

"I don't want to go."

"Please stop it," Jackie said.

"You're so lucky," Natalie said.

"Lucky?"

"You get to stay home."

"Do you even know what you're saying?" Jackie said, her voice louder now. "You think I'm home because I want to be? You think I wouldn't rather be going on with my life, going to work? Lucky? I'm not even having this conversation."

Jackie started to cry, and then Natalie started to cry. "I'm sorry," she said. "Oh sweet pea," Mark said, wrapping her into a hug, tearing up now, too. All three of them sat down for breakfast and then walked together to the bus stop. "Love you," Natalie told them, settling in a window seat next to a friend, beginning a clapping game against the window. The bus rolled up the hill, and Mark and Jackie walked back to the house. Just them now. Nobody left to come downstairs. They sat in the living room sipping coffee in silence.

It had always seemed to them that this was the perfect house, in the perfect neighborhood, in the perfect town. They had often wondered: How did they get so lucky that life delivered them here? Mark had given up a touring career in Nashville, and Jackie had decided she could drive 45 minutes each way to her teaching job in Pawling, N.Y. They had borrowed money from both sides of the family and bought an unpretentious country house on a dead-end road, with an acre of wooded land where the kids could play freeze tag and leave out leftover food for hungry raccoons.

But lately everything about the house reminded them of Daniel, comfort and affliction all at once. Up there, on the ceiling, was the sticky toy he had bought in a vending machine and accidentally thrown too high. In the kitchen was the blender Mark had used to make him a smoothie each afternoon, always with four gummy vitamins at the bottom of the glass, always, in Daniel's words, "the best one yet!" Out front was the dead-end road where he had waited for the school bus in a sprinter's crouch each morning, so he could run alongside it for a block before climbing on board. Out back was the wooden play structure where he had knocked his head and bled for the first time, which sometimes made Mark and Jackie wonder about the last time. Had it been quick? Had he been scared? Had anybody held him?

"Let's get out of here," Mark said. "Let's go get breakfast."

"Someplace new," Jackie agreed.

They drove nine miles outside of town to a small diner that a friend had once recommended. They had never been before. There were no memories here. A waitress led them to a booth by the window and handed over menus. "Perfect," Mark said. The coffee tasted good. The restaurant was empty. They were the first customers of the day. The campy decor reminded Mark of a place he had liked in Nashville. "Pretty fun vibe," he said. "I'm thinking about treating myself to the eggs Benedict," Jackie said. "Yum," Mark said.

Now another car pulled into the restaurant lot, carrying the second customers of the day, and out of all the people in central Connecticut, and all of the possible places and times for them to eat, these were two whom the Bardens recognized: a mother and her young son, who had been Daniel's classmate in kindergarten.

"Do you remember the Bardens?" the mother asked her son, bringing him over to their booth.

"Hi!" the boy said, sitting down at the table next to them.

"Let's let them enjoy their breakfast," the mother told her son, sensing the awkwardness of the moment, pointing him to another table in the corner of the restaurant. She turned back to the Bardens: "I'm sorry. He's excited. It's his birthday."

"Oh wow," Jackie said.

"So nice," Mark said.

"Seven," the mother said, following her son to the other table.

"Should we leave?" Jackie said, whispering to Mark, once the mother was out of earshot. "Would it be easier?"

"It might be," Mark said.

But instead they sat at the table and watched as the waiter brought the boy a gigantic waffle covered in powdered sugar, berries and whipped cream. They watched as the waiter stuck a candle into the center of that waffle, and as the mother sang "Happy Birthday" and took a picture with her phone. They watched as the boy swept his fingers through the whipped cream, smearing it across his mouth and face while his mother laughed. "You're so silly," she said.

This boy, who had ended up in the other first-grade class at Sandy Hook Elementary.

This boy, who had hidden in the other bathroom.

"Oh God," Jackie said, shoulders trembling, questions and doubts tumbling out as she tried to catch her breath. "Why did we wait to enroll him in school?" she said. "He could have started a year earlier. He could have been in second grade. He was old enough."

"We were thinking about what was best for him," Mark said, knowing the cycle that was starting, the blame, the need for absolution. "We wanted him to be one of the oldest."

"So he would be a leader and not a follower," Jackie said, nodding.

"So he would be confident," Mark said.

"So he wouldn't be last to get his driver's license," she said.

They sat at the booth and thought about Daniel at 16. The coffee had gone cold. The eggs sat on their plates. The boy and his mother stood up to leave, walking past their table. "We had to eat in a hurry today," the mother said. She explained that her son's name and birth date were going to be read over the loudspeaker during the morning announcements at school, and he wanted to be there in time to hear it.

"Take care," the mother told them.

"Bye!" the boy said, and Mark and Jackie watched as he ran to the parking lot.

***

A few days later, Mark and Jackie decided to go to Delaware. "Who even cares about Delaware?" Natalie had asked as they began to pack, and so they had explained to their daughter what political advisers had explained to them: that momentum for gun laws had stalled in Washington, and that the best remaining chance was to build momentum state by state, one incremental law at a time.

In Delaware that meant House Bill 58, championed by Democratic Gov. Jack Markell, who had called it "a historic and sweeping measure." But when Mark began researching the bill on his computer in the days before the trip, what he mostly noticed was the addendum of exceptions. The bill proposed to make it illegal to possess high-capacity magazines of 10 bullets or more in the country's second-smallest state — unless you only possessed those magazines at your house, which was okay; or on private property, which was also okay; or at a shooting range, which was fine; or if you were carrying a high-capacity magazine separately from a firearm, which would still be permitted; or if you were law enforcement or retired law enforcement or active military or a licensed firearms dealer, in which cases you were exempt. First-time violators would face a misdemeanor charge and a $75 fine. "Like a traffic ticket," Mark told Jackie.

The NRA had dispatched two lobbyists to the state Capitol in opposition of the bill. Markell did not want to schedule a vote until he knew he had the 21 votes necessary to pass it, and he was still three or four short.

"Your heartfelt, personal stories might still help us make history," one of the governor's aides had written in an e-mail invitation to Sandy Hook families.

At the moment, it was the only history there was to make, and the best invitation they had, so Mark and Jackie traveled with a group that included a public relations specialist, the director of Sandy Hook Promise and the parents of two other victims: Nicole Hockley, mother of Dylan; and Nelba Marquez-Greene, mother of Ana. They took a car to a train to another car to a hotel located alongside a commercial highway on the outskirts of Dover. "What brings you to Delaware?" asked a cheery 18-year-old at the front desk, and for a few seconds the parents stared back at him in awkward silence. "Life, I guess," Mark said, finally. "Bad luck," Hockley said, with a slight smile. "Is this personal travel or business?" the hotel employee said, looking at his computer. "Both. It is personal business travel," Mark said, and the parents laughed.

They went to the Capitol the next morning for a meeting with the governor's staff to discuss their trip. "Basically, we want to make sure to maximize this visit," the lieutenant governor told them, explaining that there would be a news conference, a lunch with lawmakers and dinner at the governor's residence. One of the governor's aides handed out head shots of all 41 state lawmakers, divided into who was a soft no or a soft yes. The parents' mission, he explained, was to walk the halls of the Capitol and give their children's photos to anyone who would take them. A survivor of the Virginia Tech shooting already had come to Delaware to lobby. Gabby Giffords's husband already had come. "We think you all are the extra difference," the aide said.

He said a last-minute opportunity had arisen for the parents to be recognized during a moment of silence on the House floor. Were they interested?

"We don't love those," Hockley said. "It is a little like being the exhibit in a museum."

"I understand," the staffer said. "We just want every one of these lawmakers to see you. We want them to feel your loss and understand what's at stake."

"Will they read off the victims' names?" Mark asked, dreading that.

"Yes."

"And the ages?" he asked, dreading that, too.

"Yes."

Mark looked across the table at Hockley. She grimaced and shrugged. He looked over at Jackie. She nodded.

"Okay then," Mark said.

They were led to seats in the House chamber, where a junior lawmaker recited the Pledge of Allegiance. "Today we have some special guests," she said, and 41 lawmakers turned to look. "Will our guests please stand?" she said, and the parents stood. "Please come up here," she said, and they did that, too. The room went quiet as she began reading the names.

Daniel Barden. Seven. Dylan Hockley. Six. Ana Marquez-Greene. Six. Six. Six. Six. Seven. Six. How long could one minute last? Mark looked at the lawmakers and tried to pick out the three who already had refused to meet with the Newtown parents. Could he barge into their offices? Wait at their cars? Jackie counted the seconds in her head — "breathe, breathe," she told herself — believing she was holding it together until a lawmaker handed her a box of tissues. Hockley saw the tissues and thought about how she rarely cried anymore except for alone at night, unconscious in her sleep, awakening to a damp pillow. Marquez-Greene listened to the names and pictured her daughter dressed for school that last day: pudgy cheeks, curly hair and a T-shirt decorated with a sequined purple peace sign — a peace Marquez-Greene was still promising to deliver to her daughter every night when she prayed to her memory and whispered, "Love wins."

The gavel banged. The moment of silence ended. The parents sat back in their chairs.

"Next is a motion to recognize National Nurses Week," the House speaker said. "All in favor?"

"Aye!"

"A motion to recognize women's clubs for the important role they play."

"Aye!"

"A motion to honor a champion among us, one of our own, the winner of the state peach pie eating contest ..."

"Aye!"

"A motion to recognize another special guest, here on her vacation, the mother of one of our lawmakers ..."

"Let's go," Mark said, standing up in the middle of the session, motioning for the other parents to follow. They walked upstairs into a private conference room. "This gets more surreal every day," Hockley said. "Crazy," Mark said. How was it, they wondered, that government could roll through its inconsequential daily agenda but then stall for months on an issue like gun control? They had seen polls that showed 80 percent of Delaware residents favored a ban on high-capacity magazines. Ninety percent of Americans wanted universal background checks. But in the months since the shooting in Newtown, only a handful of states with already-stringent gun laws had managed to pass stricter laws. Most states had done nothing, and the U.S. Senate had postponed another vote.

"Some of those lawmakers in there didn't want to look at us," Mark said.

"Just squirming," Hockley said.

"It's exhausting," Jackie said, rubbing her eyes.

They drove back to the hotel, where the same teenage employee was waiting for them at the front desk. "How'd it go today?" he asked. He explained that some of the hotel staff had been watching the local TV news, and they had learned the exact nature of this group's personal business. One of the employees, a bartender in the restaurant, had stayed up all night creating a tribute. She had scoured the Internet for pictures of Dylan Hockley and Daniel Barden and placed a rushed order for customized frames. "Please follow me to the bar," the front desk employee said now. The parents walked with him into a corner of the restaurant that was dark except for the glow of 26 candles, which had been placed on a table next to framed photos of their children. "Our Angel Dylan," one frame read. "Our Angel Daniel," read the other. The table was secluded behind velvet rope, and the bartender came over with a bottle of whiskey.

"Please sit," the bartender said, and the only thing the parents could think to do was to thank her, fill their glasses and drink fast before going upstairs to bed.

***

They were tired. They missed the kids. They were ready to go home. But there was still more to do. Before the parents left Delaware, they had a news conference with the governor.

They met with him privately first in a hallway at the Capitol. "Thank you for being here," he said. The parents handed him pictures of their children, and he studied each one for a long minute, repeating their names out loud. "Dylan." "Ana." "Daniel." He touched the pictures to his chest and nodded at the parents. "Look, the courage that you have shown to be here today ... well, what can I even say?" he told them.

The parents followed him into his office, which two assistants had staged for the news conference. "It's a casual and not a heavy," one of the press assistants had told the parents, explaining how they would sit with the governor and answer questions while the media taped B-roll. The governor sat at the head of the coffee table. Jackie and Mark held hands on a couch under a chandelier. Hockley and Marquez-Greene sat across from them. Fifteen cameras and 12 reporters crowded into the room. "A good turnout for a small market," the governor's press secretary said, motioning for another staffer to close the door.

"Okay. We're on," the press secretary said, nodding to the governor.

He looked up at the row of cameras. He held up the victims' pictures. He repeated their names. He touched the photos to his chest. "Look, the courage that you have shown to be here today ... well, what can I say?" he told the parents again.

Jackie sat on the couch while the governor kept talking and thought about the first time her family had discussed guns, two days after Daniel's death. Natalie had suggested something that Mark and Jackie thought was simple and beautiful: Why not collect all the guns and bury them at the bottom of the ocean, where they would rot and decay? They had encouraged her to write a letter to the president about her idea, which she had done: "My name is Natalie Barden and I wanted to tell the president that only police officers and the military should get guns," she had written.

But the past five months had taught Mark and Jackie that simplicity and innocence didn't work in politics. Neither did rage or brokenness. Their grief was only effective if it was resolute, polite, purposeful and factual. The uncertain path between a raw, four-minute massacre and U.S. policy was a months-long grind that consisted of marketing campaigns, fundraisers and public relations consultants. In the parents' briefing book for the Delaware trip, a press aide had provided a list of possible talking points, the same suggestions parents had been given in Illinois, New York, New Jersey and Connecticut.

"We are not anti-gun. We are not for gun control. We are for gun responsibility and for gun safety laws," one suggestion read.

"I am here today to honor my child's memory," read another.

"The Sandy Hook shooter used 30-round magazines. He fired 154 bullets in four minutes, murdering 20 children and six adults," read one more.

Now, at this latest news conference, the governor finished his introduction and a reporter raised his hand to ask a question. "This one is for the parents," he said. "How would a high-capacity ban prevent something like the carnage at Sandy Hook?"

Carnage? Mark squeezed Jackie's hand. She stared down at the floor. He looked up at the cameras.

"The bills on the table here make good, common sense," he said.

"This is not about banning or confiscation," Hockley said.

"We are here to honor our children," Marquez-Greene said.

"Our shooter used high-capacity magazines to fire 154 bullets," Hockley said.

"Please know, this is not about gun control but gun responsibility," Mark said, as the governor nodded in affirmation.

***

"So polished," the press secretary told Mark afterward, squeezing his shoulder, and it was true. He never lost his temper. He always made eye contact. He spoke in anecdotes that were moving and hopeful.

But sometimes the story Mark really wanted to share was the unpolished one, the one that never seemed right for a news conference, or a vigil, or a meet and greet, or the Oval Office, or a TV interview, or a moment of silence, or a Mother's Day card. Sometimes what he really wanted to tell them was what it was like in his house on another unbearable morning, like the one a few days earlier.

All of them awake again in the same room.

James to the bus.

Natalie to the bus.

And then it was upon them, the worst hour of the day, from 7:30 to 8:30 a.m., when Daniel had been alone with them in the house waiting for his bus. They had tried many ways of passing that hour: out to breakfast, back in bed, walking or hiring a trainer to meet them at the gym. A few times they had decided to wait for Daniel's bus themselves, standing at the end of the driveway and climbing the four steps to hug Mr. Wheeler, the longtime bus driver who had loved Daniel and delivered a eulogy about how the boy raced his school bus, running sideways and backward in the grass, tripping and tumbling with his green backpack.

On this particular morning, the Bardens saw their next-door neighbor on the sidewalk at 7:30 and invited her in for coffee. She was a mother of three, including a second-grade girl who had been one of Daniel's best friends. Before his death, the neighbor had come for coffee often, but lately the Bardens found it easier to see her less.

"Come visit," Mark said.

"Are you sure?" the neighbor asked.

"It will be good," Jackie said. "We've been trying to talk more about Daniel."

So the neighbor came inside, poured coffee and started to tell stories they all knew. About how her daughter and Daniel had shared so many secrets, games they played for hours in the driveway and refused to tell anyone else about. About how Daniel had excused himself from a pizza party at her house five nights before his death, because the adults were watching "National Lampoon's Christmas Vacation" in the living room, and Daniel, an old soul and a rule follower, had said: "This language probably isn't appropriate for me."

Then she started telling another story, one the Bardens had never heard before, one about that day. The neighbor said her second-grade daughter had lost her glasses while scrambling to hide in her classroom during the chaos of the shooting. The girl had clung to her teacher's leg on the way out of the school, unable to see anything, and she had still been clinging to that leg when her mother found her alive at the firehouse an hour later. She had brought her daughter home and, later that night, tried to tell her about Daniel. But her daughter had screamed not to say his name, that his name was now one of their secrets. She had sat by the window in her room and looked across the woods to Daniel's room, as she always did, and she had sobbed because she couldn't see it without her glasses.

"She loved him," the neighbor was saying now.

"Oh God," Jackie said. "It's too much. Please stop."

"I'm sorry," the neighbor said, reaching for a box of tissues. "I, I . . . I shouldn't have."

"It's okay," Mark said, but now his mind was back inside the school that morning, where it sometimes went. Jackie's imagination walked Daniel to the door of his classroom and no farther. She wanted to protect herself from the details, so she had left the box containing Daniel's clothes from that day untouched and unlooked at in the attic, where state troopers had deposited it a few weeks after his death. Mark, however, felt compelled to know. For seven years, two months and 17 days, he had known every detail of Daniel's life — the teeth that were just beginning to come in, the way his hands moved as they played "Jingle Bells" that morning on the piano — so it seemed necessary that he should also know every detail of its end. He had asked law enforcement officers to give him a tour of the school, which was still an active crime scene, and he had gone there one Friday morning while Jackie stayed home. The officers had walked him through the attack, all four minutes and 154 rounds, and because of that Mark could precisely picture the shooter, with his Bushmaster rifle, his earplugs and his olive green vest, firing six holes into the glass front door. He could hear the shouting over the intercom in the main office, where the principal had been shot, and he could hear the shooter's footsteps on the linoleum hallway as he walked by one first-grade classroom and into the next, Daniel's. He could see the substitute teacher scrambling to move the children into the corner, where there was a small bathroom. He could see all 15 of them huddled in there, squeezed together, and somewhere in that pile he could see Daniel.

Mark could see himself that morning, too, rushing out of the house at 10, knowing only that shots had been fired at Sandy Hook and parents would be reunited with their children at the firehouse. Jackie had started driving from Pawling, calling and texting him again and again. "Do you have him?" "DO YOU HAVE HIM YET?" A priest had announced that the principal had been killed, and Mark had wondered: "How will we explain this to Daniel?" Then the same priest had said 20 children were also dead, and there was shrieking and vomiting in the firehouse, and Mark had imagined Daniel running alone in the woods behind the school. He was fast. He had escaped.

Then the governor was in front of them, and he was saying, "No more survivors," and a state trooper was driving Mark and Jackie home. Mark was sitting in the passenger seat, dazed and quiet and looking over at the state trooper, who had begun to weep.

"I should have waited with you at the school until the end," the neighbor said now, in the kitchen.

"No," Mark said. "You had to get your daughter home."

"Oh dear God," the neighbor said.

"I feel sick," Jackie said, standing up and then sitting back down.

The neighbor looked at the clock and saw it was almost 8:30, time to walk her daughter to the bus. "I have to go," she said, hugging the Bardens, leaving them at the kitchen table. Jackie poured more coffee. Mark checked his phone messages. Jackie walked outside to get the mail and brought it into the living room. Mark opened a package from Minnesota that contained a Sherpa blanket and a note that read: "We will never forget."

The school bus came. The school bus went.

"What do you want to do?" Mark asked, and in that moment, the answer to both of them was clear.

"What can we do?" Jackie said.

"Nothing," Mark said, and he sank down next to her on the couch.

The Boston Globe

April 26, 2013

By Eric Moskowitz

Carjacking victim describes harrowing night

The 26-year-old Chinese entrepreneur had just pulled his new Mercedes to the curb on Brighton Avenue to answer a text when an old sedan swerved behind him, slamming to a stop. A man in dark clothes got out and approached the passenger window. It was nearly 11 p.m. last Thursday.

The man rapped on the glass, speaking quickly. Danny, unable to hear him, lowered the window- and the man reached an arm through, unlocked the door, and climbed in, brandishing a silver handgun.

"Don't be stupid," he told Danny. He asked if he had followed the news about the previous Monday's Boston Marathon bombings. Danny had, down to the release of the grainy photos of suspects less than six hours earlier.

"I did that," said the man, who would later be identified as Tamerlan Tsarnaev. "And I just killed a policeman in Cambridge."

He ordered Danny to drive—right on Fordham Road, right again on Commonwealth Avenue—the beginning of an achingly slow odyssey last Thursday night and Friday morning in which Danny felt the possibility of death pressing on him like a vise.

In an exclusive interview with the *Globe*, Danny—the victim of the Tsarnaev brothers' much-discussed but previously little-understood carjacking—filled in some of the last missing pieces in the timeline between the murder of MIT police officer Sean Collier, just before 10:30 p.m. on April 18, and the Watertown shoot-out that ended just before 1 a.m. Danny asked that he be identified only by his American nickname.

The story of that night unfolds like a Tarantino movie, bursts of harrowing action laced with dark humor and dialogue absurd for its ordinariness, reminders of just how young the men in the car were. Girls, credit limits for students, the marvels of the Mercedes-Benz ML 350 and the iPhone 5, whether anyone still listens to CDs—all were discussed by the two 26-year-olds and the 19-year-old driving around on a Thursday night.

Danny described 90 harrowing minutes, first with the younger brother following in a second car, then with both brothers in the Mercedes, where they openly discussed driving to New York, though Danny could not make out if they were planning another attack. Throughout the ordeal, he did as they asked while silently analyzing every threatened command, every overheard snatch of dialogue for clues about where and when they might kill him.

"Death is so close to me," Danny recalled thinking. His life had until that moment seemed ascendant, from a province in Central China to graduate school at Northeastern University to a Kendall Square start-up.

"I don't want to die," he thought. "I have a lot of dreams that haven't come true yet."

After a zigzagging trek through Brighton, Watertown, and back to Cambridge, Danny would seize his chance for escape at the Shell Station on Memorial Drive, his break turning on two words—"cash only" that had rarely seemed so welcome.

When the younger brother, Dzhokhar, was forced to go inside the Shell Food Mart to pay, older brother Tamerlan put his gun in the door pocket to fiddle with a navigation device—letting his guard down briefly after a night on the run. Danny then did what he had been rehearsing in his head. In a flash, he unbuckled his seat belt, opened the door, stepped through, slammed it behind, and sprinted off at an angle that would be a hard shot for any marksman.

"F---!" he heard Tamerlan say, feeling the rush of a near-miss grab at his back, but the man did not follow. Danny reached the haven of a Mobil station across the street, seeking cover in the supply room, shouting for the clerk to call 911.

His quick-thinking escape, authorities say, allowed police to swiftly track down the Mercedes, abating a possible attack by the brothers on New York City and precipitating a wild shoot-out in Watertown that would seriously wound one officer, kill Tamerlan, and leave a severely injured Dzhokhar hiding in the neighborhood. He was caught the following night, ending a harrowing week across Greater Boston.

Danny spoke softly but steadily in a 2 1/2- hour interview at his Cambridge apartment with a *Globe* reporter and a Northeastern criminology professor, James Alan Fox, who had counseled Danny after the former graduate student approached his engineering adviser at Northeastern.

Danny, who offered his account only on the condition that the *Globe* not reveal his Chinese name, said he does not want attention. But he suspects his full name may come out if and when he testifies against Dzhokhar Tsarnaev.

"I don't want to be a famous person talking on the TV," Danny said, kneading his hands, uncomfortable with the praise he has received from the few friends he has shared the story with, some of whom encouraged him to go public. "I don't feel like a hero .... I was trying to save myself."

Danny, trained as an engineer, made scrupulous mental notes of street signs and passing details, even as he abided the older Tsarnaev's command not to study his face.

"Don't look at me!" Tamerlan shouted at one point. "Do you remember my face?"

"No, no, I don't remember anything," he said.

Tamerlan laughed. "It's like white guys, they look at black guys and think all black guys look the same," he said. "And maybe you think all white guys look the same."

"Exactly," Danny said, though he thought nothing of the sort. It was one of many moments in their mental chess match, Danny playing up his outsider status in America and playing down his wealth—he claimed the car was older than it was, and he understated his lease payments— in a desperate hope of extending his life.

Danny had come to the United States in 2009 for a master's degree, graduated in January 2012, and returned to China to await a work visa. He came back two months ago, leasing a Mercedes and moving into a high-rise with two Chinese friends while diving into a start-up. But he told Tamerlan he was still a student and that he had been here barely a year. It seemed to help that Tamerlan had trouble understanding even Danny's pronunciation of the word "China."

"Oh, that's why your English is not very good," the brother replied, finally figuring it out. "OK, you're Chinese ... I'm a Muslim."

"Chinese are very friendly to Muslims!" Danny said. "We are so friendly to Muslims."

When the ordeal had started, Danny prayed it would be a quick robbery. Tamerlan demanded money, but Danny had just $45 in cash—kept in the armrest—and a wallet full of plastic. Evidently disappointed to get so little out of holding up a $50,000 car, he told Danny to drive. The old sedan followed.

"Relax," Tamerlan said, when Danny's nerves made it hard for him to stay in the lane. Danny, recalling the moment, said, "My heart is pounding so fast."

They lapped Brighton and crossed the Charles River into Watertown, following Arsenal Street. Looking through Danny's wallet, Tamerlan asked for his ATM code—a friend's birthdate.

Directed to a quiet neighborhood in East Watertown, Danny pulled up as instructed on an unfamiliar side street. The sedan stopped behind him. A man approached—the skinnier, floppy-haired "Suspect No.2" in the photos and videos released by investigators earlier that evening— and Tamerlan got out, ordering Danny into the passenger seat, making it clear that if he tried anything he would shoot him. For several minutes, the brothers transferred heavy objects from the smaller car into Danny's SUV. "Luggage," Danny thought.

With Tamerlan driving now, Danny in the passenger seat, and Dzhokhar behind Danny, they stopped in Watertown Center so Dzhokhar could withdraw money from the Bank of America ATM using Danny's card. Danny, shivering from fear but claiming to be cold, asked for his jacket. Guarded by just one brother, Danny wondered if this was his chance, but he saw around him only locked storefronts. A police car drove by, lights off.

Tamerlan agreed to retrieve Danny's jacket from the back seat. Danny unbuckled, put on the jacket, then tried to buckle the seat belt behind him to make an escape easier. "Don't do that," Tamerlan said, studying him. "Don't be stupid."

Danny thought about his burgeoning start-up and about a girl he secretly liked in New York. "I think, 'Oh my god, I have no chance to meet you again,'" he recalled.

Dzhokhar was back now. "We both have guns,'" Tamerlan said, though Danny had not seen a second weapon. He overheard them speak in a foreign language—"Manhattan" the only intelligible word to him—and then ask in English if Danny's car could be driven out of state. "What do you mean?" Danny said, confused. "Like New York," one brother said.

They continued west on Route 20, in the direction of Waltham and Interstate 95, passing a police station. Danny tried to send telepathic messages to the officers inside, imagined dropping and rolling from the moving car.

Tamerlan asked him to turn on and demonstrate the radio. The older brother then quickly flipped through stations, seemingly avoiding the news. He asked if Danny had any CDs. No, he replied, he listens to music on his phone. The tank nearly empty, they stopped at a gas station, but the pumps were closed.

Doubling back, they returned to the Watertown neighborhood—"Fairfield Street," Danny saw on the sign—and grabbed a few more things from the parked car, but nothing from the trunk. They put on an instrumental CD that sounded to Danny like a call to prayer.

Suddenly, Danny's iPhone buzzed. A text from his roommate, wondering in Chinese where he was. Barking at Danny for instructions, Tamerlan used an English-to-Chinese app to text a clunky reply. "I am sick. I am sleeping in a friend's place tonight." In a moment, another text, then a call. No one answered. Seconds later, the phone rang again.

"If you say a single word in Chinese, I will kill you right now," Tamerlan said. Danny understood. His roommate's boyfriend was on the other end, speaking Mandarin. "I'm sleeping in my friend's home tonight," Danny replied in English. "I have to go."

"Good boy," Tamerlan said. "Good job."

The SUV headed for the lights of Soldiers Field Road, banking across River Street to the two open gas stations. Dzhokhar went to fill up using Danny's credit card, but quickly knocked on the window. "Cash only," he said, at least at that hour. Tamerlan peeled off $50.

Danny watched Dzhokhar head to the store, struggling to decide if this was his moment—until he stopped thinking about it, and let reflexes kick in.

"I was thinking I must do two things: unfasten my seat belt and open the door and jump out as quick as I can. If I didn't make it, he would kill me right out, he would kill me right away," Danny said. "I just did it. I did it very fast, using my left hand and right hand simultaneously to open the door, unfasten my seat belt, jump out ... and go." Danny sprinted between the passenger side of the Mercedes and the pumps and darted into the street, not looking back, drawn to the Mobil station's lights. "I didn't know if it was open or not," he said. "In that moment, I prayed."

The brothers took off. The clerk, after brief confusion, dialed 911 on a portable phone, bringing it to Danny in the storeroom. The dispatcher told him to take a deep breath. The officers, arriving in minutes, took his story, with Danny noting the car could be tracked by his iPhone and by a Mercedes satellite system, MBrace.

After an hour or more—as the shoot-out and manhunt erupted in Watertown—police brought Danny to Watertown for a "drive-by lineup," studying faces of detained suspects in the street from the safety of a cruiser. He recognized none of them. He spent the night talking to police and the FBI, appreciating the kindness of a state trooper who gave him a bagel and coffee. At 3 the next afternoon, they dropped Danny back in Cambridge.

"I think, Tamerlan is dead, I feel good, obviously safer. But the younger brother—I don't know," Danny recalled thinking, wondering if Dzhokhar would come looking for him. But the police knew the wallet and registration were still in the bullet-riddled Mercedes, and that a wounded Dzhokhar had probably not gotten far. That night, they found him in a boat.

When news of the capture broke, Danny's roommate called to him from in front of the television. Danny was on the phone at the time, talking to the girl in New York.

THE COURSE OF THEIR LIVES

MILWAUKEE JOURNAL SENTINEL ONLINE

OCTOBER 12, 2013

By Mark Johnson

CHAPTER 1: THE FIRST CUT

The noisy, first-day-of-school chatter subsides. A hush falls over 200 students in a lecture hall at the Medical College of Wisconsin.

Already, their thoughts are drifting up a flight of stairs to the sprawling dissection lab, where in two days they will meet and become intimate with something many have scarcely encountered: Death.

Khalid Sharif-Sidi, a 24-year-old from Galesburg, Ill., who has never seen a lifeless human body beyond a few seconds at a funeral, is nervous. He wonders if it will look real or fake, if the person will have tattoos or nail polish or piercings. He wants the body he dissects to look anything but real.

Andrew Kleist, a cardiologist's son from Pittsburgh, who shadowed his father often, and last May watched him unblock a heart attack patient's artery at 2 in the morning, feels excited but uncomfortable. The 23-year-old has been thinking about the body upstairs and what he must do to it — not just a body, a person.

Hillary McLaren, a 23-year-old from Neenah who hopes to become the fourth generation in her family to practice medicine, has been steeling herself for the sight of the cadaver. Her mantra: "Don't be that girl who passes out on the first day of anatomy."

Today they begin the defining course of their medical education.

A required rite of passage on the way to a doctor's white coat, gross anatomy offers first-year students a hands-on tour of an actual human body, the chance to cut into leathery skin and sinewy muscle, to see pale, stringy nerves that run through the legs like wires, to manipulate tendons in the arms and watch the corresponding fingers move.

To hold a human heart.

To feel the moist ridges of a brain.

Before the young students meet their cadavers, they focus up front, where a projector beams the videotaped image of a woman named Geraldine Fotsch.

Fotsch is just days from her 80th birthday. She prefers to be called "Nana," in homage to her 30 grandchildren. And she has made a decision these doctors-to-be will have to consider each time they wield a scalpel over the next five months.

Upon her death, she will not be cremated or buried — not right away. She has decided instead to allow medical students, young men and women like those watching her videotaped image, to dissect and learn from her body.

It won't be these students, of course. Nana was — and is still — very much alive. But her words will be the closest this class comes to understanding the anonymous human beings they are going to take apart.

In the video, she sits beside her interviewer, Todd Hoagland, associate professor for gross anatomy and a young man himself.

What would you like the students to know? he asks.

"I would want them to know it's OK to grow old. It's great to be old."

She shakes her head vigorously, aware she is contradicting a common image of aging.

"Grandchildren are the light of your life," she says. "I would not give up this time in my life for anything."

Do you have any fear of dying?

"I'm a little apprehensive," she says. "I figure I'm not sure if I've collected enough brownie points to go directly up."

She smiles and points toward the ceiling. The students laugh.

Has it been explained what will happen to your body?

"It has," she says, "and that's fine, because I'm not around. I'm someplace else.

"This is my gift to you. Do with it what you want."

***

While much in medicine has changed over the last century, no teaching tool has replaced the gift of a human body.

X-rays, MRIs and CT scans allow medical students to see inside flesh and bone to the sources of injury and disease. Special mannequins help future surgeons hone their incision techniques. Computer programs simulate what it is like to strip off skin.

Yet gross anatomy remains a throwback to 500 years ago, when Leonardo da Vinci dissected cadavers to learn the subject of his art.

Today's embalming techniques preserve the body better. Dissection is no longer a two-day sprint to outrun decay. In most other respects, however, technology has not changed or improved the basic process.

"I don't think there's any way you could reproduce the experience of actual dissection," says Christopher Ruff, professor and director of the Center for Functional Anatomy and Evolution at Johns Hopkins University School of Medicine.

No mannequin or computer can duplicate the force it takes to guide a scalpel through fat and fascia, the connective tissue.

A computer can't capture the diversity of human bodies, the way muscle appears pale yellow in some, the color of red clay in others.

Most of all, a computer cannot fully prepare students for the difference between the beautiful color illustrations in the textbooks and the actual bones, organs and arteries they will encounter in their patients. Textbooks show structures of the young and healthy. The patients in a doctor's office are usually older and sicker.

Hoagland remembers dissecting a cadaver in medical school, studying the networks that send blood and oxygen and brain impulses through the body.

"It was the first class I'd ever taken where the light bulbs kept going off," he says. "I had been a biology major, but I didn't have a sense of how it all fit together. This was like looking at a car as a whole system, instead of just getting all of the little pieces. It's seeing how the pieces all operate in a person. If you understand the big picture, all of the rest starts falling into place."

It is a fitting place to begin. Students start with the foundations they will use their entire careers — the map and the vocabulary necessary to communicate with anyone in medicine.

But gross anatomy also provides something less scientific. Students share an experience that will bond them long after they have graduated, entered practice and forgotten most of their time in medical school.

"This is an elucidation of death and dying," Hoagland says. "It's a way for students who have never experienced that to confront it."

That first class, on a Monday in August 2012, Hoagland tells the students what he expects.

Get to class early. Be scholarly and professional at all times.

No flip-flops in the lab. No shorts. No iPods.

Students will work in teams of six. There are 36 teams; 36 bodies.

Don't talk about the donors in the elevator.

Don't discuss them at Starbucks.

"Treat them well," Hoagland says. "Be good stewards of the gift. These are some of the most altruistic people around. They donate knowing what we are going to do to the body."

***

It was six years ago that Nana Fotsch and her husband, Bill "Pa" Fotsch, first considered becoming body donors. They had two grandchildren at medical school taking gross anatomy. Also, two of their children had been through the course on the way to medical degrees.

"There was a reverence they had for their cadavers," Nana Fotsch recalls, singling out her daughter in particular. "Colleen had a cadaver. He was a priest. She thought how wonderful it was that he dedicated himself in life to his faith and society and people. And he did the same thing in death."

The Fotsches did not embark on a lengthy discussion.

"It was just a no-brainer," Nana says. "It was almost like, 'Yeah, this is what you should do.'"

Pa signed up first, Nana followed.

They'd had long, happy lives. They felt lucky. Pa and Nana were high school sweethearts at Niles Township High School in Illinois. They'd dated, decided they couldn't stand each other, then got to college and changed their minds.

In 1954, they married at Our Lady of Perpetual Help, or as kids back then nicknamed it, Old Lady's Pickle House.

The Fotsches struggled at first. When their twins were born six weeks early, before their insurance had kicked in, the couple had to borrow $500 from Pa's father. After hospital expenses "we had nothing left," Nana recalls. "We had to borrow the money just to exist."

Pa spent two years in the Army, serving as a specialist first class, shuttling back and forth between the Frankford Arsenal in Philadelphia and Washington. By then they had three little children. They lived in a tiny apartment in Philadelphia.

After his Army stint, Pa designed special machines for Kearney & Trecker in Milwaukee, then was asked by his father and two partners to run a small tool and die company near South Bend, Ind. The Fotsches skimped on food and clothing, took no vacations and eventually saved enough money to buy out the partners. Later they bought another company called Baush Machine Tool, which made automotive machinery.

The couple moved from Indiana to Wisconsin in 1965. They bought a house in Elm Grove and raised their children; there were eight of them now, a daughter and seven sons.

The Fotsches were do-it-yourselfers, remodeling, pulling the kids into various projects. They bought a vacation place in northern Wisconsin, and that meant a whole new round of repairs and upgrades.

The boys built models and learned carpentry and electrical work. Colleen learned to sew. She was cooking meals and helping her mother with housework in first grade.

"We were a nuts and bolts family," Nana says.

Pa's reverence for fixing things, however, did not extend to the human body, not for some years.

"My husband, to get him to go to a doctor, well, they were all quacks," Nana recalls. "Gradually he changed his mind."

***

Pa might have been forced to revise his view of doctors had he met the three young men and three young women who gather at Table 1 on the first day of dissection.

They are part of a medical college class that scored in the 85th percentile on the MCAT exams and graduated with a 3.76 (A) grade point average from such schools as Yale, Stanford and the University of Wisconsin-Madison. They include 19-year-old prodigies, valedictorians and published poets. They speak Farsi, Russian, Chinese and Portuguese.

These facts are a source of pride — and anxiety. At their previous schools, the students of Table 1 were all at or near the top; now, wherever they look there's someone just as smart and just as driven.On this Wednesday afternoon in mid-August, with directions given and dissection minutes away, they have little time for introductions.

Lori Wong is a 24-year-old from Los Angeles whose mother died from kidney and liver failure when Lori was a freshman at the University of Southern California. The experience left Lori a legacy of frustrations (the redundant tests, the doctors who lacked empathy) — and a firm belief that medicine can do better.

Joseph Zilisch is a 22-year-old from Kenosha, who carries this message tattooed on his back, "God will give me justice," and this one programmed on his cell phone screen: "I'm going to be a doctor." As a certified nursing assistant for several years while in college, he diapered and turned over the elderly and dealt with the naked human body until nothing about it bothered him.

Hillary McLaren, the young woman from a medical family, majored in biology and women's studies at the University of Michigan, and she talks of promoting equity in health care. Years ago an aunt learned Hillary was considering becoming a writer and offered this advice: You can always write when you're a doctor. But you can't always be a doctor when you're a writer.

Andrew Kleist, the cardiologist's son from Pittsburgh, is eager to begin dissection, to find out for himself why our bodies endure, or as he puts it, "why they don't just crap out like a Toyota after 15 or 20 years." He expects the experience to raise other questions, admitting, "I can't go to anatomy without thinking where the hell we came from."

Ashley Hinkamper is an outgoing 22-year-old from Quincy, Ill., who began volunteering at her local hospital in eighth grade. To cure herself of an aversion to needles and blood, she watched YouTube videos of blood draws. She cured herself so well that she was able to dissect a human cadaver while an undergraduate at Marquette University.

Khalid Sharif-Sidi, the son of Somali immigrants, saw his father's respect for doctors in that proud smile when Khalid gained admission into medical school. But the academic challenge Sharif-Sidi faces is never far from his thoughts: "I feel like failure is always around the corner," he says.

There is one more member of the group they have yet to meet, someone about whom each of the students has privately wondered and worried: the body.

Kleist believes he is about to disfigure a human being. He tells himself, "You signed up to be a physician, and this is part of it."

McLaren feels more at ease, especially after hearing from Nana Fotsch.

Zilisch keeps turning over in his mind what it would mean to give this gift.

"You're pretty useless lying in a casket," he says. "But I don't know if I'd want to see other people cutting up my grandfather."

The steel table before them is actually a long, raised metallic box, almost a casket. Students open two doors on top, revealing a sunken interior. They step on bars at each end of the table, lifting the interior.

Rising into view is a figure shrouded in white towels. A few pale toes jut out.

The air thickens. An odorous wave of embalming fluid washes over the room.

They unpack scalpels. They leave most of the towels draped over the cadaver, which lies face down. Only the back, where dissection begins, is uncovered. The skin is beige and wrinkly, more like a leather couch than someone's back.

The students look at each other, then at the steel table.

Who will make the first cut?

The tension reminds Sharif-Sidi of one of the last days before the start of medical school. Just a few weeks earlier, he and five friends drove to a remote cabin in the mountains of northern Tennessee.

One day they took a boat out on Norris Lake and decided to scale a steep rock and leap off it into the water. During the climb they all realized it was much higher than they'd thought. At the top, they could see the full expanse of the lake and the mountains beyond, and they waited, all of them.

Five minutes ticked by, maybe 10. Each wondered who would jump first.

That is how Sharif-Sidi feels looking down at the body. He is remembering that when the time came to jump, he waited and went second, and for one very deep breath, his feet were touching nothing at all until they slammed into the water.

So it is that Hinkamper, the only one who has previous experience dissecting a body, gently traces the first incision with her scalpel and begins.

***

Their professor is 43, but younger looking, tall with a beard and mustache, and a vivid memory of his own professor for gross anatomy.

It was the fall of 1997. Student Todd Hoagland sat in a lecture hall at Indiana University School of Medicine in South Bend listening to professor John O'Malley.

The man was an encyclopedia. He taught without a book, without even notes. Just a blackboard and chalk. A two-hour talk would flow seamlessly.

O'Malley took pains to reduce the distance between teacher and student, to make sure he was not placed on a pedestal. He addressed every student by name. He encouraged questions, praised accomplishments, challenged classes.

His face radiated an enjoyment of life.

"He had this gentle way and he knew everything," Hoagland says.

The human body was Hoagland's other teacher. He still remembers seeing the heart for the first time, how awed he was that this one muscle propels blood throughout the body.

He remembers admiring the elegance of the valves, massaging the coronary arteries with his fingers.

He remembers holding the brain, how densely packed it felt in his hands.

Until gross anatomy, so much of medicine had seemed theoretical. Picturing the work of cells and DNA requires imagination; muscles, nerves and arteries can be seen and felt.

Hoagland has taught gross anatomy for more than 10 years, the last two at the Medical College. Each time, the human body reveals something new. He has examined bodies with an extra cervical rib, an evolutionary holdover that can create a number of problems. He's come across bodies with six lumbar vertebrae instead of five.

He has noticed that different students approach anatomy in different ways. Some have been waiting years for this chance to get under the hood of the human body, to see how it's all wired. Others are nervous, uncertain of what it will feel like to see a preview of their own mortality.

And then there are the Type A students, who come to gross anatomy having led a largely goal-focused existence.

"They haven't had much time to think about their place in life. Where we go when we die," Hoagland says. "How can you not think what it is to be alive when you dissect a hand? How can you not think about who you are when you hold this brain in your hand?"

***

Hinkamper makes a gentle sawing motion with the scalpel. The skin separates. Fluid appears.

The students follow a manual of plain black-and-white drawings, which have all the aesthetic beauty of directions for putting together a crib. They also refer to Frank H. Netter's "Atlas of Human Anatomy," which has replaced "Gray's Anatomy" at many medical schools. If the manual makes the human body appear dull, Netter makes it appear impossibly beautiful, muscle the color of red wine, bones pure as ivory.

The students have one more source to guide them: Hinkamper, who has done dissection before. As she cuts, she points out fascia, pale connective tissue beneath the skin that wraps over muscles, vessels and nerves.

McLaren makes the next incision.

Sharif-Sidi pulls skin back to the right and left, laying open the inside of the back.

Using scissors, Kleist trims hair from the neck so that it won't impede the scalpel.

Zilisch squeezes skin around the waist, feeling how thick, how firm it is. Then he cuts horizontally across the lower back. Moisture — embalming fluid — seeps up and Hinkamper dabs at it with a paper towel.

Mark L. Harlow, one of five professors who pass from table to table overseeing dissection, shows the students how to let the scalpel follow the path of least resistance. The din of 36 groups of students fills the expansive room, so the members of Table 1 must lean in close to hear him.

As the professors move about demonstrating proper technique, a difference becomes clear. The students cut delicately, almost tentatively.

The professors cut briskly. They tug at skin. They dig their fingers beneath muscle or other tissue in order to reach the structures beneath.

"The idea is to find the things," explains associate professor, David Bolender, addressing the students at Table 1. "You don't need to make the dissection look like a picture in an atlas."

Gradually, the students apply more pressure as they cut. They are careful, knowing they are being graded on the quality of their dissection, knowing, too, that no tissue is to hit the floor.

Every piece must be placed inside a gray plastic tub to be cremated later with the rest of the remains.

After almost three hours when they have finished for the day, they wash the scalpels. They clean the table and reposition the flaps of skin that have been pulled back. They place the arms at the body's sides and draw the white towels over the top. Then, using the foot control, they lower the body back into the sunken portion of the table. All around them, bodies sink back into the other steel tables.

The room empties.

The students at Table 1 were so busy that they missed something. They do not know whether they are dissecting a man or a woman.

Only the next day do they notice the tag attached to their table. On it someone has drawn a little figure in red magic marker.

CHAPTER 2: THE LIVING & THE DEAD

In the second week, it happens.

While preparing to dissect the arms and shoulders of the cadaver at Table 1, the students lift the body and flip it over onto the back. As they do this, the towel that has been covering the woman's face slides off and drops to the floor.

Khalid Sharif-Sidi looks quickly. For an instant his eyes try to take in hers. But all he sees are coin-slot lids that make it look as if she's squinting.

Hillary McLaren, who is lifting the legs, sees nothing and is not bothered by what she missed — not at first anyway. As weeks pass, though, the unseen face becomes a source of anxiety.

Lori Wong, who has been meticulous about keeping the face covered, catches a glimpse. She finds it eerie. She has been telling herself the body is somehow not a real person.

"Then you see the face," she says. "It's a person's face."

Joseph Zilisch is the least uncomfortable. There is a mystery to the face that he cannot resist and cannot solve.

"If something's covered all the time, I want to see it," he says.

"That facial expression is unlike any facial expression I've ever seen any living person make. I couldn't say it's angry or sad. I couldn't put an emotion with it."

Only a few seconds pass before Sharif-Sidi swoops up the towel and places it back over her face. He too cannot forget the expression.

"Blank. Almost like the person got scared out of their body."

Sharif-Sidi pauses.

"It's like a cartoon ghost rising from a body," he says. "What makes you 'you' leaves your body after you die. I don't know what that is that makes you 'you,' or the wiring that allows it to happen. The soul, maybe."

***

The experience of dissection is so vivid it drifts into the subconscious, in dreams and daydreams. Half-asleep, Andrew Kleist can feel himself cutting connective tissue with his scalpel, touching muscle with a gloved finger.

His eyes open. He is not in lab.

And yet, in other ways, dissection becomes routine within a week or two.

The students go back and forth between the anatomical atlas with its full-color illustrations of arteries, nerves and muscles, and the body itself with its gray pallor and splotchy imperfections. They draw their own diagrams on a whiteboard to remind themselves what they're looking for and what's nearby.

At night, they read long chapters in the textbook, struggling to learn hundreds of terms, the language of the body. They worry how they will remember it all. They arrive at Table 1, hair unbrushed, eyes drooping, beards sprouting.

They come to appreciate the difficulty of their task. Dissection is like driving with a meticulously labeled street map into a city that lacks any street signs. The map is two-dimensional, but you're driving in three dimensions. Structures don't look the same as the illustrations. They hide behind fat and connective tissue.

As the students explore the cadaver's back, they apply more strength to the scalpel.

They adjust to the formaldehyde smell, though some have roommates who demand they shower and change as soon as they walk in the door.

They accept that they are cutting up a dead body, yet they never quite escape the fundamental strangeness of it.

"They are going into medicine to heal people," explains their professor, Todd Hoagland, "and the first thing they're doing is picking up a scalpel and cutting up a body when they really want to make the person whole."

Which is why sometimes the students think of Geraldine Fotsch, the woman they saw in the video that first day of class.

***

Geraldine and her husband, Bill, known to all as Nana and Pa, had no hesitation about agreeing to donate their bodies to the Medical College of Wisconsin. Just to be safe, though, Nana consulted a priest they knew, Father John Yockey from St. Jerome Catholic Church in Oconomowoc.

Father Yockey was a frequent visitor to their Elm Grove home, arriving some days in sweat pants for spaghetti dinners. When Nana asked about the Catholic Church's position on donating one's body for dissection, he put her mind at ease. Great idea, the priest said.

A year later, Pa was diagnosed with bone cancer. It was Ash Wednesday 2011. The cancer had spread to his liver. Beginning a decade earlier he'd had prostate cancer, followed by bladder and skin cancer. This time was different. The cancer was terminal.

They'd been husband and wife for 57 years. They had eight children and 30 grandchildren.

Put me in a nursing home, Pa said.

No, she replied, an answer he seldom heard.

I want you to put me in a nursing home, he insisted.

She refused.

My God, said Pa. You're like a bull.

Nana remains just as firm today. She loves old age. She does not fear death.

And she is utterly at peace with the idea that someday, when she passes from this world and leaves her body, students will take it apart and learn its secrets.

***

On Monday and Wednesday afternoons for two to three hours, they meet, the students at Table 1 and their cadaver. A relationship develops.

They do not know if the old woman was married, had children, worked. They don't know whether she was rich or poor, whether she lived on a farm or in an apartment in the city.

And yet the students are learning things about this woman that her own family and even the woman herself did not know. They know what the fatty tissue inside her lower back looks like. They've peered at the veins that carried blood through her body, the nerves that ferried impulses and sensations to her brain.

As McLaren and Zilisch cut away tissue, exposing the brachial plexus, a network of nerves that begins in the neck and shoulder, the old woman's arm juts out between them. The arm curves toward McLaren's back, the way it might if they were dancing.

Inside that arm lies a chapter of her story.

As he cuts along the left shoulder and arm, Zilisch notices that her cephalic vein seems unusually thick. In her armpits, the students discover swelling of the oval-shaped lymph nodes, part of the immune system that protects the body.

They point out these features to Hoagland.

"Aha!" he exclaims. "The story is coming together."

Dissection shows how the human body works, but also how it fails and gives out in the end. In that sense, each cadaver is a mystery with its own set of clues.

Why might the vein be abnormally large? Maybe a blockage of some kind, Hoagland suggests.

"It's like a garden hose. If you step on it, the fluid backs up. When you have a heart attack, the veins in your neck bulge and your face turns blue because blood is backing up."

The inflamed lymph nodes, he says, "probably meant she was fighting an infection. The nodes were getting larger and larger, compressing the axillary vein."

In another month, each of the 36 dissection groups will learn the cause of death for its cadaver. Until then, they search for clues.

At Table 1, the students settle into jobs without discussion. Sharif-Sidi grows a little more sure of himself — maybe failure is not what medical school has in store for him. Wong finds herself more comfortable around the body; they all do. As they're exploring the old woman's tendons and muscles, they find it second nature to look down at their own.

They begin to quiz each other, to share anxieties over the first exams, now fast approaching. And together, they search for signs the old woman might have had heart surgery, or any surgery at all.

They find no scars. The outside of the body appears unscathed.

The inside is another story. They find smaller-than-normal muscles in the arms and legs, a sign she may have gone through years of little exercise, perhaps even a long period in a wheelchair.

Then students discover a possible explanation: a metallic ball and socket buried beneath skin and muscle.

An artificial hip joint.

***

Pa's final illness was brief — Ash Wednesday to just before Easter.

Muscles wasted. His mind remained clear.

He stayed in their Elm Grove house. Nana did the nursing, most of it anyway. She fed him and helped him to the bathroom. She kept thinking, *What does he need?*

The children and grandchildren came to see Pa. Four of their sons — two from California, one from Kentucky and one from North Carolina — picked consecutive weekends to come say goodbye.

One day Nana watched Pa struggle to breathe. His chest rose slowly, then fell ... rose ... fell.

He hated the oxygen mask, but the hospice aide reached for it now.

Nana kept her eyes on his chest. She saw it stop. For weeks, a look of pain lined Pa's face. Now, the lines softened.

A short time later, their grandson Andy Lawton, one of the family's four doctors, arrived. Just to be sure, he placed his stethoscope to Pa's chest and listened. Nothing.

The body was taken to Becker Ritter Funeral Home in Brookfield. Nana had no desire for an open casket, but some of the grandchildren wanted it. Nana would not look inside.

"I didn't want to remember him that way," she says.

Nana knew Pa's wishes and her own. Young doctors at the Medical College would learn from them.

Even so, she was not ready to watch Pa's casket disappear into the hearse that took him away.

After the funeral, there was a ceremony at a dock overlooking Oconomowoc Lake, a place they'd visited on happier days. The grandchildren brought balloons decorated with personal messages and released them. A bagpiper played "Amazing Grace."

But the image of the hearse driving away — that stayed with Nana for a long time.

"Even though my faith tells me Bill was no longer there, you're human," she says. "To watch that casket go into the hearse and the hearse drive away, it's the most difficult thing. It's very final."

***

Familiar as she is, the old woman at Table 1 changes from one week to another.

It's not just the loss of skin and tissue around the triceps and forearms where dissection has focused recently. It's the way dehydration and exposure to the air slowly transform the color of her skin from beige to red clay and finally gray.

From 10 feet away, she looks sometimes like a mannequin. Up close, in certain details, she seems eerily alive. Her hands, before they are dissected, look pale and pruney, as if she'd just emerged from the bathtub. The thin hair on her head looks gently disheveled, the way it might after a long nap.

She creeps into their thoughts unbidden.

The body and the smell of the preservatives appear in nightmares that visit Lori Wong. She is the group member most familiar with death, having lost her mother several years ago to liver and kidney failure brought on by Castleman disease, a rare illness of the lymph nodes.

Ashley Hinkamper finds herself thinking of dissection when she is working out in the gym and something hurts. She pictures the human body and tries to map the pain in her own. What muscle hurts?

Kleist, the cardiologist's son, goes out to dinner one night and orders barbecued chicken wings, and as he's eating the first one, he starts to think that the best-tasting part is the connective tissue, which is what he's been cutting with his scalpel. He isn't hungry anymore.

"I don't want to know about her and what she did, because it's sort of brutal what we're doing," Kleist says. "I think cutting through her body and knowing about her are mutually exclusive. Which is weird, because that's what it's like to be a surgeon."

It is not lost on him that in some ways what they are doing is, as he puts it, "super intimate."

"That blood vessel that was really large — maybe it was important to her health and no one knew about it," he says. "We have some deep knowledge of her. No one else has seen that."

One afternoon that fall semester, a fierce, metallic whine rises above the din in the vast dissection lab. More than a dozen students crowd around one of the tables and watch as a professor cuts a small portion of the collarbone.

At first, the students were cutting too gently. Now they are learning that some tasks require an instrument a good deal less subtle than a scalpel.

A bone saw.

CHAPTER 3: A HEART IN YOUR HAND

While dissecting the woman at Table 1, medical student Ashley Hinkamper finds it is still possible to think of the human body as a grand design, amazing in its ability to coordinate the thought, energy and motion needed to blink an eye or swing a tennis racket.

She marvels at subtle peculiarities—the old woman's youthful-looking hands and Hinkamper's own, which can throw righty and bat lefty.

During the class exams at the Medical College of Wisconsin, images flash in her mind. She sees the lush color illustrations from Frank H. Netter's "Atlas of Human Anatomy."

Then, in the last week of September, Hinkamper's dissection group delves inside the old woman's chest. What they find is anything but grand or idealized.

The left lung sticks to the chest wall; it is not supposed to. And inside the organ lurks dark red, gelatinous material that should not be there.

What is all this stuff? Hinkamper wonders.

The six students at Table 1 ask themselves if there might be some connection between the material in the lung and the grossly enlarged vein they found earlier in the woman's arm.

Was this why she died?

***

Death is often private.

There are death certificates and open caskets. But few look at the certificate, and an open casket reveals little.

Imagine another view of death: You are laid out on a steel table, your demise the subject of classroom discussion.

Geraldine "Nana" Fotsch is comfortable with the role, a point she stressed in the video played on the first day to the 200 students in gross anatomy. Nana is 80 years old. She says she knows what will happen when her body is taken to the Medical College for dissection.

Not that she dwells on the inherent eeriness of young strangers seeking clues to her death.

"Weird?" she asks, then answers quickly: "No. I hope the cause of my death is that I just wore out everything that I got."

Like the students at Table 1, someday Nana's group will piece together a biography from a body. They will look for unusual veins or surgical scars or damaged organs.

They will know about her death, injuries, diseases, but not the rest: the 57-year marriage, the eight children and 30 grandchildren, the sense of humor, the Catholic faith, the whole arc of her life from childhood in Glenview, Ill., to her adult years in Elm Grove.

The mission of the students working on Nana will be to learn the map of the human body, but also to track the progression of Nana's health and figure out what killed her.

Here's one thing they will learn from Nana: She had her tonsils out in childhood. Her missing tonsils are trivial in terms of her health but revealing in what they say about medicine. Our understanding of the body remains a work in progress.

Earlier generations of doctors removed the tonsils when they were swollen. Today, doctors usually don't, believing they play an important role in the defense against bacterial and viral infections.

Aside from her absent tonsils, students will discover that Nana had a hysterectomy much later in life. And recently, at the age of 80, she had knee-replacement surgery.

Otherwise, she says, "I'm pretty much a healthy old coot."

***

As the students at Table 1 follow the networks of veins and nerves, and identify each muscle, even those controlling the eyelids, they begin to see the contradiction.

One view shows a beautiful machine; the other a broken-down wreck.

"She has no major scars," Hinkamper tells one of the professors, adding later to herself, "She had lots of problems."

The woman has no gallbladder.

She has the artificial hip joint they found.

The muscles in her arms and legs are paltry.

Her kidneys are small, and on them Hinkamper finds hard bumps, little pus-filled nodules. Inside the kidneys, the students should be able to see the medulla and the cortex, but they can't. The interior is a mess.

This is how a body looks when it breaks down.

What looks like chaos isn't random. The mess inside the kidneys clarifies something the students found earlier: an enlarged vein in the woman's arm caused by a shunt. She was receiving dialysis. Her blood was carried out of the body into a machine that cleaned out waste to compensate for her failing kidneys. Then the blood re-entered her body.

To the group, the kidney problem is another clue to the woman's death. Professor Todd Hoagland wanders over. He tells the students he made a prediction about the cause, checked the death certificate and learned he had it right.

"I'm not going to tell you the answer yet," he says. "I want you to think about it."

To one member of the group, however, the bad kidney is more than a clue to a mystery.

Lori Wong had felt anxious about dissecting a human body. She had not foreseen that the body she cut with a scalpel would bring back memories of her late mother. Both women went through dialysis.

"The thing about dialysis," Wong says, "it's not a sudden death. They actually had time to think about it and decide, 'OK, I want to stop.'"

***

The chest lies open.

A large section of the rib cage, now removed, rests at the old woman's side like a catcher's chest protector. Hinkamper and Joseph Zilisch cut through a fluid-filled sac called the pericardium.

They approach the engine of the whole beautiful machine.

"You will never again get the chance to hold the heart in your hand," the students had been told a few hours earlier by Gary L. Kolesari, a professor in the department of cell biology, neurobiology and anatomy.

In class, the professor described the four valves in the heart. He explained systole (when the heart ejects blood into the body and the lungs) and diastole (when blood refills the heart's lower chambers). Students gazed at the beautiful pictures in the Netter atlas.

But the words and the textbook pictures cannot compare with the organ itself in the palm of your hand.

The old woman's heart is a muddy beige. The size of a large fist, the organ is lighter than expected; it is filled, not with blood, but air. At the back, the heart is dense and fibrous.

Now, pinch the tissue; feel its oily-leather texture. Peer inside the dark left atrium, one of the chambers.

Picture the choreography of valves opening and closing. The parallel pumps sending blood in need of oxygen to the lungs, and blood with oxygen to the rest of the body.

"It's just amazing that it can run on its own. It knows exactly what it needs to do," Hinkamper says. "You grow up drawing pictures of hearts on Valentine's Day, but seeing the heart firsthand, I'd never been able to appreciate the four chambers before. I could hold it and imagine it pumping and blood going wherever it needs to go."

As he holds the organ, peering at the ventricles and the atria, Khalid Sharif-Sidi thinks that everyone should get to see a heart up close. But just as he's contemplating the complexity of the human body — from somewhere in his subconscious — Indiana Jones rides in.

Sharif-Sidi can't help himself. He thinks of that scene from the "Temple of Doom" movie in which a man's heart is plucked right out of his chest, still beating. And the guy stares at his own beating heart, eyes wide in fear and disbelief.

When the heart reaches Zilisch he pushes the valves with his fingers. He thinks of how much goes on in a single heartbeat, and then tries to imagine it running 60 to 100 beats every minute of every day of every year, on and on for 70 years.

"It's crazy," he says.

***

Nana has never had the opportunity she is making possible for students.

"I would be so in awe," she says. "To hold somebody's heart in your hand ... This is something that God has created and you have it in your hand."

It's not just the heart's role, but its mythology. The heart is where love resides. The heart is where we place our hand during the national anthem or Pledge of Allegiance. Is there anything that hurts more than a broken heart?

The organ has become a symbol for something so strong we can find no other word for it.

As the mother and grandmother of doctors, Nana is familiar with what the heart does, how necessary it is to life. She remembers feeling hers race the one and only time she got in a car accident, a fender-bender 15 years ago. She remembers feeling an awareness of the pulsing heart inside her during weddings and visits from grandchildren.

Someday when her heart no longer beats, a group of students at the Medical College will take turns holding it.

"I would want them to feel that this is something beautiful, not icky or gross," she says, "that it is very large — not necessarily in size."

***

In the middle of the first exam, Zilisch feels acutely aware of his own heart. It is late September and the students stand in the lab amid all the cadavers. A beeper goes off every minute, signaling that each student must move to the next body and identify the next tagged structure.

The lab is crowded yet so quiet. All Zilisch hears is the shuffling of feet, the rustling of exam papers and the sound of his heart beating inside his chest. Then the beeper sounds. Next question.

Their hearts are laboratories for the study of stress. There are twice-weekly labs and lectures, textbook chapters, long lists of structures they must know — as many as 60 on a single page of the atlas, 3,000 in all.

Before each exam, "midnight 'Hail Mary' emails" land in Hoagland's inbox. They come from students pleading for more time to study, or explaining why tomorrow's result "will not reflect my true ability." Afterward, a few sit in the professor's office, emotional wrecks.

Hoagland talks to them gently. Often he finds they are falling apart because they passed with a 75 instead of their customary 95.

Congratulations on passing, he tells them. This is a class of exceptional people. I'll take passing any day.

***

Shortly before Thanksgiving, Zilisch drives to northern Wisconsin, near Eagle River, to hunt deer.

Early one morning as the sun rises over a quiet field, he shoots a seven-point buck.

He begins field dressing the deer with a hunting knife. He works at the treeline where it meets a large meadow. There are only bird calls to break the stillness.

Usually, field-dressing is a task Zilisch performs at a brisk pace.

This time he lingers over it. He finds himself not just dressing the deer, but dissecting it, noting the layers of connective tissue and muscle, the layout of the vessels, the organ structure. He looks at the liver and the spleen.

The deer's heart doesn't look that much different from the human heart he held in his hand — just a little bigger. He dresses the deer's body for almost half an hour.

He ponders the intricacy of not just humans but all living things. He views dissecting the deer as an act of respect. "I'm eating the meat," he says, "but I'm also learning from it."

Looking out on the meadow, Zilisch utters a prayer of thanksgiving for the deer.

***

It is a few weeks before winter break and they are closing in on the old woman's face. Hillary McLaren feels uneasy.

Months ago the towel slid off the face as they were turning over the body. Some of the students at Table 1 looked. McLaren, who was working at the feet, did not.

Soon she will have no choice. And this time the students won't just be looking. They begin dissecting the skull and face right after the holiday break.

McLaren dislikes the idea that this will be how she introduces herself to the woman on the table. So, one day just before the break, as she's putting the body away following dissection, McLaren pauses.

She lifts the towel.

CHAPTER 4: THE WEIGHT OF HER BRAIN

One afternoon before the end of the fall semester, students from each of the 36 dissection teams troop over to the Medical College of Wisconsin Alumni Center, a large auditorium with a balcony. Andrew Kleist is the lone emissary from Table 1.

A projector glows in the darkened room.

Gary L. Kolesari, one of the professors helping teach gross anatomy, beams a single image onto the screen, a bland government-issue sheet of paper with little boxes, similar to a tax form.

The death certificate for the old woman they've been dissecting at Table 1. Her name is blacked out, but not the rest.

Kleist studies it. The form lists the date of birth, date of death, location of death and occupation. Students are reminded that they cannot divulge the information to anyone outside class.

Kleist has tried not to think about her life. The more he knows, the harder it is to take a scalpel to her. Yet he is intensely curious.

He looks at her date of death and tries to picture where he was and what he might have been doing at the time. He thinks how odd it is that he was going about his life that day, while someone hundreds of miles away had just died, a stranger, but a person "I would come to know in an extremely and uniquely intimate way."

"I envisioned her going about her occupation and me as a child. And I thought of the impossibility of this really specific intersection that would take place."

When he looks at her date of birth, he thinks of her age when she died — early 70s — and imagines the times she lived through. His mind fills with images of the 1960s and 1970s, but not the shots of Woodstock, flower children and anti-war marches.

Kleist places the woman into his own family's old grainy photos. She is shoveling snow from the driveway, a boat-sized Chevrolet with winged fenders in the background. He sees her blowing out birthday candles in a wood-paneled room with mustard-yellow carpets.

All of this places the old woman at Table 1 into a context.

But the one crucial piece of information on the screen is the cause of death, the answer to the mystery they've been trying to solve for weeks.

The cause is described in gradations from the most immediate (a heart attack, for example) to longer-range contributors (high blood pressure, perhaps). The certificate becomes a way to demonstrate the networks that link different parts of the body. Brain tumors often have origins outside the brain. They start as cancers somewhere else.

Kolesari discusses each certificate for a few minutes explaining the cause of death and related symptoms. His explanation confirms what the students at Table 1 had begun to suspect from the moment they discovered the evidence of a shunt in her arm and realized she'd been on dialysis.

The old woman's kidneys failed her. That is why she died.

***

The students have been telling themselves they have no emotional attachment to the old woman.

So why is it difficult to arrive at lab one winter day and find her right leg removed?

It isn't a surprise; students had been told a limb would be removed from each of the 36 bodies in gross anatomy. They know the reason. Without the leg, it is easier to see structures in the hip and pelvis.

Still, it bothers Hillary McLaren.

"I know people have been doing this for years. They have it down to a system. There's a reason (for removing the leg). It just seemed unnecessary," McLaren says. "It's sort of like it's gruesome, like it's disrespectful."

Other lab partners have a similar reaction.

Joseph Zilisch does not.

He notices there is still a little tissue connecting the limb, and he begins severing it with his scalpel. Muscles fascinate him, and, truth be told, he likes dissection. He has been doing more and more cutting for the team.

Before he came to medical school, Zilisch worked for a few years as a certified nursing assistant at St. Catherine's Medical Center in Pleasant Prairie. He saw patients with infections that went all the way to the bone. Nothing makes him gag anymore.

"I don't know if that part of my psyche is still there. I just don't access it anymore," he says. "I think it's a good thing. You don't want a doctor cringing if a patient has (a gruesome) condition."

As they go through gross anatomy, the students confront questions that go to the core of medicine.

Is it better to know your patients personally, where they come from, what they do for a living, whether they have children? Or is it better to maintain a distance from someone you might have to cut open in surgery, or treat with brutal chemotherapy drugs?

The students choose distance, yet despite their best efforts, feelings develop. And they come to realize doctors do talk to their patients, learn about their jobs, their spouses, their children.

Other questions arise. The students focus on the body at their own table, an example of our common anatomy. But professors encourage them to wander around the lab looking at the other bodies. Do we learn medicine by studying human differences or similarities? Or both?

Although humans share so many features, they also differ so much: everything from heart, liver and foot size to the color of muscle. There are anomalies only a few have: one kidney instead of two, for example. Yet a significant proportion of people have fewer veins in their arm than normal (think of that relative who complains doctors can never find a good vein for a blood draw).

And then there are all the variations that come from diet, exercise, smoking, drinking and other factors.

"This is a critical piece to medical training," says Todd Hoagland, the course director for gross anatomy. "If there wasn't so much variation, medical training would be relatively easy. As a doctor, you are not solving a class of problems. You are solving a patient's problem."

Each day the students turn another few illustrated pages in Frank H. Netter's "Atlas of Human Anatomy" trying to absorb a new language, trying to remember the names of each vein, muscle, bone and organ, its exact location and what it does. Every five weeks they prepare for two exams: the written tests and the practicals in which they identify structures on each cadaver.

There are dark circles under Andrew Kleist's eyes. His hair is bushy and unkempt. The smile on Ashley Hinkamper's face looks punchy, and sometimes it is, for example when she breaks into song: "Shake, shake, shake. Shake, shake, shake. Shake your booty."

The deeper they get into gross anatomy, the more they fill their brains. They wonder how a brain can hold any more information, but week after week it must.

"Constantly, all the time," Hillary McLaren says, "you feel like you're drowning."

***

What goes on in the brain?

This is what Geraldine "Nana" Fotsch cannot fathom, though she'd like to.

She tries to imagine the brain's inner workings. She pictures light switches and wonders what they control. She wishes she knew what's happening inside her head when she can't remember a word (more than a passing concern when you reach 80, as Nana has). She worries about Alzheimer's disease, and talks to God about it.

"When it's my time," she prays, "please let the body go, not the mind."

Like her late husband, Nana has agreed to allow students at the Medical College to dissect her body after she's dead and gone. When the day comes, the students will see what she cannot: her brain.

"To me, it's like the big controller of everything you do," says Nana. "I like to think that it's like a computer on overload."

Old age has not switched her brain to slow or pause. Her calendar is filled with appointments: the Fotsch Family Foundation, St. Camillus Foundation Board, the Elm Grove Women's Club, baby showers, birthdays. When you have eight children and 30 grandchildren, the dates add up.

Her mind is well-stocked. She can rewind decades of weddings and family gatherings. She finds it curious how her brain struggles to remember something a few hours ago, but remembers vividly those drives to Devil's Lake with her grandparents when she was only 5 years old. They'd always compete — first one to spot the Capitol dome in Madison got a nickel. She always won.

"I figured they had very bad eyesight. Those poor old people just can't see anything," she says. "But they were letting me win."

She is older now than her grandparents were then. She is determined to keep her brain limber.

Each day, she does the Jumble.

Each day, she says, "I try to read as much of The Wall Street Journal as I can stand."

***

In January, Hillary McLaren begins dissection on the old woman's face. Weeks earlier she'd peeked at it under the towel.

"I didn't want my first interaction with her to be while I was dissecting her face," she says.

She was relieved to find that the woman's face does not look real — more like a wax figure from Madame Tussauds.

McLaren dissects the side of the face, the parotid, one of the salivary glands. As she cuts away skin, she notices that the woman appears less human and less intimidating, more clinical, more like an exhibit in a museum. Later, when the nose has been bisected, the face looks less imposing still, almost like the rubbery model on which medics learn CPR.

In the second week of January, the students arrive at lab to find that a circle has been cut around the top of the old woman's skull with a bone saw. This is to make their work easier. Andrew Kleist places a chisel against the woman's head where the bone saw left its mark. He raises a mallet and hits the chisel, gently at first, then with more force.

The skull resists. He strikes the chisel harder, deeper into the bone, leveraging it like a crowbar in an effort to pry off the top of the skull. There is a sound like the ripping of packing tape.

The brain rests inside the skull, protected by three layers beginning with the dura mater, Latin for "tough mother." It is an apt description, given the way Joseph Zilisch is digging his fingers inside the top portion of the skull, trying with all his might to free the brain. He tries holding the brain, while Hinkamper wiggles the top portion of the skull, the two of them trying to twist or finesse the brain free. The rest of the team can only watch.

Hinkamper, who has dissected a body before, describes what is supposed to be happening if this were proceeding normally.

Snap. Crackle. Pop.

These sounds they should be hearing. The process should be this simple, the brain popping out from the skull with relative ease.

Instead, it takes more than 30 minutes before Zilisch finally works the brain free and Hinkamper cries out: "Whoo-hoo!"

And there it is, the brain: heavy, wet, dense.

It is spider-webbed with tiny veins and feels a little like molded Jell-O or a waterlogged mushroom. Two white nerves branch off toward the indentation where the eyes would fit.

As they did with the heart, the students take turns holding the brain and pressing the tissue with their gloved fingers.

"So now I know where Hillary Clinton's blood clot was," Khalid Sharif-Sidi says, pointing to a vein found behind the right ear.

When her turn with the brain comes, Hinkamper wonders about the experience of déjà vu, which she has from time to time while driving. Her eyes are locked on the road, but her mind is detouring down some oddly familiar lane. Where do these memories get stored and how is it they trickle back, unrequested?

Kleist holds the brain and thinks that this is where all information enters. Our brain is what makes us human. And yet, impressive as it is, the brain is a contradiction. It is far too clever and too complex to be understood even by itself.

"You can hold a brain and not know how it works," Kleist says. "You can do research for 200 years and still not know what is going on."

Feel the valves in the heart and you can picture how they work.

Hold the brain. Follow the ridges and veins. Place it on a scale and realize that all of this woman's thoughts and memories and sensations lived inside 1,275 grams, less than 3 pounds.

You can only shake your head.

"In the brain," Kleist says, "there's some hidden essence."

***

In the last few weeks, they dissect the tongue and the area where the eyes are housed and the nasal region. It is late January. The old woman looks less and less real.

And yet, the woman's humanity persists in the smallest details: a tuft of gray-brown hair behind her right ear, thick black eyelashes, the tips of her fingers.

The students are encouraged to take pride in their dissection. In preparation for the last practical exam, each group is asked to list the areas where they have done their best work. The professors will use these lists to tag the bodies for the exam.

At Table 1, students list the maxillary artery, a branch of the carotid artery that supplies blood to deep structures in the face. They also list the left orbit, the skull cavity in which the left eye rests.

By now, they are constantly quizzing each other as they perform dissection. There are whiteboards beside each table filled with terms and illustrations and anything the students think will help them to remember. At one table, students have composed a phrase to recall the branches of the carotid artery: *superior thyroid, ascending pharyngeal, lingual, facial, occipital, posterior auricular, maxillary, superficial temporal* and *transverse facial.*

Some Aggressive Lovers Find Odd Positions More Satisfyingly Tricky.

On weekends students return to the lab and visit the bodies again, going back over the structures. They worry, but also feel oddly nostalgic.

"So we're done?" McLaren asks, almost sadly, as they finish up on the final day of lab.

In the course of delving into the old woman's body, McLaren has learned about herself. She won't be a surgeon. She likes the delicate, technical work of dissection but craves a job that will allow her to build relationships with patients. That isn't surgery, she concludes.

Others have taken their own lessons from Table 1.

Sharif-Sidi did well enough on his first exam to know he could survive in medical school. He could hang with the smart kids. He sheds this one aspect of his fear of failure only to discover another. Now there is the gnawing anxiety that he has crammed so much information into his head in five months that some will slip away.

One other lesson he has learned: He is not cut out to work in obstetrics and gynecology.

"I did not like the pelvis," he says, his face tightening in a scowl. "It's your personal space, and we're invading it."

Factors just as basic — the look and the smell — have made it clear to Lori Wong that gastrointestinal medicine is not for her.

Dissection took Wong into corners of her own psyche. There is the remembrance of pain that came from discovering that the old woman died of kidney failure, one of the diseases that killed Wong's mother. And there is a strange feeling Wong admits to as the course comes to an end: She will miss the woman at Table 1.

The students scrub down the steel table, cleaning away dried pools of embalming fluid. They discuss how to leave her body — face up or face down? Up, they decide.

Finally, they draw the towels back over the old woman.

For a while, they test each other as the lab empties and classmates head to the cafeteria for lunch. The students at Table 1 finish their review and wash up.

"I think I'm going to stay for a little bit," Zilisch tells his lab partners, knowing he will not have this chance again.

As they leave, he begins a part of dissection that is optional. Using the chisel, he cuts through the temporal bone in search of the inner and middle ear.

One of the professors stays behind, guiding him, assuring him, "We should be able to see the tympanic membrane..."

**

The body has not finished teaching.

Something happens when you handle a person's final remains. Something that cannot be measured on an exam.

Todd Hoagland remembers descending into the basement of the Medical College a year ago, into a windowless, cinderblock room where he was alone with more than 400 neatly labeled white boxes, each a little smaller than a shoebox.

He tuned the radio to a classical station. The room was silent but for the music of Tchaikovsky and Beethoven.

He opened the first box.

For the next five hours, then for five hours the following day and five more hours the day after that, Hoagland processed the last remains of the bodies his students had dissected in preparation for burial.

Inside each white box was a smaller plastic box, the urn, and inside each urn was a bag of ashes.

Before they can be buried, the ashes undergo rigorous checks. Some were bound for the Wauwatosa Cemetery, others for the families.

Hoagland was meticulous. For each box, he pulled the matching file of donor records. He checked that donor wishes were being followed. He made sure the metal tag and the other donor labels matched. There could be no question about the identity of remains.

Slowly, he squeezed the excess air from each plastic bag. He placed each one inside a second bag and again removed the excess air, and when each bag was ready he arranged it on a long steel table, the kind morticians use.

Hoagland wore a respiratory mask as he worked. He could hear each breath inside his head. He could see that every bag was different. Some ashes were the color of charcoal, others battleship gray, still others the shade of wheat flour.

No two were alike. The realization shocked him.

In life, each person was unique, and somehow that uniqueness survived death and embalming and cremation.

As he worked by himself, Hoagland sensed the smallness of human beings. Our remains do not fill a 1-gallon Ziploc bag. Yet the ashes are remarkably dense. He found himself pondering why we're here and what it means to live. And he was glad he'd chosen not to delegate the task of processing remains.

"I like to be able to tell the families I did the processing myself," he would say. "It needs to be done well, and I like to be able to tell them I did that."

***

They meet once more on a bright Saturday morning in April. Two months have passed since the students set down their scalpels, since all 200 passed the course, since the team at Table 1 last saw the old woman.

"We need to give thanks for those who were our teachers," Hoagland tells the assembled crowd, "and pay respect to the dead."

It is traditional that at the course's end they hold a memorial service for the bodies they dissected — though *body* is not the word anyone uses on this day.

"A silent but brilliant teacher," Hoagland says.

"Our first patients," says Carlos Jaramillo, a student who worked with one of the other dissection groups.

From Table 1, Joseph Zilisch approaches the front of the room. Zilisch, dressed in his white lab coat, is more comfortable with a scalpel than a microphone. Still, he has volunteered to give the main student speech to a crowd of 250 that includes not only classmates and professors.

Also seated before him are relatives of the men and women the students dissected.

"By definition, death unites all living things," Zilisch says, "as a common denominator, a sort of debt to be paid for the amazing gift of life."

He tries to put into words the extraordinary closeness and the extraordinary distance they have shared, these students and their silent teachers.

They examined the brain without uncovering the personality. They peered inside the vessels of the heart without learning about the people and places that made it beat faster.

On this morning, the students have no way to find the loved ones who knew these things. They have no name to go on, nothing more than a vague description of an embalmed body and a list of medical conditions they compiled during dissection.

"Many assume that doctors will not faint at the sight of blood, get queasy at the thought of broken bones or be afraid of confronting death," Zilsch said. "Truth is, a whole lot of us were unprepared to face these challenges at the beginning of medical school and now we are better equipped to cope with these realities."

He thinks ahead to the future patients who will unknowingly benefit from all that the woman at Table 1 taught him, and on their behalf he says the only thing he can.

"Thank you."

The Manhunt: a Five-Part Series

Los Angeles Times

December 08, 10, 12, 13, 15, 2013

Written by Christopher Goffard
Reported by Christopher Goffard, Louis Sahagun,
Kurt Streeter, Joel Rubin and Phil Willon

Chapter One: Murder in Irvine

The man emerged from a charcoal-gray pickup and approached the hotel check-in counter. He wanted a room and the Internet pass code. He was 6 feet tall, with a weightlifter's build and military posture. But he could transform his soft, round face into a picture of amiability. He struck the night manager as personable and disarming

Inside Room 116 of the Hi View Inn & Suites in Manhattan Beach, he stared at his Facebook page and a lifetime's worth of grudges. It is not clear how long he had labored on the unusual document on the screen.

It was a rambling, free-associating screed in which he asserted firm opinions on politicians, journalists, comedians and television shows. It was a brew of hatreds, a sustained cry of self-pity and self-justification, and a blueprint.

One touch of a button would make it public, once people knew where to look.

It was 1:15 a.m. on Monday, Feb. 4.

Click.

***

Hours earlier, Irvine Police Det. Victoria Hurtado was crouched in the evening chill, studying an enormous diamond ring on a dead woman's hand. It was one of her first clues. "This is not a robbery," she thought.

The victim was in the passenger seat of a white Kia Optima, parked on the rooftop lot of an upmarket condo complex on Scholarship Drive. She was Asian, in a pretty blue dress. Beside her, a young black man was slumped over the steering wheel. Both were riddled with bullets, with fatal shots to the back of their heads.

Stepping carefully amid 14 shell casings scattered on the pavement, Hurtado noticed powder burns around the bullet holes in the windows. It was a close-range ambush, and as cold a scene as the detective had seen in 17 years on the force.

There was no evidence of a fight. It was as if the killer, possessed by an impersonal fury, had not known the victims at all.

Hurtado looked up at the high-rise apartments that towered above the garage. Hundreds of people would have had a plain view of the shooting, if they had peered out their windows. Hundreds should have heard it.

Five floors below, news crews were assembling. Murder was startling news in Irvine, which boasted of being America's safest midsized city —65 square miles of gleaming corporate parks and master-planned neighborhoods.

Just after midnight, the department received a call. It was from Randal Quan, a retired Los Angeles Police Department captain. He had seen the news and recognized the condo complex. His 28-year-old daughter, Monica, lived there with her 26-year-old fiance, Keith Lawrence.

Quan had grown increasingly worried. He had been trying to call his daughter. She was not answering. He came to the Irvine police station with his wife and grown son. They were a close family. Detectives led them to a private interview room.

Quan described his daughter. He had seen her earlier that day. She had been wearing a blue dress.

***

Neither Monica Quan nor Keith Lawrence seemed capable of making an enemy.

He had been a security officer at USC. She had coached women's basketball at Cal State Fullerton.

A few days earlier, Lawrence had asked her to close her eyes as he led her into their condo. He had arranged rose petals on the carpet in the shape of a heart. He knelt and asked her to marry him.

"There's no one more right for us than each other," he told her, in a scene captured on tape by her brother. "You are my winning lottery ticket."

Perhaps because she had grown up as a police captain's daughter, she was guarded about her personal life, even with the young women she coached. But before a team trip to San Luis Obispo she had displayed the big diamond engagement ring and enjoyed the screams of excitement.

Detectives considered every possible theory. They scoured police logs for reports of road rage, on the chance that an aggrieved driver had followed the young couple home. They talked to neighbors and friends, co-workers and family members.

They asked Randal Quan who might want to hurt his daughter. He had been the first Chinese American captain at the LAPD, and had run a squad targeting Asian gangs. In recent years, he had worked as a lawyer representing cops facing termination.

Did someone hate him enough to do this? Someone he had busted? A disgruntled client?

Quan struggled. He could think of no one. He saw himself as a cop who had been respectful to people he arrested. Even losing clients knew he had fought for them.

***

No one had heard anything. A police canvas of the condominium complex and surrounding buildings confirmed that baffling fact.

The couple had pulled onto the rooftop during the final dramatic minutes of the Super Bowl, when traffic was light. The entry gate recorded their arrival about 7:30 p.m. But police had not learned about the shootings until 9:10 p.m., when a resident walking to his car spotted a body slumped over the Kia's steering wheel.

How had 14 shots gone unheard? Had everybody been that fixated on the game?

Det. Hurtado would have to wait for ballistics tests to be sure, but she began to suspect that the killer had used a silencer. It was an expensive piece of equipment, the province of Hollywood spies and assassins, not real-world killers.

The possibility carried with it a sense of dread. Who were they dealing with? A professional hit man? The mob?

As the department's 18-member detective squad scrambled after leads, an investigator visited Cal State Fullerton and found a compelling clue— its significance clear only in hindsight—that someone had been stalking Monica Quan.

A few days earlier, a man had called the athletic department from a blocked number. He said his daughter played for the women's basketball team, but he was unable to reach her because her cellphone was not working.

He asked for the name of the hotel the team was using during its trip to San Luis Obispo. The request was refused. Would he care to give a callback number? The man hung up.

***

About 100 miles south of Irvine, Pedro Ruelas, 32, arrived at Sound Solutions Auto Styling to open for business Monday morning.

Some DUI arrests had cost him his job driving forklifts years back, by his account, and now he worked seven days a week at the small auto-repair lot in downtown National City, a few miles north of the Mexican border. He was the first one in, last one out.

And so, as he did every morning, Ruelas emptied the garbage, wheeling one of the gray trash cans to a small graffiti-scrawled garbage bin in the alley next to the lot.

As he approached the bin, he noticed what looked like police or military equipment lying atop the heap. Most striking was a steel-plated ballistic vest. The shape reminded him of the emblem on Superman's chest.

His first thought was that he might be able to sell the gear. But he reconsidered: The police might want to know about so unusual a find. He flagged down the first cop he saw.

***

Officer Paul Hernandez pulled on latex gloves and began to look.

One ballistic vest.

Two military-style ammunition cans, each with several hundred bullets.

Two cans of olive-drab spray paint, the kind SWAT members use to camouflage their helmets and rifles.

One military-surplus gasoline container, plastic, empty.

Two mortar-tube containers, empty. One black leather police duty belt, with thigh holsters and an expandable baton.

Two AR-15 magazine pouches.

One dark blue LAPD uniform, extra large.

One police officer's field notebook, with a cover bearing two hand-written names and serial numbers:

DORNER #37381

EVANS #31050

Hernandez placed the gear carefully in his squad car and drove to the station house.

He carried the equipment downstairs to the property room and began labeling the items for storage. Another officer might have simply filed a Found Property report and forgotten about it.

Hernandez feared that another cop had been the victim—that someone had stolen the equipment and dumped it in a panic.

At 10:16 a.m. he told the dispatcher to call the LAPD to run down the names and numbers on the notebook.

The answer came back quickly. There was no Dorner now on the force. But there was an Evans.

***

In keeping with her prework ritual, Teresa Evans had driven to the beach that Monday morning, drank a leisurely cup of coffee and read the *Los Angeles Times* on her iPad. She saw a brief story about the double homicide in Irvine.

Evans was 48, with short, dyed blond hair, an 18-year veteran of the LAPD. She was a field sergeant, athletic but unimposing, five feet tall, 115 pounds. On the street, her bulky utility belt made her seem even smaller.

Off duty, she spent much of her time hauling her teenage son and his teammates to soccer practice.

Right now, as she was preparing for her late-morning run on the beach, her phone rang.

"I'm just calling about some property," Officer Hernandez said.

She listened to the strange account of the discarded items. No, she said, she had not been the victim of a theft.

She heard the name Dorner. Anxiety gripped her.

Christopher Dorner had been her trainee six years ago, she said, a problem cop who had been fired. She had no clue where he was now, or why his gear would be in a National City trash bin.

She and Dorner had shared a patrol car in San Pedro, near the ports. He had been a probationary officer just back from a year overseas with the Navy.

She thought little of his abilities. He was sloppy and ham-fisted. He had accidentally shot himself in the hand at the Police Academy. Once, responding to a "man with a gun" call, he had walked directly toward the suspect without seeking cover.

He told Evans that the LAPD had discriminated against him as a black man, and that he intended to sue. He wept in the patrol car. She saw him as unstable, perpetually angry and frustrated, eager to see racism in every encounter.

After she warned him that he needed to improve his police work, Dorner filed a complaint that she had kicked a handcuffed, mentally ill man in the head and chest during an arrest. While being investigated, Evans was put on desk duty and prevented from working overtime or off-duty security jobs. She described the ordeal as a "nightmare."

The LAPD interviewed hotel employees, who said they had seen none of the alleged kicks. The LAPD found it fatal to Dorner's credibility that he had waited two weeks after the incident before complaining.

He sat before a Board of Rights hearing in December 2008, accused of making the story up. That session took place on the fifth floor of the Bradbury Building downtown, a place informally called "The Ovens." It is where, police said, they went to get burned.

Dorner was deemed a liar and fired. Evans knew he held her responsible. She recalled the way he had looked at her during the hearing.

It was not a scowl, not a grimace of anger, but something spookier. Her lawyer described it as the "stare of somebody whose mind is racing 100 miles an hour."

Armed guards stood watch as Dorner was led from the building.

For the next six months, she had carried her service Glock everywhere. She wore it to the bathroom, to the grocery store, to her son's soccer games. When she drove home, she circled the block to make sure Dorner wasn't following her, or waiting to ambush her.

Sooner or later, she believed, he would try to find her.

Evans said goodbye to the National City officer and hung up. She was no longer in the mood for her morning run. She wasn't sure what to do with the information he had given her, or what it might mean.

She supervised the graveyard shift on Venice Beach that night, the phone call never far from her thoughts.

***

"Is anybody going out?"

The man asking the question stood on a weather-beaten old pier at Driscoll's Wharf, amid the motley fleet of squid and swordfish boats in Point Loma. It was Tuesday morning.

Dockhand Jeremy Smith noticed the stranger's shaved head, military boots and hulking size, and thought he must be from Naval Base San Diego, a few miles south. He did not look like the ordinary visitor. Big black dude, he thought. That's way out of place.

Smith, 41, found the stranger friendly and likable.

He did not seem like the hard men he had met during his stints in lockup for DUI arrests, nor like the men he lived with now at a halfway house.

The big stranger gave his name as Mike, and said he would soon be sent to war in Afghanistan. He wanted to get in some fishing first. He was willing to pay $200 to fish in Mexican waters.

Smith thought he should help a man heading to war. He led him around the docks, past the stacks of steel-mesh lobster cages and piles of netting, looking for a boat.

Nobody was going out for marlin and swordfish; the water was cold, the fish lethargic. One captain found it odd that a man headed to war would want to spend time fishing, rather than with a woman.

Why not a sport boat? Smith asked the stranger. Why not whale-watching?

"I don't want to whale-watch," the stranger replied.

The stranger disappeared and came back with a bag of yellowtail and halibut tacos. He passed them out to the men on Pier 6 and refused to take their money.

Smith explained that he couldn't take him out on the water himself, because the terms of his jail release didn't allow him to leave the harbor. He couldn't risk being spotted by the Harbor Patrol.

"Nazis," Smith said.

The stranger sympathized. He had a friend who had been fired from the police force, he said, and he didn't like cops.

That afternoon, Teresa Evans drove to the LAPD's Pacific Area station to begin her overnight shift. She suited up and led roll call for the eight officers under her command. She and her crew headed to their cars, preparing their gear.

She overheard a group of cops chatting nearby. The subject was an officer's upcoming disciplinary hearing.

The officer needed strong representation, someone said—a good lawyer like Randal Quan, the former LAPD captain turned attorney.

Quan wouldn't be available any time soon, another cop said.

"His daughter was murdered."

The hair prickled on the back of Evans' neck. She felt vaguely sick.

Until now, she hadn't known that the young woman shot to death in Irvine two nights ago had been Quan's daughter.

She remembered that Quan had represented Dorner at his Board of Rights hearing, and she knew that Dorner had blamed everyone involved for his firing, including his lawyer. Was there a connection, somehow, to the stash of Dorner's gear in the trash bin?

It was a busy night on the Venice beach detail. Fights, drunks, homeless calls. But her mind returned repeatedly to the possibility that Dorner had killed the young Irvine couple.

No, she told herself. It's too much of a long-shot.

At the station house that night, she paused in her paperwork and told another cop, "Let me run this by you."

The other cop listened and said, "You've got to call."

By 11:15 p.m. Evans was on the phone with the Irvine Police Department's watch commander, who called the home of the detective-squad sergeant, who promptly called Evans to hear her story.

"This might be crazy," she began.

***

Det. Hurtado arrived at the Irvine station before dawn Wednesday. Her sergeant held out a piece of yellow notebook paper bearing Christopher Dorner's name.

Hurtado ran it through the databases. He had no criminal record. He was a Navy reservist. He owned a Nissan Titan pickup. He had a house in Las Vegas. He had a mother and sister in La Palma, south of Los Angeles.

He owned a lot of guns, including 9-millimeter Glocks. The shell casings at the murder scene had been 9-millimeter.

She sent two detectives to National City to examine Dorner's gear. They learned that an employee at a second auto shop—just down the alley from the first—had found more of Dorner's equipment in a trash bin. A SWAT-style helmet. A military-style backpack. A magazine with 9-millimeter bullets.

Detectives located a surveillance camera that showed Dorner pulling into the alley in his Titan early Monday, the morning after the shootings. He could be seen climbing out to toss away the items. He seemed to be in no rush.

He had picked an alley in plain view of the National City police station, as if he had hoped to be spotted and confronted.

Back in Irvine, detectives drafted search warrants for Dorner's home and his mother's home. If they found him, they were intent on taking him in.

But they were not sure they had enough to charge him with murder.

They sought a stopgap measure, to hold him as the case was being built. They found it in the expandable baton Dorner had cast away. He could be charged with possession of a prohibited weapon. When he lost his badge, he had lost his right to carry it.

Hurtado placed calls to the LAPD, trying to find Dorner's personnel file. She kept getting voice mails. People were out of the office, or on vacation.

She left her call-back number, and tried to keep the details vague. She had no contacts at the LAPD; as far as she knew, Dorner might still have friends there. If she didn't proceed cautiously, someone might alert him to her interest.

Then she called Randal Quan, and asked:

Does the name Christopher Dorner mean anything to you?

She heard silence. Then she heard him gasp and say, "Oh my God. That guy's crazy."

Quan explained that he had represented Dorner at his Board of Rights hearing. He said Dorner had blamed him for his firing and was a man obsessed with the concept of his own integrity. He possessed "kind of a hero syndrome," Quan said.

In her notebook, the detective wrote:

"Hero syndrome."

Hurtado called one of the slain couple's friends. During the conversation, an email arrived on her desktop computer. It was from a detective down the hall conducting a Web search. It had a link to Dorner's Facebook page.

"From: Christopher Jordan Dorner

"To: America

"Subj: Last resort

"I know most of you who personally know me are in disbelief to hear from media reports that I am suspected of committing such horrendous murders and have taken drastic and shocking actions in the last couple of days," the posting began.

"Unfortunately, this is a necessary evil that I do not enjoy but must partake and complete for substantial change to occur within the LAPD and reclaim my name. The department has not changed since the Rampart and Rodney King days. It has gotten worse...."

It was 1:59 p.m., Wednesday, Feb. 6. Hurtado hung up and called Quan to tell him he was in danger.

Dozens of detectives were getting the same email, reading it on desktops and smartphones. Down the hall, Irvine's police chief was meeting with his command staff. The detective sergeant ran over and stuck his head in.

"I need some help," he said.

CHAPTER TWO: FEAR AND THE CITY

Just after 2 p.m. at the LAPD's sleek, 10-story glass tower, the phones began beeping furiously.

Police in Irvine, an hour south, had alerted their Los Angeles counterparts to a terrifying Facebook post. Its author, a disgraced LAPD patrolman, had vowed to murder his former colleagues en masse.

His targets ran through the ranks. Patrol officers were targets. Sergeants were targets. Captains were targets. The chief was a target. Families were targets.

It was Wednesday, Feb. 6. An impromptu war room sprang up on the fifth floor of LAPD's downtown headquarters. Detectives in the robbery-homicide squad tore through Christopher Dorner's online tirade and tallied the names on a white board. They quickly counted 30 people who needed protection.

Sirens screamed across freeways in every direction. About 200 cops went in the first wave of protection details. Specialized units were the easiest to mobilize, so gang squads went. Vice squads went. Twenty off-duty cops from the elite Metro division went. Ordinary patrol cops went.

The potential victims were scattered across thousands of square miles —across L.A. County's far-flung suburbs, from its northern edge to deep inside Orange County, from the beach cities in the west to Riverside County in the east.

Every target would get a "scarecrow" detail: At least two cops, uniformed and visible. There was no time to ask permission of the many local police agencies whose territories the LAPD would be entering, no time to debate or negotiate.

Get there! commanders barked into radios and cellphones. Go! We'll clean it up later!

***

Dorner's 11,000-word document, which people began calling "the manifesto," was all at once a confession, an extended threat and a summing-up of the life its 33-year-old author soon expected to depart.

It was an open letter to America, and a ramble through pop culture, politics and personal grievance.

How accurately the document reflected the facts of his life is unclear. But it vividly illustrated how he perceived his life. He was a prideful man who believed the world had failed to recognize his great gifts. Victimhood was his singular theme.

No one grows up and wants to be a cop killer, he wrote. *It was against everything I've ever been...*

Dorner was raised in a series of middle-class cities where, as one of the few black kids, he felt like an outsider: Cerritos, Pico Rivera, La Palma, Thousand Oaks. His mother was a nurse. His father was absent.

In first grade at Norwalk Christian School, he wrote, the principal swatted him for punching a student who had taunted him with a racial slur. The swattings from authority figures continued through junior high, he claimed, when he dared to stand up to bigots.

When he arrived at the LAPD, he wrote, he found it a nest of racists. In the Police Academy, he complained about another recruit's use of a racial slur and was shunned. On patrol with the LAPD, he complained that his training officer had kicked a mentally ill man, and in response the department conspired to destroy him. He had dared, he said, to violate the Code of Silence.

He vowed to hunt members of the Board of Rights who had heard his case. He would hunt the LAPD hierarchy that had sanctioned his punishment. He was convinced that his former lawyer, Randal Quan, had been loyal to the LAPD rather than to him. He would hunt him and his loved ones.

I never had the opportunity to have a family of my own, I'm terminating yours...

He bragged of his marksmanship and tactical prowess. He would kill Caucasian officers who victimized minorities. He would kill black officers who belittled their Caucasian subordinates and fueled anti-black bigotry. He would kill Latino officers who victimized other Latinos. He would kill lesbian officers who degraded men.

He praised his knee surgeon, President Obama, the first lady's hairstyle, George W. Bush, Charlie Sheen, Chick-fil-A chicken and Bill Cosby. He told Gov. Chris Christie to go on a diet, and told David Petraeus that his marital failings were human. He told Natalie Portman she was beautiful. He quoted Mia Farrow on the moral urgency of gun control.

He knew he would die, and lamented what he would not get to see. He would miss "The Hangover III," and told the director not to diminish the franchise with another sequel. He would miss season three of "The Walking Dead." He would miss Shark Week.

***

From his 10th-floor office, LAPD Chief Charlie Beck was trying to coordinate the agency's response and keep his family safe. He called his wife and told her to assemble the family at home, fast.

"He has a vendetta list," he said. "We're on it."

Beck had not been chief when Dorner was fired, but he was the public face of the department. Two of Beck's kids wore LAPD badges. He ordered them pulled off duty.

Chief Beck, Dorner had written, *this is when you need to have that come to Jesus talk with Sgt. Teresa Evans and everyone else who was involved in the conspiracy to have me terminated for doing the right thing....*

Studying Dorner's words, Beck thought, "He's an injustice collector." He blamed everyone else for his failures.

Beck was struck by the length of the tirade. This was no fleeting howl of homicidal rage but the chilling product, it seemed, of months-long planning and forethought.

Dorner had invoked the most highly charged controversies of the LAPD's past. The beating of Rodney King. The Rampart scandal. The specter of Mark Fuhrman.

As chief for more than three years, Beck had helped to transform the 10,000-officer department. In black neighborhoods, its image as an occupying army had abated. Its 11% of black officers now roughly mirrored the city's demographics.

Yet Beck understood, even at a glance, the combustible elements at play. True or false, Dorner's accusations would resonate with people predisposed to believe them. And so today the chief turned to his media spokesman and asked:

"Is this the thing?"

He did not need to explain. He meant the thing that spiraled out of control so badly that it forced him from his job. He reckoned the odds at 50-50 that it would happen someday.

Everyone who served as chief in the nation's second-largest city woke up knowing today might be the day.

Beck sometimes wondered what his predecessor, Daryl F. Gates, had thought on first viewing the grainy footage of his white officers beating Rodney King. Beck had been a sergeant on the front lines in 1992 when the cops were acquitted and rioting swept the city.

Gates had been untouchable. Then he was gone.

Now, a man the LAPD had trained was promising to bring war to its doorstep. If the public turned against the LAPD in the days ahead, Beck knew, he would have to take the blame himself.

"None of us bury our past," he would say. "You don't bury it. You carry it."

***

Teresa Evans, Dorner's former training officer, was sitting in her SUV when she got the call. She was outside her home in a Los Angeles suburb, about to leave for her son's soccer game.

"It's a credible threat," an Irvine sergeant was telling her.

She looked around quickly. Would Dorner be coming around the corner, gun blazing? It would be easy for him to find her here. She had to get away, fast.

Her cellphone rang again. Two LAPD captains told her they were sending protection to meet her, and would call her back with a rendezvous point.

"Stay mobile," they said. "Don't go home."

She drove to the soccer field. There, she met her ex-husband and explained. He would watch their son for now. She hoped that if Dorner came, he would come only after her.

Back on the road, she checked the mirrors constantly. She recalled Dorner bragging about his experience in military intelligence. Was he monitoring her phone's GPS? She flipped abrupt U-turns. She pulled onto the freeway, pulled off, pulled on.

She steered with her left hand, so her right could quickly grab her duty Glock, squeezed in its holster between the driver's seat and the center console.

She called a hotel in Orange County and booked a room. She headed that way.

Her phone rang again. A security team would meet her in a church parking lot near her home.

She drove to the meeting point, but there were no officers in sight. She waited nearby, her gun close.

Then help came screaming down the block, a pack of patrol cars—10 or more, she guessed—roaring her way.

Soon there were cops with assault rifles in Teresa Evans' living room, in her kitchen, ringing her house. They drew the curtains and covered the windows with blankets. They shoved the couch against the window of her son's room, unscrewed the porch lights and deactivated the motion sensors.

She still did not feel safe. She feared that Dorner might take aim from a freeway visible from her window.

You destroyed my life and name because of your actions, he had written. *Time is up.*

She dumped her Facebook page. She turned off her phone's GPS tracker.

When her son came hobbling through the door, his ankle injured during the afternoon's soccer game, she tried to explain the presence of the SWAT team in vague terms.

Something is going on, she said, and everything will be OK.

She did not say, "Someone wants to murder us."

***

People who had known Dorner for years were shocked to see his smiling face on fliers and television screens. One of them was a San Diego police officer named Dulani Jackson. He had been friends with Dorner since they had attended Cypress High School.

Jackson, who is also black, said Dorner had complained about being bullied by racists at his former high school in La Palma. Dorner liked to say that if a girl disrespected him, he would beat up her boyfriend. Or take it out on her family.

After Dorner's firing from the LAPD in 2009, Jackson had driven to Dorner's home in Vegas to keep him company. He found him in a deep depression. Dorner blamed the LAPD for tarnishing his name and thereby sabotaging his career in the Navy. Only two days before the Irvine killings, the Navy had officially discharged him.

Dorner had abruptly cut Jackson out of his life, with a text citing a litany of long-simmering grievances. He resented that Jackson hadn't attended his graduation from Southern Utah University. He resented that Jackson hadn't visited him in the hospital, after he shot himself in the hand in the Police Academy.

Jackson could picture Dorner alone in his Vegas home, isolated from family, cut off from friends, with nothing to do but seethe. He knew that Dorner had started buying silencers about a year ago. That, he reasoned, was probably when he began to plan his murder campaign.

Like Jackson, many who knew Dorner understood that his memory for slights—real or imagined—was vast. He was always adding up the score.

A former girlfriend, Denise Jensen, remembered that he had been a perfect gentleman at first. He liked to open doors for her. He bought her a nice watch and an iPod. In a tantrum, he seized the gifts and gave them to a stranger at a gas station. Worthier of my kindness, he explained.

He made friends effortlessly but turned on them in an instant. "You just don't know until he starts turning," Jensen said.

In July 2009, months after their breakup, Dorner logged onto Facebook and used a fake name—"Mike Crawford"—to lure her to a date at a Las Vegas restaurant. He cornered her in the ladies room and left only after staff threatened to call police.

Another ex-girlfriend had posted a warning on the website Don'tDateHimGirl.com, saying: "If you value your sanity, stay away from this guy." She described him as "super paranoid always thinking somebody's out to get him."

When people asked Dorner about the multitude of firearms he kept close at hand, he would reply that trouble might come any time. J'Anna Hendricks, a manicurist who briefly rented a room from him, discovered guns hidden in the couch cushions.

At first, she found him a model of friendliness. He took her to dinner. She was white, and he jokingly called her a cracker. She called him a wheat cracker and said he was the whitest black guy she knew. She thought it was good fun, though she sensed it annoyed him. One day he invited her to his room and displayed his laptop. On it were naked photos of himself and some of his girlfriends. He seemed to be testing whether she would sleep with him. She left the room fast. Soon afterward, Dorner stormed into her room and screamed, "I want you out tonight!"

In recent months, Dorner had frequented the Lahaina Grill on the outskirts of Vegas, a dimly lit restaurant where he sat with his back against the wall. He drank bottled water and ate sushi, sharing YouTube clips on his MacBook with other patrons and holding forth on politics.

He said he favored background checks for assault-rifle purchasers, including cops. "Hey," he told a bartender, "we can snap."

***

On Wednesday night, not far from the wharf where he had been trying to charter a boat to Mexican waters, the fugitive walked onto the docks of the Southwestern Yacht Club in San Diego.

The ungated club was at the end of an out-of-the-way, affluent neighborhood. A yacht called Vivere II was moored in slip A20.

Inside, the 81-year-old owner, Carlos Caprioglio, was watching television. He would later tell police that he heard footsteps but was not automatically alarmed. He assumed it was his wife, returning from a trip to Los Angeles.

Then Dorner was there, pointing a black semiautomatic handgun at him. "I don't want to kill you," he said, "but you're gonna take me to Mexico."

Dorner took hold of the rope that moored the boat to the dock. A boater of even casual experience knew to throw the rope onto the dock. Instead, Dorner threw it into the water.

Dorner ordered Caprioglio to start the boat. The rope became entangled in the prop. They weren't going anywhere. It seemed to dawn on Dorner that he had botched his plan.

"Take my car keys," Caprioglio said. "Take my car."

"I don't want to be on the streets," Dorner said.

He found a pair of Caprioglio's shoes, and removed the laces. He ordered him to lie face-down, with his right cheek pressed to the sun deck. He tied his hands and feet with the laces, stole his cellphone and disappeared.

By the time Caprioglio had freed himself and had summoned help, just before 10 p.m, Dorner was gone.

***

With SWAT troops sitting in her darkened living room drinking soda, Teresa Evans crawled under her bedcovers Wednesday night. She thought this would prevent Dorner from seeing the glow of her iPhone—just in case he was out there, watching and waiting for his shot.

"He's going to shoot me through my window and kill me," she kept thinking.

All night she traded texts with cops and friends, searching for any scrap of news. She knew she wouldn't sleep.

Her son was down the hall. To make things easier on him, she had assured him: "It's going to be over by tomorrow."

This was a mistake she would make more than once.

Chapter Three: The Longest Night

Michael Crain's wife demanded one thing of him, whenever he put on his uniform, secured his badge on his chest and patrolled the streets of Riverside overnight.

He had to text her that he was OK. If she woke she could glance at her phone and take reassurance. He thought the ritual was silly, because he might run into trouble five minutes later, but he did it anyway.

On the night of Wednesday, Feb. 6, as he did before every shift, Crain, 34, took pains to shed every vestige of his non-cop identity. He made sure there were no family photos in his wallet, in case it flopped open in a chase. He took off his wedding ring and put it on his nightstand.

In the streets, it was best to be a man without vulnerabilities.

Suspects would see a muscular, buzz-cut, 6-foot-3 ex-Marine. Not a father who coached his 10-year-old son's baseball team, made his 4-year-old daughter breakfast every morning and learned to tie her ponytail. Not a man who liked the Food Network, Lynyrd Skynyrd and wearing zebra-striped platform shoes to disco parties.

A suspect had tried to follow him home once. This was safer.

Regina Crain had guessed he was ex-military the day they met, from the way he held out his chest and kept his hair high-and-tight. He had left the Marines before 9/11 and felt guilty he hadn't stayed to fight, but she was glad he had avoided war. Her first husband had fought in Fallujah, and she had seen too many military funerals.

Tonight, she watched him pack his duffel bag for work—backup gun, badge clip, loose change, hair gel, boot polish, Tums. She knew that he liked the graveyard shift, because it was rarely dull, and that he would be disappointed if he came home saying, "I didn't find any bad guys."

Tonight was his last shift with an officer he was training named Andrew Tachias, and he had reassured her that he was an alert, safety-conscious cop. "He's good to go," he said. "I'm basically just teaching him paperwork."

She stood on the stairway step, to reach him, and kissed him and told him to hurry home. They were approaching their second wedding anniversary. She knew he liked to get to work an hour before his 10 p.m. roll call, so he could dress at his locker and practice quick-drawing his gun.

A fanatic for safety, Michael Crain lectured his family never to leave a purse or a Gameboy in the car in plain view. At the mall, his kids knew to avoid his gun-hand side, in case the wrong person recognized him.

Before she went to sleep that night, Regina Crain checked her Facebook page. She saw that police were chasing someone named Christopher Dorner, an ex-LAPD officer who had vowed revenge against his former agency and had killed two people in Irvine.

She didn't think much about it. Los Angeles was a full hour's drive west.

At 11:43 p.m. she texted her husband: "Good night sexy man!"

She knew that if she woke up in the middle of the night, his reply would be waiting for her, assuring her he was OK.

***

In the small hours of that Thursday morning, a self-employed repo man stricken with bladder cancer was beginning work about an hour east of L.A.

Lee McDaniel, 49, the son of a retired Cleveland cop, had just left the side of his sleeping wife. Now he pulled his big Chevrolet truck up to a pump at the Arco station on Weirick Road in Corona.

Since the cancer had invaded his cells, he often felt weak, but he was determined not to lie on the couch and wither away. Work kept him busy and got his mind off his illness.

His first eight-hour chemotherapy session was to begin later that morning. He was on the road now because he wanted to exhaust himself, in order to sleep soundly as the machine pumped poison into his arm.

But first he had a few hours' work to get through, so he activated the gas pump and let it run as he walked into the AM/PM minimart to buy bottles of 5-Hour Energy. Standing in line at the counter, he felt what he described as a "hulking presence" come up behind him.

He turned. The man behind him was as big as a linebacker. They exchanged a quick look. McDaniel thought he looked vaguely familiar —maybe a neighbor, maybe someone he knew from years of coaching Little League.

McDaniel walked back to his truck, holstered the pump and slid behind the wheel. He was pulling past the door of the minimart just as the large man emerged, walking in front of the truck.

Mounted on the hood of McDaniel's truck were four license plate recognition cameras with telltale lights, the kind police use to track down stolen cars and repo men use to find cars to repossess. He saw the big man notice them.

Their eyes locked. McDaniel saw the man walk toward a charcoal-gray Nissan Titan at one of the pumps. It had a roof rack, aftermarket black rims and tinted windows.

McDaniel had seen the news. He knew Christopher Dorner was driving a Titan.

McDaniel was unarmed but accustomed to confrontations and able to function under stress. He pulled slowly past the Titan, and stuck his head out the window to get a look at the license plate. It started with an 8.

He remembered that Dorner's plate started with a 7, according to police. His truck was also supposed to be blue, and this one was gray.

McDaniel stopped his truck at the edge of the lot, close enough to escape down the street if the Titan owner pulled a gun. On his smartphone, he brought up a story about Dorner and found the plate police were distributing: 7X03191.

He typed it into his laptop, running it through a plate database. Up came a photo of a gray Nissan Titan. Roof rack, cover. It was the truck at the pump behind him.

The police had the color wrong, and McDaniel assumed Dorner had switched plates.

Now, he noticed Dorner watching him, standing at the Titan's open door, holding something McDaniel couldn't see.

McDaniel pulled onto Weirick Road. He made a U-turn. He parked across the street from the gas station.

He thought Dorner might follow him. Instead, Dorner turned right out of the station, hooked another quick right and disappeared.

McDaniel was trying to call police when he saw an LAPD patrol car pull off Interstate 15 and head into the gas station. He flashed his lights, to signal them, and drove over the median to meet them.

The officers were in Corona to protect one of Dorner's targets. The guy you're looking for was just here, McDaniel said.

At that moment, the Titan reappeared. Dorner drove past the gas station and pulled onto a freeway on-ramp.

"That's him," McDaniel said.

McDaniel saw one of the officers drop his notebook and radio as he hurried to the patrol car. McDaniel picked them up and tossed them into the police car.

The officers followed Dorner onto Interstate 15, heading north, hanging back a safe distance. They were trying to confirm it was Dorner's truck.

Five miles along, the patrol car followed Dorner down the Magnolia Avenue offramp to the street. Dorner was waiting at the curb beside his parked truck. He opened fire with his assault rifle, riddling the patrol car with .223-caliber rounds.

The officers ducked. They tried to fire back with their handguns, futilely. Dorner was about 100 feet away, with firepower that vastly overwhelmed them. His rounds pierced the squad car's windshield, punctured a tire, blew out the radiator. It was immobilized in seconds. One bullet grazed an officer's head. Dorner sped away down Magnolia.

The officers' radios were out of LAPD broadcast range. They had to rely on cellphones, one of them borrowed from a passing motorist. The delay probably cost minutes in sending a warning.

The 911 call went in at 1:24 a.m.

***

About 10 miles east, Michael Crain and his trainee, Andrew Tachias, were sitting at a red light in their Riverside Police Department patrol car. It was foggy at the intersection of Magnolia and Arlington avenues.

They had ridden together a month, and shared an easy camaraderie. Tachias had plans to marry. His father was an L.A. County sheriff's deputy, who had excited his son's boyhood imagination with stories of the job and then tried to talk him out of wearing a badge because of the toll it took on a man's personal life.

Tachias' favorite film was "End of Watch," a violent, harrowing cop drama about a pair of L.A. cops on the job. He watched it before shifts, to psych himself up.

Tonight, Tachias was in the driver's seat, Crain in the passenger seat. To their left, also stopped at the red light, a 42-year-old Riverside man sat in a Chevrolet Cavalier with flaking paint and missing hubcaps. He was a food-truck driver returning home from work. He glanced at Tachias, who smiled, looking like a man who loved his job.

It was just after 1:30 a.m. Inside the squad car, the radio crackled with news: Dorner was in the area and headed their way.

Parked at the red light, on the other side of the intersection, a 33-year-old man named Karam Kaoud was sitting alone inside a white Crown Victoria with the words BELL CAB CO. on the door.

A Palestinian raised in Dubai, Kaoud had been an American citizen for four months and driving a cab for six. He had a degree in mechanical engineering from Cal State Northridge, but couldn't find work in the field.

So he put in 15-hour shifts in his father's cab, often covering 400 miles across Riverside and San Bernardino counties. It was supposed to be temporary.

His father worried about graveyard-shift muggers and crazies. He had called this morning and said, "Please be careful."

"Inshallah," Kaoud had replied. God willing. "Don't worry, Dad."

A devout Muslim, the cabbie kept the Koran in the glovebox and prayed five times a day. When he couldn't get to the mosque, he removed the car's floor mat and flipped it over on the pavement of a quiet parking lot. Then he knelt, a smartphone app pointing him to Mecca.

He lived with his wife, parents, two sisters and his four-month-old son. He had just dropped off a customer at a Denny's and decided to head to a downtown Riverside restaurant to wait for fares.

As he pulled out of the restaurant parking lot onto Madison Street, he debated which way to go. It made sense to turn right, which would take him to the 91 Freeway and get him there fast. It didn't make sense to turn left, because the stoplights on Magnolia might cost him three extra minutes.

For reasons he couldn't explain, he had turned left. That is why he was here at this hour, facing a Riverside police car across an intersection.

He was preoccupied with his GPS when he half-noticed the Nissan Titan pulling up on his right. Then he saw the Titan moving forward, as if the light had turned green.

Reflexively, he took his foot off the brake and began to follow. Then he stopped. The light was still red. He watched the Titan cross the intersection and pull up beside the food-truck driver's Cavalier and the patrol car. At first, he did not understand what he was seeing.

He watched the cold air warped by the heat from a rifle muzzle, just outside the open window of the Titan's driver's-side window. The driver was firing over the hood of the Cavalier at the patrol car, in quick, muted bursts.

Within seconds, the Titan was pulling away down Magnolia.

The bullet-riddled patrol car rolled slowly into the intersection.

The cabbie jumped out. Inside the patrol car, he saw the wide-open eyes of Officer Tachias as he sat paralyzed behind the wheel, struggling to breathe, his foot off the brake. He noticed Officer Crain sitting bolt-straight in the passenger seat, completely still.

The cabbie had not heard the name Dorner, and he avoided trouble. He did not know if he could touch a police car; he might be sued. Still, he reached into the car and forced the gear shift into park, producing a grating sound as the car stopped.

He touched Tachias' shoulder and asked what he could do.

"The radio," the policeman managed to say. "The radio."

The cabbie reached for the walkie-talkie at Tachias' side.

"The other radio," the policeman said. He meant the walkie-talkie on the dashboard.

The cabbie grabbed it. He pushed the button on the side. He held it to Tachias' lips. Tachias struggled to form the words.

"Officer down," he said. He looked at his motionless partner.

The cabbie knew how to work the radio, because he had one just like it, but in his fear his finger was frozen on the button. His eyes darted around the streets. What if the shooter returned? What if there was more than one of them? He noticed the gun on the policeman's belt. He might have to grab it to defend himself.

"Release your hand," Tachias said.

He obeyed. A dispatcher said help was on its way.

The cabbie looked at Tachias and knew he was dying. He told him to hang on. He saw the lights of a police car, speeding toward him on Magnolia. He held his hands in the air to show he was unarmed.

He saw two policemen staring in at Crain, then exchanging a look that told him the officer was dead. He saw rescuers pull Tachias onto the ground and heard him say "I'm cold, I'm losing my breath," while a policeman said, "Keep talking to him."

Judging from the .223-caliber casings found at the scene, Dorner had fired at least 13 times with his armor-piercing assault rifle. Both officers were rushed to Riverside Community Hospital. Tachias slipped in and out of consciousness. Bullets had struck him in the back, legs and arms, blowing out his shoulder.

Crain had no pulse. Rescuers worked on him frantically for half an hour before pronouncing him dead, but he had probably died right away.

Seven rounds had struck him. They grazed his head, hit his shoulder and thigh, and severed his jugular vein.

One bullet had pierced his badge, ripped through his ballistic vest and punctured his heart. He had not drawn his gun.

Dorner had disappeared again. The Cavalier driver, Jack Chilson, had tried to pursue him but had grown afraid and stopped.

From just feet away, he had seen Dorner firing at the patrol car. He had seen the bullets punch a circle in the window the size of a paper plate.

He noticed Dorner had been wearing a heavy camouflage jacket and wraparound goggles. It looked like he had been grinning.

***

About 40 minutes after the shooting, a shuttle driver near San Diego International Airport saw a wallet in the road and stopped to pick it up. Inside was a photo ID of Dorner and an LAPD detective's badge.

The badge turned out to be real, but it was not Dorner's. He had never been a detective.

The detective who had earned it was dead; the widow could not recall how it had vanished.

Police guessed that Dorner had probably purchased it from a police-memorabilia dealer, and had used it to masquerade as a detective.

Why had Dorner dumped the wallet here, on a well-traveled route where it was likely to be spotted? Did he want them to believe he had flown out of town?

Why, soon after his first killings, had he dumped his police and paramilitary gear in two National City trash bins? Had he been scuttling possessions in hopes of fleeing the country? Or was he playing some kind of game, taunting police with scattered clues?

***

About 5 a.m. Thursday, three and a half hours after the shooting, about 60 miles west of Riverside, an aluminum blue Toyota Tacoma rolled slowly down a wide, well-lit street in Torrance.

In the back seat was Emma Hernandez, 71, who was handing copies of the *Los Angeles Times* and *Wall Street Journal* to her daughter, Margie Carranza, 46, who was driving with one hand and tossing papers onto porches with the other.

They were both small women, the mother under five feet tall, the daughter just a little taller. They were from El Salvador and spoke little English.

They had risen that morning in a Torrance tenement with a graffiti-scratched elevator. Hernandez shared the single bedroom with her granddaughter; Carranza slept in the living room near her teenage son.

The women were squirreling away money so that the boy could afford college. They did the two- and-a-half-hour shift seven days a week, 365 days a year, and held down separate jobs as housecleaners.

They drove to the newspaper distribution center to pick up their stack of 400 papers, and began their route. Their custom was to drive with headlights and hazard lights on.

The daughter noticed a police car parked at the corner of Redbeam Avenue and Norton Street, all four doors open, with no officers in sight. She was apprehensive. She never saw police here.

The women did not know that a team of LAPD officers was on the block guarding the house of a captain who had been targeted in Dorner's manifesto. The police also had just received a radio call that a truck resembling Dorner's had left the freeway and was headed their way.

The truck windows were open, and yet the women heard no orders to stop, no commands to surrender. They heard only the sound of gunfire exploding through the truck.

Glass shattered, and the air filled with splinters of plastic. Bullets flew through the seats, the headrest, the glass. "I am just the newspaper woman!" the daughter yelled, but the shots kept coming.

In the back seat, the mother saw her daughter's head sway from side to side, and feared she would be shot in the head. "No tengas miedo!" she cried. Don't be afraid.

She hugged the back of her daughter's seat, to shield her from the barrage of bullets. She did not want her grandchildren to lose their mother. "God have mercy on our souls!" she said.

One bullet went in high on the right side of her back, and emerged just above the collarbone. Another bullet struck her lower back, close to the spine. A small fragment of glass flew into her eye.

Neither woman could tell how long the shooting lasted. By one estimate, police officers—eight of them—fired more than 100 rounds, and 30 of them missed the truck altogether.

Police yelled at the women to get out with their hands up. The terrified women emerged. The daughter told her mother to stand beside her, fearing they would now be executed.

The police looked at the women and seemed to realize their mistake.

"Why did you shoot at us?" the daughter asked. They heard no explanation, no apology.

The mother was able to stand, but she felt blood pouring down her back. "I'm hurt, I'm hurt," she said. She wondered why police did not inspect her wounds or render first aid.

When an ambulance arrived, she bickered with paramedics who wanted to remove her shirt. Her daughter told her it was necessary.

Neighbors had been awakened by the gunfire, and some had crawled to their windows to peek outside. Bullets had sprayed cars and houses, roofs, garage doors, trees, windshields, bumpers, front doors.

One man heard bullets striking his front door, groped for the phone and demanded the police. The dispatcher said: They are already there.

One man found five bullet holes in the entryway to his house and voiced a common sense of bafflement. "How do you mistake two Hispanic women, one who is 71, for a large black male?"

Only a few blocks away, Torrance police had stopped a black Honda Ridgeline pickup truck. The driver, David Perdue, was a 38-year-old baggage handler at LAX. He was going to pick up a friend for a morning of surfing.

Police questioned him and told him to turn around. As he was driving away, another Torrance police car raced up and broadsided him. His airbags exploded. An officer began firing at him. Three bullets flew through his windshield but missed him. He was ordered to the pavement at gunpoint. He would complain of a concussion, spine trouble and pain that left him unable to work or lift his kids.

A white man of medium height and build, he looked nothing like Christopher Dorner.

In their attempt at an explanation, Torrance police said its officers had been responding to the shots fired by the LAPD nearby. They had perceived the surfer as a threat.

***

Regina Crain had a nightmare once, after one of her husband's colleagues on the Riverside Police Department had been killed on the job.

In the dream, she was with her husband in the kitchen, and he said, "You can't keep doing this, Gina," and she suddenly knew he was a ghost conjured from her longing. She woke up screaming and turned on the lights so she could see that he was alive.

"A cop-wife dream," she called it.

Now the doorbell rang. She went down the stairs. Voodoo, her labrador, and Pandora, her Rottweiler, were barking madly, ready to maul whoever was at the door at 4 a.m.

When her first husband was away fighting in Fallujah, she had come to dread late-night visits. She knew what they meant. She had been to dozens of Marine funerals. She had once watched a casualty-notification team walk up to a neighbor's house.

As she walked to the front door, she hoped the neighborhood was on fire. An evacuation order. Anything.

She looked through the peephole and saw a police shield and she knew.

She opened the door and saw one of her husband's friends, a sergeant. The Riverside chief was standing behind him. She told them it was a dream. She tried to close the door on them. The sergeant put out his hand and said, "No, Gina, it's real."

He asked her to put away the dogs. She took the dogs upstairs and came back down and let the police officers in. She demanded that they say her husband was fine, he was hurt and in the hospital but fine.

No.

Did he suffer?

No. It was quick.

Suddenly she remembered her phone. She raced upstairs and grabbed it. Michael Crain had sent his last text at 1:09 a.m., 25 minutes before he was shot. He had been thinking of her.

There was only one word:

"Night."

CHAPTER FOUR: A KILLER VANISHES

Det. Alex Collins was up early, with his wife and new baby, and found one story dominating the news. The reports made clear that Christopher Dorner was no longer hunting just the network of people he blamed for his firing from the LAPD. Fleeing east out of L.A. County, he was shooting anyone with a badge.

Collins was a boyish-looking 26 with an air of earnest innocence. He had married his high school sweetheart. He was the youngest of three brothers, and had followed both of them into the San Bernardino County Sheriff's Department.

Now, Collins thought of the suicides he had seen during his years patrolling Big Bear. People sought out the isolation of the mountains to end their lives. He wondered if that might be Dorner's plan.

It was Thursday, Feb. 7. Collins wasn't supposed to be working. He had been on leave for two and a half weeks, for his son's birth. His hair was longer than he liked it, and he had grown a beard.

It was still morning when his phone rang. It was his oldest brother, a patrol sergeant in Big Bear. He had information that had not yet made the news.

"Hey, I think we found Dorner's truck," he whispered. He was calling from an ice-covered mountain road where an abandoned Nissan Titan sat charred and smoldering.

Collins felt the impulse to go in. He called his other brother, who was on the SWAT team. Over the phone, he could hear him flooring his accelerator as he raced up the mountain.

Collins shaved. He put on his suit and tie.

His mom called to check on the baby. He told her he was going to follow his brothers up the mountain. He would not be able to live with himself if one of them got hurt and he was not there to help.

She sounded nervous. All three of her sons would be hunting a cop killer.

"I gotta go," he said.

***

The lock on the gate of Forest Service Road 2N10 had been snipped with bolt cutters. It lay in the snow.

The road started at an altitude of 7,000 feet and wound steeply up a mountain, parallel to the Snow Summit Mountain Resort's popular skiing and snowboarding slopes. A snowplow driver had found the truck blocking the road about 8:30 a.m., about a mile up the narrow path.

From the tire tracks in the ice, it seemed clear the driver had slid backward on his way into the mountains and found himself impossibly stuck. Deputies surmised that he had used propane to set a fire in the cab, and abandoned it in haste.

Inside the truck, deputies found the blackened parts of two AR-15 assault rifles, a charred portion of a Glock handgun, and the remains of a tent, a survival knife and a camping stove. Scattered through the truck, and in the surrounding snow, were hundreds of high-caliber rifle rounds that had exploded in the fire.

Deputies realized it could be a trap. If this was Dorner's truck, he might be in the trees now, watching them through his sniper scope. They pulled back and brought in SWAT to search the woods. An armored truck extricated the Titan from the ice, and a tow truck carried it to the resort's parking lot.

The license plate was missing, but detectives found the vehicle-ID number deep inside the truck, on a piece of steel riveted to a plate between the engine block and the cab. It was Dorner's truck.

What had Dorner been doing up here? Had he hoped to hide on the mountain? Did he know that it was law-enforcement appreciation day at Snow Summit, and cops would be all over the slopes? Had he planned to find a sniper perch and kill some of them?

Within hours, hundreds of law officers had coalesced on the mountain. Helicopters landed, and more SWAT members poured out. Checkpoints and roadblocks sprang up, resorts were closed, and businesses went into lockdown.

Dorner had an hours-long head start. He might be anywhere up here, or long gone. He might have hitchhiked off the mountain. Was the torched truck part of a diversion? Or had he burned it in panic?

Helicopters criss-crossed the mountains. Big Bear Lake had thousands of homes, many of them vacant. Searchers in ski masks crept between cabins, guns drawn. They looked in one-room shacks and in sprawling vacation homes, in campgrounds and in Depression-era cabins. They crept up long uphill driveways without cover.

Late that day, as the wind picked up across Big Bear, investigators interviewed a 45-year-old woman named Reyna Eblin, who lived down the hill from where Dorner had abandoned his truck. She said she had spotted him from her driveway that morning.

Shielded from view behind her truck, she had watched him walk down the middle of the road, in Army boots and camouflage pants, carrying something stiff under his jacket.

Bloodhounds bounded into the surrounding woods. They had Dorner's scent, sucked from a washcloth he had left in a hotel, but could not find his trail.

Darkness fell across the mountains and the cold deepened. The cloud cover and the high trees blocked the moon.

Locals stocked up on food, barricaded their doors and kept their guns and rifles close.

***

Like the Santa Ana wind that envelops millions of disparate Southern Californians in its grip, a sense of unease pervaded workaday rhythms across a vast region. On TV, on news blogs, on social media, the story of the fugitive L.A. cop gone rogue became a point of frenzied interest.

Reporters stood in the snow with microphones, updating viewers on every turn in the search. Carnage of any scale, at any place, now seemed thinkable.

On the way to work, drivers could see police staking out one freeway on-ramp after another. The thin blue line was usually invisible. Suddenly it was omnipresent and fearsomely armed. It felt like someone else's country.

Police were scared. They strapped on ballistic shields and checked their guns. They sent kids to the homes of trusted friends, erasing visible links to loved ones, yanking vacation photos from Facebook. They walked to their cars in pairs, and drove home watching the rearview mirror.

People who looked like Dorner, even vaguely, were also scared. One of them wrote on his T-shirt: "NOT CHRIS DORNER PLEASE DO NOT SHOOT."

On CNN, Anderson Cooper announced that his staff had received a package from Dorner a few days earlier. Inside was an LAPD memento coin with a bullet hole in it.

Former LAPD Chief William J. Bratton had given Dorner the coin, to honor his military service, and had later approved his firing. But he told Cooper he didn't remember Dorner.

"He clearly has a beef with you," Cooper said.

"A lot of police officers get discharged," Bratton said.

On billboards and fliers, TV screens and Internet posts, Dorner's face was everywhere. In every photo, he seemed to wear a huge smile.

"Of course he knows what he's doing," LAPD Chief Charlie Beck told the press. "We trained him."

***

To coordinate the manhunt, authorities established a command post at a secretive facility in Norwalk. It was called the Joint Regional Intelligence Center, or JRIC, which occupied a nondescript office building and was meant for large multi-agency operations, including terror attacks.

Now it was a 24/7 nerve center of ringing phones and clicking computers, a bustle of local, state and federal agencies—including more than 40 detectives—dedicated to catching Dorner.

For the U.S. marshals, who were part of the team, Dorner represented an unusual quarry in that he lacked a criminal record, which meant he had no known network of accomplices. Agents watched his mother and sister, in case he reached out. They monitored his cellphone, his bank account and his credit cards. But he had gone off the grid.

Thomas Hession, chief of the marshals' fugitive task force, was optimistic that Dorner would be captured. The question was how many people would die first.

"The fugitive that completely drops off the face of the Earth is one in a million," Hession said. "People are creatures of habit."

That is why, he said, so many high-speed chases ended in the suspect's driveway, and why he once caught a killer who couldn't give up a favorite dry-cleaner.

Dorner would probably stick to one of the places he knew, like Nevada, California or Utah. And sooner or later, wherever he was, he would make a mistake.

At the San Bernardino County Sheriff's Department, which was leading the search of the mountain, detectives wondered: Was Dorner nearly as good a tactician as he portrayed himself to be? Had the military given him specialized guerrilla or cold-weather training?

The Navy said he had gone through basic combat training, and was an expert marksman, but otherwise had not been drilled in special tactics. He had guarded an oil rig at sea, but had not been in battle. He had flunked out of flight school. He had failed to get promoted and skipped the required drills.

Somehow, he had managed to get out with an honorable discharge.

Again and again, detectives saw the gap between Dorner's boasts and his achievements. In his attempt to impress women, he had falsely claimed to be an Internal Affairs investigator, a narcotics officer or a SWAT team member. He had displayed grisly war photos, passing himself off as a combat vet.

His LAPD record showed that he had struggled through the academy—it took him 13 months to graduate, rather than the customary six. He had punched one recruit and tried to choke another. He had fired a bullet into his own hand. Even in his 30s, he admitted to friends, he relied heavily on his mother for financial support. In his flight from the law, he had been unable to steal a boat from an 81-year-old man.

***

On Friday, cabdriver Karam Kaoud drove to Riverside Community Hospital and parked.

He walked up and found a security guard. He wasn't family, he explained, but he wanted to know if he could see the young Riverside police officer who had been shot by Dorner the day before.

He didn't say that he had witnessed the shooting, and that he had used the police radio to help save Officer Andrew Tachias' life.

The guard left and came back and said no. Tachias was under guard.

Back in his cab, Kaoud called Riverside police. Would they let him see the officer?

The dispatcher who answered the phone asked if he was related.

"No," he said. "I just wanted to know if he is OK. This is important to me."

"He's getting better."

***

Det. Alex Collins had joined the search on the mountain. He was in his detective's suit and tie, freezing. He and his partner set up motion-sensing cameras, bolting them to trees and telephone poles.

Collins and other detectives searched cabins for surveillance cameras, hoping that one of them had captured Dorner. They studied video footage from gas stations, hoping that Dorner had been seen pumping gas. They searched the trunks and back seats of cars coming and going on the mountain. Nothing.

As night fell Friday, searchers trudged back to the command post after 14-hour shifts in a state of taut-nerved alertness. Their exhaustion was exacerbated by the knee-high snow, 60-pound vests and the thin, high air. Now, with snow piled up to the doors of their trucks, they passed around shovels.

***

As the manhunt wore on, the LAPD's threat-assessment team—including detectives, commanders and the department's top shrink—met twice a day in the big, wood-paneled conference room on the 10th floor of headquarters.

On the white board, the names of potential targets had grown to 77. Protection details were working 12- to 14-hour shifts.

Traps were set outside the houses of some top-level targets. A single black-and-white would be stationed outside, to give Dorner the impression of light protection. Positioned in the surrounding neighborhoods were 16-man undercover teams.

This required officers with specialized training, however, and their ranks were fast depleted.

Some people on the target list felt stifled by their guards, and wanted to be left alone. Most stayed in town, a fact that didn't surprise the department's head psychologist, Kevin Jablonski. "They are armed," he said. "Their personalities say, 'Don't run.' "

The psychologist thought Dorner was hunkered down in a cabin in Big Bear, "not hidden in the snowbank like James Bond." He tried to make sense of Dorner's actions. The attempt to get to Mexican waters. The drive into the mountains. The abandoned truck. Were they part of a master plan? Or were they the actions of someone in way over his head and prone to panic?

Jablonski studied Dorner's language and saw a man who expected to die. He advised the San Bernardino County SWAT team to assume that he was booby-trapped, should he appear to be surrendering. They should approach him as if he would fight to the last breath.

He had some advice for his own department. Don't use the terms "mentally ill" or "psychopath" in public about Dorner, he explained. It might further inflame him.

"This guy doesn't want to be blamed for anything that's going on," Jablonski said. "He's delusional. But don't make him a Looney Tune."

Chief Charlie Beck and his spokesman heeded the advice, but it did not stop others from pronouncing publicly on Dorner's mental health. "He's entitled, he's narcissistic," said one former police psychologist. Another added that he suffered from a "psychiatric illness."

Jablonski had more advice for his chief: Announce that the case leading to Dorner's firing would be reopened. This might give Dorner some pause, maybe enough to catch him.

**

In one sense, Dorner's killings had already achieved their desired effect. People were reading his splenetic screed, and more than a few had already bought into his self-portrayal as a righteous man wronged.

On Facebook, pages had sprung up praising Dorner as a folk hero who had dared to defy the law enforcement establishment. Police were portrayed as gangsters in uniform who had again shown their disregard for civilian life in the two Torrance shootings.

"Christopher Dorner For President," one page was entitled. Another admirer called him "Chocolate Rambo." On social media, people vented about bad experiences with police, unjust workplaces, lost jobs, lying bosses, discrimination.

To many familiar with the history and culture of the LAPD, some of his accusations seemed plausible, at least on their face. He claimed the agency had railroaded him for reporting a supervisor's misbehavior. Others had complained about such retaliation for years, citing a Blue Wall of Silence that forbade cops to snitch on other cops.

He portrayed the agency as a caldron of racism, and this resonated among those who remembered the Rodney King beating, the aggressive round-ups of black men during the gang wars of the 1980s, and LAPD Det. Mark Fuhrman, whose incendiary racist rants surfaced at the O.J. Simpson murder trial.

***

To the people hunting him, Dorner's lionization was an outrage. For his first victim, they pointed out, the supposed crusader for racial justice had selected a defenseless young black man and shot him in the back of the head.

Riverside Police Chief Sergio Diaz, who had stood over Crain's body at the hospital, called support for Dorner "ignorance and hate masquerading as intellectualism."

There was nothing ambiguous about it, Diaz said. He was a murderer, plain and simple. "For this knucklehead, this cockroach to become an icon..."

Some of the cops hunting Dorner studied his manifesto for clues about what he might do next.

Justin Musella of the San Bernardino County Sheriff's SWAT team concluded that Dorner would probably stay hidden until the heat died down.

"We have to handle him totally separately from anything we've ever dealt with," he said.

His SWAT colleague, Chad Johnson, read a few pages and tossed it aside.

Its author had hunted down and murdered a man's daughter.

"That's all you need to know," he said.

***

On Saturday morning, Det. Alex Collins and his partner methodically checked the cameras they had spread around the mountain. No hits.

The sky over the mountain was a marvelous blue. Tourists were coming back, lured by the promise of 18 inches of fresh snow. They reasoned that Dorner must be gone.

Helicopters continued to criss-cross the mountains with cameras so sensitive they could detect a rabbit from the air. No sign.

Collins and other detectives visited utility companies, trying to determine if any of the cabins had seen a sudden spike in water, gas or electricity.

An address in Big Bear Lake jumped out, and soon Collins was in a helicopter looking at footprints in the snow around the cabin.

SWAT went in by Snowcat. No Dorner.

***

Charlie Beck was waiting for the shooting to start again.

An elite team of officers was guarding his home, set on two acres of winding horse trails at the end of a San Gabriel Valley cul-de-sac. At night it grew bitterly cold. He put space heaters in the garage for them; his wife brought cookies.

Beck's three grown children were staying at the house, two of them cops themselves. "I need you guys to take care of each other," he told them. "Think of yourself as a line of defense."

Beck saw the adulation for Dorner as partly a reflection of Americans' deep-rooted affection for anti-heroes. A lone rebel versus the LAPD's Evil Empire—people who cheered Dorner seemed to want the story to fit that convenient template.

The real story was something else, thought Beck. It was about a failed cop, angry and paranoid and perhaps mentally ill, who blamed everyone but himself for his shortcomings.

On Saturday, the fourth day of the manhunt, Beck announced that he would reopen Dorner's termination case. It was "not to appease a murderer," he said, but to assure people that the LAPD was "fair and transparent."

"I am aware of the ghosts of the LAPD's past," Beck said, "and one of my biggest concerns is that they will be resurrected by Dorner's allegations of racism within the department."

***

The announcement stunned Sgt. Teresa Evans, who had been in hiding with her teenage son for four days. The whole case stemmed from Dorner's accusation—determined by the LAPD to be a lie—that she had kicked a suspect.

She felt betrayed. Would she have to relive what she called the "nightmare"? For most of a year, she had been forced to work behind a desk, barred from earning overtime as she tried to clear her name.

"Are they saying they don't believe me now?" she asked her lawyer over the phone.

Her lawyer said the chief was playing to public perceptions.

Evans wondered how long it could possibly continue. The first day she had felt too vulnerable at home. Reporters were assembling outside. It meant Dorner could find her too. On the second day, SWAT extracted her and her son, rushing them—both hidden under hooded jackets—into an unmarked van.

Now, with cops stationed in the hall outside, she and her son had adjoining rooms in a hotel with a view from a high floor. She had packed his Xbox, a MacBook, an iPad and some underwear.

Hour after hour, Evans played video soccer with her son. She let him watch a little TV, so he understood the outlines of the situation, but tried to shield him from the details.

SWAT brought her lattes and turkey sandwiches. She picked at the meat. She threw up when she tried to eat. She was 115 pounds and shedding weight by the day.

She did not think Dorner could still be on the mountain. Someone must be helping him elude the dragnet, she thought. What if he was never caught?

She would have to quit the police work she loved. She would have to leave the country with her son. She would have to find a new home, maybe in Ireland, with relatives.

She told no one where she was, not even her ex-husband. She refused to stray outside the hotel room into the hall. Someone might notice her and snap a photograph and post it online. As quickly as that, the location of the safe house would be exposed.

She traded texts with her lawyer and friend, Robert Rico, who was also under heavy guard. Considering Dorner's record, Rico thought, the real question wasn't why the LAPD had fired him but why he hadn't been fired sooner.

Evans and Rico kept returning to a disturbing realization: Sooner or later, their protection details would be pulled. "At some point," Evans would say, "they're going to dump me out the door and say, 'Good luck to you.' "

***

Hundreds of tips poured in, most of them useless. One night, police stationed snipers at windows around an apartment building in a rundown San Bernardino neighborhood after a 911 caller claimed Dorner was inside with a stash of guns. It was a fake call, but some wary police still wondered: Was Dorner staging a diversion? Was he watching?

On Sunday, Los Angeles Mayor Antonio Villaraigosa stood with Beck and Diaz, the Riverside police chief, to announce a $1-million reward for Dorner's capture.

"We will not tolerate this reign of terror," the mayor said.

By the next day, nearly a thousand bad tips had poured in. There were false Dorner sightings from Denver to Chicago.

They found nothing Sunday. They found nothing Monday.

Then it was Tuesday, and as the manhnt entered its seventh day, the Riverside Police Department was nervously preparing to bury Officer Michael Crain.

The memorial service at Grove Community Church, and the burial at nearby Riverside National Cemetery, were expected to draw 8,000 to 10,000 people, many of them cops.

It had been five days since anyone had seen Dorner. "You got a guy who has all kinds of high-powered weapons and a desire to kill," recalled Riverside Police Department Deputy Chief Jeffrey Greer, who was organizing the service. "I am sweating bullets."

If Dorner planted himself in the low-lying mountain range overlooking the church, he would have a direct line of sight in a sniper scope. Police tried to calculate if rounds from a .50-caliber rifle might reach mourners from that distance. They sent helicopters into the hills, looking for heat signatures.

They staked out high positions on buildings along the seven-mile stretch the caravan would travel from the church to the cemetery. There were 200 cops lined up to work security, and agencies from everywhere were volunteering manpower.

Dorner was not their only worry. He might have an acolyte, with a gun and a plan.

On the mountain, search teams were being pulled out.

Dorner might be dead somewhere under the snow, and wouldn't be found until the snow melted in weeks or months. But if he was still up there, the large crowds attending the upcoming Presidents' Day weekend —combined with the lighter police presence—would give him a chance to slip away.

Just down the road from the spot where Dorner had abandoned his truck, Jim and Karen Reynolds were cleaning the 13-unit resort they managed in their retirement.

Around noon, they approached Room 203. Jim inserted the key.

CHAPTER FIVE: THE MOUNTAIN

Everyone hunting him understood the equation. If Christopher Dorner was still alive, he would get the first shot.

Jeremiah MacKay was 35, a large, boisterous, red-haired detective on the major crimes squad of the San Bernardino County Sheriff's Department. He had a wife, an infant son and a 6-year-old stepdaughter. It was hard to find a room in which he was not the loudest man.

MacKay had been searching Big Bear for days. He had grown up nearby, and knew the mountains well.

A fireman's son with Irish roots, he liked pints of Guinness, expensive Scotch and wearing a kilt on St. Patrick's Day. He played the bagpipes in the honor guard at police funerals. In his nearly 15 years on the job, he had seen more cop widows and cop orphans and grieving cop parents than almost anyone.

Out of uniform, he preferred not to mention his job, so people would be themselves. He introduced himself as a salesman for a fictional pickle company, with a dirty pun in the title. "They sell them at Trader Joe's," he would say. "A gourmet brand."

As he hunted for Dorner that week, he received a call from a buddy on the force.

"Whoever finds him is gonna get killed, because he gets to act first," the friend said. "Whoever opens that door...."

"I'm gonna get him," MacKay said. "He's a cop killer."

***

Jim and Karen Reynolds were about to find Christopher Dorner.

The couple, married 36 years, lived above the office of the Mountain Vista Resort on Club View Drive, which they ran with their grown daughter.

Jim was 66, a former Navy man and IBM system engineer, tall, lanky, and white-haired, with wild, bushy eyebrows. Karen was 56, a former nurse, small, sweet-faced and bespectacled.

Their resort was a cluster of 1980s-era brown condo units, with maple trees and a towering Ponderosa pine. They were going room to room, stripping sheets and collecting towels, when they came to Room 203.

Five days before, when Dorner's pickup was discovered up the road, Jim had methodically checked the doors and found this cabin locked. It had been unlocked earlier for repairs, he knew, but he assumed one of his family members had re-locked it.

Now, Jim opened the door and they entered, climbing the red-carpeted stairway. It led upstairs to a living room with an old stone fireplace, a kitchenette and a sliding-glass door that opened onto a snow-covered balcony.

Jim went to the window to examine the curtain rod, which needed repairs. Karen was heading toward the hallway that led to a bedroom, looking for fresh linens.

Dorner emerged from the hallway, pointing a handgun.

Karen recognized him at once. She yelled and ran back down the stairs toward the entrance. She had the door open. She was partway through. She hesitated.

She couldn't leave her husband. She couldn't risk leading Dorner to her daughter, who was somewhere on the property. She thought of her own life: If you go out that door, he has to shoot you.

In a moment Dorner was on her, digging his fingers into her forearm.

Upstairs, Jim fumbled for the smartphone in the rubber case on his waist, but couldn't get it free in time to dial 911. He hid it in the sofa cushions.

Dorner came back up the stairs with Karen and said, "I know you know who I am."

Jim thought they were as good as dead. It was an hour's drive, at least, to get off the mountain. His only chance of escape was to kill them.

By appearances, Dorner had been there for days. There were trail mix wrappers and containers for ready-to-eat meals. There were footprints on the snow-covered balcony. He had used a towel in the downstairs shower.

Jim thought Dorner looked well-rested, with a couple days' growth of beard, and composed like a man trained to handle tense situations.

After abandoning his truck, Dorner would have had to walk only a short distance to reach Club View Drive. From there, at a brisk pace, past log cabins and gracious A-frames and porches adorned with antlers and carved wooden bears, he would have made it to their resort in five minutes.

The San Bernardino County sheriff would insist that searchers had checked it, but had found no signs of forced entry, and were not authorized to kick down the door. The Reynoldses said deputies never contacted them to ask permission to go inside.

However it happened, Dorner's presence had been missed. From the room's porch window, he could have seen his truck towed into the parking lot of the ski resort across the street.

He could have seen police helicopters landing and taking off, and an army of law enforcement—police, sheriff's deputies and federal agents—coming and going from the command post. Along with fleets of reporters and cameramen, they would have passed easily within range of his sniper scope.

Because the room had an Internet hookup and cable, he could have watched the manhnt unfold live, and learned that the massive effort was dwindling.

"I just want to clear my name," Dorner told the Reynoldses.

The couple was shaking with fear. Dorner explained that he had spared the San Diego yacht owner, and would spare them too. They were merely means to an end.

Jim thought of mentioning that he had been a Navy man himself. Maybe this would endear him to Dorner, and increase the odds of survival. Then he remembered hearing that Dorner's stint with the Navy had ended badly.

Jim thought fleetingly of throwing himself on Dorner, maybe distracting him just long enough for his wife to escape. But he doubted she would leave him anyway. And trying to overpower a bigger, younger, stronger man seemed a fool's errand.

"Do you have a car?" Dorner demanded.

Yes, they said, it was parked in front of the office with a full tank of gas. A purple-maroon Nissan Rogue. He took the key.

Dorner ordered them to kneel on the sofa with their faces against the wall, their ankles crossed and their hands up.

Dorner said he had seen Jim shoveling snow a few days earlier.

"You are good, hard-working people," he said.

They felt Dorner tightening zip-ties around their wrists. Dorner took Karen's cellphone out of her jacket pocket. He ordered them to their feet, and told them to go down the hallway toward the bedroom.

"Don't look around," he said. "Look at the ceiling."

In the bedroom, atop a small dresser, Jim noticed pieces of carrots and a dull-bladed butcher knife from the kitchen. He is going to hack us to death back here, he thought.

Dorner ordered them to lie face-down on the floor, then tightened zip-ties around their feet. Searching Jim's pockets, Dorner found a Hershey bar and asked if he was a diabetic.

"Yes," he said.

"Oh s---," Dorner said.

He put the chocolate between them on the carpet.

He left the room and returned with washcloths to stuff in their mouths. He pulled pillowcases over their heads. He found electrical cords and tied them around their heads, to hold the gags in place. He jerked their heads back.

"Say the alphabet," Dorner ordered her.

"A...B...C...D...E...F...G...H...

I...J...K..." She slurred and mumbled more than necessary, to convey the impression the gag could be no tighter, and Dorner seemed satisfied when she reached "K."

He pushed them face-down on the carpet. They could hear him packing a bag. He asked calmly if they would be quiet long enough for him to escape.

For the first time, Karen understood the literal truth of the concept of being paralyzed with fear. But she managed to nod.

They heard his footsteps in the hallway. They listened for the thump of the front door closing. Instead, they heard Dorner's voice, now tinged with panic: "These aren't car keys!"

It was a keyless car, they explained through their gags. Just push the starter.

Dorner disappeared again.

Karen was terrified that he would run into her daughter, who was on the property, maybe in the laundry room just below. She felt her hands and feet swelling from the zip-ties. She maneuvered her head down to Jim's hands. His fingers fumbled uselessly as he tried to get the pillowcase off her face.

She scooted and wriggled until her hands were at Jim's head, and her fingers found purchase and removed his pillowcase. Then he was able to pull off hers.

She rocked back and forth, struggling to her knees and then her feet. She saw the butcher knife on the dresser and got its handle in her teeth. Maybe the edge would cut the zip-ties.

She dropped the knife toward Jim, hoping he could grab it. She heard a noise through the door. She kicked the knife against the wall, where it would be hidden behind the door if Dorner returned.

They waited. Dorner did not return. She pushed down on the door handle and hopped into the hallway and into the living room. With her hands still tied behind her back, she grabbed the land-line and tried to dial 911 but couldn't manage it.

She noticed that Dorner had inexplicably left her smartphone on the coffee table. It was a new phone, and it took awhile to find the speaker-phone button.

She dialed 911. She got an operator. Dorner is in Big Bear, she said. He has our car. It was 12:23 p.m. He had a head start of 15 to 30 minutes.

***

Det. Alex Collins had spent the morning searching the woods near the condo, trying to rethink his assumptions about where the fugitive might be. He and his partner were back at the Big Bear station, about to head to lunch, when the radios crackled: Dorner was near Big Bear. He was driving a stolen purple Nissan Rogue.

Collins and his partner grabbed their tactical vests and rifles and jumped into the truck. On his iPhone, Collins Googled "Nissan Rogue" so he could be sure what it looked like.

There were only a few ways off the mountain, and they reasoned that Dorner would not risk California Highway 18, which would take him through town.

They guessed he would try to sneak out the back way, on California Highway 38, toward Redlands.

***

Deputy Jeremiah MacKay was at his office at the Yucaipa station when he got the word. That morning, detectives had visited his office to seek his help on a drug-related homicide, but the talk had quickly turned to Dorner.

The men knew the mountain, and batted around ideas about where he could be. It seemed outrageous that one man could hold law enforcement hostage like this.

MacKay said what he had been saying all week: "I want to get him."

He raced up the mountain.

***

On Highway 38, near Glass Road, four law enforcement officers—two San Bernardino County deputies and two state Fish and Wildlife wardens —were setting up a checkpoint and laying spike strips.

They noticed a pair of school buses coming down the narrow, winding highway, headed west. The Nissan Rogue was following close behind, as if to guard against the spike strips. Dorner was at the wheel.

The officers jumped into their cars and gave chase. Dorner swerved around the buses and accelerated. In the time it took the pursuing cars to get around the buses, Dorner had vanished.

They guessed that he had hooked a hard right on Glass Road, which twisted downhill through thick, snow-covered forest toward the community of Seven Oaks.

They raced down, rifles out the window. About a mile down the road, they found the Rogue smashed against a snowbank, the windshield cracked, the air bags deployed. Inside, Dorner had abandoned a package of Quickclot, meant to pour on wounds, and a small arsenal: smoke grenades, tear-gas canisters and a silencer-equipped Remington sniper rifle bearing the word VENGEANCE.

Nearby, on the same road, a 62-year-old man who ran a local Boy Scout camp was driving by in his silver Dodge Ram when Dorner walked out of the trees aiming his assault rifle. The driver parked and raised his hands.

"I don't want to hurt you," Dorner said. "Just get out."

Three wardens, stationed down the hill at Seven Oaks, were now racing up Glass Road in two separate trucks, lights flashing and sirens blaring.

They were looking for the purple Nissan, not the stolen Dodge pickup in which Dorner was now hurtling toward them.

Dorner crossed paths with the first warden, who noticed Dorner behind the wheel and radioed a warning to the second truck.

Dorner raised his AR-15 and fired at the second truck, a four-door Chevrolet pickup. Inside were two wardens and a German shepherd, Reno. Bullets struck the windshield. The roof. The driver's window. The door jamb. Glass shattered on the wardens.

They knew a rule from the academy: Drive through an ambush, then get back into the fight.

One of the wardens, Ben Matias, an ex-Marine, jumped out of the truck, ran to a berm and spotted Dorner taking sharp turns down the hill. He took aim with his .308 assault rifle and emptied a 20-round magazine at the fleeing truck. It disappeared.

***

Det. Alex Collins, racing to the scene, received calls in quick succession from both his older brothers. Like him, they were San Bernardino County sheriff's deputies hunting for Dorner. They told him the same thing: Be careful. Don't rush in alone. Wait for us.

With his partner driving, Collins was scanning the woods around Glass Road over the top of his Mini-14 semiautomatic rifle, forest rushing by on both sides. They passed the Fish and Wildlife truck with the blown-out driver's side window.

They hung a left at the bottom of Glass Road. On the right, at 40700 Seven Oaks Road, stood an empty one-story wood cabin. A stone fireplace rose above its east side. It sat amid a towering forest of white oaks, black oaks and cedar pines.

Trucks of law officers hurtled past the cabin. Collins and his partner stopped just west of it and climbed out.

They were looking for the stolen truck. Where they found it, they knew, they would find Dorner. But there was no sign of it anywhere around the cabin.

They did not know that Dorner had sent it to the bottom of an embankment behind the cabin.

They did not know that he was now inside the cabin, waiting for a target.

Collins was side-stepping along the road, head tilted over his aimed rifle, when he saw a flash. He had the sensation of being punched in the face. A round from Dorner's assault rifle entered just under his left nostril, crashed through the roof of his mouth, shattered his front teeth, split his tongue and exploded bone as it emerged from his lower right jaw. His face went numb.

The bullets seemed to be coming from a cabin window, but the muffled pop pop pop from Dorner's silencer made it hard to pinpoint where. Another round struck Collins just below the left kneecap. A round passed through his left forearm. A round struck his chest.

He scrambled behind the back wheel of another cop's silver Dodge Durango and collapsed. Bullets were flying all around him. Rounds sailed through the truck. Shattered glass from the Dodge fell at his feet.

Dorner seemed to be shooting carefully, whenever he saw an exposed human shape. He was firing at the pavement under the truck, trying to kill with ricochets.

Collins thought: "In seconds, I'll pass out and die."

He was choking on his blood and teeth. He was sure the burning in his chest was a high-powered AR-15 round that had pierced his ballistic vest.

He thought: "It wasn't supposed to happen like this."

He'd been running scenarios through his head all week, preparing himself. What if he found Dorner on the road? In a car? In a closet? He'd tried to imagine how he would react. And now he was close to death with no idea how it had happened.

Trim and athletic, he ran three miles a day, and he knew how to push through pain. But the pain in his leg was excruciating, and he thought: "If I am going to die, God, let me go now."

He felt he had let everybody down. He thought of how furious his brothers would be at him.

He had to call his wife. He would spend his last seconds telling her he loved her, and explaining that he wouldn't be home tonight, that he was sorry he let this happen, sorry for leaving her alone with a brand-new baby.

He reached under his ballistic vest. He kept his iPhone in a jacket pocket over his heart. The phone was shattered. Angrily, he hurled it away.

Seconds passed, and he realized he wasn't dead yet. He heard yelling and gunfire.

He thought: "Don't panic. Don't freak out."

He thought of his training at the Sheriff's Academy, where cops who had been shot spoke of the Will to Live, of never giving up. He thought of the Navy SEAL in one of his favorite books, "Lone Survivor," who had survived horrific injury in Afghanistan.

He leaned forward on his arm, to allow the blood filling up his throat to pour onto the pavement.

A few feet away, Deputy Jeremiah MacKay had scrambled behind another wheel of the Dodge and was firing at the cabin. A rescue chopper was overhead, and MacKay got on the radio to tell the pilot which structure Dorner was firing from.

"It's gonna be right from where you're at now," MacKay said, his words captured on a dispatch recording. "Right ahead of you—right ahead of you—directly underneath you right now —"

Seconds later, as he tried to direct the helicopter, MacKay lost just enough of his cover to give Dorner a target.

The bullet went in at a high angle, right above MacKay's ballistic shield, and ricocheted into his chest. He was dead almost instantly.

A few feet away, Collins watched his own blood pooling on the pavement. Then something happened that he did not understand. He turned his head and saw that he was completely exposed to the cabin. The Dodge Durango that had been shielding him had vanished. He saw his rifle in the road, but couldn't reach it. He waited for a bullet to hit his head.

A hasty rescue attempt had cost him his cover. One cop had intended to drag the shot deputies out of the line of fire, using the Dodge—driven by a second cop—as a moving shield. Amid the fear and pandemonium and flying bullets, the truck was driven off, and the downed deputies left in the road.

***

They called it the kill zone, a wide-open stretch of road in the direct line of Dorner's assault rifle, and now Collins and MacKay lay in the middle of it. For perhaps 20 or 30 yards, there were no cars, no trees, no sources of cover at all.

"Shots fired. Officer down...."

"Automatic fire coming in-bound...."

"Officers still down in the kill zone...."

San Bernardino County Sheriff's SWAT Sgt. John Charbonneau raced up in his truck. In the seat beside him was Det. Justin Musella, who had fought as an Army Ranger in Afghanistan, and who now recognized the faint THWUP THWUP THWUP of silenced high-powered rounds flying from the cabin.

"Sergeant, stop! We're getting shot at!"

They jumped out and opened fire at the cabin. More cops arrived, and raced to find cover behind trucks and trees. Glass fragments flew outward from the cabin as Dorner fired. There was the rustle of a curtain in one of the cabin's east windows.

Officers poured in rounds. Dorner's bullets zipped overhead. They thwacked into trees and pierced the sides of cars. The smell of gunpowder saturated the thin, cold air.

The two downed deputies still lay motionless in the road, and for the men who could see them every second was excruciating. Instinct told them to race out and retrieve their brothers; logic told them this would guarantee their own quick death.

They needed an armored vehicle to provide cover for the rescue, but nobody could say how long it would take to get it there.

Musella sprinted closer toward the cabin, taking cover behind a small, wooden, free-standing game room across the driveway. He tossed a smoke grenade toward Dorner, but it landed in the snow. The smoke churned upward; the wind blew it back toward the officers.

He threw another. This time, the smoke rose and created a wall between the cabin and the downed deputies.

On the west side, SWAT deputies Daniel Rosa and Larry Lopez locked eyes. This was their chance.

Lopez ran into the road first, as officers laid down a barrage of cover fire. He grabbed the first deputy he came to, MacKay, a big man, and dragged him 25 to 50 yards until they were behind a shield of trucks. Breathing hard, he grabbed his rifle and looked at Rosa.

"Your turn," he said.

Rosa sprinted out to Collins. He grabbed his vest and started dragging.

***

Tell my brothers I love them, Collins was saying. Tell them I'm sorry I screwed up.

He felt himself being loaded into the back of someone's pickup truck, and then a blaze of pain as MacKay's body was loaded on board partly on top of his wounded leg. He saw himself bleeding into a pair of spare boots. He thought: Someone will be mad.

He was aware of a gurney beneath him, of men carrying him into a rescue chopper.

Put me on my stomach, he managed to say, or I will choke on my blood.

On the way to Loma Linda Hospital, he clutched his cloth sheriff's badge in his fist. He did not know why. He was still conscious when the emergency room staff cut off his clothes and boots.

Doctors examined his chest. The high-powered round had pierced his ballistic shield and been deflected by the iPhone in his jacket pocket. It had saved his life.

***

Around the cabin, after perhaps 10 minutes of furious gunfire, everything slowed down. There were 30 or 40 officers with assault rifles forming a perimeter to ensure that Dorner wouldn't escape. They passed around fresh ammunition magazines.

A dozen cops were trapped, hunkered behind a row of trucks in front of the cabin. When an armored personnel carrier finally reached them, 45 minutes after the shooting had started, they scrambled inside and got away.

Deputies received word, from the cabin owner, that the property was not occupied, dispelling worries that Dorner might have a hostage. They learned the cabin had a basement.

A team of LAPD SWAT officers had taken command of a fire helicopter and flown to the mountain. They were deposited on a ridge about a half-mile north of the cabin.

"I'm not sure if they were invited or not, or if anyone's controlling them," a sheriff's deputy said over the radio.

Not only had the helicopter presented another target for Dorner's rifle, but the local deputies lacked direct radio contact with the LAPD team, which created the possibility of confusion and chaos.

Was the LAPD so zealous because Dorner had been one of their own? Did they doubt their San Bernardino counterparts could handle the crisis? A "miscommunication," the LAPD called it, a result of bad cellphone and radio coverage in the mountains.

Whatever the reason, San Bernardino County sheriff's commanders were furious. They ordered the LAPD team not to get any closer.

***

From the SWAT truck, an amplified voice boomed an order to surrender: You are surrounded. You have no chance of escape.

No response.

They fired canisters of tear gas into the cabin. Still no sign of Dorner.

At 3:45 p.m. a sheriff's deputy rumbled toward the cabin in an armored tractor and tore into the east wall with an extendable claw. The claw ripped out a door and some windows. A camera mounted on the tractor appeared to show a wall covered in blood.

Police later surmised this was not blood but the orange-red burst of pepper spray from a gas canister.

At 4:05 p.m., greenish smoke emerged from the cabin. Dorner had popped his own smoke canister, apparently expecting that the SWAT team would be rushing into the house. The smoke would blind them, and give him an advantage.

This meant Dorner was alive. Nobody rushed in.

SWAT command decided to shoot in canisters of CS gas, called burners. Also known as hot gas, or pyrotechnic tear gas, it had a propensity to spark fires.

Critics would question this decision. Why not just wait Dorner out?

Dorner had shown no willingness to surrender. He had not attempted to communicate with deputies. He was well-armed, and possibly equipped with rations, meaning the standoff could go on indefinitely. His manifesto made it clear he planned to die.

The shadows of the tall pines were lengthening. Every minute represented further risk to the law officers, risk that would multiply when darkness overtook the snowbound mountains. Dorner might possess night-vision goggles that would enable him to find targets.

On their radios, deputies orchestrated the end-game.

"We're going to go forward with the plan, with the burner...."

Hot gas went in at 4:09 p.m. Flames began to spread. They waited for Dorner; he did not emerge.

"Seven burners deployed, and we have a fire."

"We have a fire in the front and he might come out the back...."

At 4:20 p.m., from the cabin, there came the sound of a single gunshot.

"No. 4 side fully engulfed...."

A firetruck was told to hang back a couple hundred yards. Ignited by fire, ammunition was exploding inside the cabin.

"This thing's well-constructed.... I still have ammo popping here...."

"Fully engulfed...."

"More ammo going off...."

"I'm told that there's basement in that cabin.... I'm going to let that heat burn through that basement."

"Good call...."

The fire wasn't spreading to nearby homes or trees. They let it burn.

***

Live on television, people watched the climax of the Dorner manhunt play out in flames.

At Dorner's favorite watering hole in Las Vegas, bartenders and customers watched.

At the manhunt command post in Norwalk, an army of cops watched.

At LAPD headquarters, the chief stood with the mayor and watched.

At a secret hotel room, Dorner's former training officer, Teresa Evans, watched.

At Grove Community Church in Riverside, where a viewing was underway for Michael Crain, people had been trying to shield his widow Regina from the news, because it had not been confirmed that it was Dorner in the cabin.

But Regina kept asking where her husband's friends on the SWAT team were, and finally someone told her they were on the mountain.

At 8 p.m. they still had not shown up, and she pleaded with the church to keep the viewing open a little longer. A few minutes later the SWAT team entered, their faces smeared with camouflage paint.

They took turns hugging her.

"We got him," one of them said. "It's OK. We got him."

***

Michael Crain's 10-year-old son walked slowly behind his father's flag-draped casket the next day. He looked tiny among the police pallbearers, his palms pressed against one end of the casket.

A woman from the neighborhood watched the long caravan of police cars pass by, lights flashing. She told her twin granddaughters: "Put your hands over your hearts."

Regina Crain received the folded American flag from the police chief, and watched as her husband was buried.

Later, she would ask commanders for the badge her husband had worn the night of his death, so she could put it in a place of honor. They were reluctant, and she knew why: A bullet from Dorner's AR-15 had torn through her husband's badge, and the shield, on the way to his heart.

***

Teresa Evans still did not feel safe.

Maybe the dead man in the cabin was a Dorner look-alike, an accomplice. It did not seem crazier than what had already happened.

"What seemed impossible before is no longer impossible," she said. "My reality is, I'm not really sure what could happen at any time."

Back home alone, she coped with her nerves by cleaning. She took down the sheets over the windows. She put the furniture back in place. She couldn't eat.

Even after experts confirmed that the charred body in the basement was Dorner—first by dental records, then by comparing a sample of Dorner's DNA kept by the Navy to marrow from the femur of the charred corpse—she remained apprehensive. What if someone tried to finish what he started?

One day, she found that someone had removed her window screen and tried to get inside her house.

Another day, she saw graffiti on a wall near the police station: TERRI EVANS IS A LIAR. On the Web, some people hailed Dorner as a hero and said she deserved whatever she got.

She thought about changing her name, but it would be easy to find the new one in public records. She knew her name would be visible, on her uniform, as long as she wore one.

Not long ago, she drove up the mountain and stared at the blackened hole in the ground where Dorner had died. She badly wanted to talk to the families he had hurt. But she dreaded what they might think. What if they held her responsible for pushing him over the edge?

"I don't know how people feel about me," she said. "I don't know who blames me, and who doesn't."

So far, she hasn't returned to work. Even at the LAPD, she can't be sure who is her friend.

***

By his charred corpse, police found the 9-millimeter Glock that Dorner had used to put a single bullet through his temple.

Ballistics analysis matched the gun to the shootings of Keith Lawrence and Monica Quan. The charred AR-15 assault rifle found in the basement was matched to the slayings of Michael Crain and Jeremiah MacKay, and the shootings of Alex Collins and Andrew Tachias.

In Dorner's wallet, along with a fake police badge, an LAPD business card had survived the cabin fire. On it, he had written the names of two of the police captains who oversaw his Board of Rights. Their addresses were included, and the names of their wives.

***

For the LAPD's mistaken shooting of Emma Hernandez and her daughter, Margie Carranza, the newspaper delivery women received a $4-million settlement from the city.

Of the two, Carranza is the more traumatized. She is afraid of police, and afraid to go out at night. When she takes her children to the movies, she sits separately from them.

Her logic is simple. If someone comes with a gun to kill her, she does not want her children to die too.

***

Alex Collins spent two months in the hospital, an armed deputy standing guard day and night. A conference room was outfitted with a recliner and a baby crib, so Collins' wife and infant son could stay close.

His wife wondered what would have happened if he had worn his smartphone in his back pocket that day, instead of over his chest. One day, in his hospital room, he and his wife caught a glimpse of the television news. A man was getting Christopher Dorner's face tattooed on his arm.

Collins underwent 20 surgeries. The roof of his mouth was repaired, his tongue sewn together, his obliterated teeth replaced, his shattered leg embedded with pins. Plastic surgeons erased the mark of the bullet hole under his nose. He learned to stand with a walker, and finally to do without the walker, and now his limp is barely visible.

He returned to police work in September, in the intelligence division. His son will turn 1 in January.

***

Riverside Police Officer Andrew Tachias lives in constant pain from Dorner's bullets. He has no movement in his left arm, and little in his right. He has grown reclusive, and has trouble talking about the shooting that took his partner's life.

"He hasn't healed at all," his father says.

The cabdriver who helped save Tachias' life insists he did nothing extraordinary.

"If you are at same place and same time, I believe you are gonna do the same," says Karam Kaoud, then thinks about it some more and says, "Actually, I don't know."

He still drives a cab, only now he hates to be stopped at red lights. He doesn't want to be a target.

***

"I don't defend what Dorner did, but like many in the community, I believe what he said," a man told Charlie Beck.

The LAPD chief was standing before a crowd in South Los Angeles. The speaker's sentiment was no surprise. For those who remembered similar community meetings from 20 years ago, what seemed remarkable was the softer tone. No one shouted at the chief; no one cursed him.

"We hire from the human race and we hire the best people we can, and sometimes they make mistakes," Beck said.

Recently, the LAPD completed its review of Christopher Dorner's firing. The conclusion was the same. He had told a lie about his training officer, and his badge had been properly stripped.

***

Randal Quan drove to the Irvine Police Department to meet the chief detective who had worked his daughter's killing.

He was there not to discuss the case, but because he had requested the jewelry his daughter had been wearing when she was killed. He wanted to bury her in it.

Usually, the transfer of such property took time. There was red tape.

Det. Victoria Hurtado wanted to ensure he received it without delay. She walked to the property room. She removed Monica Quan's engagement ring, necklace, bracelets and watch from the sealed evidence bags.

The jewelry was caked with blood.

She found a brush and paper towels, and went to the sink. She began cleaning.

How WE REPORTED THE STORY

Chapter One: Murder in Irvine

1. *The man emerged...* The account of Dorner's actions at the Hi View Inn & Suites is based on interviews with Irvine Det. Victoria Hurtado.

2. *Murder scene:* The account of the Irvine murder scene, and of the investigation into the deaths of Monica Quan and Keith Lawrence, is based on interviews with Hurtado, Irvine Police Sgt. Bill Bingham, Lt. Julia Engen and Det. J. Sanders.

3. *Detectives led them to a private interview room...* The details of the exchange between Irvine police and the Quan family are based on an interview with Hurtado.

4. *Neither Monica Quan...* The portrait of Monica Quan is based on interviews with Alex Thomas and Tailer Butler, who played for Quan on the Cal State Fullerton basketball team, and with Marcia Foster, who coached the team.

5. *Nor Keith Lawrence...* The portrait of Keith Lawrence is based on an interview with his father, Kevin Lawrence.

6. *About 100 miles south...* The account of the discovery of Dorner's gear is based on a police report and on interviews with Pedro Ruelas and National City Police Cpl. Michael Harris.

7. *Officer Paul Hernandez...* The account of Officer Paul Hernandez's actions is based on interviews with Hernandez.

8. *In keeping with her prework ritual...* The account of LAPD Sgt. Teresa Evans' thoughts and actions, here and throughout the story, is based on an interview with Evans. Details of Dorner's history with the LAPD and of his disciplinary hearing are drawn from a transcript of the hearing.

9. *"Is anybody going out?"* The account of Dorner's visit to Driscoll's Wharf is based on interviews with witnesses Jeremy Smith, Mike Flynn and Shawn Collins.

10. *A second auto shop...* The account of the discovery of Dorner's gear in the second trash bin is based on interviews with Irvine police and with Platinum Auto Sports manager Majid Yahyai.

11. *They sought a stop-gap measure...* The account of the plan to charge Dorner with possession of a prohibited weapon is based on an interview with Orange County prosecutor Ebrahim Beytieh.

12. *She called Randal Quan...* The conversation with Randal Quan is based on an interview with Det. Hurtado.

13. *The detective sergeant ran over...* The detective sergeant's actions are based on an interview with the detective sergeant, Bill Bingham.

Chapter Two: Fear and the City

1. *The phones began beeping...* The account of the LAPD's actions after learning of Dorner's manifesto is based on interviews with Chief Charlie Beck and with LAPD Assistant Chief Michel Moore and Cmdr. Matt Blake.

2. *From his 10th-floor office...* The account of Beck's thoughts and actions throughout the manhunt is based on an interview with Beck.

3. *Teresa Evans, Dorner's former training officer...* The account of Teresa Evans' actions, here and throughout the story, is based on an interview with Evans.

4. *One of them was a San Diego police officer...* Dulani Jackson's account is drawn from an interview with Jackson.

5. *A former girlfriend...* Denise Jensen's account is drawn from an interview with Jensen.

6. *He cornered her in the ladies room...* The details are drawn from a police report of the incident.

7. *At first, she found him a model of friendliness...* J'Anna Hendricks' account is drawn from an interview with Hendricks.

8. *Dorner had frequented the Lahaina Grill...* Dorner's behavior at the bar is based on an interview with bartender Amber May.

9. *The fugitive walked onto the docks...* The account of Dorner's attempt to hijack the boat is based on an interview with San Diego Police Capt. Terry McManus.

Chapter Three: Longest Night

1. *Michael Crain's wife...* The portraits of Michael Crain and his wife and of his last night alive are based on interviews with Regina Crain.

2. *In the small hours...* The portrait of Lee McDaniel and of his experience at the Arco station is based on interviews with McDaniel.

3. *The patrol car followed Dorner...* The account of the Corona shooting is based on interviews with LAPD supervisors and investigators close to the investigation.

4. *His trainee, Andrew Tachias...* The portrait of Tachias is based on an interview with his father, Anthony Tachias.

5. *A 42-year-old Riverside man...* The account of the Cavalier driver is based on an interview with the driver, Jack Chilson.

6. *A 33-year-old man named Karam Kaoud...* The portrait of cabdriver Karam Kaoud, and the account of his actions, is based on interviews with Kaoud.

7. *Judging from the .223 caliber casings...* This detail is based on an arrest warrant affidavit filed by the Riverside Police Department.

8. *A shuttle driver near the San Diego airport...* The account of the discovery of the LAPD badge is based on interviews with Irvine Police Det. Victoria Hurtado and Sgt. Bill Bingham.

9. *An aluminum blue Toyota Tacoma...* The portrait of newspaper delivery women Emma Hernandez and Margie Carranza, and of their experiences that night, is based on interviews with Hernandez , Carranza and their lawyer, Glen Jonas.

10. *By one estimate...* The estimate is based on an interview with Glen Jonas.

11. *Now the doorbell rang...* The portrait of Regina Crain learning that her husband had been killed is based on interviews with Regina Crain, Riverside Police Sgt. Ryan Wilson, and Riverside Police Chief Sergio Diaz.

Chapter Four: A Killer Vanishes

1. *Det. Alex Collins was up early...* The portrait of Det. Alex Collins and his family is based on interviews with Collins and his wife, Lila.

2. *The lock on the gate...* The account of the discovery of Dorner's truck is based on an interview with San Bernardino County Sheriff's Sgt. Trevis Newport.

3. *Hundreds of law officers had coalesced on the mountain...* The account of the manhunt is based on interviews with Newport, Collins and fellow San Bernardino County sheriff's deputies Larry Lopez, Justin Musella, Daniel Rosa, Chad Johnson and Sgt. John Charbonneau.

4. *A 45-year-old woman named Reyna Eblin...* Reyna Eblin's account is based on an interview with Eblin.

5. *For the U.S. marshals...* The account of the U.S. marshals' actions and strategy is based on interviews with fugitive task force chief Thomas Hession, Los Angeles Regional Task Force supervisory inspector Bert Tapia and Agent Andrew Haggerty.

6. *At the San Bernardino County Sheriff's Department...* The account of the San Bernardino County sheriff's investigation into Dorner's background is based on an interview with Newport.

7. *The Navy said...* The background on Dorner's Navy service is based on military records and on interviews with Navy spokesmen Lt. Greg Raelson and Lt. Shawn Eklund.

8. *On Friday, a cabdriver...* The account of Karam Kaoud's visit to the hospital is based on interviews with Kaoud.

9. *Det. Alex Collins had joined the search...* The account of Collins' actions during the manhunt is based on interviews with Collins.

10. *The department's head psychologist...* The account of the thoughts and actions of psychologist Kevin Jablonski is based on an interview with Jablonski.

11. *Riverside Police Chief Sergio Diaz...* Diaz's remarks are drawn from an interview with Diaz.

12. *"We have to handle him totally separately..."* Musella's quote, and the account of his actions, are drawn from an interview with Musella.

13. *His SWAT colleague, Chad Johnson...* Johnson's quote and the account of his actions are drawn from an interview with Johnson.

14. *Charlie Beck was waiting for the shooting...* The account of Charlie Beck's thoughts and actions is based on an interview with Beck.

15. *The announcement stunned Sgt. Teresa Evans...* The account of Evans' thoughts and actions is based on an interview with Evans.

16. *A fearful-sounding woman...* The account of the fake tip is based on interviews with Riverside Police Det. Jim Simons and Lt. Bruce Blomdahl.

17. *The Riverside Police Department was nervously preparing...* The account of the funeral preparations is based on interviews with Riverside Police Department Deputy Chief Jeffrey Greer.

18. *Jim and Karen Reynolds...* The Reynoldses' account is based on interviews with the couple.

Chapter Five: The Mountain

1. *Jeremiah MacKay...* The portrait of Jeremiah MacKay and descriptions of his actions during the manhunt are based on interviews with San Bernardino County sheriff's deputies Roger Loftis, Randy German, Trevis Newport, Stan Wijnhamer and John Hayes, as well as with his father, Alan MacKay, and his wife, Lynette.

2. *Jim and Karen Reynolds...* The account of the ordeal of Jim and Karen Reynolds is based on interviews with them.

3. *Det. Alex Collins...* The account of Collins's actions, here and throughout the story, is based on interviews with Collins.

4. *On Highway 38...* The account of the shootout with Fish and Wildlife wardens is based on an agency report about the shooting and on an interview with Department of Fish and Wildlife Assistant Chief Dan Sforza.

5. *They called it the kill zone...* The details of the shootout at the cabin and of the attempt to rescue Collins and MacKay are based on interviews with Riverside Police detectives Jim Simons and Michael Medici, and San Bernardino County sheriff's deputies Larry Lopez, Justin Musella, Daniel Rosa, Chad Johnson, Capt. Gregg Herbert and Sgt. John Charbonneau.

6. *The LAPD wanted to get a SWAT helicopter into the air...* The account of the helicopter is based on an interview with LAPD Assistant Chief Michel Moore.

7. *Deputies orchestrated the end-game...* The account of the radio traffic is based on audio recordings released by the San Bernardino County Sheriff's Department.

8. *At Grove Community Church...* The account of Regina Crain at the funeral home and of her actions in the months that followed is based on an interview with Crain.

9. *Teresa Evans still did not feel safe...* The account of Evans' thoughts and actions is based on an interview with Evans.

10. *Police found the 9-millimeter Glock...* The account of the ballistics conclusions is based on an interview with Sgt. Trevis Newport.

11. *For the LAPD's mistaken shooting...* The account of the aftermath for Emma Hernandez and Margie Carranza is based on interviews.

12. *Alex Collins spent two months...* The account of Alex Collins's recovery is based on an interview with Collins.

13. *The cabdriver...* The account of the after-effects of the shooting on cabdriver Karam Kaoud is based on an interview with him.

14. *"I don't defend what Dorner did..."* The account of Beck's appearance at a community meeting is based on a column by *Los Angeles Times* columnist Sandy Banks.

15. *Randal Quan drove...* The account of Irvine Det. Victoria Hurtado cleaning Monica Quan's jewelry is based on interviews with Hurtado.

A Mother Helps Son in His Struggle With Schizophrenia

The Washington Post

Sunday, May 26, 2013

By Stephanie McCrummen

Every day is unpredictable for Naomi Haskell and her son, who has schizophrenia. But the constant is her love for Spencer — and the worry about his future.
"Wait — You described it as a cloudy feeling?"
"Yeah. Cloudy. It feels like these winds are blowing inside my head."

In Houston

The mother drives her son everywhere because he is not well enough to drive. He sits next to her, and at the red lights she looks over and studies him: how quiet he is, how stiffly he sits, hands in his lap, fingers fidgeting slightly, a tic that occasionally blooms into a full fluttering motion he makes with his hand, as if clearing invisible webs from his face. He is 19 years old, 6 feet tall, 250 pounds. His eyes are more steady than bright at this particular moment; his mouth is not set in a smile or a frown but some line in between.

"How're you doing, sweetie?" Naomi Haskell asks.

"Fine," Spencer says.

It has been 10 years since he began thinking his classmates were whispering about him, four years since he started feeling angry all the time, and two years since he first told a doctor he was hearing imaginary voices. It has been 20 months since he was told he had a form of schizophrenia, and 15 months since he swallowed three bottles of Benadryl and lay down to die, after which he had gotten better, and worse and, for a while, better again, or so Naomi had thought until an hour ago, when they were in the therapist's office and Spencer said that his head was feeling "cloudy."

"Wait —" she said, interrupting. "You described it as a *cloudy* feeling?"

Cloudy was the big, flying red flag that she had learned to dread. It might simply be a side effect of one of his five medications. But it could also be the quiet beginning of her firstborn son falling apart again, of hallucinations, or of a dive into depression, or some other dimension of his illness that Naomi has yet to fathom.

"Yeah," Spencer said. "Cloudy. It feels like these winds are blowing inside my head."

A light turns red, and she glances over again.

"You're feeling okay, baby?" she asks.

"Yeah," he says, staring straight ahead.

This is what it is like to be the mother of a son with a severe mental illness—an hour-to-hour, minute-to-minute vigil. At a time of increasing public concern about the role mental illness might have played in mass shootings in places like Newtown, Conn., and Aurora, Colo., Naomi's worry on a Tuesday in Texas is different. It's about keeping her son well.

"Dear Friends and Family ..." she had written last year, explaining her son's illness and his suicide attempt. "I don't believe I have fully processed the horror of my child suffering a level of torment so deep that it caused him to want to end his life. I'm afraid of what will happen to me if I think about it too much."

So what Naomi is thinking about now is helping Spencer make it until Friday, when he has another therapy appointment, and when the effect of a new medication he has just started taking might become clear.

TUESDAY AFTERNOON

They are driving across suburban Houston, a landscape of gray four-lanes, brick strip malls and beige office parks that Naomi knows as the place where the therapist's office is, or the doctor's, or the drugstore, or the ramp to the highway that goes to the psychiatric hospital.

She asks Spencer if he wants to go with her to the drug store and then the community college library where he likes to study when he feels able.

There is a pause before he answers, a dash whose length Naomi measures as a sign of how lost he is in his own world at any moment—one, two, three seconds. She looks over if he doesn't answer at all.

"Okay," Spencer says. "I need to get my backpack."

They drive to the apartment where he moved in January, when Naomi had thought Spencer was stable enough to leave the home where he had been living with her, his step-father and his younger brother. He had made it through the busy Christmas season working as a cashier, handling his symptoms with promising self-assurance, telling a customer who wondered who he was talking to not to worry, he just had a thought disorder.

Naomi knew that he wanted to get back to everything he had been doing his senior year in high school, when he was first told he had early-stage schizophrenia, a diagnosis later refined to schizoaffective disorder, bipolar subtype with obsessive-compulsive elements. He wanted to study math, go to college, go out with girls. He wanted independence, and Naomi thought the apartment would be a step toward that.

Then the first week he was there he got the cloudy feeling. He said that his brain felt like it was "under a hair dryer." He told Naomi he felt "unsafe." He checked himself into a psychiatric hospital.

When he was released 11 days later, he insisted on returning to the apartment rather than home, because he wanted to keep moving forward. Naomi's 70-year-old mother moved in with him, setting up a single bed in the living room in front of a balcony three stories high and over a sidewalk, a drop that Naomi tries not to think about.

She parks the car. She watches her son trudge up the three flights of open-air stairs, a slow, lumbering figure in jeans and a sweatshirt.

The signs she looks for: how he walks, whether he is quick or slow or heavy or aimless. How he talks — crisp or sluggish, or perhaps angrily to no one, as he had done in December, when he yelled "Stop following me!" down an empty hallway. Spencer had become deeply religious during the advent of his illness, and Naomi checks his Facebook page to see how many posts are there about Revelations, or Deuteronomy, or other biblical arcana. More than two or three is a warning sign, not because it is religious but because it is obsessive.

She checks his text messages, though she isn't always sure how to take them.

"I figure," he wrote around the time of the cloudy feeling in January, "a few hundred years after the resurrection, it will be like a sci-fi novel, and we'll have spaceships and everything and all sorts of crazy stuff. ... I will probably be an old man then but with reincarnation it is possible to go through childhood again, the right way. The Lord will make all things anew."

She watches little things, such as whether he dries off with a towel after a shower or walks naked and dripping to his bed and rolls around. She watches whether he remembers to put on deodorant, how he eats, whether he is being considerate.

He comes back down, his backpack full of books for his computer programming and math classes, and they drive to the library.

"It's right here," he says as Naomi gets near the campus.

"I know, baby," she says.

"I just thought you might subconsciously drive past it," Spencer says.

Naomi waits out the two hours in a coffee shop next to the library, leaving only briefly to get a soda. When Spencer comes back, he smiles faintly for the first time all day.

"I did this week's computer science assignments," he offers. "And I read the reading for next week."

"You must be feeling less cloudy," Naomi says.

"Yeah," Spencer says.

At lunch, she glances at the news blaring on the TV. A young man has just stabbed 14 people at a community college campus.

She is sure that in the coming days, it will come out that the young man had an untreated mental illness, and that the parents had tried to help or didn't know. With Newtown, Aurora and Tucson and so many other violent episodes, she had felt the same, horrible way. She felt devastated for the victims' families. And she felt devastated for the parents who, she imagined, had struggled in their own way just like her to save their sons.

"My heart bleeds for those parents — it literally bleeds," Naomi says at such moments, along with a prayer. "There but for the grace of God ..."

But she doesn't see that kind of violence in Spencer, not at all. She has read statistics that show her son is more likely to be a victim of violence than a perpetrator of it. She has also read about the elevated risk of violence among people with schizophrenia, and knows the statistics that show their risk is higher if severe symptoms such as paranoia or hallucinations are not controlled, or if they have a history of violence or drug abuse. But that isn't her son.

As she says one day when he is not there: "I don't see that in him. And I hope I'm not fooling myself. What I see is a kind, loving, empathetic boy struggling to regain his footing in this world. That's who my son is."

Now she turns away from the TV and watches Spencer eat a huge hamburger. She drives him back to his apartment and watches him bound up the three flights of stairs.

WEDNESDAY

Wednesday morning, he lumbers down. He piles into Naomi's car in sweatpants and a T-shirt, and they drive toward the psychiatric hospital near Houston for his electroconvulsive therapy appointment, a treatment for severe depression.

"How are you feeling?" Naomi asks her son. "It seems like you didn't want to wake up?"

A long pause; he stares straight ahead, eyes steady.

She turns on the radio. "Are you still feeling yuck?" she asks.

No response. Spencer keeps staring ahead. Cars are whipping by on the highway. Naomi glances over at him again and again and tries to make conversation about her cellphone, about the traffic, about anything, but Spencer does not engage.

They park in front of the low, sprawling psychiatric hospital. At the front desk, Spencer does the drill for the security lady: pockets inside out, pants legs up. He walks through the metal detector and holds out a wrist for the paper hospital bracelet. They go into the waiting area for ECT patients—a brightly lit, plastic-smelling space with a sagging plant and a man in an expensive-looking suit sitting in one of the mauve chairs, eyes to the white linoleum floor. Two women sit next to him, one blinking slowly toward sleep. A young woman who works at a coffee shop leans against her husband.

"How's he doing?" she asks Naomi with Spencer sitting right there.

"He's better," Naomi says, looking at her son. "Wouldn't you say, Spencer?"

He doesn't say. A few minutes later, he reaches over and pets his mother's head.

"Mommy," he says in a soft voice.

"Baby," she says, looking at him.

A nurse calls him in, and Naomi stays in the prep area as he gets ready. He takes off his black T-shirt, puts on a hospital gown and lies on a white-sheeted bed. The nurse takes his blood pressure, pulse and temperature, tapes the IV tube to his hand and starts a saline drip. Then he waits. He has never complained about ECTs, never said he was nervous about them.

Naomi is sure that he is, though, because of how he stares straight ahead when he is in the prep area, focusing on a single point on the wall. She knows because of how her son breathes so consciously, and because he does not want her to talk to him, but does not want her to leave him, either. She stays until they wheel him into the next room.

First comes the anesthesia through the IV, which he can feel moving through his hand and up his arm and then dissolving through his system. He had tried to resist sleeping before, but the feeling was so uncomfortable that he has learned to just give in. Next comes the gel, which is swabbed on his head, and then the electrodes pressed into the gel, and the electrical current, which triggers a controlled seizure, which requires placing a guard in Spencer's mouth to keep him from biting his tongue. The seizure, it is hoped, will trigger a change in his brain chemistry that might bring some relief.

They roll him into the recovery area to wake up while Naomi waits on the mauve chairs. After awhile, a nurse comes out.

"He's ready," she says.

Naomi pulls the car around to a back door, and the nurse rolls Spencer out in a wheelchair. He stands up and wobbles into the car.

"How are you feeling, my love?" his mother asks.

"Okay. My jaw hurts," he says, woozy, rubbing his jaw. "I have a headache."

She hands him a Tupperware container with his morning dose of pills, which he takes later on ECT days. He struggles to open it and hands it back to his mother, who opens it easily and hands him a bottle of water. He pops in the antipsychotic to keep hallucinations and paranoia at bay, the mood stabilizer to even out his highs and lows, and two antidepressants, including the new one. He washes them all down with thirsty gulps of water. He pulls off his hospital bracelet.

They go eat lunch then drive back to the apartment. Spencer wobbles up the stairs holding both sides of the railing and goes to bed.

Two hours later, he wakes up.

"Hi," he says to Naomi and his grandmother, who are waiting in the living room.

"How are you feeling?" Naomi asks.

"Less cloudy," he says. "I think each time my brain heals a little."

He walks to the refrigerator and gets a huge bowl of Jell-O. He sits on the couch and props his feet on a coffee table stacked with books he's reading: Matthew Henry's 2,000-page, 17th-century "Commentary on the Whole Bible"; "The Words and Works of Jesus Christ"; "God's Glory in Salvation Through Judgment."

He opens his laptop and checks the online Jerusalem Post, because he finds life in Israel more interesting than life in America. He watches a scene from a Japanese anime cartoon in which a beautiful female character says a long goodbye to a male character who appears to be dead or sleeping in a hospital bed.

He checks his Facebook page, where he has posted a photo of himself when he was 4, blond and bright-eyed with his little brother, and another one from his senior year in high school, when he was thinner and fitter but also sicker.

"What's going on, baby?" Naomi asks after awhile. "You want to take another nap?"

"Let's go to the gym," Spencer says.

"The gym?" Naomi asks.

He hasn't felt like going to the gym in weeks.

"Yeah," Spencer says.

So Naomi drives him to the gym. She sits in the lounge area and watches her son who was slumped in a wheelchair only four hours earlier load weights on to a bar. He benches 250 pounds. He runs on the treadmill. He walks over to the punching bag and starts hitting it with his fists.

Naomi starts to cry. If he is feeling better, she knows it might be the start of a manic phase. If he is feeling worse, she knows he is trying to hide it. Maybe the medicine is working. Maybe the psychiatrist has finally hit on the magical formula and what she is seeing right now is the start of a period of stability, the start of the life she wants for her son to have. Maybe she will get a phone call tonight that he has taken his life. The one thing Spencer had told her that she believed unconditionally was that if he ever decided to commit suicide again, he would make sure that no one suspected it.

He finishes and walks over to her, breathing heavy and sweating.

"I did back, abs and 13 minutes of cardio," he says.

"That's great, baby," Naomi says.

They drive home, and Naomi watches her son walk into the kitchen, pile a tower of crackers onto a plate, smear them with butter and drench them in syrup. She watches him walk to his desk and eat them with a fork and his fingers.

It is getting late. His grandmother has gone to teach ballet. Naomi has to get home.

"How are you feeling?" she asks.

"I feel relaxed, I feel good," Spencer says. "The headaches are mostly gone away."

His eyes are bright and animated. His body seems relaxed.

"You feel okay to be here by yourself tonight?" she asks, getting her purse.

"Yeah," he says. "I'll be okay."

"You can come home with me, bring a change of clothes," she says, moving toward the door. "I'm about to leave—you sure?"

"Yeah," he says.

She wants to trust him.

"And you'd tell me if you weren't okay?" she asks.

"Yeah," he says.

They hug, he pats her on the head and she shuts the door.

Thursday

On Thursday morning, Spencer doesn't see his mother. Instead, while she is away, he talks about his life.

He says it's been almost three years since a miracle happened. He says he was a junior in high school and developed a crush on a girl who was a Christian, which led him to become a devout Christian himself, which allowed him to begin to see his intense, manic anger and paranoid thoughts as "delusional beliefs," which opened the door to understanding he had an illness.

He says it has been two years since he first heard voices — what he describes as "whispers" that would come mostly at night, along with brief flashes of images he describes as demons. If his mother was afraid of him, he says, it was because he had become terrified of himself. He says he tried to manage by working out, by doing martial arts, not because he enjoyed beating people up but because it felt good, somehow, to get beaten up, and when nothing worked he asked his mother to take him to the doctor, where he heard words like "psychotic," which terrified him even more.

He says he was angry at his mother, at his teachers, at everyone for not figuring out what was wrong with him sooner.

"Like if somebody had been watching me throughout my first year or two in high school, at school or in my personal life, I think the mental illness would have been easily recognized," he says. "But my family was oblivious."

He says that he wanted to escape all of it. He says he started researching gluten intolerance and an array of other illnesses looking for any explanation other than the one the doctor had given him, which was that he was on the cusp of full-blown paranoid schizophrenia.

He says he moved briefly to Austin to attend college and study math, because he had somehow managed, even as he was becoming sicker, to get the highest score on the most difficult Advanced Placement calculus exam. But then he says he started "freaking out" that the world was going to end, which led him think he should learn carpentry to help Jesus rebuild after the apocalypse, which he now understands was one of his first psychotic episodes.

He says he understands why, when his mother found out, she went to a court and convinced a judge that her son was a danger to himself or others, then tricked him into getting on a bus back to Houston, where he was handcuffed and taken to the psychiatric hospital, where he began to accept that he would have to manage delusions and paranoia and mania and depression for the rest of his life.

He says he understands why he couldn't go back to college, and why the psychiatrist recommended a transitional program in Idaho for young adults with mental illness.

He says he moved there with his medications, and soon after that, something like the cloudy feeling began, and got much worse. He says he noticed that he was crying for several hours a day, and that he began feeling an intense pain that he describes as like having "a burning coal on my heart." He says he tried to draw it away by inflicting pain on other parts of his body, that he pressed a knife blade against his arm, and scalded himself with hot water. He says he began to realize that his favorite part of the day was going to sleep, when he felt nothing.

He says his medication was changed and he got better, and then he got much worse, and all the bad feelings came rushing back.

"I looked at the past and the future and I decided there was no way out of it," he says, and that was why he walked out of the facility one December day into the freezing cold and kept walking 15 miles to a Target, where he bought the Benadryl, and then went to a Wendy's, ate several burgers and chicken sandwiches and washed down three bottles of the pills with a Diet Coke, and then went to a mall and walked in circles until he got sleepy, then looked for a place he could die, and went into a dressing room at Sears.

He says the third-to-last thing he remembers thinking is that he was making a mistake, the second-to-last thing he remembers thinking is that he didn't care, and the last thing he remembers is raising an arm and saying a prayer.

He says he was found vomiting and seizing, and that four days later he woke up in an intensive care unit. He says people told him it was the best Christmas present ever, but he was not so sure. He says he came home, which is when Naomi told him about what she did in the days before:

She had made sure the gun at home was locked in its safe. She had put away the kitchen knives and then found herself wondering whether she should also remove the forks, and maybe the cleaners, until she started to see everything as a hazard — the trees in the yard, the car, the traffic on the road. She told her son that she loved him, and that she wanted to help improve his odds of surviving his illness, but that she knew that she could not ensure it, that it was ultimately up to him.

He says he understands that, which is why he is willing to bear the electrical currents, the pills, the constant shuffling to doctors and the constant scrutiny, and why he wants also to pull away from all that, to get in shape, to be better, to get back to studying math, to college, to driving, to everything he was doing when he first got sick.

He says he wants to reach the point that he knows is possible for people like him, where he can manage his illness instead of the other way around.

"I'm really not afraid of breaking down anymore," he says. "I've gained a lot of knowledge and control. I'm not afraid I will relapse into chaos."

He says all that, and then he takes a shower, uses a towel to dry off, and puts on his khaki pants and blue polo shirt. He packs his backpack — a sandwich, a Bible, his glasses — and goes to work.

FRIDAY

On Friday, Naomi picks Spencer up early for his therapy appointment, and he hustles down three flights of stairs.

"Hi, my baby," Naomi says.

"Hi, my mommy," Spencer says.

"Did they give you a hard time for missing work?" she asks, referring to the days he has missed because he has not felt well.

"They were happy to see me," Spencer says.

"Everybody's happy to see Spencer," Naomi says.

They are driving across suburban Houston, and she is somewhat relieved. He seems better. All Naomi wants is for her son to be well.

What she does not know is that the day before, without telling anyone, Spencer quit his job, believing that it was interfering with studying and going to the gym.

Eventually he will tell Naomi, and when he does, her anxiety will soar and her heart will sink because the last time Spencer quit a job was when he was paranoid and having hallucinations two years ago. She will check his Facebook page and see several religious postings. She will tell him that a lie of omission is still a lie, and that trust is important, and that she needs to be able to trust him. She will tell herself that it is okay, that he is struggling to become more independent, but she will not really be sure.

For now, though, at a red light, Naomi is looking over at her son, and in this hour, in this minute, his eyes are brighter.

"You still feeling cloudy?" she asks. "Or are the clouds clearing?"

"The clouds are clearing," Spencer says.

The Lobotomy Files / Forgotten Soldiers: When America Lobotomized Its Vets

The Wall Street Journal

December 12, 13, 14, 2013

By Michael M. Phillips

Part One

LA CROSSE, Wis. —Roman Tritz's memories of the past six decades are blurred by age and delusion. But one thing he remembers clearly is the fight he put up the day the orderlies came for him.

"They got the notion they were going to come to give me a lobotomy," says Mr. Tritz, a World War II bomber pilot. "To hell with them."

The orderlies at the veterans hospital pinned Mr. Tritz to the floor, he recalls. He fought so hard that eventually they gave up. But the orderlies came for him again on Wednesday, July 1, 1953, a few weeks before his 30th birthday.

This time, the doctors got their way.

The U.S. government lobotomized roughly 2,000 mentally ill veterans —and likely hundreds more—during and after World War II, according to a cache of forgotten memos, letters and government reports unearthed by The Wall Street Journal. Besieged by psychologically damaged troops returning from the battlefields of North Africa, Europe and the Pacific, the Veterans Administration performed the brain-altering operation on former servicemen it diagnosed as depressives, psychotics and schizophrenics, and occasionally on people identified as homosexuals.

The VA doctors considered themselves conservative in using lobotomy. Nevertheless, desperate for effective psychiatric treatments, they carried out the surgery at VA hospitals spanning the country, from Oregon to Massachusetts, Alabama to South Dakota.

The VA's practice, described in depth here for the first time, sometimes brought veterans relief from their inner demons. Often, however, the surgery left them little more than overgrown children, unable to care for themselves. Many suffered seizures, amnesia and loss of motor skills. Some died from the operation itself.

Mr. Tritz, 90 years old, is one of the few still alive to describe the experience. "It isn't so good up here," he says, rubbing the two shallow divots on the sides of his forehead, bracketing wisps of white hair.

The VA's use of lobotomy, in which doctors severed connections between parts of the brain then thought to control emotions, was known in medical circles in the late 1940s and early 1950s, and is occasionally cited in medical texts. But the VA's practice, never widely publicized, long ago slipped from public view. Even the U.S. Department of Veterans Affairs says it possesses no records detailing the creation and breadth of its lobotomy program.

When told about the program recently, the VA issued a written response: "In the late 1940s and into the 1950s, VA and other physicians throughout the United States and the world debated the utility of lobotomies. The procedure became available to severely ill patients who had not improved with other treatments. Within a few years, the procedure disappeared within VA, and across the United States, as safer and more effective treatments were developed."

Musty files warehoused in the National Archives show VA doctors resorting to brain surgery as they struggled with a vexing question that absorbs America to this day: How best to treat the psychological crises that afflict soldiers returning from combat.

Between April 1, 1947, and Sept. 30, 1950, VA doctors lobotomized 1,464 veterans at 50 hospitals authorized to perform the surgery, according to agency documents rediscovered by the Journal. Scores of records from 22 of those hospitals list another 466 lobotomies performed outside that time period, bringing the total documented operations to 1,930. Gaps in the records suggest that hundreds of additional operations likely took place at other VA facilities. The vast majority of the patients were men, although some female veterans underwent VA lobotomies, as well.

Lobotomies faded from use after the first major antipsychotic drug, Thorazine, hit the market in the mid-1950s, revolutionizing mental-health care.

The forgotten lobotomy files, military records and interviews with veterans' relatives reveal the details of lives gone terribly wrong. There was Joe Brzoza, who was lobotomized four years after surviving artillery barrages on the beaches at Anzio, Italy, and spent his remaining days chain-smoking in VA psychiatric wards. Eugene Kainulainen, whose breakdown during the North African campaign the military attributed partly to a childhood tendency toward "temper tantrums and [being] fussy about food." Melbert Peters, a bomber crewman given two lobotomies — one most likely performed with a pick-like instrument inserted through his eye sockets.

And Mr. Tritz, the son of a Wisconsin dairy farmer who flew a B-17 Flying Fortress on 34 combat missions over Germany and Nazi-occupied Europe.

"They just wanted to ruin my head, it seemed to me," says Mr. Tritz. "Somebody wanted to."

The VA documents subvert an article of faith of postwar American mythology: That returning soldiers put down their guns, shed their uniforms and stoically forged ahead into the optimistic 1950s. Mr. Tritz and the mentally ill veterans who shared his fate lived a struggle all but unknown except to the families who still bear lobotomy's scars.

Mr. Tritz is sometimes an unreliable narrator of his life story. He describes himself as "mentally injured, not mentally ill." For decades he has meandered into delusions and paranoid views about government conspiracies.

He speaks lucidly, however, about his wartime service and his lobotomy. Official records and interviews with family members, historians and a fellow airman corroborate much of his story.

It isn't possible to draw a straight line between Mr. Tritz's military service and his mental illness. The record, nonetheless, reveals a man who went to war in good health, experienced the unrelenting stress of aerial combat—Messerschmitts and antiaircraft fire—and returned home to the unrelenting din of imaginary voices in his head.

During eight years as a patient in the VA hospital in Tomah, Wis., Mr. Tritz underwent 28 rounds of electroshock therapy, a common treatment that sometimes caused convulsions so jarring they broke patients' bones. Medical records show that Mr. Tritz received another routine VA treatment: insulin-induced temporary comas, which were thought to relieve symptoms.

To stimulate patients' nerves, hospital staff also commonly sprayed veterans with powerful jets of alternating hot and cold water, the archives show. Mr. Tritz received 66 treatments of high-pressure water sprays called the Scotch Douche and Needle Shower, his medical records say.

When all else failed, there was lobotomy.

"You couldn't help but have the feeling that the medical community was impotent at that point," says Elliot Valenstein, 89, a World War II veteran and psychiatrist who worked at the Topeka, Kan., VA hospital in the early 1950s. He recalls wards full of soldiers haunted by nightmares and flashbacks. The doctors, he says, "were prone to try anything."

Born in Portage, Wis., in 1923 to Albert and Anna Tritz, young Roman had a strict upbringing. Two of his seven sisters were allowed to finish high school, but the three sons who survived to adulthood (one died in infancy) were expected to leave school after eighth grade and help on the family farm.

"The father is the boss," recalls Dorothea Tritz, 83, who grew up on the next farm over and married Mr. Tritz's younger brother. Albert's credo, according to Dorothea: "If you work hard and got a strong back, you can accomplish anything."

Roman was mild-mannered and quiet, relatives say. His blue eyes, now watery and startled, were warm and smiling back then. He played euchre and tinkered with engines.

After leaving school, he helped his father with the cows. But he dreamed of flying and joined what was then called the Army Air Forces.

The Army trained him to pilot the B-17 Flying Fortress, a four-engine bomber bristling with machine guns. He shipped out to England in the fall of 1944 to join the 728th Squadron of the 452nd Bombardment Group, which conducted daylight raids in continental Europe. Mr. Tritz would sometimes fly in huge formations of B-17s stretching across the skies like immense migrating geese.

Earlier in the war, airmen had to fly 25 missions to earn a ticket home. By the time Mr. Tritz arrived, the requirement was up to 35. Crewmen died or were captured at a rapid pace: The group lost 110 aircraft on 250 missions.

After the war, Mr. Tritz told his sister-in-law Dorothea he would look around the barracks and wonder who would be there the next night. "Every time you went, you thought this might be the last one," Mr. Tritz recalls.

He remembers one mission in which antiaircraft fire hit the cockpit and a metal fragment slammed into his helmet, fracturing his skull and rendering him unconscious. That incident, though clear in his memories, doesn't appear in his military records, which report no battle injuries. His recollections of other raids, however, match descriptions in military records and from a fellow crewman.

On Jan. 17, 1945, the squadron was dispatched to bomb U-boat bunkers in Hamburg, according to Richard Muller, a military historian at the U.S. Air Force School of Advanced Air and Space Studies. Mr. Tritz was co-pilot that day in a plane called Puddin's Pride. On its nose was painted a pinup image of a bombardier's wife lounging suggestively in high heels and a bathing suit.

The planes flew into black, shrapnel-filled clouds of antiaircraft fire. Directly over the submarine pens, Puddin's Pride got caught in turbulence, rolled onto its side and plunged 2,000 feet before Mr. Tritz and the pilot steadied it. The military sent a news release to the *Portage Daily Register and Democrat* detailing the hometown boy's near-miss.

"The worst moment was turning over with a full bomb load," says Gordon Skordahl, 91, who was manning the top gun turret that day. "That kind of disturbed me."

On April 7, 1945, Mr. Tritz's squadron bombed an airfield complex at Kaltenkirchen, home to new jet-powered fighters the Germans hoped would reverse their flagging fortunes. For bombing accuracy, the B-17s flew at 18,000 feet, instead of the usual 27,500 feet, making them vulnerable to counterattack.

German fighters swarmed the bombers with orders to ram any plane they couldn't shoot down. The attack lasted 40 minutes until the bombers turned for England.

Flying back, Mr. Tritz thought he was out of harm's way. Then he saw a German fighter slam into a nearby B-17 and shear off the bomber's tail section. He watched an American crewman tumble out of the opening and into thin air.

"That gives you a hell of a feeling," Mr. Tritz recalls. There were several reports of American fliers falling out of the sky as a result of German suicide attacks that day, according to Prof. Muller.

Four of the unit's 38 planes went down and 13 more suffered battle damage, military records show. Gen. Dwight Eisenhower signed a citation noting the unit's "unwavering devotion to duty" in the face of "continuous, aggressive, and fanatical attacks."

After his final bombing raid on April 19, 1945, Mr. Tritz returned home to Portage, where he got work assembling Quonset huts. Military doctors discharged him with a clean bill of health.

When World War II began, the U.S. military thought it knew how to stave off the psychiatric issues that had ravaged men in the trenches in the previous world war. It began screening potential recruits for psychological trouble signs and ultimately rejected some 1.8 million American men for World War II service on that basis.

Nevertheless, the military and VA soon found their hospitals over-flowing. A 1955 National Research Council study counted 1.2 million active-duty troops admitted to military hospitals during the war itself for psychiatric and neurological wounds, compared with 680,000 for battle injuries.

Desperate for an effective treatment for the worst-off patients (including some mentally ill World War I veterans) the VA embraced lobotomy. At the time, tens of thousands of the procedures were being performed in civilian hospitals, a wave inspired by two of lobotomy's most avid promoters, neurologist Walter Freeman and neurosurgeon James Watts.

"In practical use, the operation has been found of value in eliminating apprehension, anxiety, depression and compulsions and obsessions with a marked emotional content," VA Assistant Administrator George Ijams wrote to his boss in July 1943, urging the agency to approve the procedure.

Within a month, VA headquarters set guidelines. It ordered doctors to limit lobotomies to cases "in which other types of treatment, including shock therapy, have failed" and to seek permission of the patient's nearest relative.

In the late 1940s and early 1950s, there existed no diagnosis of post-traumatic stress disorder, a term that came into vogue after the Vietnam War. Back then, the term was "shell shock" or "battle fatigue." Many lobotomy patients, however, exhibited symptoms that might now be classified as PTSD, says Dr. Valenstein, the former VA psychiatrist.

"Realistically looking back, the diagnosis didn't really matter—it was the behaviors," says psychiatrist Max Fink, 90, who ran a ward in a Kentucky Army hospital in the mid-1940s. He says veterans who couldn't be controlled through any other technique would sometimes be referred for a lobotomy.

"I didn't think we knew enough to pick people for lobotomies or not," says Dr. Fink. "It's just that we didn't have anything else to do for them."

In a standard lobotomy, a surgeon pulled back the forehead skin, sawed two holes in the skull and inserted a rotating tool or spatula-like knife. The surgeon then severed pathways between the prefrontal area behind the forehead, and the rest of the brain. These fibers were thought by practitioners to promote excessive and compulsive emotions.

Dr. Freeman, the neurologist who popularized lobotomies, also pioneered a more controversial technique in which he hammered an ice pick beneath the upper eyelid, through the thin bone of the eye socket and into the brain. He would make the cuts by toggling the pick.

Immediately after his return from England, Mr. Tritz seemed healthy enough to his sister, Regina Davis, now 83. By the late 1940s, his behavior became alarming.

Their parents worried Mr. Tritz would attack Regina, according to medical records. "He had voices telling him that maybe he should come into one of the other rooms where one of us might be," says Mrs. Davis, who lives in Chilton, Wis. "What he had in mind, I don't know."

Mr. Tritz's sister-in-law, Dorothea, remembers visiting the family farm in 1949 and noticing something amiss. To this day, she recalls an exchange she had with Mr. Tritz.

"How are you doing?" she asked.

"Does anybody really care?" she remembers him saying.

Mr. Tritz complained of being persecuted by the Federal Bureau of Investigation and the Air Force, medical records show. Relatives tried to persuade him the conspiracies were imaginary. The senior Tritzes, devout Catholics, took him to a priest.

"The family is quite worried that patient might, because of his thoughts, commit a mortal sin and be damned to eternal hell," a VA medical report said. The priest sent him to a Catholic psychiatrist, who recommended electroshock therapy.

In 1949, Mr. Tritz's parents had him committed to the VA hospital in Tomah, which specialized in psychiatric cases. They struggled with the decision, according to Mrs. Davis. "I think that's partly why my mom and dad felt it best that he be committed—for the safety of the family," she says.

Medical records describe his insulin shock treatments, electroshock and the high-pressure water sprays. "Sometimes the patient would be very alert and would respond immediately when spoken to, and other times would continue to stand in place and grimace as [if] he had never been spoken to, apparently anticipating the shock of the cold water as it hits his body," medical staff reported in 1952.

"Condition improved slightly," the staff concluded.

Within months, doctors began to build a case for lobotomy. During one examination, a brain surgeon reported that Mr. Tritz stared straight ahead, refused to speak, turned his arms and hands "in various bizarre positions," and seemed to be hearing voices.

One neuropsychiatrist warned Mr. Tritz might not get great results from the surgery. "I doubt that social rehabilitation will follow," she wrote. It is unclear from the records whether such doubts were shared with the Tritz family.

Mr. Tritz's father authorized the lobotomy, and his mother signed as witness.

The day of the procedure, an anesthesiologist rendered Mr. Tritz unconscious with sodium pentothal and at 11:05 a.m. the surgeon made the first incision into his scalp. By noon the doctor had stitched his head with black silk sutures. Mr. Tritz's lobotomy was done.

After, Mr. Tritz's sister and mother found him bandaged and writhing in agony on the bed. "He was in so much pain," says Mrs. Davis, his sister. "It was hard to see him like that."

Mr. Tritz remembers having "an awful headache, about as bad a headache as anybody could have."

Among the VA staff who recommended the Tritz lobotomy was David Merrell, then a 29-year-old psychology doctoral candidate and VA trainee. In a 1953 report he said a lobotomy for Mr. Tritz "should be helpful in lowering the intensity of the disrupting emotional impulses and enable the patient to function more efficiently."

Dr. Merrell himself had served as a medic during the bloody Allied landing at Anzio, Italy, in 1944. For years after the war, his night terrors would jolt his wife, Ivy, from her sleep.

Now 88, Dr. Merrell remains troubled by his role in Mr. Tritz's case, the only lobotomy he recommended before leaving the VA. "Looking back at it, it was a terrible thing that came out of the psychiatric medical field at the time," he says of lobotomy. "But it did allow for control of hospital patients—aggressive, combative patients—without having to hurt them."

At the time, Mrs. Merrell, 81, was a psychiatric nurse at Tomah, where she worked on the violent ward, playing cribbage and softball with psychotic vets. "I wasn't a believer back then, and I'm not a believer now in lobotomies," she says. "I didn't like the fact that you were messing with somebody's brain that was already messed up."

In the immediate postwar period, lobotomy wasn't viewed with the uniform revulsion it inspires today. Newspapers and magazines often portrayed it as a miracle cure for the severely mentally ill. Some parents of soldiers even sought out the treatment for their troubled sons.

In 1950, a Fresno, Calif., woman wrote to the San Francisco VA pleading with doctors to hurry up and lobotomize her hospitalized son, whose operation had been delayed. "When his draft no. came up in '42 he answered the call and enlisted," she wrote—and then asked: "Why can't he have this operation" without further delay?

Some families credit lobotomy for improving vets' lives. Relatives of Maurice Dusseault believe his lobotomy helped him resume something close to a normal life after he suffered a breakdown while serving in the 756th Military Police Battalion. Following the operation, he lived with his sister in Manchester, N.H. — a bottle of Old Grand-Dad bourbon near at hand, according to relatives—and held down a job at an airfield and another as a deliveryman for the family grocery store.

"My whole life, I had a lot of respect for lobotomy because the only patient I knew was Maurice, and it worked for him," says his nephew, Eugene Rheault, 78.

Doctors reported that violent patients became calm and no longer needed restraints. They seemed less suicidal. Some could leave the hospital and live with their families.

But VA doctors were also keenly aware that they were often trading their patient's personality for emotional stability.

"These patients as a group remind me of a watch that has stopped," Jay Hoffman, a psychiatrist, wrote in 1949 of 42 veterans lobotomized at the VA hospital in Bedford, Mass. "If one shakes it vigorously the watch is apt to tick a few times, and the tick sounds like that of a watch in good repair, but it runs down almost immediately and stops."

In 1949, the VA distributed a 37-point take-home guide for families—a pamphlet that, in essence, warned a soldier's relatives that the man they sent to war was returning to them a child. "He may say anything that 'pops into his head,' thus embarrassing you," the pamphlet says. "Like a young child he may say, 'I won't' to everything you suggest. If you will joke with him, offer him something new, talk about something else, he will probably forget his 'I won't.'"

The lobotomized vet might masturbate openly or "bathe or play in the tub for hours and at the same time may not get himself clean."

"When will he be well?" the VA asked. "We cannot answer this question."

The VA did try to determine whether the benefits outweighed the risks. And the risks were severe. Overall, 8% of lobotomized veterans died soon after the operation, according to a 1947 document. One hospital reported a 15% fatality rate.

In 1953 a neurosurgeon at the Roseburg, Ore., VA hospital sought to test whether the operation had a real or placebo effect. He cut holes in the skulls of four mentally ill veterans and although he didn't touch their brains, he told them afterward that they had had lobotomies. The surgeon reported that none showed "even slight improvement."

The doctor later reopened their skulls and completed the operations.

It wasn't until the mid-1950s that the VA finished a five-year study of 373 veterans. Half were given lobotomies and the rest served as experimental controls. But by the end of the study, many of the test subjects were taking new antipsychotic drugs, muddling the conclusions.

Despite the absence of hard evidence, there persisted at the VA a belief that the operation left patients better off. Two nurses at the VA hospital in Northampton, Mass., wrote in 1949 that lobotomy offered the possibility—where none existed before—that a vet could someday leave the psychiatric ward and go home again. "It is difficult to put into statistics what it means to say 'Good-bye' to a man who a few months before lived in a dark world from which there seemed no exit save death," they wrote.

Mr. Tritz recovered slowly from his operation. Six weeks after surgery, he gave a loud cry in his sleep and his entire body convulsed. It was the first of a series of seizures that doctors concluded had likely been caused by the lobotomy.

By September 1953, though, he had brightened, working jigsaw puzzles and playing checkers with other patients. But he soon withdrew again and alarmed doctors by referring to himself as "the Prince of the Universe."

In January 1954, doctors allowed him a trial stay at the family farm. It went badly. His father whispered to a visiting VA social worker that he was scared to drive his son alone back to Tomah, records show. In the end, the sheriff returned Mr. Tritz to the hospital.

During swimming-pool therapy that spring, Mr. Tritz "was very confused and catatonic," according to his records. Doctors ordered him to undergo 30 more rounds of high-pressure water treatments to "motivate" him into activity in the game room, records say.

Another home trial in 1955 ended when he had a seizure and foamed at the mouth. Doctors again blamed the lobotomy.

A final home trial in 1956 went better. He spent evenings playing cards with his parents. When they drove into town, though, he refused to get out of the car. A VA social worker reported the senior Tritzes "believe he fears having to return to the hospital."

The VA formally discharged him on March 30, 1957, after 2,272 days of being institutionalized.

After his mothers death in 1958, Mr. Tritz lived alone with his father, who grew increasingly worried about a renewal of his son's psychiatric symptoms and the return of the voices in his head. "They" were telling him which electric roaster to use, his father told the VA. "They" wouldn't let him go to a particular store to buy overshoes. Mr. Tritz forced his father to empty his underwear drawer to show that he hadn't taken one of Roman's pairs.

In 1960, Mr. Tritz's father checked into a sanitarium, diagnosed with tuberculosis. Mr. Tritz's sister delivered him back to the Tomah VA, where he spent most of the following year.

From his own sickbed, Albert Tritz wrote to a VA social worker: "He showed no personal interest in many of the everyday activities that do happen and occur, it was very clear to me, to the neighbors and to the friends around us, that Roman very definitely slipped into a world by his own and there was no way known to me how to design a way to get him out of the rut that he is in."

The VA placed Mr. Tritz in the care of farm families and boardinghouse operators into the early 1960s. He would do rough carpentry work, clean the barn and help with the milking. He had another seizure in 1962, so he wasn't allowed to drive a tractor.

In 1963 he moved to La Crosse to study at a technical school. "He says he is a little more self-confident than he was one year ago," a doctor wrote.

At first, people refused to hire him because of his history of seizures, according to VA records. But Mr. Tritz eventually found work in machine shops, cutting airplane and plumbing parts. He started at $70 a week.

His symptoms ebbed and flowed over the decades that followed. He grew separated from family and wary of friends, persecuted by thoughts of government conspiracies and the magnets he believes were placed in his head.

For more than 30 years, he has eaten alone, twice a day, at the King Street Kitchen, a La Crosse restaurant. Regulars joke they set their watches by his 10:30 arrival for breakfast, usually a ham-and-cheese omelet, hash browns and two strips of bacon. He rarely speaks to other patrons. Mr. Tritz's self-isolation is so complete he didn't know that another restaurant regular was also a B-17 crewman during the war.

He won't use a phone. So out-of-town relatives visit when they can and check on him by calling the restaurant to make sure he is showing up for meals.

"I gotta come here to eat because if I don't I'll give into the gol-darned Federal Bureau of Investigation," Mr. Tritz explains.

Mr. Tritz is convinced he was in the diplomatic corps and the Secret Service; that the FBI broke up his two marriages (his relatives are confident he never married); and that he met Osama bin Laden. He also says he served in Vietnam, though he seems to know he is walking a fuzzy line between memory and fantasy. "I'd be dreaming of flying a B-52 and all of the sudden I'd wake up home in bed," he says.

He says there are several Roman Tritzes, but he isn't one of them. He believes he was born in England and spirited away to America by the FBI into a forced adoption by the Tritz family.

Asked what effect the lobotomy has had on his life, Mr. Tritz wanders into the cul-de-sacs of his mind: "I had a bad head injury while flying. That was put in suspended animation like it never happened. Now I feel confused and stuff like that, and that's about all I can say about it. I don't know."

At the same time, he leads an independent life on Social Security benefits and annuity payments from his machinist days. He drives his blue Chrysler when he doesn't feel like walking to the restaurant.

Mr. Tritz's one-room rental apartment has stale air and grimy walls that were once cream-colored. There is a single bed with no headboard, an array of aluminum trays filled with tools and a closet jammed with boxes that contain military records, letters from the VA and a presentation box with his Air Medal and four Oak Leaf Clusters. Each represents six combat missions.

This summer, VA doctors urged Mr. Tritz to undergo surgery to treat an intestinal condition. For months, he refused. He was reluctant to let VA doctors near him with a knife.

Corrections & Amplifications

Elliot Valenstein is a biological psychologist who worked at the Topeka, Kan., Veterans Administration hospital in the early 1950s. A Page One article on Thursday about the VA's use of lobotomies incorrectly described him as a psychiatrist.

PART TWO

As World War II raged, two Veterans Administration doctors reported witnessing something extraordinary: An eminent neurologist, Walter J. Freeman, and his partner treating a mentally ill patient by cutting open the skull and slicing through neural fibers in the brain.

It was an operation Dr. Freeman called a lobotomy.

Their report landed on the desk of VA chief Frank Hines on July 26, 1943, in the form of a memo recommending lobotomies for veterans with intractable mental illnesses. The operation "may be done, in suitable cases, under local anesthesia," the memo said. It "does not demand a high degree of surgical skill."

The next day Mr. Hines stamped the memo in purple ink: APPROVED.

Over the next dozen or so years, the U.S. government would lobotomize roughly 2,000 American veterans, according to a cache of forgotten VA documents unearthed by The Wall Street Journal, including the memo approved by Mr. Hines. It was a decision made "in accord with our desire to keep abreast of all advances in treatment," the memo said.

The 1943 decision gave birth to an alliance between the VA and lobotomy's most dogged salesman, Dr. Freeman, a man famous in his day and notorious in retrospect. His prolific—some critics say reckless—use of brain surgery to treat mental illness places him today among the most controversial figures in American medical history.

At the VA, Dr. Freeman pushed the frontiers of ethically acceptable medicine. He said VA psychiatrists, untrained in surgery, should be allowed to perform lobotomies by hammering ice-pick-like tools through patients' eye sockets. And he argued that, while their patients' skulls were open anyway, VA surgeons should be permitted to remove samples of living brain for research purposes.

The documents reveal the degree to which the VA was swayed by his pitch. The Journal this week is reporting the first detailed account of the VA's psychosurgery program based on records in the National Archives, Dr. Freeman's own papers at the George Washington University, military documents and medical records, as well as interviews with doctors from the era, families of lobotomized vets and one surviving patient, 90-year-old Roman Tritz.

The agency's use of lobotomy tailed off when the first major antipsychotic drug, Thorazine, came on the market in the mid-1950s, and public opinion of Dr. Freeman and his signature surgery pivoted from admiration to horror.

During and immediately after World War II, lobotomies weren't greeted with the dismay they prompt today. Still, Dr. Freeman's views sparked a heated debate inside the agency about the wisdom and ethics of an operation Dr. Freeman himself described as "a surgically induced childhood."

In 1948, one senior VA psychiatrist wrote a memo mocking Dr. Freeman for using lobotomies to treat "practically everything from delinquency to a pain in the neck." Other doctors urged more research before forging ahead with such a dramatic medical intervention. A number objected in particular to the Freeman ice-pick technique.

Yet Dr. Freeman's influence proved decisive. The agency brought Dr. Freeman and his junior partner, neurosurgeon James Watts, aboard as consultants, speakers and inspirations, and its doctors performed lobotomies on veterans at some 50 hospitals from Massachusetts to Oregon.

Born in 1895 to a family of Philadelphia doctors, Yale-educated Dr. Freeman was drawn to psychosurgery by his work in the wards of St. Elizabeth's Hospital, where Washington's mentally ill, including World War I veterans, were housed but rarely cured. The treatments of the day —psychotherapy, electroshock, high-pressure water sprays and insulin injections to induce temporary comas—wouldn't successfully cure serious mental illnesses that resulted from physical defects in the brain, Dr. Freeman believed. His suggestion was to sever faulty neural pathways between the prefrontal area and the rest of the brain, channels believed by lobotomy practitioners to promote excessive emotions.

It was an approach pioneered by Egas Moniz, a Portuguese physician who in 1935 performed the first lobotomy (then called a leucotomy). Fourteen years later, he was rewarded with the Nobel Prize in medicine.

In 1936, Drs. Freeman and Watts performed their first lobotomy, on a 63-year-old woman suffering from depression, anxiety and insomnia. "I knew as soon as I operated on a mental patient and cut into a physically normal brain, I'd be considered radical by some people," Dr. Watts said in a 1979 interview transcribed in the George Washington University archives.

By his own count, Dr. Freeman would eventually participate in 3,500 lobotomies, some, according to records in the university archives, on children as young as four years old.

"In my father's hands, the operation worked," says his son, Walter Freeman III, a retired professor of neurobiology. "This was an explanation for his zeal."

Drs. Freeman and Watts considered about one-third of their operations successes in which the patient was able to lead a "productive life," Dr. Freeman's son says. Another third were able to return home but not support themselves. The final third were "failures," according to Dr. Watts.

Later in life, Dr. Watts, who died in 1994, offered a blunt assessment of lobotomy's heyday. "It's a brain-damaging operation. It changes the personality," he said in the 1979 interview. "We could predict relief, and we could fairly accurately predict relief of certain symptoms like suicidal ideas, attempts to kill oneself. We could predict there would be relief of anxiety and emotional tension. But we could not nearly as accurately predict what kind of person this was going to be."

Other possible side-effects included seizures, incontinence, emotional outbursts and, on occasion, death.

Goateed and bespectacled, Dr. Freeman toured state hospitals and spread the gospel of psychosurgery. At first, he found himself welcomed by glowing media profiles. "A world that once seemed the abode of misery, cruelty and hate is now radiant with sunshine and kindness to them," said the *Saturday Evening Post* in 1941, describing lobotomy patients.

In the summer of 1952, Dr. Freeman operated on 225 people in 12 days during a lobotomy tour of West Virginia, according to his unpublished memoir. One patient in Iowa in 1951 died when the doctor chose an inopportune moment to stop for a photo and the surgical instrument penetrated too far into the patient's brain, Freeman biographer Jack El-Hai wrote in "The Lobotomist."

VA hospitals around the country vied for Dr. Freeman's time, offering him and Dr. Watts $50 a day each (roughly equivalent to $450 today) in consulting fees, according to documents at the George Washington University, where Dr. Freeman taught neurology. Dr. Freeman served on the Committee for Lobotomy at VA headquarters, helping guide the agency's use of the surgery. He also advised Walter Reed Army Hospital in the early 1950s.

The VA knew it was taking a risk in signing on with Dr. Freeman. In 1946, as the VA was deciding whether to hire him as a lobotomy consultant, an internal agency memo noted that "there are certain objections to an appointment of Dr. Freeman on the grounds that he is 'a biased enthusiast.'"

"It is my opinion that if the situation were properly handled the advantages of being able to use the services of Dr. Freeman would outweigh the disadvantages," Dr. Pearce Bailey, chief of the VA's neurology division, wrote to a senior VA psychiatrist, Dr. Daniel Blain.

Dr. Blain agreed, adding a handwritten note to the bottom of the memo saying that, despite the "many psychiatrists" skeptical of Dr. Freeman, he is "probably the best man."

Lobotomies "may do a tremendous job for VA in chr[onic] cases," Dr. Blain wrote.

In early Freeman operations, often called standard lobotomies, his surgeon partner, Dr. Watts, would cut holes in the patient's skull. Dr. Freeman—a neurologist, not a surgeon—would usually stand about two yards behind the patient's head for a good line of sight, and then verbally guide Dr. Watts as he inserted an instrument and sliced the neural fibers.

That open-skull method gave doctors a peek into the mystery of which part of the brain controlled which bodily functions. It also provoked a controversy within the VA in 1947, when the agency's Seattle office asked headquarters in Washington, D.C., about the feasibility and legality of removing, for research purposes, one cubic centimeter of live brain tissue during lobotomies.

"One might, of course, obtain the relatives' permission for such a procedure," a Seattle VA doctor wrote to headquarters. "However, I am afraid that one might run the risk that removal of brain tissue would be misinterpreted and that the relatives will feel that the patient is used as a 'guinea-pig.'"

VA headquarters sought the advice of several medical experts, including Dr. Freeman, who responded that he saw no objection. "I have frequently urged Dr. Watts to do this in order that our own biopsy studies be carried out and I have seen no ill effects as a result," he wrote.

In the end the VA rejected Dr. Freeman's advice. "We are extremely afraid of such a procedure," a senior doctor at VA headquarters wrote to the Seattle office.

Dr. Freeman's aggressive championing of lobotomy unsettled other, less interventionist, doctors. In 1948, Dr. Florence Powdermaker, chief of the VA's psychiatric-education section, inserted a pink note in the files expressing her strong doubts about Dr. Freeman, whom she accused of having "liberal ideas" about brain surgery. In unusually sarcastic language for a government memo, she made the quip about how he might even find lobotomy suitable to treat "a pain in the neck" and mused about whether Dr. Freeman had "shown any disposition to modify his idea that lobotomy is useful for practically everything."

At a meeting of the Washington, D.C., Psychiatric Society the following year, Dr. Winfred Overholser, superintendent of St. Elizabeth's Hospital in Washington, where Dr. Freeman began his career, gave a pessimistic report on patients lobotomized there. "I am sorry to say that even when they are improved, they are still nothing to brag about," he said. "We are not enthusiastic."

Dr. Harvey Tompkins, chief of the VA psychiatric division, was in the audience. He said the agency had already performed 1,200 lobotomies at that point but that VA doctors couldn't say whether the surgery worked, according to a 1949 Newsweek article about the medical conference.

At the end of 1950, Dr. Francis Gerty, chair of the lobotomy committee at the VA hospital in Hines, Ill., reported to headquarters that, out of an abundance of caution, his hospital hadn't performed any lobotomies. "Much more careful research will have to be done on many fundamental aspects of this problem before we would be justified in using it very much," Dr. Gerty wrote.

In 1946, Dr. Freeman took a new path into the cranium. He used electric shocks to jolt a female patient into unconsciousness and, using a hammer, drove an ice pick—one taken from his own kitchen—into her brain through the thin bone of the eye socket called the orbit. He then swiveled the pick to the side to make the desired cuts.

He saw the operation as one that could be done as an office procedure without a surgeon's assistance, and he went on to perform thousands of ice-pick operations, usually without gloves or mask. His methods so alarmed Dr. Watts that their partnership collapsed in 1948, and Dr. Watts moved out of their shared office in Washington.

At one medical conference where Dr. Freeman expounded on the virtues of the ice-pick approach, Dr. Watts stood up to criticize his old friend on its use. "I thought it was wrong," Dr. Watts said years later.

When an operation went badly, Dr. Freeman discussed the outcome in detached, matter-of-fact terms. "On two occasions I was embarrassed by having the tip of the instrument break and while in neither case does it seem to have done any harm, the patient received no benefit from [the] operation," he wrote in one undated document.

"In a later case when I thought I had a stronger instrument, the shaft broke at the 6 centimeter mark and lacerated the eyeball of the patient so that not only was she not benefited by [the] operation but she lost the sight of her eye and had to be operated upon for removal of the steel fragment," he wrote.

The incidents motivated Dr. Freeman to commission a hardier ice pick, dubbed an orbitoclast. He described it as strong enough to place "in the keyhole of a door and practically lift the door off its hinges without bending it or breaking it."

Dr. Freeman's ice-pick method provoked an uproar at the VA.

In 1948, the VA hospital in Tuskegee, Ala., invited Dr. Freeman to demonstrate ice-pick lobotomies on 15 or 20 veterans, "whom we will presumably have at hand by that time," a Tuskegee doctor wrote to VA headquarters. To compare the results, Dr. Freeman suggested giving another group of veterans electroshock therapy, but no lobotomies.

A month before the visit, however, VA consultant Francis Murphey, a former Army neurosurgeon and respected Memphis doctor, raised objections. "So far as I know [Dr. Freeman] has published no article on the subject in the national literature and as a result I know nothing about the dangers, complications or results" from ice-pick lobotomies, Dr. Murphey warned Dr. Raymond Crispell, chief of the VA neuropsychiatry division in Atlanta.

Dr. Murphey was troubled that a doctor using the ice-pick method couldn't see the area of the brain being cut. "I am surprised that you have written me for my approval of such a procedure which departs so radically from standard surgical procedures, since you know how we have labored to throw every safeguard" around lobotomies, Dr. Murphey wrote.

At first, VA headquarters approved the Freeman visit, but insisted patients' families be informed the doctor was using an unorthodox technique. The contretemps intensified when Dr. R. Glen Spurling, national neurosurgical consultant to the VA, was quoted by a colleague as saying that only "over his dead body" would a nonsurgeon such as Dr. Freeman be permitted to perform a lobotomy at a VA hospital, according to a letter in the National Archives.

The VA retracted the invitation.

Dr. Crispell sent an apology to Dr. Freeman, saying his would-be hosts were "greatly disappointed, distressed, and embarrassed." He added that a government hospital couldn't proceed without approval from headquarters and that the risk of misunderstanding was high, "especially at Tuskegee"—which treated only black patients—"where it might be said that we were experimenting on our colored veterans." (The VA wasn't behind the infamous U.S. Public Health Service syphilis study at the Tuskegee Institute, launched 16 years earlier, in which government researchers left African-American men untreated for the disease.)

Three years after the decision against the ice-pick method at Tuskegee's VA hospital, the issue arose again. Dr. F.M. Cook, manager of the VA hospital in Lexington, Ky., wrote to headquarters asking permission to use the technique, citing Dr. Freeman's view that the operation need not be performed by surgeons. Psychiatrists could master the procedure with two or three weeks of training, Dr. Cook wrote. "It would occur to us that considerable money could be saved," Dr. Cook wrote.

The doctor promised the hospital would supervise such procedures carefully so "as to not let such a program get out of control."

At first, the VA's psychiatric chief, Dr. Tompkins, quashed Lexington's hopes. Only the VA hospital in Bedford, Mass., was authorized to perform ice-pick lobotomies, and only as part of a study, he wrote.

A year later, the VA had reversed course. In a second letter, Dr. Tompkins ruled that, while VA doctors were "sharply divided" over the method, it was up to the hospitals themselves to decide which procedure to use.

Dr. Freeman's star began to fade with the advent of antipsychotic drugs, and the public began to see lobotomy as mutilation, not miracle cure. Lobotomy's popular image darkened further with Ken Kesey's 1962 novel, *One Flew Over the Cuckoo's Nest*, in which the mental-patient hero is lobotomized for his rebelliousness.

In 1954, Dr. Freeman left Washington for California, where he continued to perform ice-pick lobotomies at the shrinking number of hospitals that would allow him to operate.

His son, Prof. Freeman, remembers his father showing up at a medical conference in the 1960s with a large box of Christmas cards from grateful patients and families, evidence he hoped would persuade other doctors that his surgery brought positive results. In his later years, Dr. Freeman roamed the country in a camper, taking photos of former patients, as if reassuring himself of the same thing.

"He redoubled his efforts to explain it and justify it in the eyes of the public," says Prof. Freeman. "He was a fighter."

Walter Freeman, who died in 1972, performed his last two operations on a single day in 1967. One patient "has done well," he wrote in his unpublished autobiography. The other, a woman who'd had two previous Freeman lobotomies, died of a hemorrhage three days later.

PART THREE

This summer, Donald Peters searched the shed outside his Texas home for the old foot locker that holds the memories of his brother Melbert.

Inside the metal trunk, he found Melbert's air medal, awarded for World War II combat. And the American flag that covered Melbert's coffin in 1988.

But he found no photos of Melbert there. The mice had eaten them. Gone were the only pictures Donald had of the brother who had left for war a happy-go-lucky teen and returned home a 20-year-old plagued by guilt, violent anger and mental illness.

Now, what remains are six decades of bitterness at the oldest Peters brother, Jimmy, who, in the early 1950s, gave government doctors permission to give Melbert not one, but two, lobotomies.

Jimmy "kind of thought it was funny that [Melbert] had a double lobotomy—he laughed about it," says Donald Peters, 81 years old. "That's what really burned me up."

Melbert Peters was one of some 2,000 mentally ill veterans lobotomized by Veterans Administration and state hospitals during and immediately after World War II, according to a trove of documents uncovered by The Wall Street Journal.

It was an episode now erased from public memory. Even the VA itself forgot long ago about its use of the controversial operation to treat psychiatric conditions.

But the families of those who underwent lobotomies can't. Today, some still struggle with the doubts, anger and sorrow that sprang from the decision, made more than a half-century ago, to allow doctors to cut into a young man's brain and sever neural fibers then thought to contribute to uncontrolled emotions.

At 93, Edna Schauer still weeps when she speaks of how war and lobotomy robbed her brother of the chance to be an artist. At 64, David Nigro remains angry that his mother didn't tell him his real father was an Army veteran killed by a botched lobotomy. His mother, now 84, just wishes she could forget the whole thing—the violent husband, the brain surgery, the deception that followed. The family of Emil Kauzlarich treated his lobotomy as a secret to be kept from the children, who wondered why their uncle's face went blank when told a joke.

During World War II, lobotomy had a reputation, fueled by outspoken doctors and laudatory media reports, as the best hope for improving the lives of people with severe mental illness, the kind that might otherwise keep them locked up for life in VA psychiatric wards. Some veterans' parents even demanded the procedure for their troubled sons.

Many learned too late, however, that lobotomy could be a mixed blessing. The operation might reduce a patient's violence and angst, but it could also leave him forever scrubbed of personality and stripped of independence.

"He wasn't able to function the way he was before," says Donald Rawlings, whose uncle Eldon Rawlings, a Navy veteran, was lobotomized by the VA and spent his final years pushing a mop at a Utah rest home. "He was all scrambled up in his brain."

Melbert Peters: Guilt, Grudges and Lincoln Logs

Under the VA's rules, it was usually family who gave the final go-ahead for a lobotomy. For patients such as Melbert Peters, that meant a radical treatment with ambiguous prospects for success. For his family, it meant decades of doubt and resentment.

Mr. Peters grew up in Morton, Wash., a varsity baseball and basketball player in high school who dreamed of being a surveyor. He served as a radio operator on a B-24 Liberator bomber. Once he went down in the English Channel after his plane was crippled by enemy fire on a bombing mission, according to his younger brother Donald.

His niece Bea Cooper recalls him buying her ice cream and show tickets before the war, the gentle acts of a favorite uncle. "When he came home, he was very reclusive, and he would get violent—I guess when he had flashbacks," says Ms. Cooper, now 75 years old.

He obsessed over the Germans he had killed from the air. He drank too much and fought too easily. "It was a sad story as far as I was concerned," says Donald, who was still in junior high school when Melbert left the Army. Being the youngest, Donald says, "I didn't know how to handle a lot of it."

In the late 1940s, Melbert checked into the VA hospital at American Lake, Wash., where he was diagnosed as schizophrenic and, eventually, given a lobotomy. The operation wasn't deemed a success, so doctors performed a second one.

Melbert wasn't considered competent to authorize his own surgery. So it fell to Jimmy, as the eldest brother, to give the doctors permission. "That's why [Jimmy] and me didn't get along too good," says Donald.

One of the operations was likely an ice-pick lobotomy, in which the doctor punched a probe through Melbert's eye sockets and into his brain to cut neural fibers. "He had two big black eyes, so I'm sure they went in through his eyes," says Donald. Bruised eyes were a typical side-effect of the ice-pick method.

"When they first did the lobotomy, he was like a zombie," says Ms. Cooper. Later, he alternated between docile and angry, she says.

Donald's son, Daniel Peters, now 58, remembers visiting with his uncle years after the operations. "He didn't speak a whole lot about anything," says Daniel. They would play with Lincoln Logs together, the child and the childlike man.

Melbert Peters was in and out of the VA hospital into the 1970s, "considered incompetent," his medical records say. He spent his last days at the Washington Soldiers Home in Orting, scavenging bottles for deposit money.

Melbert died at age 63, struck by a car as he stepped off a bus. Jimmy died last year at 94. Donald is widowed and ill, living in Hawley, Texas, unable to get over Melbert's fate or forgive Jimmy's fateful decision.

"I always hated the thought of lobotomies," Donald says. "They were messing with something they didn't know or understand."

Harvey Bailey: A Secret That Still Splits Mother and Son

Harvey Bailey's lobotomy shattered his family, and the lies that followed still echo between his wife and his son.

Mr. Bailey, then a 19-year-old from Madera, Calif., went AWOL for 111 days after his draft board ordered him to report for training in 1943, military records show. When he turned himself in, military doctors weren't sure what to make of him. Over a period of a few months, they described him alternately as "mentally normal" and a "constitutional psychopath." They diagnosed him as a sleepwalker. They recommended a psychological discharge.

Instead, the military attached him to the 123rd Armored Ordnance Battalion and ultimately sent him to France. There, Technician 5th Grade Bailey served as an ambulance crewman and collected body parts from the battlefield, his relatives say. After the fighting ended, he served in the occupation force in Germany.

At his discharge in 1946, Army doctors declared him psychologically "normal."

Back home, however, Mr. Bailey grew convinced someone was trying to poison or shoot him. He forced his young wife, Alice, to taste his food. He locked her and their toddler son, David, in their house. Relatives recall how an uncle had to rescue them.

"He was having all kinds of flashbacks," says Stan Matli, 73, Mr. Bailey's nephew.

Alice grew frightened and regretful. "I thought I was going to get away from home," she says of her marriage to Mr. Bailey. "It was a mistake from the beginning."

Because of his outbursts, she had her husband committed to a civilian mental hospital in San Jose. There, he was diagnosed as a paranoid schizophrenic.

Dolores Hartsell, his niece, used to drive relatives to the hospital for visits in her 1949 Chevrolet. Ms. Hartsell, now 81, says Mr. Bailey would beg to be brought home. "I don't belong here," she recalls him saying. "I know I don't belong here."

Around that time, Alice Bailey left town, remarried and became Alice Nigro. Young David Bailey became David Nigro.

Back at the mental hospital, Mr. Bailey's condition worsened, and his mother authorized a lobotomy in 1953, relatives recall. The surgery went wrong, and infection spread through Mr. Bailey's brain, according to his death certificate. He died soon afterward, on David's fourth birthday.

David's memories of Harvey Bailey gradually faded until he came to believe that his stepfather was his actual father.

David says his mother didn't correct him. When David's half-sister stumbled across his birth certificate in a shoebox, and noticed the mismatched surnames, Alice put it down to a clerical error, the sister says.

"I spent my adult life trying to forget," says Alice, who lives in Ontario, Calif.

Only as a teenager did David learn about his birth father's existence, and how he died. David says his mother's deception shook his faith in her. His father's lobotomy shook his faith in the government.

"It really devastated me when I found out," says David, now a math teacher living in Shasta Lake City, Calif. "He was my father. He was a World War II vet, and he never received any kind of recognition for what he had done. That's what hurts me the most."

Says David: "I would like to have known him, good or bad."

David avoided the Vietnam draft when his number came up in 1970, working at a defense contractor to get a deferment and faking a hearing disability when his deferment ended, he says.

"There was no way in hell I was going to go to Vietnam after what happened to my father," he says.

Emil Kauzlarich: A Brother's Haunting Choice

In 1951, Fabian Kauzlarich agreed with VA doctors who wanted to lobotomize his older brother Emil, a Coast Guard veteran with profound mental illness. In the decades that followed, Fabian couldn't shake the feeling that he had made a terrible mistake.

"Later on, [Fabian] would talk about it with guilt," says Frances Malzahn, Fabian's daughter. "At the time, they thought it was the best decision for him."

Chief Machinist's Mate Emil Kauzlarich, of Roslyn, Wash., began showing signs of mental illness in July 1945, while patrolling off Alaska, the scene of naval clashes between the U.S. and Japan. The commander of the Coast Guard Cutter *Cyane* wrote that Emil "was mentally confused and, when questioned, made the statement that no one liked him and his buddies thought he was crazy."

At one point, Emil dived off the ship in uniform, military records show. Commanders sent him to a Coast Guard infirmary in Ketchikan, Alaska, where doctors diagnosed him with "psychoneurosis, depressive type." One night, he became so volatile that medical staff put him in the brig to restrain him.

At a Navy hospital in Seattle he refused food for three days. "I don't deserve to eat because of the way in which I lived," he said, according to medical records. Navy doctors declared him "a menace to himself and others."

The Coast Guard discharged him in 1946 and sent him under guard to a VA hospital.

Married during the early years of the war, he lost touch with his wife and daughter after he returned home ill, according to Ms. Malzahn.

Six years of psychiatric treatment—including electroconvulsive and insulin-shock therapies—failed to improve Emil's health. So in 1951, Fabian and his parents jointly agreed to the VA's recommendation that Emil undergo a lobotomy, according to Ms. Malzahn, 45, of Granger, Wash.

Ms. Malzahn wasn't told until she was an adult that Uncle Emil had been lobotomized. But she grew up thinking there was something off about him.

Fabian, now deceased, would reminisce proudly about the math skills his older brother had exhibited before the war, and how he had risen through the Coast Guard's ranks. But Emil lived out his years in group homes and managed care. He was generous and usually subdued—until his anger flared in the form of temper tantrums. He often stared uncomprehending when told a joke.

When the family took a road trip along the Pacific coast, Emil insisted on wearing the same shirt for the whole journey. "Come on, Emil, it's time to change that shirt," Fabian would chide him, according to Ms. Malzahn. Instead, Emil would go to a drinking fountain and splash himself with water.

"His whole frame of reference emotionally was bracketed," says his nephew Joe Minerich, 63.

Ms. Malzahn recalls a car ride years after Emil's 1984 death, during which her father opened up about the regret he felt about allowing the VA to lobotomize his brother. "The guilt came from the realization that it wasn't as great as it was supposed to be and that he wasn't able to be independent," says Ms. Malzahn. "They thought it would make things all better, and it didn't. In some ways, it made it worse."

Eugene Kainulainen: A Sister Loses Her Protector

For years, Edna Schauer's brother was all she had. And then she lost him, too.

Eugene Kainulainen was Edna's shield from a hard world in Kitsap County, Wash. The family fell apart when their father returned from a fishing trip to find their mother—who sang Finnish songs on local radio—sitting on another man's lap. Edna, then 4 years old, and Eugene, then 6, witnessed the bloody knife fight that ensued, according to Ms. Schauer.

After that, Edna and Eugene were shunted among friends and relatives. Mr. Kainulainen assumed the role of his sister's protector, and she, in turn, adored him. "He looked after me," says Ms. Schauer, who lives in Port Orchard, Wash.

Eugene drew pictures for his high-school yearbook and dreamed of attending art school, a goal interrupted by the arrival of his draft notice in 1942, when he was 23. Within months, Pvt. Kainulainen was overseas with the 450th Military Police Co. in North Africa, where U.S., British and French forces were fighting desert battles to dislodge Germans and Italians.

In 1943, Mr. Kainulainen contracted syphilis. He soon exhibited signs of psychological stress, as well. He reported "tenseness, apprehensiveness, battle dreams, insomnia and vague abdominal complaints," records say. He tried to shoot himself.

Military doctors linked his mental symptoms to childhood tendencies toward "nightmares, somnambulism, temper tantrums and [being] fussy about food." The Army sent Mr. Kainulainen to a hospital in Algeria for treatment, then shipped him back to the U.S. and discharged him in 1944.

He returned home fond of drink and quick to anger. The combination got him institutionalized at the VA hospital in American Lake, Wash., where their mother authorized a lobotomy in 1953, says Ms. Schauer.

With the brain surgery, he became sweet-tempered and emotional, apt to break down in tears. "You're as beautiful as a movie star," he used to tell Ann Marie Brown, Ms. Schauer's daughter.

He was also unable to fend for himself.

Around Christmases and birthdays, Mrs. Brown's husband would pick up Eugene at a rest home, stop to buy him a sympathy beer and deliver him to the family home, where he would sit quietly and smile vacantly. He died in 1977.

"He never had a life," says Mrs. Brown. "He never had a family. He never had anything but institutions. It was the end of it, really."

Some of the toughest moments came soon after the lobotomy, when Ms. Schauer and her daughter showed up at the hospital with a potato-salad-and-ham picnic for Eugene. Edna's protector had no idea who she was.

"I loved him so," says Ms. Schauer, her voice cracking. "I wish he could have gone to art school."

James Oberman contributed to this article.

TAKEN UNDER

THE VIRGINIAN-PILOT

OCTOBER 20, 2013

By Aaron Applegate

Hurricane Sandy swelled beyond the horizon, but the tall ship's crew had faith in its experienced captain, who had battled and beaten harsh storms before

The ocean buried one side of the tall ship in a foamy froth. Deckhands exhausted from hours of fighting the hurricane huddled in a wet clump on deck. Some slept sitting up, deaf to the wind clattering through the rigging.

Those awake in the dark October morning felt the sickening angle of the ship and watched the sea rush toward them. They were 100 miles off the Outer Banks of North Carolina.

Drew Salapatek tugged at the arm of his sleeping girlfriend.

"Hey, it's time to go," he said to Jessica Hewitt, as if rousing her from a nap on the couch. "She's going over."

Jess snapped awake. The couple, wearing climbing harnesses over neoprene survival suits, scrambled to find level footing as the ship tilted toward the sea.

"We got to go!" Jess screamed. "We have to get out of here!"

Her mind flashed through emergency training drills, but there had been nothing for this. Jess clipped a short rope from her harness onto Drew's. Tethered, they jumped into the sea.

The 180-foot wooden ship *Bounty* had been a refuge against weather and water for 16 people. Now it was the most dangerous thing in the ocean. The ship's three wooden masts, each more than 100 feet tall and bisected with three spars loaded with sails and tangles of thick lines, slammed up and down as the ship rose and fell with the waves.

Jess and Drew struggled to swim out of range, but part of the heaving ship caught the rope that joined them, dragging them underwater. It felt as if the entire weight of the ship was pulling them beneath the dark waves.

I don't have a chance, Jess thought. A voice in her head pleaded: Not like this. Nobody is going to know.

She clawed at the harness but couldn't rip it off.

She gnawed at the metal clip linking the rope to it, shearing off part of a tooth.

Underwater, her world slowed down. She thought about a comedian she liked who did a bit about terrible ways to die. Drowning was one of them.

Her body wanted her to breathe, breathe, breathe. The voice said: No, no, don't breathe! She couldn't help it. She inhaled the ocean.

At the other end of the rope, Drew snapped his head above the water and gasped for air. The ship yanked him down again. He wriggled his thin hips, pushing down on the harness until it slipped off. The pressure was released.

He and Jess shot to the surface.

She came up vomiting seawater. It tasted like tar and diesel fuel. Her ears ached. She was alone.

Drew popped up to see the ship's masts and rigging pounding the sea dangerously close. Water rushing into the ship had created a current that seemed to be sucking him in.

Over his shoulder, spread out across the sea, he saw tiny bodies in identical red survival suits, each locked in its own struggle to escape the *Bounty*.

The *Bounty* was perhaps the best-known tall ship in the world. Its black hull, yellow trim and window-covered stern framed by hanging lanterns created a striking presence in any port.

When the crew climbed high into the rigging, spreading out on yards to unfurl square sails, the ship evoked a bygone age. The *Bounty*'s longtime captain, Robin Walbridge, also seemed to hail from another era.

He loved nothing more than shutting off the *Bounty*'s engines and navigating by the stars as the ship harnessed the power of a fair wind.

For 17 years, Walbridge had poured his soul into the *Bounty*, more than once saving it from the death by decay that awaits all wooden vessels.

While his crew of mostly young sailors changed every year, Walbridge and the *Bounty* were constant companions, fused over time by the peculiar intimacy that bonds men and ships.

Together, captain and ship had crossed oceans, ridden out violent storms, and survived equipment failures, each scrape increasing Walbridge's faith in himself and the *Bounty*.

In the end, there was a final lesson: Sea and sky are indifferent to the confidence of men.

Four days before the *Bounty* went down, on the afternoon of Thursday, Oct. 25, 2012, the ship's 15 sailors met with Capt. Walbridge on the deck.

The *Bounty* was tied to a dock in New London, Conn., on the Thames River, a short tidal estuary with quick access to the Atlantic Ocean.

Like most crews of historical wooden ships, the group was a motley collection of aspiring professional mariners and young men and women seeking the adventure of a lifetime. Some people call tall-ship sailors the "hippie navy."

Most of the crew had some experience on historical ships; others were new to sailing. All wanted to learn from Walbridge, one of the world's few experts on the art of sailing traditionally rigged ships.

Above the sailors' heads, the *Bounty*'s masts reached into a brilliant blue sky. The day's breeze had died down to a whisper.

Many of the crew had heard about the approaching storm.

Hurricane Sandy had just thrashed Cuba. Meteorologists were predicting that the storm would travel offshore along the East Coast before turning west into land unusually far to the north. Sandy's winds weren't particularly strong for a hurricane—it was rated Category 1— but the system was big and getting bigger.

If the *Bounty* was going to sail toward St. Petersburg, Fla., as planned, on its last major ocean passage of the year, Walbridge would have to find a way around or through the expanding disturbance.

Jessica Hewitt, 25, was annoyed when a text message from her mother arrived in several long chunks in backward order. Were they still going out, with the hurricane coming? She ignored the message, chalking it up to maternal worrying.

Her friend and fellow deckhand Claudene Christian, 42, had been keeping track of the storm.

Sandy was a strange one. It just kept growing. Two other weather systems were poised to interact with it. With Halloween just around the corner, a meteorologist had dubbed the coming collision "Frankenstorm."

"The global models show Sandy remaining a very deep cyclone and the wind field expanding," a National Hurricane Center bulletin said that afternoon.

"You know how most hurricanes look like this?" Claudene asked Jess, holding up a balled fist to represent a tightly packed storm. "Well, Sandy is more like this." She opened her fist and spread her fingers wide.

"We're going to have to go to Europe to avoid it," Jess joked.

It didn't occur to her to investigate Sandy more. As a graduate of Maine Maritime Academy and former captain of her high school sailing team on Cape Cod, Jess had respect for the chain of command and trusted her superiors.

After tiring of the repetition of sailboat racing, Jess had fallen in love with long sea voyages, the reward of feeling like a traveler and not a tourist.

She'd learned while on an academy schooner voyage to the Arctic that you follow orders on a ship or risk the whole thing falling apart.

The weather was the captain's problem.

The previous winter, the tall ship she had been working on was moored in the Virgin Islands at the same time as the *Bounty*. Jess toured the *Bounty* and met Drew Salapatek, a sailor with blond-streaked hair that trailed past his shoulders.

Drew, 29, was a carpenter, bike mechanic and a former upright-bass player in a bluegrass/punk band from Chicago. An annual counter-cultural event, Brew Not Bombs, started in the backyard of his rented house with gallons of home-brewed beer, live bands and a vegan chili cook-off.

Drew started sailing in 2010 when he volunteered aboard a wooden schooner that transported medical supplies from Florida to Haiti after the country's devastating earthquake. The next year, he joined the *Bounty* for a voyage to Europe, which began with a 36-day crossing of the Atlantic Ocean.

The ship was a popular attraction, especially in England. The *Bounty* was a replica of an English coal ship purchased by the Royal Navy and dispatched to Tahiti in 1787 in search of a cheap food source for slaves in the country's Caribbean sugar plantations.

During the voyage, the ship's first mate, Fletcher Christian, led what became the world's most famous mutiny, against the *Bounty*'s Capt. Bligh.

In 1960, Metro-Goldwyn-Mayer built a real wooden ship to film *Mutiny on the Bounty*, starring Marlon Brando as Christian. Movie executives contracted with a shipyard in Nova Scotia that employed men who still knew how to wield adzes and broadaxes and sew large sails.

Ten thousand people crowded docks in Lunenburg to witness the launch of the ship. The new *Bounty* was 120 feet on deck, about one-third bigger than the original, to accommodate engines and movie cameras. With the pointy bowsprit, its full length stretched to 180 feet.

The shipyard owner's wife smashed a bottle of water from Tahiti across the bow for good luck. A politician wished the ship a "happier fate than the original."

Brando, the story goes, threatened to walk off the set if the *Bounty* was burned, like its namesake, and the ship was spared.

On the *Bounty* in New London, Drew didn't think much of the approaching hurricane. He figured it would be a wet, bumpy ride.

But he had noticed something strange that morning. The ship's bilge pumps didn't seem to be working right. Bilge pumps expel water that seeps into boats during normal use. Drew reported the problem to a ship's officer, who seemed to know about it. Drew didn't realize that other deckhands also had reported malfunctioning pumps.

Walbridge started the crew meeting with a question: "What would you want to know about a hurricane?"

At 63, Walbridge cut an unlikely figure for a sea captain. He wore large glasses and hearing aids and tied his scraggly hair into a small ponytail that he often tucked under a ball cap.

One of his teaching techniques was to assign tasks without giving instructions. He issued soft-spoken orders and almost never raised his voice, a rare quality for any captain. Many crew members had never heard him yell.

Walbridge insisted on washing his own dishes. The crew, which called him Robin or Capt. Robin, was under orders not to point him out in port.

The informal mannerisms didn't dilute his authority.

In the rare instances when he was challenged, he would remind sailors that the ship was not a democracy. "Some of you are under the impression you have a vote," he once said. "You have a voice."

Over the years, Walbridge had supervised three major renovations of the *Bounty*, rebuilding the ship in stages from the keel up. Maintaining a large wooden vessel is a never-ending and costly enterprise. Water and wood are natural enemies.

The *Bounty* was always short on money, and Walbridge found ways to keep it sailing, even if it meant sometimes cutting corners on materials or maintenance. Some people called Walbridge the "MacGyver" of the traditional tall-ship fleet because of his creative solutions, but it wasn't always a compliment.

To make money and keep the *Bounty* sailing, Walbridge conceived numerous schemes, and executed some, sailing to unusual places where the ship was a novelty and people would pay for a tour.

He contemplated navigating the icy Northwest Passage, a voyage that other tall-ship captains considered risky, and a trip to Dubai that would have taken the ship near the coast of Somalia, an area notorious for piracy.

"A giant, slow-moving American boat full of diesel and interesting supplies? A whole bunch of us were, like, 'We're going to opt out. You have fun with that,' " said former *Bounty* crew member Samantha Dinsmore. "Robin seemed to believe the *Bounty* was the stoutest thing ever."

Walbridge did motor the *Bounty* through the Erie Canal in New York. The ship is one of the largest to have bumped through the narrow passage that is part of a route from the Great Lakes to the Atlantic.

His unorthodox notions extended to crew selection. He was unimpressed by formal credentials and often said the main quality he was looking for was a person's desire to be on the *Bounty*. "If you think you should be here, you should be here," he sometimes said.

In a way, that was how Walbridge had lived his life.

During the Vietnam War, Walbridge, a conscientious objector, briefly attended a community college while he worked for an airline manufacturer. He took two classes—algebra and art—and told his older sister he'd learned all that college could teach him.

After a brief stint in long-haul trucking based in his home state of Vermont, he started working on boats in his early 20s. He bounced around marinas mainly in Florida and eventually began crewing on tall ships, climbing the ranks as he gained experience.

In nautical parlance, Walbridge was a classic "hawsepiper," the increasingly rare seaman who becomes an officer without the education of a maritime college or academy. He took over as captain of the *Bounty* in 1995.

In 1996, a Navy captain asked Walbridge to train him and his crew to sail the Constitution, also known as Old Ironsides, for a celebration. The ship, used during the War of 1812, had not sailed in more than 100 years.

Walbridge trained Capt. Mike Beck and his crew on the *Bounty* and was at Beck's side when Old Ironsides sailed in 1997 to commemorate its 200th birthday.

"I said, 'Robin, you're my right hand,'" Beck recalled. "If I do anything wrong, I want you to tell me."

On the *Bounty* in New London, a few deckhands ventured to answer Walbridge's question on what they'd want to know about a hurricane.

I'd want to know its predicted path, one said.

Its size, said another.

Walbridge said nothing. He'd seen his share of heavy weather.

In 2008, the *Bounty* rode out a hurricane in the Gulf of Mexico.

"We got on its coattails and used its wind after it had gone by to get us to where we wanted to go," said former *Bounty* sailor Rebecca Twombly, who was aboard.

Two years later, the *Bounty* survived 40-foot waves in a December nor'easter while sailing from Maine to Puerto Rico. The storm ripped a sail, and the *Bounty* took on water after a bilge pump broke.

Walbridge initially felt the ship could continue the trip, but after talking with officers, he detoured to Bermuda for repairs.

Last year, Walbridge said in an interview, "We say there's no such thing as bad weather; there's just different kinds of weather."

Walbridge asked the crew another question: Is a ship safer at sea or in port?

I know this one, Jess thought. It's safer at sea, where you can maneuver or heave to—a stalling tactic used to ride out storms. In port, a ship could get smashed against the dock. That's what she'd always been taught in her classes.

Walbridge had come to believe a ship was safer at sea.

In Baton Rouge, La., in 2002, the *Bounty* weathered a storm while moored to a barge tied to a dock. The wind pushed the ship into the barge and bent iron pieces on the hull.

The next year, the *Bounty* ducked into Lunenburg, Nova Scotia, to hide from Hurricane Juan. The morning after the storm, Walbridge told the crew that a tall ship they'd spent the summer sailing with had sunk at a Halifax dock.

Walbridge surely knew about the time, before he was captain, that the *Bounty* had left a Florida dock to ride out a hurricane.

In 1992, temporary captain Stanley Hausman assembled a five-man crew, took down the sails, filled the ship with 3,000 gallons of diesel and 1,500 gallons of water for ballast and motored into Hurricane Andrew.

"Following seas were making it very hard to keep from broaching," Hausman wrote in the trip log. "With a little experience, we found holding full left rudder seemed to produce the right balance for the 80 to 100 mph winds and with the 15 to 20 ft. following seas off the starboard quarter."

The rough seas lasted about three hours, Hausman said. A day after setting out, the ship was back at a dock in Miami with the start of a reputation: The *Bounty* likes hurricanes.

A crew member answered Walbridge's question: A ship is safer at sea.

Walbridge told the crew that his plan was to sail southward and eastward until Sandy committed to a course. Then he'd pick a route, either coming back toward the coast if the hurricane swung out, or traveling farther out to sea if it veered toward land.

Walbridge ended the meeting with an offer to the crew: "If you want to get off the ship, you can," he said. "Nobody will think any less of you."

The deckhands had various reasons for staying aboard: They didn't want to let the group down. They didn't want to miss an epic trip. They wanted to test their nautical skills against the storm. They didn't think anything bad would happen.

Mostly, though, they trusted the captain, with all his years of experience, to make the right decisions and keep them safe. No one left the ship.

The deckhands didn't know what had happened just before the meeting. The *Bounty* 's chief mate, John Svendsen, 41, had pulled Walbridge off the ship to say he was worried about Sandy.

"It appears to be a very large system of historic proportions, and I think we should evaluate other options," he told Walbridge. Two other ship's officers had expressed concerns to Svendsen.

Walbridge said he believed that the waves would not be larger than 30 feet and that the winds would be at Category 1 strength, 74 to 95 mph, conditions he and the ship had been through before.

He told his chief mate: "This is the best option."

He ordered deckhands to start taking off dock lines.

Too Quiet

When the *Bounty* set sail from New London, Conn., toward Hurricane Sandy, it was a glorious time to be at sea. The sky was bright blue, the fall air crisp. That night, sailors gathered on deck to gaze at a giant ring surrounding the nearly full moon as the ship slipped through gentle swells. Jessica Hewitt tried to wake her boyfriend, Drew Salapatek, so he could take in the moon, but sleep trumped natural beauty, and he waved her off.

On Friday morning, the sky broke clear again, streaked with wispy clouds. Deckhands climbed into the top of the ship's rigging to take down the highest sails, which would not be needed during the storm.

Despite the gorgeous weather, Jess felt uneasy aloft, high above the deck, where the rolling of a ship is exaggerated, like movement at the end of a teeter-totter. She was spooked when another deckhand casually swung from the rigging, suspended only by the line attached to his harness, squealing, *Wheeee!*

Lunchtime on deck came as a relief. Afterward, the crew gathered around Capt. Robin Walbridge.

The meeting began cryptically. Walbridge said he'd never thought much about retirement when he was young, but someone evidently had. The sailors waited to see where the story was headed.

"Now, Jess here has been saving for retirement," he joked, looking at the deckhand, who was wearing a pair of ripped-up jeans, her favorite since seventh grade. The crew chuckled.

The captain's attention was flattering. Once, Jess had summoned the courage to challenge Walbridge to a game of chess. His prowess was legendary, and he agreed on the condition that he play two other crew members simultaneously. Still, Jess wasn't sure he knew who she was.

Walbridge moved on to more serious matters. It's calm now, he said, but we know there's a storm coming. How would sailors of the past, without our technology, have known a hurricane was out there?

Drew gazed at streaky cirrus clouds drifting across the blue sky. Maybe the cloud structure was the beginning of a low-pressure system, he thought. But maybe not. It didn't look like much to him.

Jess noticed that the clouds were coming from the south. It seemed to make sense that they could be the start of the hurricane.

Walbridge didn't offer an analysis of the weather. That didn't mean he wasn't worried.

"Sandy looks like a mean one," Walbridge emailed the *Bounty*'s home office administrator Friday using the ship's satellite system.

He asked for help.

"Right now I do not want to get between a hurricane and a hard spot," he wrote. "If you can send us updated track info (where it is projected to go) that would be great. We know where it is, I have to guess (along with the weather man) where it is going."

It was starting to look as though the storm would be everywhere at once.

The origin of Hurricane Sandy had been textbook. It had started two weeks earlier as a pulse of thunderstorms off the coast of western Africa and hitched a ride on trade winds to the warm waters of the Caribbean Sea.

On Saturday, Oct. 20, the first primitive bands of Tropical Depression 18 had taken shape and begun circulating in a telltale counterclockwise direction.

"The depression is located in an environment that is highly conducive for strengthening," a National Hurricane Center bulletin said.

Two days later, an Air Force "hurricane hunter" plane clocked wind speeds of more than 40 mph. It was pronounced Tropical Storm Sandy.

"Remaining nearly stationary over the warm waters of the southwestern Caribbean Sea is never a good sign for this time of year," said another National Hurricane Center update.

On Wednesday, the day before the *Bounty* set sail, satellite images picked up the eye of the storm 80 miles south of Jamaica. It looked like a red ring you could stick your finger through. Sandy was officially a hurricane.

As the storm spun northward, meteorologists watched two other weather systems poised to interact with it.

In the North Atlantic, a large dome of high pressure moving south from Iceland was cutting off the normal west-to-east flow of the high-flying band of air known as the jet stream.

This system, called a "blocking piece" by meteorologists, was positioned to prevent Sandy from veering northeast out to sea. It looked as if the blocking piece would channel the storm up the East Coast farther north than usual.

At the same time, a large low-pressure system over most of North America was marching eastward on a collision course with Sandy.

Systems like this can weaken a hurricane, shredding its bands and blunting wind speeds. But that doesn't always happen.

Sometimes a weather system's counterclockwise rotation can mesh with a hurricane's, fusing into a giant storm.

If that happened, the violent union would take place off the coast of the Carolinas, where the warm waters of the Gulf Stream would feed Sandy even more energy.

Two days after leaving New London, on Saturday, the *Bounty*'s sailors felt the arrival of Hurricane Sandy off the coast of Virginia. White-capped waves had grown to 10 to 12 feet, and the wind was building.

The crew fastened safety lines across the deck to serve as hand-holds. The lookout watch post, normally at the bow of the ship, was moved to the middle, out of the spray of breaking waves.

The *Bounty* always took on water, especially in heavy seas, but deep in the ship, water was rising unusually fast. The bilge pumps, powered by two diesel generators, were running almost constantly but couldn't keep up.

Jess busied herself stowing loose items in cabins below deck: bins of T-shirts, tools, books. She was annoyed that the drawers of a large bureau didn't have clasps to keep them closed. She wished they'd had more time to stow things before getting under way. A pot shook loose in the galley and was clanging around, rattling her nerves.

Around 10 a.m. Saturday, Walbridge ordered a major change in direction. The *Bounty* turned from its southeastward course, out to sea, toward the southwest and North Carolina's Outer Banks.

Walbridge told a ship's officer that he wanted to sail to the west of Sandy. This put the *Bounty* on course to cross its path. The decision might seem odd, but sailing to the western side of an approaching hurricane is the textbook way to navigate through a storm that can't be avoided.

On that side, winds are generally less intense because the counterclockwise rotation of the storm generates gusts that move southward, against the direction the storm is heading.

Sandy defied the rules.

As the *Bounty*, now somewhere off the coast of Virginia Beach, sailed toward the storm, Sandy was transforming into what meteorologists call an extratropical hurricane. This type of storm produces a huge wind field, and, unlike a traditional hurricane, its strongest gusts are often on the western side.

Walbridge, relying on weather faxes and information relayed from the home office, probably didn't realize he was sailing the *Bounty* into the height of Sandy's fury.

That night, normal tasks on the ship became impossible.

Jess slipped into the galley to cook an egg. She tried to microwave it for 45 seconds, but the egg careened inside the oven, smashing against the door. As she was giving up, Walbridge came in to warm a cup of water for tea. His cup slid around in the oven, sloshing out water, and he, too, gave up.

That night, Walbridge acknowledged the enormity of Sandy.

"I think we are going to be into this for several days, the weather looks like even after the eye goes by it will linger for a couple of days," he wrote in an email to the ship's office. "We are just going to try to go fast and squeeze by the storm and land as fast as we can. I am thinking that we will pass each other sometime Sunday night or Monday morning. All else is well."

In the ship's small navigation shack, Drew glanced at weather reports being spit out by the fax machine. Hurricane Sandy was aimed at the

Bounty, which was headed for Cape Hatteras, the beaklike protrusion of the Outer Banks.

The seas off Cape Hatteras are notoriously unpredictable, largely because of the Gulf Stream, the massive river of warm water that flows up the coast. A modest breeze of about 20 mph working against the current can create hazardous waves in the "Graveyard of the Atlantic."

In 1803, the federal government built a sandstone lighthouse powered by whale oil on Hatteras Island. It did little to curtail shipwrecks.

In 1862, the *Monitor,* the ironclad warship that earlier in the year had clashed with the Confederate ironclad *Virginia,* formerly known as the *Merrimack,* at the Battle of Hampton Roads, sank while being towed in a gale off Cape Hatteras. Sixteen of the ship's 62 crew members died.

An 1899 hurricane off the cape sank or ran aground 15 ships, killing more than 50 sailors, including four on the Baltimore merchant ship *Priscilla* on its way to Brazil. The ship was "broken into pieces and driven ashore by the tempest," according a report by the U.S. Lifesaving Service.

The captain of the *Priscilla,* who was rescued, later said, "It was blowing a hurricane from the northeast, and the seas were running mountain high."

The weather faxes Drew gazed at showed that the *Bounty* was headed into an enormous storm. One dispatch Saturday night showed Sandy moving offshore up the East Coast: "HRCN SANDY, MAX WINDS 65 KT, gusts 80 KT, SEAS TO 40 FT."

Drew felt a sudden kinship with past mariners.

Huh, he thought. *How did I find myself in this position?*

SMACK INTO SANDY

Late Saturday, Oct. 27, 2012

Jessica Hewitt awoke just before midnight to the sound of rushing water. The gurgling grew louder as the ocean trapped inside the ship advanced, then quieted as it ebbed. The *Bounty*'s wooden hull groaned, its planks flexing against the building sea. Jess climbed onto the deck for her midnight-to-4 a.m. duties. The wind had built to about 52 mph. The waves were bigger and mashing together haphazardly, like water sloshing in a bathtub. In the engine room below, the generators running the bilge pumps roared. After her shift, Jess returned to her cabin to discover her sleeping bag was dripping seawater. When the *Bounty* rolled, water from the bottom of the ship sloshed up the side and dripped down onto her bunk. She tried to sleep but felt as if she were under attack.

Jess climbed the steps to a communal room at the rear of the ship called the great cabin, where she slept on a settee. She awoke later when a huge wave rolled the ship and slid her off into a standing position.

"Good morning!" Capt. Robin Walbridge said. He was meeting in the cabin with the ship's officers.

Jess listened in. Walbridge was saying the *Bounty* should have time to cross Hurricane Sandy's path. He reduced daily duties on Sunday because of the rough seas.

After the meeting, Jess dozed again. A loud crack jolted her awake. A large wave had rolled the *Bounty* and thrown Walbridge into a table. He lay wincing on the cabin floor.

"I'm going to be OK, but I'm going to hurt," he told her. Jess thought: *That's what guys say when an injury is really bad.*

Jess gave Walbridge the wet towel she'd been using as a blanket for a pillow. She felt bad that it was all she had to offer, but Walbridge seemed to appreciate the slight comfort.

On deck, her boyfriend, Drew Salapatek, was trying to steer the ship. The waves had grown to about 20 feet, and the blowing sea spray soaked his long hair. The pressure of the waves on the rudder made it difficult to turn the vessel. Drew had to put all his weight into the *Bounty*'s wooden spoked wheel. At noon, he went below to rest.

When Jess came on deck around the same time, she found Claudene Christian smiling brightly.

Claudene was the greenest crew member, but what she lacked in technical skill, she made up for in enthusiasm. She was the ship's unofficial chief morale officer, always in a good mood, often bobbing her blond head as if listening to music.

A former dance team member at the University of Southern California, the 42-year-old spent more time on her appearance than most sailors. The first time Jess met her, Claudene was wheeling a carry-on bag down the dock. Jess thought she was leaving the ship, but the bag was full of makeup and hair accessories that Claudene was rolling to the shower. On cold mornings, Claudene used a blow dryer to warm up before starting her shift on deck, a trick Jess adopted.

After a few months of volunteering, Claudene had been promoted to a paid deckhand. Her first paycheck was in the mail. She was already thinking of making a movie about the ship, continually jotting down ideas for it in a journal.

"This is awesome!" Claudene yelled to Jess. "I'm having the time of my life!"

Jess looked at her. *What do you mean, you're having the time of your life?* she thought. *I'm exhausted. Where do you get that energy?*

Jess's routine ship check began with a disturbing discovery. A glass fuel-level indicator in one of the tanks had broken, allowing most of the diesel to leak out.

She reported the finding to an officer and took the helm to steer, trying to hold the course. Another deckhand joined her. It helped having two people gripping the wheel. It was better for morale, too.

"We're sailing right to the bar!" Jess shouted.

"What are you going to get?" the deckhand yelled back.

"My first beer is going to be a shotgun as I enjoy a big plate of mozzarella sticks!"

"I'm getting nachos!"

A patch of blue opened in the gray sky.

"Let's steer for that!" Jess said.

Clouds quickly snuffed it out.

Lowering her gaze, Jess saw the big sail on the ship's forward mast rip down the middle.

Walbridge limped on deck and ordered the most experienced sailors aloft.

The female bosun and three male sailors scaled the rigging. Jess felt a sisterly surge of pride. She joked to Walbridge that he could've sent Claudene up. He didn't say anything for a moment.

Finally, he said: "No, actually, she's done very well."

Walbridge helped Jess wrestle with the wheel. Sea spray coated his glasses, blinding him. He told her: "I'm just holding on!"

Twenty feet above, sailors furled the torn sail as Claudene watched from the deck, gripping an orange life ring in case anyone fell overboard.

Walbridge spent much of Sunday afternoon in the engine room dealing with one problem after another. The engineer, who was on his first tall-ship voyage, had gotten seasick and couldn't work much.

The generator drawing fuel from the broken tank had cut off. The other generator sputtered. Inside the ship, lights flickered. One engine shut off.

Jess poked her head into the engine room. The noise was deafening.

Walbridge pointed to his hearing aids and yelled: "You don't want to end up like me!"

Seawater hissed into the ship through loose seams between planks. The water kept rising.

That afternoon, Walbridge told an officer: "I believe we are losing the battle against the bilge water."

No one seemed to know why the bilge pumps weren't working.

Drew had reported the problem to an officer on the day the ship left New London, Conn.

A few days before that, another deckhand had interrupted Walbridge and an officer to say that something was wrong with the bilge pumps. Walbridge had said he'd think about it.

The deckhand had reported the problem again to the same officer on the day after the *Bounty* left New London. The officer reminded him that Walbridge was thinking about it.

The *Bounty* had another problem that not everybody knew about. Rot had been discovered in the frame a few weeks earlier when the ship had been hauled out of the water for repairs in a Maine shipyard.

A shipyard supervisor had told Walbridge. It was impossible to tell how widespread the rot was without removing lots of planks, which would be time-consuming and expensive.

Walbridge had said he'd investigate it during the next maintenance period, and he had the crew cover the rot with house paint.

As Hurricane Sandy engulfed the *Bounty* on Sunday evening, normal routines broke down.

Dinner was dictated by whatever the cook could dish up inside the rocking ship: macaroni and cheese, hot dogs, Goldfish crackers. When the cook tried to warm up frozen peas, sparks shot from the microwave, then smoke.

Walbridge ordered the ship to "heave to" —a holding pattern sometimes used to ride out storms. The sails are taken down, and the rudder is fixed in place so that steering becomes unnecessary.

Walbridge hoped that tilting the ship to one side would make the water pool and give the bilge pumps a better chance to get it out.

Drew strapped the helm down. The *Bounty* was angled so that its port side, the left, rode higher than the starboard side.

Jess tried again to sleep in the great cabin, wedging herself into a high spot on the left side. Waves smacked the ship's overhanging stern with loud booms, and water was leaking through the windows.

Chief Mate John Svendsen went into the great cabin and told Walbridge he thought they should call the Coast Guard to report the *Bounty*'s predicament. He said he'd learned in his training that shipwreck survivors always say they wished they'd called for help earlier.

Walbridge said no; he wanted to focus instead on getting water out of the ship.

Jess went to tell Drew what she'd overheard. She found him on his way to help out in the flooding engine room.

"If the ship goes down," she said, "don't lose me."

"I won't."

The sun sank behind gray clouds on Sunday night, and Sandy cranked up. Jagged waves rolled the *Bounty* with a violence that sent pots, paint cans and tools flying with crashing thumps.

Jess opened a cabin door to see drawers from the bureau she'd tried to secure earlier hurtling at her face. She slammed the door and taped a message to it: *Do Not Open.*

With the *Bounty* in a holding pattern, there was no reason for sailors to be on deck. Every few minutes, Drew popped his head up through a hatch to check on the ship. He saw the wind tugging a large sail loose from its furl. A sail catching air uncontrollably is dangerous in heavy wind.

Drew and three other sailors rushed up into the rigging to rein in the ballooning sail. The wind was so strong, it pinned them in place. The rain flew sideways and pelted them like bullets of salty hail. The sailors turned their heads to protect their eyes.

The wind teased more of the sail loose, cracking it like a whip. Drew tried to grab the flapping canvas.

Twenty feet below, on the *Bounty*'s rolling deck, he saw an officer yelling at him, but no sound seemed to come from the man's mouth. Drew heard only rushing wind. He yelled to the other sailors: "It's too dangerous!" They climbed back down. The hurricane shredded the sail into wet ribbons.

Right after they hit the deck, a piece of wood close to 10 feet long that had supported a sail at the back of the ship snapped in half and swung around wildly.

Drew and the other sailors crawled to the stern, timing each movement with the rolling of the ship.

They corralled the swinging piece of wood with rope and lashed it to a mast. An officer held up a wind gauge. It read 90 knots—104 mph. Then it broke.

The *Bounty* crew had no way of knowing, but Hurricane Sandy was peaking. The change of course had taken the ship into the full rage of the storm, west of its eye. Below, in the great cabin, Svendsen again suggested that they contact the Coast Guard and the ship's owner. This time, Walbridge agreed.

Svendsen climbed on deck into the howling wind and sea spray to get a satellite phone connection.

He had a garbled conversation with the *Bounty*'s owner, businessman Bob Hansen, and tried calling different Coast Guard numbers. He couldn't be sure whether he was talking to someone or leaving a voice mail.

Coast Guard Cmdr. James Mitchell was at home searching the Internet for a restaurant to take his wife to for their anniversary when his phone rang. It was about 8:45 p.m.

"Sorry to bother you on Sunday night, but I have kind of a bizarre case," the command duty officer said.

"What do you mean by 'bizarre'?" asked Mitchell, the Coast Guard's search-and-rescue coordinator for North Carolina.

He learned about the *Bounty*. The Coast Guard had no direct communication with the ship, so it was hard to know what was going on, the officer said. All the information was coming secondhand from the office of the ship's owner in New York.

That's strange, Mitchell thought. He felt that perhaps the sailors didn't know what they were getting into.

Mitchell ordered his office to email the *Bounty*, instructing the crew to set off a locating device known as an Emergency Position Indicating Radio Beacon, or EPIRB. The beacon beams a distress signal to satellites to pinpoint a vessel's location.

At 9:06 p.m. Sunday, the Coast Guard's Rescue Coordination Center in Portsmouth picked up a signal from WDD9114, the call number of the *Bounty*. The ship was about 100 miles southeast of Cape Hatteras.

Mitchell had his staff check to see whether any Coast Guard or Navy ships were nearby, but the closest was 260 miles away, too far to help.

They had all steered well clear of Sandy. A Danish oil tanker was closer, but the captain told the Coast Guard that his ship was pitching 25 degrees in 20-foot seas and 60-knot winds and needed to get out of the weather.

The *Bounty* was on its own.

FEAR AND FLIGHT

Sunday night, Oct. 28, 2012

The *Bounty* was heeled over, trying to ride out the hurricane in the darkness. Waves pounded its wooden hull, each slap forcing more of the Atlantic into the ship. Below, the water level rose. Drew Salapatek made several trips onto the deck and into the wind and spray to retrieve survival suits and haul them below. The thick, red neoprene suits are designed to keep shipwreck survivors warm and afloat. Each has a hood, a hose to add air by mouth for buoyancy, and built-in gloves and booties. In theory, the suits can keep an adrift sailor alive for three to four days. Drew tried to move calmly as he piled up the suits. *Man*, he thought, *I hope this doesn't make anyone worried.*

Coast Guard officials in North Carolina faced a dilemma. Should they send an airplane into Hurricane Sandy?

Information about the *Bounty* was spotty, coming secondhand from the ship's home office in New York. Cmdr. James Mitchell, North Carolina's search-and-rescue coordinator, wanted eyes on the ship. It wasn't his decision to make alone, though.

Mitchell joined a conference call with Capt. Joe Kelly, commander of the Coast Guard's Elizabeth City Air Station, to make his case. C-130s, large surveillance aircraft that can fly for more than 12 hours, are based there.

Mitchell quickly outlined what he knew about the *Bounty*'s situation. As many as 20 people were aboard. No one was in the ocean, yet. The ship was about 100 miles off Cape Hatteras. It was taking on water. Its bilge pumps couldn't keep up. The rest was confusing, he told Kelly. We need direct communication, he argued.

Mitchell's idea was to send a C-130 close enough to establish radio contact and relay information to the command center.

Kelly was concerned. "You're asking my crew to go into a hurricane."

Mitchell said he knew it would be risky. "Can we just get close?"

"OK, I'll ask the crew," Kelly said. He called Lt. Wes McIntosh, a pilot. Earlier in the day, McIntosh's crew had flown a C-130 to Raleigh-Durham International Airport, where runway alignments gave the plane a better chance to take off should it be needed during Hurricane Sandy.

The 60-knot wind—almost 70 mph—estimated near the *Bounty* was at the upper limit of the plane's capacity, but McIntosh said he was willing to give it a shot.

Kelly told him he didn't have to put eyes on the ship.

"Your job is simply to establish communication," he said. "You have the authority to turn around if you need to."

At 9:34 p.m. Sunday, McIntosh and seven crew members took off. Almost immediately, wind slammed into the plane, flexing its wings and causing it to rise and fall drastically. It wasn't long before crew members strapped into the back of the plane began vomiting.

Using night-vision goggles, McIntosh flew toward a massive cloud wall illuminated by a nearly full moon. That was the edge of the hurricane. He circled outside the wall, hoping he was close enough.

In Chicago, Jim Salapatek, Drew's father, checked his cellphone just before going to bed on Sunday night. A Google alert made him sit up straight. The *Bounty* had set off its emergency locator beacon.

He got dressed and quickly crossed the street to his TV repair shop. In a back room littered with circuit boards and old manuals, he fired up a computer and two television sets to see what he could learn.

The three days since the *Bounty* had left New London, Conn., had been busy for Jim. Word had spread quickly online that the ship was heading toward Hurricane Sandy. Mariners on Internet discussion boards criticized the decision to leave port.

"Sure, let's take a wooden-hulled sailing ship out into a hurricane. What's the worst that could happen?" one person wrote.

Jim managed the *Bounty*'s Facebook page and rose to Capt. Robin Walbridge's defense. He wasn't a sailor, but he had taken several trips on the *Bounty* with his son, and he liked the skipper.

He posted: "Rest assured that the *Bounty* is safe and in very capable hands. *Bounty*'s current voyage is a calculated decision...NOT AT ALL... irresponsible or with a lack of foresight as some have suggested. The fact of the matter is... A SHIP IS SAFER AT SEA THAN IN PORT!"

Despite his apparent optimism, however, Jim knew his words were largely an effort to make himself, and others, feel better about the danger. He was determined to be a voice of hope.

The seawater in the *Bounty* kept rising as Sunday night wore on. Walbridge managed to send off several emails to the *Bounty*'s home office.

At 10:15 p.m., as the Coast Guard's C-130 was bucking its way toward the vessel, he wrote: "We are taking on water. Will probably need assistance in the morning. Sat phone is not working very good. We have activated the epirb. We are not in danger tonight but if conditions don't improve on the boat we will be tomorrow...The boat is doing great. We can't dewater."

Forty minutes later, Walbridge was feeling less confident. He wrote: "My first guess was that we had until morning before having to abandon. Seeing the water rise I am not sure we have that long. We have two inflatable life rafts. We have activated our epirb."

Below, in the engine room, Drew had never seen the water so high. It was ankle-deep and causing the plywood floor to float.

The water, pooled on the *Bounty's* right side, drowned the starboard engine and generator. The machinery died in a grand finale of arcing sparks.

Walbridge went into the engine room and got the port generator running by bypassing a kill switch, but it quickly died again. He went back on deck.

Drew worked frantically with the second mate on the generator. The water was now waist-deep, and it spilled into toolboxes mounted on the ship's side.

At 11:07 p.m., Walbridge wrote to the office, asking about the Coast Guard.

"Do they know we are in trouble? I am probably going to lose power shortly."

The office forwarded the message to Coast Guard officials, who wrote back to Walbridge. They told him to activate the ship's second EPIRB if the *Bounty* was in distress.

In the engine room, Drew had to stand halfway up a ladder to stay dry as he handed tools to the officer working on the generator.

"You got a couple more moves before we're underwater," he said. The generator roared to life. Drew and the officer yelled in triumph, slapping hands.

Then it spewed sparks and died, this time for good. The water was just too high.

Drew and the officer retreated up the ladder and out of the engine room just as a wave rolled the *Bounty*. The surge of water ripped off the ladder. Drew helped drag it from the engine room so it wouldn't punch a hole in the ship.

At 11:41 p.m. Walbridge emailed the Coast Guard:

"we have lost all dewatering abilities.

estimate 6-10 hours.

when we lose all power we will lose email there should be a second epirb going off. water is taking on fast

we are in distress

ship is fine we can't dewater

need pumps"

Six minutes later, he wrote: "WE HAVE JUST SET OFF THE SECOND EPIRB."

It was the last email sent from the ship.

Just after midnight on Monday, McIntosh flew his C-130 into radio range of the *Bounty*. He was at 9,000 feet, fighting against 60 knots of wind.

"HMS *Bounty*, HMS *Bounty*, this is the Coast Guard on Channel 16. HMS *Bounty*, HMS *Bounty*, this is the Coast Guard on Channel 16."

John Svendsen, the ship's chief mate, responded. McIntosh learned that the ship had6 feet of water inside it. The generators that powered the bilge pumps weren't working.

Basically, they're dead in the water, McIntosh thought. It was worse than he expected. He felt that he needed to see the scene for himself. He spotted a small break in the wall of clouds and turned the plane into the outer bands of Hurricane Sandy.

Winds blowing at 92 mph slammed into the side of the aircraft, knocking out the autopilot function. McIntosh was now in the clouds, wings flexing up and down, flying blindly.

He descended to 1,000 feet, but all he could see was a wall of gray. He dropped to 500 feet—the lowest that a C-130 should fly. The wind picked up and dropped the plane, 100 feet at a time. The crew in the back started vomiting again.

Finally, the plane broke through the clouds. McIntosh saw huge waves, their crests being torn off by the wind. Sea spray filled the air.

His co-pilot spotted the *Bounty*.

"What does it look like?" McIntosh asked.

"It looks like a pirate ship in a hurricane," the co-pilot responded.

McIntosh thought, *There are going to be 16 people in the water soon.*

FULL TILT

Sunday-Monday, Oct. 28-29, 2012

The *Bounty* was dead in the water, drifting in the darkness. The crew retreated to the ship's middle section, called the 'tween deck. It was mostly dry, but water was coming up fast. A last-ditch effort to start a small portable pump failed miserably. Nobody seemed to know how it worked. The pump had been stowed away, unused, for two years. Capt. Robin Walbridge's theory was that it would be fresh if needed. Walbridge had other unorthodox notions about maintenance. He mostly ran one of the *Bounty*'s two generators, instead of alternating them, to reduce maintenance schedules and save money.

He'd had the crew use unusual and inexpensive compounds to seal the *Bounty*'s caulked seams. At the time of the storm, half of the *Bounty*'s seams under the waterline were sealed with something from Home Depot, the other half with a construction sealant. He was experimenting to see which worked better.

After the engine room flooded, deckhand Drew Salapatek heard an officer suggest to the captain that a bucket line be formed.

"No," Walbridge said. "Now is the time to rest."

He estimated the sea was rushing into the *Bounty* at 2 feet per hour.

Drew sat down for a break. He felt a shift in purpose.

This was no longer about saving the ship and limping into Florida. This was about getting off alive.

Walbridge hadn't given up on the *Bounty*. He had one last hope: If the Coast Guard could bring pumps, maybe he could save the ship.

Coast Guard pilots in a C-130 circling the *Bounty* radioed back to the command center: "The vessel said, if they can get water off the ship, that they could get it under control and make it to shore."

Walbridge had reason to hope. He'd been in this situation before.

On Oct. 3, 1998, the *Bounty* was taking on water in a storm off the coast of South Carolina as it headed toward St. Petersburg, Fla.

The main bilge pump had blown a rod. Rising water had shorted out two backup pumps. After 30 hours of flooding, the crew tried in vain to fix the machinery in waist-deep water.

Walbridge radioed the Coast Guard. A helicopter, two cutters, two Navy ships and a tugboat responded to deliver emergency pumps. A Navy damage-control team boarded the ship to help remove water. A Coast Guard survey later found that the ship had been taking on 20 to 40 gallons per minute.

A Coast Guard investigation report had described the *Bounty*'s flooding as "uncontrolled" and from "multiple areas."

The report had concluded that the *Bounty* was taking on water because the storm had loosened seams in the ship's planking and because the bilge pumps had stopped working. It said Walbridge had misjudged the severity of the ship's leaks before leaving port.

Jessica Hewitt and Claudene Christian peered down through a hatch at water rushing through the sleeping cabins.

"I wish I'd grabbed my journal," Claudene said. It was loaded with ideas for a movie about the *Bounty*.

Jess had taken it upon herself to retrieve personal items for fellow sailors, making several trips into the flooding cabins. She'd grabbed glasses for Drew and a wad of cash that another deckhand kept under his pillow.

She'd paused in her cabin to consider what she should take. She remembered being asked by students in a sailing class she had taught, *If your ship was sinking and you could only take one thing, what would it be?*

"My black cardigan," she'd answered.

I can't be a liar, she thought, picking up the sweater. Then she put it down and grabbed another one that a friend had loaned her. She wanted to return it. She also grabbed a hair band, thinking: *After we're rescued, I'll need something for my hair.*

On Jess's earlier trips below, the water had been lower, swirling around her feet and knees, depending on the roll of the ship.

Now, as she made a run for Claudene's journal, she lowered herself into waist-deep water. Chunks of plywood floorboards sloshed around.

She waited for the ship to roll and then charged through, stepping in a hole where the floor had been. Water rushed up to her neck.

Swimming from the hole, she ducked into Claudene's cabin and climbed onto a bunk above the swirling water. A pair of socks and a padded pushup bra favored by one of the youngest deckhands floated by.

Under Claudene's pillow, she found the journal. Yes! she thought, briefly savoring a minor victory. Jess grabbed a large bag that looked like Claudene's purse and fought back through the water. She climbed up to the middle deck, where she ran into Claudene and handed her the journal.

"I have surprise for you," Jess said, showing her the bag. "I grabbed your purse!"

"That's not my purse," Claudene said. "That's my makeup bag. I don't need to worry about that." She scrunched up her nose in a show of determination. "No, not today."

Walbridge wanted pumps, but Coast Guard officials weren't sure they could deliver them safely.

Lt. Wes McIntosh was piloting a C-130 through 70 mph winds early Monday. At sea level, it was blowing at about 46 mph.

Without power, the ship would have no way to maneuver to pick up pumps if they were dropped into the sea.

And dropping them directly onto the deck would be like bombing the vessel. The command center asked McIntosh, "When the *Bounty* is DIW (dead in the water) and on battery power, how do they see the possibility of passing a pump?"

McIntosh knew it was impossible.

At 1:41 a.m. Monday, the Coast Guard ruled out trying to deliver pumps with the plane.

Officials considered trying to send in a ship but decided it couldn't get there in time.

At 1:48, the Coast Guard emailed the first news release about the *Bounty:* "The vessel is reportedly taking on water and without propulsion." The story was out.

Back in Chicago, Jim Salapatek, Drew's father, who was scouring the Internet for any word on the ship, found a link to the release.

He posted on the *Bounty*'s Facebook page: "Your prayers are needed."

Coast Guard officials discussed launching a helicopter to lower pumps to the ship. It seemed a better option than having to rescue 16 people in the darkness.

Walbridge estimated the *Bounty* could stay afloat until 8 a.m. Monday. The Coast Guard started planning for a 7:30 evacuation, though officials were skeptical the ship would last that long.

"What I've seen with them, they overshoot all their guesses," one official said just before 2 a.m.

McIntosh relayed to the *Bounty* the idea of a helicopter delivering some pumps called P100s.

At 2:23, the *Bounty* responded: P100s could be a good start, but P250s would be much better.

McIntosh and his co-pilot exchanged an amused glance. The captain was obviously familiar with emergency pumps.

Jess gazed through a hatch at water coursing through the *Bounty* like a river. She couldn't believe what she saw trapped in an eddy: Swirling pink, green and purple lights. Then a bunch of sunglasses floated by. It was the glow sticks and goofy shades she'd stuffed into her sea chest to break out for a party when they reached Florida.

She stared down, mesmerized by the odd beauty and shocked by the thought of the force of water needed to crack the sticks so they'd glow.

She went to find Drew, who was resting.

"You've got to see this," she said.

Drew got up and peered into the hole.

"Whoa. It's like a party down there."

At 3:16 a.m. Monday, the Coast Guard prepared to launch a helicopter from Elizabeth City to deliver pumps to the *Bounty*.

Officials held a conference call to discuss the plan. It was determined that pumps could not save the ship, just delay its sinking. Still, there could be value in buying time.

At 3:37, however, the Coast Guard decided that the flight would be too dangerous. Their color-coded risk assessment came up red: "Risk outweighs gain," the rescue log noted.

The C-130 pilots told Walbridge that there would be no rescue pumps.

Walbridge repeated his intention to abandon the ship in daylight.

Coast Guard officials in Elizabeth City were skeptical.

"How confident are we about their rate of flooding and the time in which the vessel can make it?"

The command center acknowledged that seawater flooding into the ship's hull could hasten its demise.

The Coast Guard planned to launch two helicopters at first light. They would arrive at 7:30 for an 8 o'clock rescue.

On the *Bounty*, Walbridge gathered some of the crew in the small navigational shack.

He was visibly hurting from a fall the day before. His glasses were askew. His hearing aids were soaked.

"What went wrong?" he asked. "At what point did we lose control?"

Most of the deckhands, including Jess and Drew, weren't there to hear his questions. Those who did had no answers.

Water crept into the 'tween deck, and Walbridge ordered the crew to get into survival suits.

Jess was uncomfortable putting hers on below decks. The order went against her training, which said suits should be donned on deck to keep crew members from getting trapped below by their buoyancy in the event a ship quickly flooded.

"Aren't we supposed to be doing this on deck?" asked Claudene, one of the ship's novice sailors. Even she knows, Jess thought. She wasn't sure she trusted Walbridge anymore.

Claudene noticed a plaque hanging on a wall with the names of the crew members who sailed on the *Bounty*'s first voyage, in 1962.

"Should we take this?" she asked Jess. They didn't have a screwdriver, so they left it.

As the water rose, the sailors climbed, one by one, out into the hurricane.

There was nowhere else left to go.

At 4:07 a.m. Monday, the *Bounty* radioed the Coast Guard that all 16 sailors were on the ship's deck wearing survival suits, with two 25-person life rafts nearby. "Their main concern is the wind," the rescue log noted.

Coast Guard officials told the *Bounty* to activate an EPIRB, an emergency locating device, if anything changed. They still hoped for a daylight rescue. "For all parties involved the safest effort would be at sunrise," the log said.

Jess sat next to Drew on the port side of the ship. A slurry of sea spray and rain blasted across the drenched deck. Through gauzy strips of clouds, they saw the nearly full moon and the lights of the circling Coast Guard plane.

Drew busied himself getting used to the bulky survival suit. He practiced reaching the carabiner on a harness he was wearing, and the hose that would inflate the suit with air.

Jess looked at the life rafts, still packed in their canisters on deck. *How are we going to get into those?* she thought. The waves were so big, and the life rafts looked so small.

A deckhand sitting next to her offered her a drink. Irrationally, she thought it was vodka.

"No, I'm cool," she said.

"You got to hydrate one sip at a time," he said.

She realized it was water and drank some.

She leaned against Drew.

"What are you thinking about?" she said.

"I don't know."

"I'm thinking about snow. Walking in the snow."

"Walking in the snow sounds nice."

Empty minutes passed. Jess fell into a daze. She thought about throwing a ball to a friend's dog, over and over, as she drifted to sleep.

Drew started to nod off. He lifted his head, thinking: *The ship is sinking.* Then he fell asleep and woke up: *The ship is sinking.*

He felt the *Bounty* roll to the right five or six times. Each time, it came back up.

Jess and Drew didn't know it, but the chief mate, John Svendsen, was telling Walbridge it was time to abandon ship. Not yet, Walbridge replied.

A few minutes later, Svendsen again said that it was time. He thrust an arm into his survival suit, which he had been wearing up to his waist to keep his hands free.

Another big wave rolled the *Bounty*. This time, the ship didn't come back up.

Seawater rushed up the deck, washing the chief mate backward into the navigation shack.

He clawed against the current, screaming into the radio to the C-130 pilots that the crew was abandoning ship.

It was 4:26 a.m. Monday, nearly three and a half hours before Walbridge's planned evacuation.

Drew and Jess scrambled to stand on the side of a compartment, which was now horizontal because the ship was listing so severely. They watched the deckhand who'd given Jess a drink jump into the ocean.

"We have to get out of here!" Jess screamed.

She clipped a short rope from her harness into Drew's. Tethered, they stepped into the sea.

The *Bounty's* mast and rigging slammed up and down against the waves. Part of the ship snagged on the rope that joined Jess and Drew, dragging them underwater.

Drew squirmed free of his harness, and the pressure was released.

Coast Guard officials ordered the launching of two rescue helicopters from Elizabeth City. With sailors in the water, the gain now outweighed any risk.

DELIVERANCE

Early Monday, Oct. 29, 2012

Jess vomited seawater and looked around. *Where's Drew? He's not here! We're not attached!* She could think of only one horrible explanation. In the darkness, she oriented herself on waves by the rising or falling feeling in the pit of her stomach. From the crests, she could spot bodies in identical red survival suits trying to free themselves from the *Bounty*. When she plunged into troughs, she saw only walls of black water. Jess wished someone bigger and stronger would pluck her from the sea. The sound of her ragged, wet gasping filled her ears. Her inner voice urged: *Just keep breathing.*

Near her, one of the *Bounty's* booms thrashed the water. She got stuck in its rigging. She lifted the lines and swam free only to get stuck again. Lift, swim, lift, swim, over and over.

From the top of a wave, Jess saw somebody about to get pummeled by a spar on the heaving ship. He had long hair. Chief Mate John Svendsen yelled and put an arm up to protect his head.

Jess thought: *Remember that voice. I'll have to tell someone how he died.*

She slid down the face of the wave. Another picked her up, and she caught a glimpse of a group of people but lost sight again as she plunged into another foamy trough.

"Just keep breathing," she told herself. She had a comforting thought: *I can make it three days in a survival suit. Just keep breathing.* Again, she saw red suits, this time closer.

A shout rang out: "Jess, dig your fingers in!" She grabbed on to a fragment of the ship. It was deck grating, about 3 feet by 4 feet, and four other sailors were clinging to it.

Over the roar of rushing waves, she heard the *Bounty* cracking apart. *This is sad,* she thought. *We're the last people to walk across the deck of that ship.* She held tight to the wood.

A big wave broke nearby, and there was Drew. He grasped the chunk of wood, holding his breath as waves broke over him.

The sea was littered with equipment from the ship: coolers, life jackets, unused survival suits. The sailors clinging to the wood watched one of the ship's life-raft canisters bob by. It had washed off the ship, and the wind was sweeping it away.

Trailing from the canister was a long rope with a parachute-like sea anchor at the end. Jess, Drew and the others decided to swim for the raft. They linked arms in a circular chain and backstroked slowly away from the bobbing piece of wood.

"Always the bridesmaid and never the bride," Coast Guard helicopter co-pilot Jenny Fields joked to veteran pilot Steve Bonn.

It was about 5 a.m. The pilots had been called in to the station in Elizabeth City immediately after the Coast Guard learned the *Bounty* had gone over.

Lt. Cmdr. Bonn, 44, chuckled. He'd been the co-pilot—second in command—of the first Coast Guard helicopter to respond to the 2008 sinking of the *Alaska Ranger*, a fishing boat that went down in the icy Bering Sea with 47 people aboard, including five who died.

Now, with another big rescue mission in the works, he'd be flying the second helicopter out to the *Bounty*. They could hear the roar of the first one warming up nearby.

Bonn knew it was luck of the draw. Pilots can go their whole careers without a dramatic mass rescue.

The *Bounty* was the first big mission for Lt. Fields, 26. Until then, her specialty had become the useful but routine plucking of sick passengers off of cruise ships.

At the rescue briefing, Fields was surprised to see the *Bounty* looked like an old sailing ship. It reminded her of the *Eagle*, the Coast Guard's square-rigged tall ship she'd trained on.

Bonn, Fields, a rescue swimmer and a flight mechanic lifted off and made a climbing right-hand turn over the Pasquotank River. Clouds whizzing by looked green through their night-vision goggles. Beads of rain streaked the windows.

A 65 mph tailwind propelled the helicopter to about 160 miles an hour. The air speed indicator warned the pilots that they were in the upper limits of safe flying.

Bonn flew low, at 300 feet, down the middle of the river and across the Albe marle and Currituck sounds. He slid around Roanoke Island to avoid any towers and shot over the Outer Banks.

Stack after stack of mountainous waves rolled in from the Atlantic, pounding the narrow barrier islands.

Jess, Drew and four other sailors reached the rope trailing behind the life-raft canister and yanked it. The carbon-dioxide-charged canister exploded into a hexagonal rubber raft with a canopy.

They used the rope to pull themselves, hand over hand, to the raft. A nylon ladder hung out its door but didn't go very deep into the water.

After Jess caught her breath from the swim, she thought, *I'm going to be the first one in. I'm totally going to dominate this raft.*

She tried to heave herself up the ladder, but the water trapped in her survival suit made her too heavy.

When Drew tried to pull himself into the raft, the water in his suit rushed to his bootie-clad feet. The higher he pulled himself, the heavier his feet got. It was exhausting work. Nobody could get into the raft.

The suits were supposed to keep water out, but they likely had filled up because of the sea's frenzy and the time that Jess and Drew had spent underwater.

The sailors clung to a rope circling the outside of the raft, ducking as 20-foot waves crashed over them.

Drew had a morbid recollection. After a group of Norwegians sailing in the Antarctic Ocean had disappeared in 2011, the boat's life raft was found, inflated and unused.

Jess clung to the raft and felt a tug, then another. Her head went underwater. She was tangled in the raft's anchor line. *I'm going to die holding on to a life raft,* she thought. But the other sailors were able to free her.

Clinging to the bobbing raft, the sailors considered just holding on to conserve energy, but they decided to try another plan.

Drew would pull himself up the ladder while everyone else pushed him from behind.

He got his torso up over the edge of the raft and squirmed partway in, but his head flopped into a few inches of water that had accumulated on its rubber floor. He couldn't breathe. He was stuck, his weight balanced between his waterlogged feet and his upper body.

This is ridiculous, he thought. *I'm not going to drown in a puddle of water inside a life raft.*

He strained to lift his feet so the water in the suit flowed toward his head, and that tipped the rest of his body into the raft. Drew then pulled in another sailor, who helped him yank the four others from the ocean.

The sailors leaned back against the raft wall, breathing hard as their eyes adjusted to the new surroundings.

Co-pilot Fields was amazed at the size of the waves as the helicopter zoomed over the Outer Banks. *This is big,* she thought.

"So this is like Alaska?" she asked Bonn, the pilot.

"Yep," he said. "A little colder there, but this is it."

That made her feel better. *This is doable,* she thought.

Bonn asked whether she'd been to the Coast Guard's Advanced Helicopter Rescue School in Oregon, where the Columbia River drains into the Pacific Ocean. The confluence creates giant waves that the Coast Guard uses for extreme training. She hadn't.

He gave her a crash course. Her job would be to call out large approaching waves. A rogue wave could easily swamp a helicopter hovering during a rescue at 30 feet.

They sped through the clouds. The pilots flipped on the helicopter's searchlight but, like a car's headlights in heavy fog, it was useless. They switched it back off.

Inside the life raft, Jess, Drew and the four others looked through its stock of emergency equipment. There were packages of food and water; a first-aid kit; fishing line; covers for the doors.

Suddenly, they heard a whooshing sound. A big wave broke over the raft, folding it like a taco shell and slamming the sailors into the walls.

The raft popped back open. A gust of wind caught the canopy so that it flapped violently. Then all was quiet.

We're in the raft, Drew thought. *I hope the wind doesn't tear the roof of this thing. I hope a wave doesn't rip off the sea anchor and tear a hole in it.*

Another big wave collapsed the raft, and again it popped open. That quickly became the routine: Hear a wave, hold on, and wait for the raft to collapse and regain its shape.

The instruction booklet in the raft said to cover the doors with squares of fabric. But when Drew fastened the doors shut, the canopy caved in.

"Quick! Quick! Get them open!" they yelled, ripping off the door covers. The raft's canopy popped back up. The doors needed to be open to allow the wind to pass through.

The sailors made a rule: No sleeping. Every few minutes, someone would shout, "Hey! How is everybody? Say something!"

When the C-130 passed over the raft, Drew and others stuck their heads out.

The plane gave Drew reassurance. *People know we are here,* he thought.

The first hint of Monday's sunrise bloomed over the ocean.

Bonn and Fields flew the helicopter into radio range of the C-130. A second plane had arrived to relieve the first, and its pilots were getting an update.

Fields overheard that the first helicopter to reach the *Bounty* was rescuing a survivor from the water.

With dawn breaking, she pulled off her night-vision goggles. She saw nothing but gray. Gray sky, gray ocean, gray clouds, gray sea spray. Without contrasting color, it was hard to get any perspective. *Was that a big cloud far away, or a small cloud up close?* she wondered. Spooky.

Fields heard on the radio that the other helicopter was now flying at 300 feet. They dropped to 150 feet. Nothing would be worse than two rescue helicopters colliding.

She could hear the C-130 but couldn't see it, even though it was less than 2 miles away.

Finally, the plane broke through the clouds in a left-hand turn, a wingtip pointing at a life raft. Fields saw three little heads pop out. Then, frantic waves.

Inside the raft, sailors were yelling, "It's a helicopter! We made it!"

Drew stuck out his head and recited the play-by-play action.

"The helicopter is here!"

"There's a swimmer coming down!"

"He's in the water!"

"He's coming toward the raft!"

Then Dan Todd popped in.

He looks like an Abercrombie & Fitch model who snuck into a Red Bull commercial, Jess found herself thinking. *He's perfect. Does he pluck his eyebrows?*

Todd said, "I hear you guys need a ride."

Hovering above, pilot Bonn spotted a monster wave heading for the raft. It grew bigger and bigger. *Oh, man,* he thought. *This is not going to be good.* The wave crested, pounding the top of the raft. Bonn was surprised it didn't flip.

The impact of the wave sent the rescue swimmer flying. His helmeted head smashed into Drew's face like a punch, knocking out one of his contact lenses.

"Well, that sucked," Todd said.

"Welcome to our world!" a sailor shouted.

Todd swam off towing a deckhand to a rescue basket dangling from the helicopter, and then he came back for Jess. She jumped into the ocean, and he put his arm around her to tow her. It felt like the strongest arm ever. She didn't know she was inside the basket until it was around her.

Above, in the helicopter, Bonn didn't like what was happening.

The wind had blown the raft behind him. He didn't want to be upwind because the rotor wash was now buffeting the raft.

But with a swimmer in the water with a survivor, Bonn had to hold his position.

He had a sinking feeling. Sure enough, the life raft flipped over, with people inside it.

Where the raft doorway had been, Drew now saw only green ocean. *This is not how this is going to happen,* he thought. *I am not going to drown inside a life raft with a helicopter above me.* He swam for the exit.

Now inside the helicopter, Jess looked down and saw the overturned raft. Finally, heads surfaced—one, two, three, four.

When the rescue swimmer came for Drew, he went limp with relief as he pushed off from the raft and into Todd's arms.

The six sailors collapsed in wet heaps at the back of the helicopter. Bonn and Fields passed around something small and white.

Medicine? thought Drew. He popped one into his mouth. It was a mint. He smiled and yelled, "Hey! It's a Life Saver!"

Bonn flew to another raft. The first helicopter had left because it was low on fuel, but there were still sailors in the water.

The Coast Guard hoisted three more into the helicopter. The survivors from different rafts compared stories. They couldn't account for everyone.

Capt. Walbridge, Chief Mate Svendsen and deckhand Claudene Christian seemed to be missing.

Not Claudene, Jess thought. The captain and chief mate, she understood. But not Claudene. *Goddamn it, not Claudene.*

Bonn turned over the controls to Fields for the flight back to Elizabeth City.

The nine sailors in the helicopter, a tangle of wet neoprene, didn't say a word.

They caught their first sight of land. Over the Outer Banks, sea spray from pounding waves drifted high above the barrier islands.

In Chicago, Drew's father tried to keep his phone line clear. Parents of *Bounty* crew members kept calling, trying to figure out what was going on. All he knew was that the Coast Guard had rescued most of the sailors, but not all. He didn't know who was missing.

He braced for one of two phone calls. It would either be his son, or someone from the Coast Guard with bad news.

Drew paced around the Coast Guard station with a borrowed cellphone, composing himself to call home. He made small talk about the sandwiches Coast Guard officials had handed out. The coffee. Anything to feel normal.

Drew thought his family knew nothing, just that he was off sailing.

He didn't want to shock them with his call. He decided he wouldn't say: "I'm alive! The boat sank! The Coast Guard rescued us!" No, that would be overwhelming.

He dialed.

Jim Salapatek saw the North Carolina area code pop up on his cellphone. The waiting was over, but he paused, staring at the ringing phone. He felt he might crumble to pieces. Finally, he picked up.

"Hey, how you doing?" Drew said.

"Where are you?" his father said cautiously.

"I'm here with some friends in North Carolina," Drew said. "We're just eating some lunch."

Jim called his ex-wife on the office landline and put his cellphone over the receiver. Drew's sister picked up at her mom's house. She heard Drew's voice and started crying.

Drew choked up. He held his breath.

It was hard to find the words: Yes, I didn't die.

Fourteen of the *Bounty*'s 16 sailors had arrived at the air station in Elizabeth City. Svendsen, 41, who some sailors thought was missing because he never made it into a raft, was among them. At sea, the Coast Guard continued to search.

Coast Guard officials handed out matching blue jumpsuits to the crew and arranged for a trip to a store so they could buy dry shoes and clothes.

Drew wandered Wal-Mart's bright, wide aisles, dazed with euphoria and nearly blind. He'd lost both contact lenses in the shipwreck.

He couldn't be sure whether he was looking at men's or women's clothing until he pulled labels inches from his face. Soon, he gave up. It felt ridiculous anyway. Two hours after nearly dying at sea, he was shopping for pants.

Jess was inspecting neon-colored sports bras when news flashed on a store TV that Claudene had been found.

"We made it!" she said to a crew member.

A few minutes later, in the shoe aisle, the truth emerged. Claudene had been found, but she was dead.

Jess, Drew and other sailors formed a small circle in the Wal-Mart, hugging and crying. A couple shopping for tube socks came over to comfort them.

For four days, the Coast Guard conducted 22 searches covering 11,000 square miles for Capt. Robin Walbridge. At sunset on Nov. 1, the search was called off. His body was never found.

Some survivors said they last saw Walbridge struggling in the water near the *Bounty*.

As one sailor swam away from the ship, a light on a survival suit could be seen disappearing under the waves and fading away, down into the sea.

Epilogue

One month after the *Bounty* sank, Capt. Robin Walbridge and Claudene Christian were honored in Fall River, Mass., the ship's former homeport.

Tall-ship captains have widely criticized Walbridge's decision to sail into Hurricane Sandy.

"The main thing is, most of us are just scratching our heads because none of us would have done the same thing," Walter Rybka, captain of the tall ship Niagara, said in an interview.

Jan Miles, captain of the Pride of Baltimore II, in an open letter to Walbridge after his death, called the decision to sail "reckless in the extreme."

Walbridge's family remembered him as a gentle teacher and skilled seaman who stressed safety aboard the *Bounty*.

"One little part of me is glad my brother is gone because he would have been devastated he lost the ship and Claudene," said Lucille Walbridge Jansen, one of Walbridge's sisters.

In February, the Coast Guard held a formal hearing in Portsmouth. *Bounty* survivors recounted their experiences. Tall-ship captains, Coast Guard officials and shipwrights also testified. The Coast Guard's investigation is ongoing.

The family of Claudene Christian has filed a lawsuit against *Bounty* owner Robert Hansen. The official cause of death was drowning. A medical examiner's report showed bruising over her right eye.

Coast Guard swimmers Randy Haba and Daniel Todd were awarded the Distinguished Flying Cross, one of the service's highest commendations. The award cited Haba and Todd for "extraordinary heroism" in swimming through 30-foot waves and gale-force winds to save the sailors. Twenty-four other service members—the crews of the C-130 and rescue helicopters—also received awards.

Jess and Drew broke up a few months after Sandy.

Drew spent the summer working on a tourist schooner in Lake Michigan and is now an officer on the Pride of Baltimore II.

After the Coast Guard hearings, the *Bounty*'s former chief mate, John Svendsen, called him to ask what he had learned from the shipwreck. The mate was making a list for the Coast Guard. Drew wasn't sure how to answer.

"I don't know what I learned," he said. "What is there to learn? It's like losing friends in a car accident. What did you learn? Oh, I don't know. It's something that happened to me."

Jess struggled in the months after the *Bounty* sank. Waves of grief and anger crashed over her unexpectedly.

"It's not like I can sit down and say, 'I'm going to let it all out now' —it just comes," she said.

After the *Bounty* sank, she joined the crew of a tall ship in Puerto Rico. When it was time to cross the ocean to Florida, she flew back to the States instead. She didn't feel that the ship had the proper safety equipment.

She is still working on tall ships, most recently the schooner Liberty Clipper.

Jess is sometimes angry at Walbridge but says she understands why he made the decision to sail.

"It makes sense that once you've been through some really bad conditions, you would say, 'Well, I've seen worse.' "

She said it would have been hard to get off the *Bounty* before it set sail.

"When you're young, you don't expect bad things to happen. It's just the innocence of youth," she said.

"I know I didn't sink, but sometimes it feels like a lot of me did."

A Mother, at Her Wits' End, Sets out to Find Help for Her Sick Son

Milwaukee Journal Sentinel Online

July 20, 2013

By Meg Kissinger

CHAPTER 1: A Quest for Care

San Francisco — Rob Sweeney sucked on an unlit cigarette while his mother stood at the car rental counter, trying to negotiate a better deal.

His legs twitched. His eyes darted right and left. His head bobbed to a beat no one else could hear.

After two airplane flights, he was antsy.

"Want to get some vodka and watch movies in my hotel room?" he asked the stranger sitting next to him.

Rob, 25, has been diagnosed with schizoaffective disorder, a catch-all term for a brain disease that causes a combination of delusions, paranoia, depression and mania. He has spent the past six years churning through

Milwaukee County's troubled mental health system, cycling week-to-week from house to hospital to homeless shelter.

Now he and his mother, Debbie Sweeney, have come to California in a desperate search to find a safe place for him to live.

Rob does things that make his mother sick with worry.

He walks into traffic, spits on people's cars, yells racist slurs out bus windows, writes suicide notes, puts cigarettes out on his forehead and cuts his arms to make himself feel better.

He imagines people are trying to kill him.

Rob once ran into a stranger's house in West Allis at two in the morning, convinced he was being chased.

In the past few years Rob has taken to keeping a knife in his pocket to keep the "evil people" away. When Debbie found a butcher knife under his bed, she told Rob he couldn't stay at home any more. But he still sneaks into her house from time to time and stands by her bed late at night. Debbie has taken to locking her bedroom door.

"That's what this disease does to you," she said. "It tears a mother away from her son."

No one has put these things together in a case file and taken Rob before a judge to say that he needs intensive treatment and supervision. Six psychiatrists who were asked by the Journal Sentinel for their opinion on the best way to care for Rob said this is what should be done.

"He sounds like a powder keg waiting to explode," said Steven Moffic, a retired psychiatrist who managed outpatient clinics for the Medical College of Wisconsin for 20 years.

Rob does not get any of the treatment the doctors recommended. He does not get therapy. He is not taught coping skills. He sees a psychiatrist four times a year for a maximum of 15 minutes each time, the standard for Milwaukee County's mental health care.

Like thousands of other people in Milwaukee County, Rob lives in a twilight zone — too sick to make it on his own, not getting the help he needs. A 2009 analysis by the county's Behavioral Health Division found at least 3,200 people with chronic and persistent mental illness who would qualify for services if they were available.

If the county had the kind of community care available in places like Madison, a team of professionals — a doctor, a social worker, an occupational therapist — would check him daily to provide enough support to keep him safe.

In Milwaukee County, the only option is commitment until he is well enough for community care. Debbie doesn't know how to make that happen on her own. The system won't help her figure it out. Instead, she is told Rob has the right to be mentally ill.

Rob actually gets more care than most.

Since 2008, he has been enrolled in one of the 1,264 slots for the county's Community Support Program, the most intensive level of support a patient can receive short of being hospitalized. A case manager, Steve Seidl of Transitional Living Services, delivers Rob's medicine, keeps charge of his finances and tries to help him find places to live.

There is only so much Seidl can do.

Unlike most mental health systems—including the one for Milwaukee County's youth—the adult system does not provide full-service health management for patients. In Milwaukee's "brokered system," case managers try to link patients to services for housing and medical care that are provided by other agencies. Case managers have limited authority. Families find it impossible to learn who is responsible for what.

In Rob's case, his mother and caseworker, who declined to be interviewed, are often at odds.

Email from Seidl to Debbie:

"I don't think Rob should continue to be rewarded for his not cooperating with treatment."

Debbie to Seidl:

"I don't rescue him Steve...he shows up at my house, repeatedly, because you won't find him a place to stay. He can't be homeless!!"

Seidl to Debbie:

"He tells you things to manipulate you, tug at your heart strings and make you feel sorry for him."

Debbie to Seidl:

"This is ridiculous that he is mentally ill and has no place to sleep. He has no food, he doesn't even have his medicine!!! At the very, very least you should be driving out to him to give him his daily medication."

Rob had a mental breakdown midway through his second semester of college, a time many mental illnesses emerge, especially in men.

In the six years since, police have hauled him to Milwaukee County's psychiatric emergency room at least 12 times. He stays in the hospital for a few hours, or a few days, depending on what he wants or what his insurance coverage will allow, then he's back on the streets.

Rob can't find a landlord in Milwaukee who will rent to him anymore. He makes too much noise and too much mess. He's been kicked out of homeless shelters for breaking curfew and smoking cigarettes. He lives out of motel rooms—when he can afford it and where they will allow him—with money from his federal disability account. Or he sleeps under bushes or begs his mother to let him sleep on her couch.

Debbie knows it's not very logical to travel across the country where they don't know anyone, hoping to find some kind of answer to this very complex problem.

But Rob has talked since he was in grade school of moving to Silicon Valley to write programs for computer games. California could offer him a change of pace, a clean slate, the chance to realize his dreams. Maybe he will accept treatment there.

"I know it's a little crazy," Debbie said. "But there is nothing for him here."

An executive assistant at a downtown insurance company, Debbie has planned for this trip since September. She clipped coupons and shopped for specials. She set aside most of her vacation days and dug into savings.

In February, she paid $483.60 for airfare for herself and Rob to San Francisco. She booked a room for them for nine nights at the Ramada Inn in Sunnyvale, near San Jose, and scoured the Internet for programs there for people with mental illness.

They would leave April 22.

Debbie hoped to come back to Milwaukee alone May 1, but bought a round-trip ticket for Rob, just in case.

Her fiancé encourages her to do what she thinks is best for her son. Her daughter sends her emails of comfort.

But this trip is Debbie's lonely burden to bear.

A right to be mentally ill

Twenty years ago, Debbie might have had more allies. The National Alliance on Mental Illness was founded in Madison in 1979 after the state changed its commitment laws and thousands of patients who had been hospitalized were released, often to the streets.

The group was designed to help families navigate the new system and advocate for safer care. But in recent years the Milwaukee chapter has served as more of a patient advocacy organization, fighting changes to state law that might make it easier to compel unwilling patients into care —including those who don't understand what is wrong with them.

The law allows family members or others to make their own case that a loved one should be committed for care. But it is rarely done, since the standards are so difficult to meet.

NAMI has helped Debbie learn about the symptoms of her son's illness, but no one has helped her figure out how she might take his case to court to get him the intensive treatment doctors say he needs. The six psychiatrists each say community care is not enough for Rob right now. He can't cook for himself or do laundry and doesn't know how to avoid dangerous situations. He needs to be stabilized and supervised, the doctors say.

"How do you even do that?" Debbie said.

The way the system is designed, it's Rob's decision if he wants treatment or not, or if he will take his medicine. He hates Zyprexa, the medicine that makes the voices go away. It makes his arms and legs feel heavy, like he's swimming in a pool of oatmeal.

He often refuses to take it and starts to hallucinate within hours. Debbie has suggested to Seidl, the caseworker, that they try a different drug—Clozapine.

Seidl agreed that it is the most effective medication available. Still, he shot down Debbie's idea.

"The only way we could venture a trial of this without Rob's approval and to do it most safely would be in an extended in-patient stay, and he was on a Commitment, neither of which is a likely scenario for Rob at this point," he wrote in a recent email.

Case managers have told Debbie that her son has a right to be mentally ill; Debbie doesn't understand that. Why would anyone want to be terrified the way Rob is when he imagines people are chasing him or getting inside his brain? Why would anyone want to be too scared to get out of bed? Or to be kicked out of the library for vagrancy or stopped by police for walking down the street?

The other day Debbie found Rob lying on the bathroom floor crying.

I'm sick, Mom, he told her. *I'm so sick and I can't think straight.*

Rob is getting worse.

"I am slowly watching my son die."

Early signs of trouble

Rob Sweeney was born July 16, 1987, after a frantic delivery. Debbie had been in hard labor for more than 12 hours when the lines on the fetal heart monitor jumped, showing signs of distress. The doctor called for a forceps. They would have to hurry.

His father stood waiting to cut the umbilical cord, but a nurse whisked the newborn away to a warming table in the corner. He was blue and not breathing. Debbie lay nearby, heart pounding, waiting to hear her baby cry.

"Once he started, he barely stopped," she said.

Rob was a fussy baby. He startled easily and had trouble nursing. He didn't like being held and wailed at the slightest noise or touch.

"I couldn't put him in anything with wool or corduroy," Debbie said. "It had to be real soft."

Rob was 3 the first time he got in serious trouble.

He threw a chair over the balcony of Hales Corners Lutheran Preschool that landed a few feet from where other children were playing.

No one was hurt, but school administrators said Rob could not continue there. They didn't have the resources to handle a child with his problems.

Debbie begged them to reconsider. She was raised Lutheran and wanted her children to go to Lutheran schools. She liked the values they taught — do unto others as you would have them do onto you.

We're going to start seeing more and more of these crack babies, one of the teachers told her.

Debbie was shocked; she had never taken drugs.

This was the first of many humiliations she would learn to endure.

Debbie stopped going to church.

She took Rob to see a psychiatrist who diagnosed him with attention deficit hyperactivity disorder and put him on 5 milligrams of Ritalin three times a day, a dose he maintained for the next ten years.

Once Rob got to school, administrators developed an individualized education plan for him and assigned a team of teachers and social workers who met regularly to review his case.

One of the school counselors suggested Rob might have autism, because of his poor ability to relate to other people, but the idea was dismissed, Debbie said, because Rob scored so high on intelligence tests.

By eighth grade, he refused to take the Ritalin, too embarrassed to go to the school nurse for his midday dose.

"We noticed the difference immediately," Debbie said. "Even his handwriting changed."

It seemed like he got into trouble every day, for lipping off, forgetting to turn in his homework, fights on the playground.

Debbie and her husband divorced when Rob was 7. She wrote off a lot of the bad behavior as an effect of trauma from the breakup. Three years ago, Brian Sweeney moved to Florida. He rarely sees or talks to Rob.

Rob never was much for soccer or baseball or swimming. He wasn't able to concentrate. He didn't have the dedication or the discipline to practice.

Computers were his passion.

He and his friends would spend hours at the local computer store building their own networks and playing games. Rob struggled in his other classes, but soared in computer class. During his senior year, he took classes at ITT Tech, a private college offering classes in computer technology and engineering.

Rob made it through Whitnall High School with just enough credits to graduate in 2005. Debbie had high hopes for him studying computers at the community college in Shreveport, La., where her mother lived. Rob moved in with his grandmother, but the arrangement only lasted a few weeks.

"It was a disaster," Debbie said.

Debbie traveled to Louisiana to get him settled in his own place.

The following spring, she got a call from Rob saying that he couldn't think straight. He was hearing voices. He drove himself to the nearest hospital, where they admitted him to a locked psychiatric ward.

Three days later, Debbie got a call from a nurse saying Rob had sneaked out.

Debbie tried to get Rob to go back to the hospital. Instead, he got into his car and drove back to Milwaukee, pulled over by police outside Chicago for driving 118 mph.

For the next several months, Rob lived at home in Franklin and worked a variety of jobs — fast food restaurants, phone sales, yard crews. None of the jobs lasted more than a few months. Debbie recently counted 28 places where he had worked since high school.

By the summer of 2008, the voices in Rob's head had become more menacing.

"He thought the cars were talking to him and that there was someone hiding in the backyard playing a drum," Debbie said.

He moved to an apartment on W. North Ave. in Milwaukee with a friend from high school.

One day, Debbie got a call from Rob's roommate saying Rob was lying on the couch laughing uncontrollably and not making any sense. Before long, he started to imagine that the man next door was controlling his brain. He was petrified and refused to get out of bed.

Debbie persuaded Rob to go to the hospital for a few days. Eventually, he was enrolled in the county's targeted case management program. As he grew sicker, he was put in the most intensive program the county offers. The federal government declared him to be disabled and awarded him monthly payments of $880.

Debbie resolved to learn all that she could about ADHD and schizoaffective disorder and brain synapses and medication levels. She signed up for parent education classes.

"In the end, he's my responsibility," she said.

California air

Maybe this trip to California would shake something loose for Rob. Maybe someone would take pity on him and give him a chance.

If nothing else, maybe Debbie could get Rob's federal disability benefits transferred to California and find a group home there that would take him and where he would obey the rules.

She had to do something, and this was the last thing she could think of.

"If Rob kills himself, which he's talked about a lot lately," she said, wiping the tears from her eyes, "I have to know that I did all I could for him."

At the airport's car rental counter, Debbie decided on a white Jeep. She'd dreamed of tooling around the West Coast in a convertible, but couldn't afford it. Dinner most nights of the trip would be a bag of nuts from Costco, a power bar and a bottle of soda.

They rolled down the windows and took off in search of the motel.

"Oh, man, feel that air," Rob said.

His mother giggled.

"It's 71 degrees at 9 o'clock at night," she said, glancing at the car's temperature gauge.

Everything seemed better here.

"I'm going to get a job and make $500,000 a year and go to college," Rob declared. "And I'm going to hang out with movie stars."

But first, a stop at the liquor store.

Rob grabbed a six-pack of vodka lemonade and a pint of rum.

Debbie knew it was not a good idea for Rob to mix alcohol with Zyprexa. Still, what 25-year-old man doesn't want to cut loose a little? "That better last the week, honey," she said.

Unsettled mission

Debbie woke up that first morning in California ready to roll. Rob was another story. For all his bluster the night before, he just wanted to sleep.

She tried coaxing him for hours, but he wouldn't budge.

Finally she got him in the car to look for lunch. They pulled into a nearby shopping mall in search of Taco Bell, Rob's favorite restaurant. But the best Debbie could do was a sandwich shop that served hummus and sprouts and carrot juice.

"This is California, Rob," she said. "They eat healthy out here. You better get used to it."

While Debbie went inside to buy the food, Rob paced the parking lot.

Back and forth. Back and forth.

When Debbie returned, he grabbed his food and found a spot by himself at a far-away table.

"You want anything else, Rob?"

He shouted over his shoulder:

"Yeah, I want a house and Porsche and $500,000."

Throughout lunch, Rob badgered Debbie, shouting across the patio: "Take me back to the motel."

Eventually, Debbie relented. Angry that the swimming pool was closed for repairs, Rob headed straight back to bed, slamming the door in Debbie's face.

The motel is about 20 minutes from San Jose, where Debbie had researched their options.

"It's supposed to have some of the best mental health care in the country," she said.

Debbie had talked to a case manager for Santa Clara County's mental health agency who said a move might work, especially because Rob was on federal disability. The case manager talked of getting Rob a job, even gave Debbie a list of agencies and places to live.

But as the trip drew closer, the woman — Victoria — was less specific about how it all could be done. Now she wasn't returning Debbie's calls.

Debbie set out for downtown San Jose to find her. She found the office, a 10-story building in the midst of a huge medical center campus. She stood before the lobby directory, scanning it for Victoria's name.

No listing.

She tried calling. This time Victoria picked up.

"We're here in the lobby," Debbie said.

Victoria refused to see her and wouldn't tell Debbie what her office number was.

"It's confidential," Victoria said.

She gave Debbie the names of drop-in centers she could try.

On her way back to the car, Debbie's cell phone rang. It was Rob.

"Want to know what I figured out, Mom?" he said. "It doesn't matter if we're in a crappy motel room. I'm lucky we're here at all. This is costing you a lot of money.

"Thanks, Mom. I love you. Stay safe."

Debbie smiled.

"Just when I'm ready to kill that kid, he does the sweetest things."

CHAPTER 2: THE RUN-AROUND

Debbie Sweeney was still shaking two hours after she found the ripped-up notes her son, Rob, had thrown all over their motel room.

I am going to Heaven no matter what!!!!!

This is the last time everyone. I am going to a better place

I listened to the right ear and still they took it all away from me

Rob had written things like that over and over again, and it always left Debbie worried about suicide.

When Debbie would call police, they would take Rob, 25, to the county's psychiatric emergency room. But doctors there have never asked a court to order him to undergo long-term care, saying he does not meet the standard of being an imminent danger to himself or others.

He is released once he agrees to take his medication.

But Rob hates his medication. And when he stops taking it, the hallucinations return.

Rob has been hospitalized 10 times in the past six years.

If Rob had a brain tumor, he'd have a team of doctors examining his scans and coordinating his care. Few people would question the cost.

Rob has a different problem affecting his brain. He has been diagnosed with schizoaffective disorder, a condition that causes him to have delusions, paranoia, mania and depression.

Often, due to privacy laws, Debbie can't even get a doctor or nurse to talk to her about Rob's case.

They had been in California three days and Rob would not leave the motel room except to walk down the block to a liquor store. He was still wearing the same black sweatpants and gray hooded sweatshirt, smeared with taco sauce and smelling rank.

Debbie's flight home was just six days away.

She tried again to get Rob moving, but he pulled the covers over his head.

"Leave and don't come back," he said.

Debbie had arrived back at the motel the night before to find the room was a wreck. Rob had eaten most of a large pizza she had ordered for him, then thrown up in the sink. The room reeked of vomit and cigarette smoke.

Rob was curled up asleep on her bed. His was a mess of knotted up sheets.

Bill Bishop, Debbie's fiancé, had warned her, time and again: If Rob is not accepting his illness, no one anywhere is going to be able to help him.

But that assumes, like everyone seemed to do, that an ill brain can think rationally — that a person hearing voices can convince himself they're not real.

Rob's illness is severe.

He cannot shop, cook or care for himself. He can't maintain a job, hasn't held one in years. He gets into fights, gets mugged, often lives on the streets.

Debbie has begged Rob's case manager, Steve Seidl, to find him more structure, more treatment.

"He tells me I am taking away Rob's freedom," Debbie said. "What freedom? The freedom to die on the street?"

Seidl tells Debbie he is frustrated, too.

"I cannot neglect the rest of my duties and the other 200 plus clients we serve when he finally calls," Seidl recently wrote in an email. "I understand your frustration and feel it, but the resources are limited."

Staying focused

With meticulous notes, Debbie tracks every spot Rob has moved over the past six years, 38 in all. She researches drugs and treatments, programs and policies, logging each phone call and conversation.

Debbie often worries about whether Rob's mental illness is her fault. Did something in the genetic code cause her son to suffer like this?

She took a class on the symptoms of mental illness at the Milwaukee chapter of NAMI, the National Alliance on Mental Illness. It helped to understand the science, though there is so much unknown about what causes schizoaffective disorder, the disease Rob has.

Debbie's doctor warned her not to let Rob's struggles overwhelm her.

"You need to step back," her fiancé, Bill, has told her.

Mental illness takes a huge toll on families who are embarrassed or feel guilty. Unlike other illnesses, diseases that affect the way people think and behave are still widely considered the patient's fault or a byproduct of bad parenting. Family members often distance themselves from loved ones, to avoid being consumed by their problems and struggles.

"The person who jumps in to save a drowning man might well drown, too," said Florence Mahoney, who ran a NAMI support group for families for more than 20 years.

"Then what good are you?"

Those who join the group get Mahoney's set of rules to live by and are urged to read them every day.

We release all feelings of guilt concerning this mental illness for we are not to blame for the illness or its effects.

We choose to be healthy and lead a balanced life. We choose to return to a healthy focus on ourselves.

We believe that we have inner resources which will help us with our own growth and will sustain us through crisis.

Debbie taped the list to her refrigerator.

Recovery is possible

It was clear Rob would not budge. So, once again, Debbie decided to go look for help without him.

The Zephyr Drop-In Center in San Jose is a place where people with mental illness can come and hang out, four days a week. David Sisson is a peer specialist there. He spent years in and out of various mental hospitals, thinking of ways to kill himself.

"I finally learned I needed to take the medicine," he told Debbie. "I could have saved me and my family many years of heartbreak if I'd gotten that message earlier. Recovery is possible."

Debbie explained to Sisson that she had read many wonderful things about mental health care in San Jose, and she would like to find a place for Rob around here.

"Don't think we are able to do miracles," he said.

"He's getting virtually no help in Milwaukee," she said. "So, at this point, the littlest things are miracles to me."

Then Debbie told him about the notes she had found that morning. His eyes widened.

"You need to get him into urgent care," Sisson said. "I would take him in today."

She pulled out a notebook and wrote down the phone numbers he read her from his computer screen. He printed out a map.

"How are you going to manage leaving him here?" Sisson asked. "It's very difficult to do this by remote control."

Debbie blinked.

"This is his dream, to be in California," she said. "There is nothing for him back home."

She wished she could get Rob into urgent care that day. But she knew it would be a waste of time. Rob wouldn't agree to go to the hospital voluntarily, and the suicide notes wouldn't be enough to persuade a doctor to order Rob into long-term treatment.

As in Wisconsin, Rob would need to be considered an imminent danger as evidenced by a recent act of violence or overt threat.

"You really have to make a case that he is dangerous," Sisson said.

Debbie remembered the time Rob ended up in the emergency room at West Allis Memorial Hospital after police found him hiding behind bushes, babbling about marrying Kelly Ripa, the morning television show host. The emergency room doctor didn't think he was dangerous enough to be held. So, the officer drove him to the Milwaukee County Mental Health Complex while Debbie followed in her car.

"When we got there the cop kind of winked at me and said, 'He said some really wild stuff,' " Debbie said. "I could tell he was exaggerating, but that's what it took."

She didn't have that kind of inside track here.

And Debbie admitted she didn't have the guts to make the case against her own son.

Nowhere to go

The next morning, Debbie was on the phone by 8 a.m., still trying to find an agency in San Jose that would help Rob.

A woman at the call center said that unless Rob was an imminent danger, he would have to wait.

"Three business days," she said.

It was Friday.

"But I am leaving next Wednesday," Debbie said. "I was hoping to have this wrapped up by then."

By 10 a.m., Debbie and Rob were on the road with a page of addresses and phone numbers to see what they could find.

A brown accordion-style folder wedged between the seats was stuffed with notes on places to check out. The GPS was turned on, an iPad close by.

Rob sat in the front seat tapping his feet, staring out of the window.

After spending days trying to get him out of bed, Debbie decided not to give Rob the Zyprexa, hoping he would be more alert.

But without the drugs, Rob was more anxious and more likely to lash out.

He begged Debbie to take him to McDonald's. Lunchtime was still three hours away.

"I told you. You have to eat the free breakfast in the lobby. The budget is tight."

"MOM!" Rob shouted. "Why are you so (expletive) evil?"

Debbie blinked and kept driving.

Rob bobbed his head and started to grin. Then, he gave a sinister chuckle, like a playground bully laughing at someone getting hurt.

Their first stop was a yellow Victorian house on San Jose's south side, a racially mixed neighborhood with some tired houses with busted concrete sidewalks and others that were neatly tended with rosebushes and yard ornaments.

Rob refused to get out of the car.

"This is ghetto," he said. "I'm not living in a ghetto. Take me back to Silicon Valley, please. NOW."

Rob cranked the radio to the highest level.

"Rob, we are running out of time," Debbie said. "You have to go in and meet with these people or you won't have any place to live."

He turned his head away. "Your breath stinks."

The Bill Wilson Center offers transitional living for troubled teens. Rob is too old, the woman told them.

She sent them two miles down the road to the Boccardo Regional Reception Area, a homeless shelter with mental health services.

"My son is in the car and won't come in," Debbie said. "He's 25 and has schizoaffective disorder. He's homeless."

The intake worker sneezed a few times, wiped her nose with her sleeve and shrugged.

Without a doctor, a case manager and a number, Rob had one choice: He'd have to try his luck at urgent care. That would mean going to the hospital.

"He's not dangerous enough," Debbie told the worker.

Back to the car. Two more stops. Both busts. No one can see him without a case number, and he can't get a case number until his federal disability benefits are transferred to California.

Debbie doesn't want Rob to fill out the paperwork to transfer his benefits until they are certain he can get some kind of treatment and housing here.

"Let's eat," she said. "Then let's go back to the motel and take a big nap."

They drove around Silicon Valley, past miles of sprawling office buildings, each with manicured lawns and a household name: Facebook, Google, Amazon, Netflix. Rob was looking for McDonald's.

Atari. E-Trade. Dell.

"Look Rob!" Debbie said and pointed. "eBay!"

No response.

Fading hopes

Reality was starting to sink in for Debbie Sweeney.

After five days, she had not found a place for her son.

"Sometimes I feel like running away," she said. "I'd like to get in the car and just drive as far as it'll take me and never come back."

She had high hopes that this trip would give Rob another chance at a reasonably happy life. She sees Rob's friends around town — some of them college graduates, married, with kids of their own. Debbie knows Rob will never have that life.

"But I thought the fresh air and sunshine and the warmer weather would help," she said.

Except for a few hours of fruitless driving around, Rob has been holed up in a motel room with drapes drawn, smoking cigarettes and sleeping. At night, he slams doors and paces the parking lot, talking to himself, listening to heavy metal music on his headphones. One night he showered three times.

He could just as well be in Omaha or St. Louis, or at home in Franklin.

With all the health offices closed for the weekend, Debbie tried to coax him to go see the ocean. No luck.

She'd been singing that old Dionne Warwick song all week: *"I'm going back to find some peace of mind in San Jose."*

Debbie was going to go to the ocean even if Rob was not.

Her ears popped as she drove over the mountains to Santa Cruz, past massive oaks and towering redwood trees. Is there any place more breathtaking than northern California in April?

She slowly made her way to the beach, stopping every 10 feet or so to take another picture. Flowers everywhere: wisteria, yellow poppies, azaleas, fuchsia.

"It's heaven," she said.

The beach was filled with Saturday afternoon excitement. Kids jumping in the waves, a boy making a sandcastle. Volleyball games. A baby toddling along with his dad.

She kept driving.

Just outside of Monterey, a pod of sea lions lay stacked up like bags of sand. A sea otter swam by, hamming it up for the crowd. He was in no hurry, swimming on his back with a fish on his belly. What a show-off! He circled around right where Debbie stood.

For the first time that day, she chuckled.

Sea otters are known for their playfulness, the guidebook said: "They appear to engage in behavior for the sheer enjoyment of it."

Debbie checked her watch, then winced.

Rob would be needing his medication.

CHAPTER 3: WAITING FOR AN ANGEL

Rob Sweeney woke up Monday morning and told his mother there was no way he was going back with her to Milwaukee.

Go back for what? To live on the streets, get hassled by cops, risk getting thrown into that awful mental hospital again?

They had come to California, hoping to find a better way for Rob to live.

Debbie Sweeney's plane was leaving in 36 hours.

And she had a long list of things she needed to get done:

Find a safe place for Rob to live.

Get someone to make sure he takes his daily dose of his anti-psychotic drug.

Transfer his disability benefits from Wisconsin to California.

Get him lined up with a doctor.

Rob had his own list:

Recharger for iPod.

New sunglasses — baby blue with black trim.

A card to buy medical marijuana.

A haircut.

In the car outside Great Clips, Debbie started her daily round of phone calls: Homeless shelters, halfway houses, social service agencies.

They each told her something different.

Apply for local benefits. Don't apply for local benefits.

Get an appointment with a doctor. Go to urgent care. Call 211 and get your name in the system.

"Our first appointment is in two weeks," one woman said.

Debbie sighed.

These were the same answers she had been getting for years in Milwaukee, which was what sent them to California in the first place.

As Debbie sat outside the barbershop waiting for Rob, her cell phone quivered.

Gabrielle Dietz, a supervisor with Santa Clara County's Mental Health Department, was calling to say that they were working on Rob's case. The agency was one of more than a dozen places she had called seeking help.

"Oh, that's terrific," Debbie said, grabbing her pen.

She scribbled and smiled.

"This is the first real hope we have had in a week," she said.

"Your case is complex," Gabrielle told Debbie. "Let's see what we can do."

Debbie was giddy. She marched into the barbershop to tell Rob.

"This might work," she told him.

"Okay," he said. "Cool."

Rob told the stylist to give him the works — shampoo, haircut, mousse. Debbie even gave him permission to buy the styling gel.

"Live a little," she said.

A new caseworker

Dietz assured Debbie that someone would be calling back to set up an appointment, and that a caseworker could get Rob's federal benefits transferred to California. Still, Debbie wasn't taking any chances.

She and Rob headed over to the Central Benefits Office to see how they could get Rob's benefits transferred themselves.

"It's lunchtime now," the woman at the desk told them. "Take a seat and we will call you when someone comes back."

So, they sat.

And sat.

By 1:30 p.m., the room was full of people looking for help.

Debbie's phone rang again.

"Oh, that's fantastic," Debbie said. "Yes. Yes. Okay."

The caller was Abe Hughes, who would be Rob's caseworker.

Yes, he would transfer Rob's benefits and get him in to see a doctor. Yes, they have therapy sessions. Yes, there was a spot in a rooming house where they serve two meals a day, plus snacks.

Debbie put Rob on the phone and he and Hughes set up an appointment for 8 a.m. the next day.

She was ecstatic.

Just one problem:

Rob would have to share a room.

"I'm not doing it, Mom," he said. "Put an ad in Craigslist. Find me a place of my own."

Debbie's face tightened. For the past eight days — really the past six years — the two had been riding separate emotional roller coasters. Every time she was up, he was down.

Eventually, Rob agreed to meet the woman who ran the rooming house. He would have to promise to follow the rules.

Debbie wanted to go to a Mexican restaurant to celebrate. Rob was in no mood.

"Take me back to the motel," he told her.

"You sure you won't come?"

Rob didn't answer.

He glared out the window, bobbing his head. Until a familiar sign came into view.

"Look, Mom," Rob said, pointing. "Intel!"

Ready to go

The next morning, Rob was up early and ready to go. He tried eating the free breakfast of cereal and danish in the motel lobby but felt too nauseous. He hadn't slept well.

Rob jumped out of the car when they pulled up to the Sunnyvale Behavioral Health Complex, where they had an 8 a.m. appointment with Rob's new caseworker. Rob frantically searched for his cigarette lighter.

The complex was set in a new, sparkling building with a meditation garden out front and soothing artwork inside.

"Rob?" a man said, extending a hand.

Abe Hughes, who has been a mental health caseworker for 13 years, pointed them toward his office.

"I want to go to college and get a job and get a house and maybe meet some girls," Rob told him.

Then he turned to Debbie.

"Mom, I'm never going to see you again in my life."

Hughes laughed.

"Well, first things first," he said. "Let's get you a roof over your head and maybe something to eat."

He gave Rob several forms to fill out authorizing the transfer of his federal disability benefits from Wisconsin to California.

Rob glanced at his mother, his legs twitching.

"I think I found a real nice place for you," Hughes said. "It's in one of the nicer parts of San Jose."

The place was called a "board and care." Rent would be $750 a month for a shared bedroom.

Rob received $880 a month in disability benefits in Wisconsin, but would get more in California when Social Security workers adjusted his payment for the higher cost of living.

The house had four bedrooms and several rules:

No smoking.

No alcohol.

No street drugs.

"Have you ever been evicted?" Hughes asked Rob.

Debbie kept her head bowed. Rob looked at his shoes.

"No," Rob lied.

As Rob's caseworker, Hughes would check up on him a few times a week, but it would be Rob's responsibility to take his medication.

"Yeah," Rob said. "About that."

Debbie interrupted.

"Mom," Rob said, fingering his unlit cigarette. "Don't talk."

But Debbie persisted. "I need to say this. Every time you go off of your medication you end up in the hospital."

Rob nodded.

Hughes would deliver the medication each month and the landlady would keep it locked in the kitchen closet, but Rob needed to swallow that pill every day.

"Sometimes people need medication even if they don't like to take it," Hughes told Rob. "You know how people with diabetes need to take insulin so they don't end up in the hospital? It's the same with some kinds of mental illness."

Hughes stepped out to make a copy of Rob's driver's license.

"I don't love you, Mom," Rob said. "You're evil. You're going to burn in hell for the things you say and do to me."

Too good to be true?

Fifteen minutes later, Rob was all set — with one more condition:

He needed to pass inspection with the landlady. They pulled up to the house, a gray stucco Prairie-style house on a tree-lined street down the block from a park.

"This is it?" Debbie said, voice filled with disbelief.

"Mom, this is nicer than your house," Rob said.

They walked through the house, gawking at the Rococo-style living room and the tapestry on the wall. They made their way to the back porch and a yard dotted with a lemon tree, an orange tree and a big bush of bright red roses.

"Look, Rob," Debbie said, pointing. "A hummingbird!"

Brett, 51, who has stayed in the house for the past six months, came out to eat his breakfast, a large bowl of noodles.

"It's the best of the best," Brett said. "You're not going to find a cleaner, nicer place in all of San Jose."

He listed just two drawbacks: It was a 15-block walk to the closest store and the traffic from the highway can be noisy.

"I have schizophrenia," said Brett. "So I almost never sit out here in the back. I hear voices in the traffic, and it scares me."

Back inside, they waited for the landlady to arrive. Sun poured through the big front windows.

Rob stretched out on the bed in the room nearest to the kitchen, the one that would be his to share with another 25-year-old, a man named Tony.

"Is she going to let me stay here, Mom?" Rob asked. "It seems too good to be true and, in my world, when something is too good to be true, it really is."

Maribel Galsim moved to California from the Philippines 20 years ago. In addition to running the board and care, she operated a day care center out of her home with her mother and her sister.

Rob could stay, she said, if he agreed to follow the rules.

"If I'm good, can I stay for a long time?"

Rob was smiling, nodding, standing tall.

"I'm real helpful," he said. "You want me to get you something at the store? I like this place so much."

Debbie agreed to pay Galsim $775 in cash — $750 for rent and $25 for the first night. They would check out of their motel, pick up some things at Walmart and be back in an hour or so. She would find a new hotel closer to the airport to catch her 6 a.m. flight home.

Rob was no help at the motel. As Debbie packed their clothes and cleaned out the ashtrays, Rob paced in the parking lot, smoking one cigarette after another.

"I love this place," Rob said. "I really want to stay here. Maybe for the rest of my life."

When they arrived back at the board and care, Rob headed straight for his bed while Debbie put away his things.

She handed the cash to Galsim — slipping in an extra $150 for cigarettes, laundry detergent and other small items Rob might need.

Debbie circled around the kitchen, into the backyard, then back to Rob's room. She straightened his shirts, fluffed his pillow.

Rob's eyes were closed.

"Goodbye, Mom," he said.

She leaned down and gave him a hug and then a kiss on his cheek, which he wiped away.

"Can you just go now?" he asked.

Debbie got in the car, promising herself she would not cry.

She would go back to Milwaukee and get her garden started. Bill, her fiancé, could use help with his new Texas barbecue restaurant. She and her daughter, Michelle, would have more time together. Everything would work out.

Ninety minutes later, Debbie arrived at the new motel and checked into a nonsmoking room.

She rolled her suitcase down the parking lot, swiped her card and shut the door.

Then she lay on the bed and sobbed.

CHAPTER 4: No Place Left to Turn

Debbie Sweeney had been back home in Franklin less than 72 hours when she got the call she had been dreading.

Her son, Rob, was back on the street.

At the group home in San Jose, he refused to take his anti-psychotic medication and was breaking the rules.

He was not supposed to go outside past 10 p.m. but he did — often — and the neighbors were complaining.

The landlady gave Rob his money back, minus $75 for the three nights he had stayed there.

She drove him to the train station where he bought a $562 ticket to Milwaukee. He would board the train at 8:23 p.m. Saturday and, after switching trains in Portland, Ore., was due to arrive at 2:07 p.m. Tuesday.

Debbie felt like a failure.

"All that time," she said. "All that money."

Her friends at work told her the trip had not been a waste. She had wanted to give her son a chance and she did. Debbie told herself that no matter what happened, she would know that she did that much for her son.

How could she ever have thought this would work?

Come Tuesday, the train was delayed by an hour. A few rumpled passengers trudged up the hallway. A lady with a limp. A man with a long beard. A mother with two little kids.

No Rob.

After 12 minutes, the train pulled away.

No safety net

Milwaukee County's mental health system had failed Rob before.

Now it was Debbie's only option.

The system has been criticized for years for having some of the worst practices in the country. It emphasizes short-term emergency treatment over effective long-term care. Community services are poorly coordinated and overwhelmed by the demand.

Without adequate help in the community, patients return to the emergency room at an alarming rate, lost in the depths of their disease. Many cycle back dozens, even hundreds, of times.

At the center of the system is a public psychiatric hospital that has been cited by federal authorities eight times since 2006 for endangering patient safety.

Consultant reports on how to fix the system stack up and task forces grind on, with members spending dozens of hours discussing ways to combat the stigma of mental illness, the importance of treatment providers being culturally sensitive and the value of peer support.

Debbie has more urgent issues: Her son is delusional, suicidal and homeless. He carries a knife, cuts his arms to feel relief and burns himself with cigarettes.

Mental health administrators and county politicians have been promising reforms since Rob threw that chair over the balcony in his nursery school classroom.

After more than two decades, they haven't constructed a safety net strong enough to catch him, or hundreds of others like him.

Safe for the moment

Frantic when Rob was not on the train, Debbie called his Milwaukee case manager, Steve Seidl.

Two hours later, they had their answer.

Rob was at the Shasta Mental Health Center in Redding, Calif., 255 miles north of San Jose.

The nurse told her that Rob wasn't talking when he first arrived, and they had no idea who he was or where he was going until they found his driver's license in the lanyard he wore around his neck.

He was confused about what happened but said he was kicked off the train at 2 a.m. "in the middle of nowhere."

When Debbie spoke to Rob on the phone, he said he had been awake for five days, though only two days had passed. He thought he had been in a motel somewhere, but couldn't remember.

The nurse told Debbie that Rob might remember more once he was stabilized. They were going to try a new medication, an anti-psychotic called Invega Sustenna.

The medication is given by injection once a month so they wouldn't have to worry about him skipping a dose. But it can have some dangerous side effects — hives, difficulty breathing, uneven heartbeat, numbness, weakness, fever and chills. They would need to keep him in the hospital for a few days to see how he would tolerate it.

Rob was being treated as a voluntary patient. If he decided to leave, the doctor could sign a petition asking a judge to order treatment.

The plan was to get Rob well, the nurse told Debbie. So he can come home.

Rob was in a psychiatric hospital, but at least he was safe.

That night, Debbie had her first good night's sleep in a week.

Dazed and wandering

The relief was only temporary. Debbie got a call the next day from a woman named Ada at the hospital in Shasta.

They were thinking about discharging Rob.

You can't do that, Debbie said. It's too soon.

When Debbie called a few hours later to talk to Rob, a nurse named Adrian told her it was too late. They had already released him.

Rob had urged them not to call her, apparently worried that she would beg them to keep him hospitalized. When Debbie demanded to speak to the nurse in charge, she was told they weren't authorized to discuss Rob's case. Rob had not given them permission to speak to her. Debbie couldn't even find out if they had given him the injection.

"They gave him snacks and took him to the Amtrak station," Debbie said.

The train was scheduled to leave in 12 hours, at 3:06 a.m.

Arrival in Milwaukee was scheduled for 2:07 p.m., on Sunday, Mother's Day.

Debbie's phone rang at 12:30 a.m. that morning.

This time it was a nurse from the emergency room at the University of California-Davis Medical Center. She said Rob had been brought in by ambulance. Police had found him wandering dazed around downtown Sacramento. He had gotten on the wrong train.

The police had filed an emergency detention order that would allow them to hold Rob for 72 hours. Doctors gave him Risperdal, an antipsychotic medication.

Debbie booked a flight back to San Francisco. She would leave that Saturday.

"Whatever you do," Debbie told the nurse, "don't put him back on that train."

'Here to pick up Rob'

When the plane landed, she went back to the same car rental counter where she and Rob had stood 3½ weeks earlier, full of hope, and rented another white Jeep.

Debbie noticed the rosebushes along the highway, so lush on her first trip, were beginning to wilt.

She drove right past the sign for Sierra Vista Hospital, pulled into a nearby shopping mall and got out. She walked around the parking lot, once, twice, again. She took deep breaths, tried to focus, then headed to the hospital.

"We're here to pick up Rob Sweeney and take him home," Debbie said into the metal box on the side of the door.

First a buzz, then a click.

Debbie had been inside many psychiatric hospitals visiting Rob over the past six years. This one seemed especially chaotic.

A slight woman with messy hair and a black eye who looked to be in her 40s shuffled down the hallway in her nightgown muttering to herself and crying. A second woman, younger, with neatly styled blond hair, stood at the nurse's desk demanding help translating a description of the hospital into Spanish.

"I must have this in Spanish," she said in precise English. "These are my rights. I demand my rights."

As Rob stood waiting for the nurse to retrieve his shoelaces and driver's license, a third woman, no older than 20, was pulling on his sleeve.

"You like the Goo Goo Dolls, Rob?" she asked. "Do you?"

Their voices echoed in the darkened hallway.

"Let's get you out of here, Rob," Debbie said.

Rob grabbed the plastic bag from the clerk and headed for the door.

"Freedom!" he shouted as he burst into the afternoon sun. "It feels like I've been in that place for five weeks."

Five minutes on the road, Rob asked: "Mom, can I live with you for a few weeks until I get settled?"

Debbie shook her head.

"Please."

"It's not even open for discussion."

He sat in silence for the next two hours.

When they arrived at the group home to pick up his stuff, Rob would not get out of the car.

Rob's suitcase was waiting near the door.

"He was fine the first day," the landlady told Debbie. "But he just wouldn't take his medicine after that."

Rob didn't say a word on the 90-minute drive to Redwood City. He stared out the window.

Debbie went to check in, and when she came back to the car to get the suitcases, she found Rob curled up on the curb, sweatshirt hood pulled over his face, head between his knees.

He was crying.

Rob said he didn't know what he did or how he had gotten kicked off the train. He was sorry for all the trouble he caused her.

"Is there a heaven, Mom?" he asked, staring at her with his brown eyes the way he did when he was a little boy.

"I hope so, Rob."

Rob knotted his fists. His knees were shaking.

"Will I get to go there?"

Back in Milwaukee

It was 4 a.m. Monday when Debbie and Rob set out for the airport. Her nerves were shot.

Rob had refused to take Ativan, the sedative the doctor gave him in Sacramento. He was up all night pacing around the motel. The Redwood City police knocked on their door just before midnight after some guests down the hall saw him stalking outside their window.

Debbie had not slept more than 10 minutes all night, worrying what to do if Rob refused to get on the airplane, if he had a panic attack once they were airborne.

She missed the exit for the airport, then left her purse in the rental car. Rob laughed as Debbie scurried down the escalator, hoping they would not miss the flight. Before they got on the plane, Debbie pulled out Rob's bottle of Ativan and popped one in her mouth.

They had less than 30 minutes during a layover in Denver, but Rob managed to find a bar and guzzle two beers that he bought with the $20 Debbie gave him for food. As they made their way down the jetway, Rob punched Debbie in the arm and tried to grab her purse. He wanted her phone and more money.

Debbie shook him off. They boarded, Debbie sitting a few rows ahead of Rob.

When they finally landed in Milwaukee a little after 1 p.m., she was pale and her hair was a mess. She didn't know which baggage claim area to go to. Her face was pinched.

She pulled out her phone to call Seidl to find out where to take Rob.

No answer.

She called again.

No answer.

She found the luggage claim area and sat on a bench next to a man with a gray ponytail who had been seated near her on the plane.

"Ma'am is everything OK? I noticed that young man over there was being very rude to you."

"That's my son," Debbie said softly. "He is mentally ill."

The man nodded. "I understand."

Rob paced back and forth.

"Life is hard sometimes," the man said.

"Yes it is, sir. Yes, it is."

Home remains a dream

Debbie only got as far as a Citgo Station at S. 60th St. and W. National Ave.

Rob grabbed her phone and jumped out of the car. She didn't have any energy to chase him. She drove home.

Rob was back on her doorstep at 6:30 the next morning, ringing the bell again and again.

He said he had been kicked out of the Rescue Mission and had roamed the streets all night.

In mid-June, Debbie went on disability from her job. Her arms and legs ached. She could barely get out of bed.

"I was becoming very forgetful and crying all the time," she said.

She lies on the couch for hours, getting up when one of her three dogs needs to go out or to water the rosebushes in the backyard.

"I thought this would give me some peace, to know that I tried," she said. "But it's not enough. I actually think I made Rob's life worse."

Rob continues to sleep in motels near the airport with money from his federal disability check or, when that runs out, what Debbie will provide. Sometimes he ends up in his mother's garage. Debbie has spotted him a few times walking along the highway.

Debbie has a new idea. It's the only thing she can think to keep her son from harm. If no one else will take him in, she could build a place for him.

She described it like this in an email:

Perhaps an extra concrete room attached to the house (but interior doors locked so he can't get into our main home while we're away). Due to his smoking, it would just be a concrete floor, although the rules would be no smoking in his "room."

We'd also need heavy duty insulated walls for minimal noise. I'd have some sort of back door attached to this room so he could go in and out for his pacing in the backyard and for smoking.

He would have minimal furniture (bed, dresser, chair, and TV). He'd have his own refrigerator, microwave and bathroom (for his constant showers). Then I'd have to fence in the entire backyard so he would be safely enclosed and have his privacy to walk around whenever he wanted to.

In late June, Seidl found Rob a temporary spot at the Jabez Residential Treatment Center, a rehab facility for alcoholics and drug addicts on the city's north side. The place was named in a 2010 federal criminal complaint as the hub of a drug operation perpetrated by the owner's family.

It is scheduled to close at the end of July.

Last Voyage of the Bounty

Tampa Bay Times

October 27, 30 and November 3, 2013

By Michael Kruse

DAY 1: SAFER AT SEA

In the dark, in the wet, whirling roar of Hurricane Sandy, on a ship tipping so badly the deck felt like a steep, slick roof, the desperate, damaged sailor searched for a spot from which to jump. Close to the stern, he gripped the helm, now all but touching the water's high black churn. He let go and paddled and kicked in the buoyant but clumsy blood-orange suit he had wiggled into not long before. The ship spat up a heavy wooden grating, and it landed on his head. *Crack.* His adrenaline surged. He thrashed, straining to get away from the heaving ship, her three masts of tree trunk heft rearing up and slamming down like lethal mallets, her thinner, sharper spars piercing the surface like darts, the ropes of the rigging like tentacles, grabbing, yanking. *Pfffffft.* The tip of a spar sliced down, catching the sailor, pushing him below. He gasped, choking on water, struggling back to where there was air.

His focus narrowed.

Next breath.

Breathe.

He kept swimming away, and finally Adam Prokosch was clear of the ship, away from his home of the last eight months, away from his 15 fellow crew members who felt like family, no longer together, now all alone, in the middle of the deafening noise, the needles of rain, the frothing, cresting waves.

He couldn't see the captain who had decided to sail toward the storm. He couldn't see the first mate get bashed by a spar. He couldn't see his good friend get tangled and wrenched so far under he started saying sorry to his mother. He couldn't hear the voice of the woman shrieking she was stuck.

Up in the sky, 500 feet high and 90 miles from shore, under the menace of the thick swirl of clouds in the early morning of Oct. 29, 2012, the men in a Coast Guard C-130 airplane made radio calls, repeating the name of the ship, hoping her crew could hear.

... Bounty ...

... Bounty ...

... Bounty ...

***

More than a month before, down one of the winding roads of hilly Boothbay Harbor, Maine, the masts of the 169-foot replica of one of the most famous ships in the world stretched toward the sun. Winched out of the water, wedged into a dry-dock railway, the *Bounty's* bottom was exposed, her wooden hull ready for routine repairs.

She was one of the last of her kind. It was amazing she was still around. And she was sailing more than she had since the earliest stages of her 52 years of life.

The main reason was one man, St. Petersburg resident Robin Walbridge, who had been the captain for 17 years.

For most of his early adulthood, Walbridge had been curious and itinerant, flitting from job to job, but gradually gravitating from land to sea — truck driver, marina mechanic, operator of paddle boats, master of smaller, wooden schooners around Florida. His whole life, even as a boy in Vermont, he read and re-read John Masefield's poem *Sea Fever — I must go down to the seas again, to the lonely sea and the sky, and all I ask is a tall ship and a star to steer her by* — and in the *Bounty* he had found his ship.

He had, he thought, the best possible job. Officially, the owner of the *Bounty* was Robert Hansen, the head of an air conditioning company on Long Island, but really the ship belonged to Walbridge, who had been with her longer than Hansen, and longer than anybody on board. With that longevity came credibility, and confidence—confidence others had in him, and that he had in himself. Typically dressed in jeans, Teva sandals and a green baggy *Bounty* hoodie, and with a bald spot ringed with wispy hair he kept in a stubby ponytail, glasses with strings on the stems and hearing aids on which he sometimes turned down the volume, Walbridge spoke softly and sparingly.

"I truly believe …," he often said.

He truly believed wooden, square-rigged ships had changed the world, the tractor-trailers and space shuttles of their time.

He truly believed that sailing this kind of ship, not just getting on a boat and flipping a switch, was a dying art that needed to be preserved.

He truly believed that a ship like the *Bounty* was a uniquely fertile learning environment and that the sailing was but a portion of the education.

"It's one thing to stand on shore and look at the mast and the sails," Walbridge once said. "It's quite another thing to be 115 feet in the air in a violent storm and you're dependent on other crew members and other crew members are dependent on you."

"What you are learning," he liked to say, "is how to live with yourself."

Walbridge, 63, had started talking about retirement. He was introducing his possible successor. You'd be crazy to take the job, he would tell the first mate, and you'd be crazy not to. He wanted to see more of his wife of a decade and a half, Claudia McCann, who spent months by herself in their bungalow in St. Pete. He called her every day he had a cell phone signal. He hid notes at home, saying he missed her, loved her.

But it was his devotion to the *Bounty* that friends and colleagues considered "extreme." They thought of the captain and the ship as almost one and the same, inseparable, him and her, their identities inextricably linked.

And there was so much Walbridge wanted to do still. He wanted to take the *Bounty* up the Arkansas and down the Mississippi. He wanted to guide her through the Northwest Passage, the treacherous Arctic route, because he wanted to do with her what was supposed to be impossible.

It would be, he thought, a great way to cap his career as the captain of the *Bounty*, a fitting last chapter.

***

Walbridge had been at the shipyard in Boothbay Harbor before. The first time, in the summer of 2001, the *Bounty* showed up in deplorable condition, not dead but close, taking in through leaky seams 30,000 gallons of water an hour. Hansen, the owner, who had just purchased her, paid $1.5 million to replace every plank of wood below the waterline. The next time, to replace every plank above it, cost even more. These latest repairs, Walbridge said, were just "a shave and a haircut."

Time spent in yard was different from time spent at sea. Often crews thinned out because summer was over and winter was on the way and because the work felt more like drudgery when it wasn't broken up by the fresh sights of travel.

For Walbridge, though, it was nonetheless a chance to teach. A middle child, the only son of two teachers, his style of instruction reflected the way he liked to learn. During high school in Montpelier, Vt., he focused more on his job at the local Howard Johnson, working to learn how to do everything — how to open and how to close, how to order food and how to cook it, how to clean the equipment and how to keep the books. He took a couple of classes at a community college in Connecticut, algebra and art, and decided that was sufficient. He taught himself how to build furniture, kayaks, jewelry boxes for his wife, his wife's daughter, her daughter. He was a devotee of antique tools, antique trades and the increasingly antique practice of apprenticeship, a more organic and intimate exchange of knowledge, he thought, than contemporary methods stamped with certificates. Where else but a ship like this could he use all these disparate interests, hobbies and skills?

Reprimands started with questions. "Now, Lee, why did you think that was a good idea?" He didn't give lectures. He told stories.

He knew where the best used book stores were in all the ports, immersing himself in tales from the golden age of sail, when ships like the original HMS *Bounty* ventured into the unknown, with no idea how long they'd be gone, or if they'd return.

His only requirement for crew members was that they wanted to be there. Those with more experience taught those with less until they, too, became those with more. He encouraged deckhands to become able seamen, able seamen to become mates and mates to become captains.

He asked them to do things they hadn't done.

He asked them to be things they hadn't been.

They were loyal because of it.

So in Boothbay Harbor during this yard period, he asked them to scrape algae and barnacles off the hull, to make some new spars called yards, to caulk the leakiest seams between planks, and they did. They installed new fuel and water tanks. They did touch-up painting. They worked 12 hours a day, six days a week.

They also found patches of rotted wood above the waterline—in the planks, in essence the ship's skin, and in the frames, her ribs. They found the rot spots, ranging from golf ball-size to softball-size, on both sides of the ship. It was confounding, thought Todd Kosakowski, the shipyard's project manager, because this had been new wood only five years before. Such rapid deterioration was abnormal, and alarming, he thought, because of how it looked—dried out, brittle, "almost charred-looking."

Kosakowski estimated 75 percent of the frames above the waterline could have rot. That would undermine the ship's dependability. But there was no way to know without removing more planks. He recommended Walbridge extend the *Bounty*'s stay. Walbridge agreed with Kosakowski, but staying, he said, would mean more of two things the *Bounty* didn't have: money and time. The chill of winter was in the air. The *Bounty* needed to be in New London, Conn., Oct. 24 and 25, for a day sail with the crew of a Navy submarine. The ship was due in St. Pete for tours Nov. 10 and 11 at the Pier in the city where the *Bounty* had significant history, where the captain lived and his wife was waiting.

Stay or go?

Walbridge made the decision he almost always did.

He had the crew pull out the visible pieces of rot and replace them with healthier wood. He had them paint over the planks with oil-based primer even though yard workers said that would do next to nothing. He told Kosakowski they'd do a thorough inspection next year. Kosakowski couldn't make them stay. He advised Walbridge, however, to pick his weather wisely. Before they left he took pictures of the rot. He also kept a few chunks of the strange, blighted wood, putting them in a box he slid under his desk.

And as the *Bounty* traveled south from Boothbay Harbor to New London, Prokosch and other crew noticed something else that was worrisome: In the engine room, the bilge pumps didn't seem to be working as well as they usually did. All wooden boats leak. Water works its way through the tiniest slits. That's what pumps are for, and the *Bounty* had five: two electric pumps, two backup hydraulic pumps that still needed power to run and a portable gas pump. Prokosch had worked on almost a dozen ships. "Sailors don't wear gloves," the 27-year-old with a sturdy build once said. "We grow them." An able seaman and an aspiring captain —he already had a captain's license for smaller boats—he had joined this crew in March. Now his experience told him something wasn't right.

He mentioned it to the second mate. He told the captain. They were looking into it.

***

She was built in 1960 in the coastal village of Lunenburg, Nova Scotia, to be in MGM's 1962 version of *Mutiny on the Bounty*, starring Trevor Howard as Capt. William Bligh and Marlon Brando as lead mutineer Fletcher Christian. She was built because of a story, a true tale of adventure and human nature. This *Bounty*, though, had a story of her own. She was a third bigger than the original, but faithfully rendered, using the British Navy's original plans. She was not a prop. The craftsmen gave her modern amenities: diesel engines, running water, even air conditioning. They built spacious 8-foot ceilings on the tween deck — the middle of the three levels — to leave room for bulky cameras, assuring the ship would straddle the line between authenticity and practicality.

Once eased into the water down rails greased with cow fat and fish oil, the first thing she did was sail 7,327 miles to Tahiti in the South Pacific. She looked like a copperplate etched from an earlier epoch, *National Geographic* wrote, her 60-foot bowsprit leading the way, the windows of her signature stern cabin glowing in the dark.

After a publicity tour on both sides of the Atlantic, she settled in the late '60s into a mostly sedentary life in St. Pete's Vinoy Basin, subsisting as a "marine-historical attraction," a tourist site with a gift shop. The ship was a downtown draw at a time when there weren't that many. People in the city came to think of the *Bounty* as their own.

Media tycoon Ted Turner bought her by accident in 1986 when he acquired the MGM film library.

Seven years later, he gave her for a tax break to Fall River, Mass., where a group of enthusiastic businessmen wanted her to sail from port to port with the name Fall River painted on her stern, an attempt to alter the image of their small, run-down city. They hired Walbridge, a mate on the *Rose*, a similar ship. Expenses, though, proved too much for local coffers. By 1999 she was sinking at her dock.

That's when Hansen bought her.

He had her hole-riddled hull swaddled in a diaper of sorts, and she was towed by a tug to Boothbay Harbor, starting the high-priced repairs. Hansen was like Walbridge. He wanted her to sail.

With Hansen's millions in improvements, the *Bounty* visited American and Canadian ports, still spending some winters in St. Pete. The *Bounty* got better, and so did her crews.

And everywhere she went, no matter which other ships were present, she was the star. After her initial '62 title role, she played herself, or some facsimile, in movies from *Yellowbeard* to *Treasure Island* to *Pirates of the Caribbean* sequels. Older people wanted to touch the helm Brando touched. Younger people wanted to do it because of Johnny Depp. The wind ship of antiquity had the modern credibility of celebrity.

The Coast Guard, though, called the *Bounty* something else. At a dock, she was a "moored attraction vessel." On the water? She was essentially a private yacht. The classification meant minor oversight. It meant she couldn't charge for sailing tutorials or take paying passengers. To make money she had to go, go, go, in search of new batches of gawkers at 10 bucks a head. The artifice paid for the art.

The eclectic collection of people who chose to go with the *Bounty* included commercial mariners who saw value in learning traditional seamanship, retirees who sought something greater than golf or gated ennui, twentysomething adventurers for whom a cubicle equated to something close to death, or slightly older meanderers hoping for what the author of the 1840 book *Two Years Before the Mast* termed a change of life.

They had one thing in common: They sought something on this ship that they hadn't found on shore.

They lived for the holy moments of leaving a port under sail, engines off, nothing but wind and water carrying them, one knot, two knots, three knots, all but soundlessly back to where they felt they belonged. They navigated through the Erie Canal, the Cape Cod Canal, the Panama Canal. They traveled through the Chesapeake Bay and Long Island Sound and up the Hudson River and down the St. Lawrence. They went to the Canary Islands and the Galapagos. They saw dolphins frolic. They saw plankton-gorging basking sharks and right whales and pilot whales and minke whales. Here, whaley, whaley, whaley, Walbridge would say, trying to take their picture. They hung hooks and pulled up mahi-mahi for the freshest-ever sushi. In squalls, they clambered up the rigging to furl sails, knowing by instinct where to put their hands and feet. In the dark, they watched the water around the ship radiate with bioluminescence, sparkling streaks of yellow, green and blue.

Through the night, crew members woke up their counterparts for the next watch, not with alarm clocks' blare but with whispers about stars and which sails were set. The coffee in the pot sloshed the way the ship sat.

They stood watch, four hours twice in every 24-hour cycle. They watched the way wind filled sails. They watched the water level in the bilge at the bottom of the boat. They watched for what was ahead. They watched after each other. Divorced from land's more distracted existence, these watches ordered their days, fostering a marriage of surroundings and self.

Sometimes they stopped smack in the middle of the Atlantic and jumped in. Because who gets to do that?

On longer transits, out in the open ocean, Walbridge liked to tape over the screens of the ship's 21st-century positional aids and announce with a wink that they had experienced "major electronic failure." Then they used old-fashioned sextants for celestial navigation, determining the angle between the sun and the horizon, doing math to calculate their latitude and longitude.

They learned from the *Bounty*, and her captain, the self-affirming ability to determine where they were, their place in space, their moment in time.

***

They arrived in New London the evening of Oct. 23. The next afternoon, a bunch of them ended up at Hanafin's, a pub blocks from the dock. From behind the bar, nearing the end of her shift, 26-year-old Amanda Sherer found the crew's camaraderie so intoxicating that when she got off she joined them. They drank beer and bourbon and shots from the owner's private bottle of Green Spot whiskey. So boisterous and spontaneous, Sherer thought — but one of them stuck out.

Claudene Christian.

She was different from the start, since she got on in Wilmington, N.C., in the middle of May, when her parents dropped her off. She was a 5-foot-1 41-year-old with blond hair, blue eyes, pressed-on, white-tipped nails and pink luggage, marching up the gangplank into a setting more accustomed to dreadlocks and duffel bags.

She came on strong, all ardor and words—according to Prokosch, "a faceful of Claudene."

It felt like she wanted to say everything to everybody. She had the confidence of an only child of doting parents, who from the time she was little said she could do whatever she wanted. She used to be Miss Alaska National Teenager! She used to be a Song Girl cheerleader at the University of Southern California! She used to own a doll company! She used to own a house near the beach!

And she was the great-great-great-great-great-granddaughter of the mutineer! Of Fletcher Christian!

True? Who knew? But everybody could see it was true to her.

I live, work & Travel the Sea aboard the HMS Tall Ship Bounty, she announced on Facebook. *I'm sure my ancestor would be proud.*

Before boarding, she sang in bands, played video games on a vintage Atari and roller skated on the hardwood floors in her house in California. She drank, mostly wine, sometimes too much. She dated a lot. She was a nocturnal journal keeper. She was diagnosed as bipolar but sometimes she didn't take her medication because she didn't like the way it made her feel. She lost her house. She moved in with her parents in Alaska. She moved with them when they moved to rural Oklahoma, where she volunteered at the sheriff's office, cheerfully filing papers and sending faxes. She was a sister to her mother and a mother to her father, who had diabetes. She started writing them a song about how much she loved them but didn't finish it. She felt landlocked. She had her parents take her to the *Bounty*.

Tell me anything! she told her fellow female deckhands, most of them half her age. Think of me as your hip mom!

They didn't expect her to last. Christian was a volunteer, not even making the regular deckhands' paltry weekly rate of $100. She could've gotten off wherever, whenever.

Tarring the shrouds left black gunk in her blond hair. The fake nails peeled away. She sent her mother pictures.

I am on a TALL SHIP AT SEA, she tweeted on June 6.

I am in LOVE with my ship, she tweeted on June 23.

She texted a friend in California: *It is seriously SOO much work, I've done a lot of questioning what I'm doing ... But the one thing I do know for sure, is that ... my head, my heart, my body and soul are aligned ... And I've really found peace ...*

She loved how beautiful the sky was at night, surrounded by so much sea, under the moon and the stars and no other light.

In Nova Scotia, she helped organize a private tour for some of the *Bounty's* builders and earliest sailors, her eyes glistening with tears because of how much it meant to them.

By the time the *Bounty* arrived in Boothbay Harbor, her parents told her they would come pick her up — they were always willing to come pick her up — and she almost let them. Her grandmother was ill. But Christian said no. She still had her blow dryer, an appliance that earned eye rolls, but now she used it to warm her clothes in the nippy Maine mornings. Working in Boothbay Harbor, she had bounced from one menial task to the next, striking Kosakowski, the project manager, as the happiest deckhand he had ever seen. She told a fellow crew member who had started the season as a volunteer, too, that she was proud of them for sticking it out.

I want to see this through, she said.

She told some other crew she didn't know how she would handle it if she got off. Would she be okay?

Some fuzzy notion of the romance of the sea might get you on a ship. Something else keeps you there. And just before they left Boothbay Harbor, after months of fiddling with her phone when checks were distributed, she had been told she'd be paid. She beamed. The money didn't matter as much as the validation. *Good news*, she wrote in a text message to her mother. Oct. 18 was her birthday, 42 now, and Christian was moving in a direction she liked.

In New London at Hanafin's, the night before they were slated to leave, she clicked with the bartender and so did the crew. They asked her to join them. She would fit in, they said, and that meant a lot to her. Born here, raised here, lived here — Sherer looked at the crew of the *Bounty* and saw "freedom." She said she'd think about it and see them the next day. That night, though, Christian and Sherer drank at the bar and stepped outside in the unseasonable warmth to stand on the sidewalk and smoke American Spirits. They sang *Me & Bobby McGee*, belting out that *freedom's just another word for nothin' left to lose.*

***

The next afternoon, toward the end of the day sail with the crew from the Navy sub, some civilian passengers asked Walbridge about the storm developing in the Caribbean. Sandy, expected to cause catastrophic damage along the East Coast, was a hurricane now. They knew the captain was leaving that evening, headed in that direction.

Walbridge held up his hands to explain his strategy. Depending on where the storm went, he said, its strong winds could help propel the *Bounty* to Florida. That, he believed, was better than waiting, tied to a dock, where the ship might get damaged. He didn't sound cocky. He sounded, they thought, like he knew what he was talking about.

And who were they to say any different?

He was the captain.

A little later, his wife called from her hotel in Rome, where she was finishing a vacation in Italy. It was Oct. 25. She wished him happy birthday. She could tell he was excited about the day sail and a visit to the sub — she could hear the joy in his voice — but she mentioned the threat of the storm. If it got too bad, he told her, he could turn and head north.

On the dock, away from the others, the first mate wanted to talk to the captain. John Svendsen was concerned. This, he said, was a potentially historic hurricane. Svendsen, serious but easy-going, and nonconfrontational — not unlike Walbridge — suggested some options.

Up the Thames River. Nearby ports that offered more protection. Or they could stay.

Walbridge said no. Waves weren't supposed to be higher than 30 feet, he explained, and he and the *Bounty* had seen that. Ships, he said, are safer at sea.

Svendsen relented. At least, he said, the crew should know the situation. Walbridge agreed.

The captain gathered them around the capstan, a large, spool-shaped gearbox by the helm, their meeting spot near the stern.

I know many of you are hearing from your families about the weather out there, Walbridge said.

He outlined his experience with rough weather. He said he used to go out in the Gulf of Mexico to pull crews off oil rigs before and even during hurricanes, and he had been in hurricanes on the *Bounty*, too. He often played chess against crew members, three or four at a time, almost always beating them all — and he was approaching this, he told them, like another game, success a question of making the right moves at the right times. His plan, he said, was to head south and east until Sandy either targeted land or veered to sea. They would go the opposite way, keeping sufficient distance from the storm. He reiterated what he had told the day sail civilians and Svendsen: Ships are safer at sea.

Usually, at capstan meetings, Walbridge told a story or two and asked questions — What would you do if? — but now there was no time for that.

We need to leave immediately, he said.

He added something none of the crew could remember him ever saying. He gave them the opportunity to get off. I won't hold it against you, he promised.

The New London train station was visible from where they stood. Amtrak to anywhere.

The crew looked at each other.

The second mate, Maine Maritime Academy graduate Matt Sanders, had started dating Christian. The third mate, Dan Cleveland, was dating the boatswain, Laura Groves. Deckhands Jessica Hewitt and Drew Salapatek also were dating. The engineer, Chris Barksdale, had been on the ship for only a month, and the cook, Jessica Black, had gotten on just that day. She'd been working on yachts in the Caribbean. The *Bounty* sounded "more interesting." Able seaman Doug Faunt, the oldest member of the crew, wondered if he had enough time to gather his belongings even if he did want to get off. Mark Warner, Anna Sprague, Josh Scornavacchi, John Daniel Jones, and Christian, too — all first-season deckhands, the crew with the least experience—looked at the crew with more. This was sure to be an uncomfortable voyage, miserable and wet, but was there reason for greater alarm?

Prokosch had gotten on the *Bounty* specifically to learn from the captain. Walbridge's 17 years of experience — for Prokosch, that was a powerful pull. He was confident, too, they were ready to solve any problem that might come up. He also was interested in decisions. How they're made. Why they work or why they don't. He wanted to see how this one turned out.

Svendsen said nothing. Rigid hierarchy has eased drastically since earlier eras of sailing, when the captain was king, but chain of command still matters. The ship's potential next captain chose to respect it.

Walbridge seldom seemed concerned. He didn't seem that way now.

The crew felt like family — some of them considered the bonds closer than that — and they didn't want to let each other down. They trusted each other. They trusted Svendsen. They trusted Walbridge.

The choice they were being asked to make was one they had already made. Sailors who make a habit of walking off ships aren't sailors for long. These sailors preferred the uncertainty at sea to the uncertainty on land.

Nobody got off.

The meeting had taken roughly 20 minutes. It was just before dusk. The crew secured the gangplanks and turned on both engines close to full power. They left in a hurry.

Standing at the bottom of State Street, holding a cup of coffee, was Sherer, the bartender from Hanafin's. The previous evening had been magic, but now something felt off. The sun started to set, and she watched the *Bounty* disappear.

***

The ship maneuvered around the tip of Long Island, using engines and sails and heading fast, more than seven knots instead of the standard five, on a south-southeast course. The crew of 16 was a tad short-handed, and tired, Faunt thought, from Boothbay Harbor plus the day sail. The air was calm and getting cooler. Chili simmered on the galley stove.

A deckhand texted the *Bounty's* plan to Jim Salapatek, Drew Salapatek's father, who from his home near Chicago posted updates on the *Bounty's* Facebook page.

Bounty has departed New London CT ... Next Port of Call ... St. Petersburg, Florida, the update read. *Bounty will be sailing due East out to sea before heading south to avoid the brunt of Hurricane Sandy.*

Hewitt called some people to say bye. They said they would pray for her. She thought that was a bit much.

Christian called her mother. She had just gotten out of a doctor's appointment with Christian's grandmother.

Can I call you back? her mother said.

No, no, Christian said. I want to tell you how much I love you.

Why are you saying it like that?

Just in case something happens. We're already on the water. I'm afraid I'll lose service.

On the phone, she sounded agitated, her mother thought, but she sent her a series of text messages.

Really we're not too worried about the hurricane, Christian wrote. *The Capt loves hurricanes and we're going to make sure to go outside on the East side.*

I love you mom & dad, don't worry, we'll be fine! she added.

Our capt has 30 yes experience and our ship is strong. They say Bounty loves hurricanes.

Christian's mother wrote back: *We love you sooo much!!!! Please be careful!!!*

Christian responded: *And just be sure that I am ok and HAPPY TO BE HERE on Bounty doing what I love ... And if I do go down with the ship & the worst happens ... Just know that I AM TRULY GENUINELY HAPPY!! And I am doing what I love! I love you.*

She updated her Facebook: *HEADED STRAIGHT THROUGH THE PATH OF HURRICANE SANDY!!*

As they continued south — much more south than east — they lashed down what might move in rougher weather. They used extra lengths of rope to secure sea-stowed sails. One deckhand even reinforced the jar that housed his fighting fish. Prokosch loved the energy of the crew. They were buzzing. Some were excited by the prospect of sailing into a hurricane. They had enjoyed pleasant weather all year, and the storm would be a chance to test their training. Prokosch viewing this almost like a big game against a tough opponent. In good weather, he thought, ships and sailors could get lax — not in bad weather.

On both sides of the ship they ran jacklines, on the top deck and also in the tween deck, or the tweens, making something for crew members to hold onto. Losing somebody overboard, Walbridge often told them, was his biggest worry. It was why they did man-overboard drills more than they did abandon-ship drills.

Christian had a question for Prokosch.

What do you mean by storm-tight?

Prokosch tugged on rope. No slack. Storm-tight, he said.

As a girl, Christian twirled her hair in the dark to soothe her nerves, and as an adult, living with roommates, she often climbed into bed with a girlfriend when a boyfriend wasn't spending the night. Even on the *Bounty*, she strung lights around her bunk, so her space was never pitch-black.

And yet over the course of the summer she had taken to an onerous task called flaking the chain. It required her to squeeze into a dark compartment at the front of the ship to organize the anchor chain as they pulled it back in. She would emerge wet with mud, seaweed and sweat, her face streaked with makeup, her blond hair a frizzy mess. She did it so much some of the crew asked her why. She wasn't the most experienced sailor, but she could be a good shipmate, she said. She could help the cook. She could flake the chain.

Now she bounced around the ship, checking on what she stowed. She called to Prokosch.

Storm-tight! Storm-tight!

Is it hurricane-ready? Prokosch hollered.

Hurricane-ready! Christian yelled back.

Late that night, though, she checked the report from the *Bounty's* weather fax and looked at the picture of Sandy, the storm's building bands now covering most of the Atlantic. She showed it to Hewitt. This thing's huge, Hewitt said. One of the key parts of the captain's plan — watch where the storm went, go where it didn't — seemed impossible. The storm was going to be practically everywhere.

Where they were, south of Long Island about 100 miles off shore, Walbridge wrote Friday morning in an email to his wife, *one would never know there was a raging storm out there. It is a beautiful morning. Sun shining. Not a cloud in the sky.*

The storm, meanwhile, had grown to almost 2,000 miles wide and moved north at about 10 miles an hour. The ship moved south at about the same pace.

Near Chicago, Jim Salapatek tracked the paths on his computer. *This will be a tough voyage,* he posted.

On Facebook, and on related message boards, people wondered what the captain was doing out there.

Sandy looks like a mean one, Walbridge wrote in an email to Hansen, the owner, and Tracie Simonin, his assistant. *Right now we are on a converging course. I am actually headed to the dangerous side of it. ... We are running trying to stay on the east side of it. Bad side of it until we get some sea room. If we guess wrong we can run towards Newfoundland. If it turns and wants to tangle with us that means it is pretty far off shore and we can turn and go down the west side of it. I need to be sure it is well off shore before we can take advantage of the good weather for us. Right now I do not want to get between a hurricane and a hard spot. If you can send us updated track info (where it is projected to go) that would be great. We know where it is, I have to guess (along with the weather man) where it is going.*

Simonin responded that she would send him updates. She asked him to do the same, *so I don't have to worry about you all weekend.*

***

Good morning, Miss Claudia, Walbridge wrote to his wife. Saturday now. Oct. 27.

The *Bounty* was 250 miles east of the Chesapeake Bay. Sandy was no longer a discussion around the capstan or a picture on a printout. The ship entered the storm's ragged edge. Waves climbed to 15 to 20 feet. Winds surged to 40 miles an hour.

I am still waiting to see what the storm wants to do before we try and sneak around it. I do not want to get caught between it and the rocks if it did an unexpected turn to the west. We were able to set squares this morning — the biggest, lowest sails — so we will have a good ride. I think we will pass each other Sunday night or Monday morning.

If all goes well with the storm, he added, before signing off by telling her he loved her, *we should be in St. Pete a day or two early.*

Walbridge, thinking the *Bounty* still had satisfactory space from the storm's center, decided early in the afternoon to change course. Sufficient sea room, or distance from shore — the rocks, as he called it in the email to his wife — is important. Too much, though, can be a problem, especially in hazardous weather. A ship that founders hundreds of miles from land is a ship on her own. Maybe that was part of his thinking. If it was, he didn't tell the crew. So now, instead of mostly south and a little east, the *Bounty* shifted to mostly west and a little south. They were heading toward Hatteras Canyon, off the coast of North Carolina, where the crashing currents of the northbound Gulf Stream create notoriously dangerous conditions even without the water-whipping forces of a hurricane.

The message board second-guessing spiked:

... that they'd choose to take this risk is criminal.

Rogue wave machine right there.

He needs to be removed from his duties if they make it through tonight in one piece. The buoy off of Hatteras is reporting 24-foot seas right now with the center of the storm still south.

I worry that he has young people on there.

Jim Salapatek on Facebook tried to counter: *Rest assured that the Bounty is safe and in very capable hands. Bounty's current voyage is a calculated decision ... NOT AT ALL ... irresponsible or with a lack of foresight as some have suggested. The fact of the matter is ... A SHIP IS SAFER AT SEA THAN IN PORT!*

The crew took down all sails except one, the lowest sail on the mast closest to the front of the ship, the fore course. It's the sail that tends to lift the bow — the most necessary sail to keep a ship stable in a storm.

In the engine room, members of the crew worked the bilge pumps hard. Usually they used one of two electric pumps. Now they were using both. The water level in the bilge wasn't critically high, but it wasn't going down, either. The pumps sucked, then stopped, sucked, then stopped. Walbridge came down to help, an indication to the boatswain that this was getting serious.

Barksdale, the engineer, hadn't been on the *Bounty* long enough to know if this was normal. He found it increasingly difficult, though, to remain in the engine room for longer than 15 minutes. He was seasick, as he had been on the journey from Boothbay Harbor to New London, but now much worse. The ship's lurching and rolling had dislodged one of the generators. Barksdale used a wrench to tighten its bolts. He also checked on the fuel filters for the generators. He had pledged to be vigilant because Simonin in New London had dropped off the wrong ones. They needed 20-micron filters. The filters they had gotten were 2-micron. This meant they might clog quicker.

Barksdale felt nauseated when he finished and went to the top deck to get some air. A big wave made the ship shudder, and Barksdale grabbed for something, jamming his right hand, rendering mostly useless two of his fingers. Still queasy, now injured, the engineer sat on the steps leading down to the ship's navigational cabin, or nav shack.

As evening approached, the equation was becoming clear: Even with both electric pumps working constantly, water was coming in faster than it was going out. It wasn't yet above the sole boards, the surface on which they stood to work, and it was hard to say exactly how high it was because the ship kept pitching back and forth, sending the water sloshing up the walls.

Walbridge asked the crew to start the backup hydraulic pumps. They hadn't used them all year long. It showed. The fittings were corroded.

Good evening Miss Tracie, he wrote in an email to the owner's assistant.

I think we are going to be in this for several days, the weather looks like even after the eye goes by it will linger for a couple days. We are just going to keep trying to go fast and squeeze by the storm and land as fast as we can.

All else is well, the captain concluded.

In the nav shack, Prokosch looked at the automatic indicator system, which shows ships in the area. Usually, there were as many as 15 on the screen, but now it was blank. The *Bounty* was out there alone.

DAY 2: RISING WATER

They could see the seawater seeping through the sides of the ship. Every time the *Bounty* rolled, riding high waves in stiff winds, they could hear leaks between planks. *Sssssss.* More every roll. *Sssssss.* Capt. Robin Walbridge, the *Bounty* and 15 crew members had left New London, Conn., Thursday evening, Oct. 25, 2012, trying to get to St. Petersburg for dockside tours at the city's Pier. It was now early Sunday morning, Oct. 28, and they were headed toward Hatteras Canyon off North Carolina's coast, on track to traverse the Gulf Stream perilously close to Hurricane Sandy. They were running the two main electric pumps and the two backup hydraulic pumps — which hadn't been used all year — but still they were taking in more water than they were getting out.

At the morning meeting of the mates they talked about Walbridge's decision the previous day to change course. They had been going mainly south and somewhat east, trying to go out to sea to put sufficient space between them and the storm. Now they were going southwest in an effort to make it between the worst of the storm and the shore. The aim — the hope — was to harness the powerful counterclockwise winds to shoot to St. Pete. They were crossing Sandy's path, and already were well within the storm's sprawling reach. It made sleep almost impossible. First mate John Svendsen told the crew to try to rest when they weren't on duty for watch. He said they could expect waves of up to 30 feet and winds of 80 mph or higher. It was going to be a long day.

Good morning, Miss Claudia, Walbridge wrote in an email to his wife shortly after 8:30. She had just gotten home to St. Pete from her vacation in Italy. *I am thinking we will have the worst of the storm in the next 24 hours and then we should start to come out of it. Can't wait to see you.*

On the *Bounty*'s Facebook page, Jim Salapatek, the father of deckhand Drew Salapatek, posted an update: *So far so good! Bounty has now positioned herself to pass on the west side of Hurricane Sandy.*

The Facebook post had acknowledged the course change but not its potential pitfalls. At woodenboat.com, on the message board, second-guessers monitored the track of the ship and looked at weather radar. Sandy's west side was a swirl of clouds over land. They were aghast.

Cutting it close, especially if something goes wrong.

Basically no options and no redundancy.

I'm still stupefied.

Other than the occasional tanker, made of metal and many times larger, the *Bounty* was the only ship anywhere near the storm.

The ship had been built in 1962 as a larger replica of the HMS *Bounty* to star in MGM's retelling of the infamous mutiny. The original *Bounty* was built in Hull, England, in 1784. Her life was spectacular but short — she left England and never came back. First mate Fletcher Christian took the ship from Capt. William Bligh in 1789, and the mutineers burned her in 1790. The *Bounty* replica had plenty of history of her own — different owners, different captains, different missions. Ups and downs. Her close calls were legion.

On her first voyage, before she even got to the movie set, the engine room caught fire. Within two years, the *Bounty* nearly collided with a steamer in the English Channel, a squall split sails on her way to France, and in the Caribbean she found herself surrounded by six waterspouts, one of which chased her wake, only to veer off at the last instant.

In 1965, on the way from New York, where she had been docked at the World's Fair, to St. Pete, where she would become a tourist stop, an unexpected storm spawned 35-foot waves and sent water cascading over her deck. *Life seemed fuller,* one of the crew members later wrote, *now that we had gone to the edge and made it back.*

Walbridge, too, had gone to the edge.

In 1998, also in October, also on the way to St. Pete, the captain and a crew of 21 ended up not far from Hatteras Canyon, off the coast of North Carolina, water rising in the engine room. The sun was out. The sea was calm. The *Bounty* was sinking.

Walbridge called the Coast Guard for help. Helicopters dropped pumps. Cutters arrived with more. Two nearby Navy vessels showed up. Walbridge chose not to abandon ship, and the *Bounty* got towed to shore. A Coast Guard report concluded the captain had misjudged the severity of the leakage through the hull, but that's not how he saw it.

"This is a wooden ship," Walbridge told a reporter. "There are thousands of places where the planks come together. It's normal for a wooden ship to take on water.

"We basically refused to evacuate because that would have been the wrong thing to do," he added. "The ship was in no danger of sinking."

Twelve years later, on the way from Boothbay Harbor, Maine, to San Juan, Puerto Rico, the *Bounty* and a small crew got a scare when two storms converged on top of them. Sails ripped. A mast broke. So did one of the pumps in the engine room. Three of the newer members of the crew left the ship in Bermuda, too spooked to keep going. In Puerto Rico, finally, the remnants of the frazzled crew celebrated with a spaghetti dinner, over which they gave thanks and recalled an old seafaring saying: Take care of the ship, and the ship will take care of you.

In 2011, on the Baltic Sea, the *Bounty* saw waves higher than 20 feet and winds of 70 mph with gusts stronger than that, and on the way back the water in the bilge splashed uncomfortably high. That had been the crew's standard for high water in the *Bounty*. Until now.

Ssssssss.

"We say there's no such thing as bad weather," Walbridge had said in August to a reporter in Belfast, Maine. "There's just different kinds of weather.

"We chase hurricanes," he crowed, before clarifying: "You don't want to get in front of it. You want to stay behind it. But you can also get a good ride out of a hurricane."

Sandy's center was now 260 miles southeast of Hatteras, N.C., about 200 miles from the *Bounty*. But hurricane-force winds extended up to 175 miles.

Sssssssss.

In the engine room members of the crew looked to their captain. Walbridge had been in charge of the *Bounty* for 17 years. Some of the crew had gotten on specifically to learn from him. A story circulated in the tall ship community that he once fixed a generator with pieces of a microwave. Even those who sometimes questioned his judgment acknowledged his resourcefulness. Richard Bailey, a friend who had hired Walbridge as a mate on the *Rose* before the *Bounty* had hired him as captain, considered him a "mechanical genius." Walbridge, thought third mate Dan Cleveland, who had worked with him for five years, always exuded a quiet confidence, and it transferred, he believed, to the rest of the crew. They never saw him get anxious or flustered. They didn't see it now.

After a while ships develop personalities, not unlike people, say those who come to love them. Ships are fast or slow. They are wet or dry. They are finicky or forgiving or fearless or tough.

Walbridge sometimes used a different word for the *Bounty*.

Lucky.

***

Up for her Sunday morning watch, walking through the tween deck, the ship's middle deck, Claudene Christian approached Doug Faunt. She told him she was concerned. The pumps were pumping and pumping — were they pumping enough? The generators — were they going to hold up? No generators, no power. No power, no pumps. No pumps ...

She felt people were ignoring her when she raised these worries, because she was Claudene, ex-cheerleader, ex-owner of a doll company, 42-year-old, blue-eyed, blond-haired novice sailor.

Faunt, an able seaman and one of the *Bounty's* most seasoned crew, told her people were listening — she just wasn't telling them anything they didn't already know. Everybody, he said, was really busy working on the problems.

Christian, Faunt thought, looked reassured.

Meanwhile, in crew quarters, water dripped down walls, leaving bunks wet.

In the galley, a cereal bowl skidded across the table, and water leaked on appliances' wires. The cook noticed smoke wafting from the top of the stove. The air reeked like burning plastic. Walbridge was behind the cook, and she called to him. The captain calmly walked to the fuse box and flicked a switch. He told her to cover the oven with plastic bags when she wasn't using it.

In the sweltering engine room, Chris Barksdale, the *Bounty's* new engineer — unsteady, seasick and using a hurt right hand because of a fall the previous day — took a second stumble when the ship rolled. He caromed into a steel work table, gashing his left arm and bruising his shin.

Approaching noon the port engine and the port generator shut down. Maybe it was because of a fuel leak. Maybe it was because water had splashed them. Tough to tell. Without power, the *Bounty* would be more like its 18th-century namesake, at one with — and at the mercy of — her surroundings.

Faunt climbed the ladder out of the engine room and walked through the nav shack and up to the deck to get some air.

He saw Christian. She was alone near the rear of the ship. Her fellow crew members thought of her as a fun-seeking extrovert, but those who knew her best considered her cautious, even fretful. In California, she booby trapped her house with chairs, bells and cans. She slept with a gun. In Oklahoma, where she had been living with her parents before she left to board the *Bounty*, she urged her mother to look both ways before driving across railroad tracks. In her first month as part of the crew, the ship used a surge of wind to dash through the Chesapeake Bay, the rail practically in the water, thrilling her more experienced hands. Christian, wary, wore a life jacket. Now, though, Faunt watched her, sitting on the stern grating, sporting a harness which she had clipped into one of the safety lines. She was fastened to this lurching ship. Grinning.

Christian, Faunt thought, was having way too much fun.

***

Matt! 'Course!

Able seaman Adam Prokosch stood at the helm early in the afternoon, steering the ship. He shouted at Matt Sanders, the second mate, over the rain and wind. Sanders couldn't hear.

Prokosch pointed.

Look!

The fore course, the big, square sail set low on the mast closest to the bow — the sail that steadies the ship in storms — had ripped at the middle seam. Gusts whipped loose pieces.

All hands on deck!

Walbridge wanted his most reliable and nimble furlers to clamber up the rigging to corral the parts of the sail. He asked for his "best men." That meant Prokosch and several others.

Not Claudene? deckhand Jessica Hewitt joked to the captain.

No response. Maybe he hadn't heard in the noise of the storm. Maybe his hearing aids weren't working in the wetness.

I'll take that as a no, Hewitt said.

Walbridge spoke up. She has actually done quite well for herself, he said.

The furlers started scaling the rigging. A deckhand grabbed a life ring just in case.

Furling a sail in a storm is dangerous. In the 18th and 19th centuries, in the era of the original *Bounty*, death doing this was so commonplace it typically merited no more than a note in the captain's log. Sailors slid off spars and into the sea and were never seen again. Herman Melville called it *the speechlessly quick chaotic bundling of a man into eternity*. The members of the crew of the 21st-century *Bounty* weren't out here courting death. And they weren't just running from, or postponing, "real life," as some said. There are far easier ways to do that. If they were running from anything, it was the falsity of constant convenience, the illusion of stability. They weren't looking to die. They were looking to live.

More than 50 feet up, the rain pelting their skin and stinging their eyes, the heavy, sodden tatters slapped at their faces and arms. They tied up the pieces and hurried back to the deck.

In the engine room the water approached the sole boards, the floor above the bilge, meaning the bottom of the ship was filled with almost 4 feet of water. The strong wind slowed them down. Faunt worked to get the port generator started again. The bilge alarm wailed throughout the tween deck. Walbridge asked Faunt to disable it. The alarm was there to let the crew know water was too high. The crew knew. The ship's sides hissed. *Sssssss. Sssssss.* Shortly after 3, the starboard generator surged, power fluctuating around the ship, flickering on and off. Then off.

Almost an hour later, with Walbridge now in the stern cabin, a wave jerked the ship. The captain lost his footing, flying across the room, his lower back crumpling against the side of a bolted-down table. Hewitt, using a towel as a pillow on the cabin's floor due to her soaked bunk, woke to the thud.

Barksdale, startled by the force of the blow, helped Walbridge to his feet.

I'm going to be sore, the captain said, but I'll be okay.

Hewitt got up and went to find Salapatek, her boyfriend, who was heading to the engine room.

If the ship goes down, she told him, don't lose me.

***

In the engine room, Sanders, wearing a headlamp, worked furiously to restart the starboard generator. Power. Power for the pumps. He took apart the hydraulic backups, cleaned their parts again, reassembled them and turned them back on. Walbridge told Cleveland at the start of his watch at 4 that he believed they were "losing the battle against the bilge water" and to "heave to."

"Heaving to" essentially brings the ship to a halt — an effort to push pause. The maneuver here shifted the focus from making progress to staying afloat. They lashed down the wheel of the helm, hard over, toward the wind. If they didn't get more water out of the bottom of the ship, and fast, it wouldn't matter where they were. Prokosch couldn't remember ever heaving to on the *Bounty*, but he knew doing it in a hurricane, and with "bare sticks" — no sails — was a way to try to weather the storm, hoping for the best. His commitment, though, didn't flag. He was tired but buzzing. A true test is what he wanted. Here it was.

Walbridge asked some of the crew to brace the stern cabin windows with 2-by-4s. Up on the deck, as late afternoon waned, Cleveland's handheld anemometer measured Sandy's winds at 80 mph, 90, 100 — then it broke. The line holding down the *Bounty's* rubber dinghy snapped and the loose boat scudded into the rigging; the thick, stout spanker gaff attached to the mizzenmast cracked; the shreds of the fore course blew out of their furl — a rapid series of calamities.

Crew members ran to the boat to tie it down. A deckhand waited in the nav shack to call man overboard if one of them didn't make it back.

Prokosch and others wrestled the spanker gaff to the deck.

They climbed aloft again to try to fix the fore course's broken furl. The wind pasted them to the rigging. They looked down. Cleveland was shouting something. It looked like he was saying to come down. This was too dangerous.

The sun started to set on the *Bounty*.

The *Bounty's* satellite phone didn't work below deck. Svendsen went up to the main deck and dialed Tracie Simonin, owner Robert Hansen's assistant on Long Island. He couldn't hear in the rain and the wind. Was it ringing? Was he talking to Simonin? Was he leaving a voicemail? He screamed into the phone.

In the nav shack, Faunt, the crew member with ham radio expertise, tried different forms of communication. High-frequency, single-sideband — didn't work. He tried a system called Winlink, a radio-based email program the *Bounty* often used — that worked. Walbridge, seated on a stool because it hurt his injured back to stand, entered Hansen's email address. He typed a 93-word message and hit send.

Svendsen also activated an emergency position indicating radio beacon, or EPIRB, hoping to send the *Bounty's* location to the Coast Guard.

The second mate, the engineer and a host of deckhands worked in the engine room to troubleshoot the generators and pumps. Floating in the water was an array of debris — flecks of wood, strands of string, plastic bags — and Prokosch used a pasta colander to scoop. In college in Olympia, Wash., he studied science, history and leadership. Later, he worked as a counselor at wilderness camps and traveled the Pacific Northwest in a green Volkswagen van, hiking, climbing, exploring. He liked books about survival, drawn to the central credo of outdoorsman Tom Brown — one wave at a time, be here now. They might end up having to abandon ship, and the ship might sink, Prokosch thought, but he could fight for extra hours, minutes, seconds. He was an able seaman — and proud of that designation — and these were things an able seaman did. A deckhand came down and asked if he could help. Prokosch gave him the colander. He saw the cook on the ladder at the top of the engine room, offering the crew bottles of water, apples, oranges and Goldfish crackers. Prokosch asked her to help him get another colander.

The cook walked across the tweens toward the galley. Prokosch followed. A wave staggered the ship. The cook clung to the jackline. Prokosch tried to stutter step but the floor that had been under his feet was no longer there. He fell across the tweens, a drop of some 25 feet, head-first into the starboard wall. The impact separated his right shoulder, broke three ribs and fractured two vertebrae in his lower back. He exhaled a guttural moan. The cook ran to him. Prokosch, woozy, was obviously injured. Don't go to sleep, she told him, concerned about a concussion, and she ran to get the first mate. Prokosch tried to breathe and assess what hurt. His back pulsed with spasms, and he had trouble controlling the movement of his limbs.

Svendsen arrived and touched Prokosch's legs and feet. He could feel that. He wiggled his toes. Svendsen told him to stay still, on his back, tight against the wall that had stopped his fall.

Christian came to him. Now it was just the two of them, the ship listing, the lights flickering as the power came and went. She gave him a bottle of water and placed a flashlight on his chest.

Here's our light, she said. We're getting out of here together.

***

Around 9, the Coast Guard district command center in Portsmouth, Va., received the signal from the *Bounty's* EPIRB, transmitting its location and confirming distress. The command center also got a call from Simonin. The shift commander in the Coast Guard's North Carolina headquarters in Wilmington read the email from Walbridge.

We are taking on water, the captain had written in the nav shack. *We'll probably need assistance in the morning. Sat phone is not working very good. We have activated the EPIRB. We are not in danger tonight, but if conditions don't improve on the boat we will be in danger tomorrow. We can only run the generator for a short time. I just found out the fuel oil filters you got were the wrong filters. Let me know when you have contacted the USCG so we can shut the EPIRB off. The boat is doing great but we can't dewater.*

The shift commander Sunday night in Wilmington tried to parse this note. There was a word, he thought, for a ship that was taking on water and couldn't get it out. The word wasn't *great.* The word was *sinking.* The shift commander needed to know more. He checked, and no ships were close to the *Bounty,* so he called the Coast Guard's Elizabeth City, N.C., airbase.

Wes McIntosh, a pilot of a C-130, had moved his plane inland to Raleigh to make sure he could take off in case somebody needed help. He got word from Elizabeth City a ship called the *Bounty* was foundering 90 miles from Hatteras. The Coast Guard wanted to establish communications to determine what to do next.

McIntosh and his crew of six drove in a rented minivan to the airport. One of the "dropmasters," the members of the crew that specialize in dropping pumps or rafts out the back of the plane, Googled the *Bounty* on his phone.

According to Capt. Walbridge, said the ship's website, *Bounty has no boundaries. As her captain, he is well known for his ability and desire to take Bounty to places that no ship has gone before.*

Capt. Walbridge, the site continued, *is a quiet, self-effacing individual; yet, when you stop to consider all he has done in its entirety, collectively, it and he are pretty amazing.*

To Robin, it said, *Bounty is an extension of himself.*

In an airport office, McIntosh and Mike Myers, his co-pilot, looked at the radar, checking the weather around the coordinates gleaned from the *Bounty's* EPIRB. The screen was surly with swirls of green, yellow and red. The *Bounty,* they concluded, was about to be in the worst of the storm.

McIntosh, Myers and the crew got into the plane, and the white, sturdy C-130 taxied on the runway slick with rain. It was 10:15 Sunday night. In Raleigh, the weather was wet and windy, but not as bad as it was closer to the coast. The radio chatter still was almost nonexistent. No other planes were taking off.

Hey, the Raleigh air traffic controller said to them. Are you guys heading out to Hurricane Sandy?

We are, McIntosh said.

Well, good luck, the controller said.

The turbulence was immediate and got worse the closer they got to the storm. McIntosh and Myers climbed to 7,000 feet for not quite an hour.

At 10:29, Walbridge sent an email to his wife, home in St. Pete. *Yes we are in trouble,* he wrote. *The boat would be doing fine but we can't dewater. We will be okay, probably have to abandon ship. Everyone knows we are here. It is not the storm that is getting us. It is the pumps.*

He signed off. *Love you.*

At 10:55, he sent an email to the Coast Guard, giving the *Bounty's* position and saying there were 17 people on board — a wrong number — adding he didn't know how long email would work. *My first guess,* he wrote, quickly and with sketchy punctuation, *was that we had until morning before have to abandon seeing the water rise I am not sure we have that long.* He said the ship had two inflatable rafts.

Half an hour later, from Jim Salapatek on Facebook, an incongruous update: *One of Bounty's generators has failed ... they are taking on more water than they would like. THE CREW AND BOUNTY ARE SAFE. ... The captain will await till morning to determine if Bounty is in need of any assistance.*

In the C-130, wearing night vision goggles, or NVGs, which turn the field of vision into green and black, contrasts between light and dark, the pilots approached the ominous, swirling clouds of Sandy, more black than green, before slowing at the storm's southwestern edge. McIntosh radioed down, hoping somebody on the ship already would be able to hear.

Calling to the *Bounty,* he identified himself as Coast Guard Rescue 2004, "two-zero-zero-four," a C-130 at 7,000 feet, approximately 40 to 50 miles away.

The response from the ship was immediate. Coast Guard C-130, this is the *Bounty.* We have you loud and clear.

Can you confirm your current position, McIntosh radioed down, the number of people on board and the nature of your distress?

Svendsen, talking into the radio in the nav shack, told them their latitude and longitude. He said there were 16 people on board. He said both generators had failed again, there was 6 feet of standing water, they were taking on water at a foot an hour, and they were running the radio on dwindling battery power.

The pilots confirmed the right number — 16, not 17 — but what stood out to them was the same thing Christian had worried about. No generators, no power. No power, no pumps. No pumps ...

They also were concerned about the battery-powered radio. It meant they could lose contact with the ship at any moment. They decided to go find the *Bounty*. To fly into Hurricane Sandy.

To the south they saw scattered clouds but mostly clear skies. A full moon. To the north: the angry, twisting bands of the storm, stretching from as high as they could see to as low as they could see. Sandy's southern edge.

The plane shuddered and rattled at the wall. The 45-mph winds became 90-mph winds. The autopilot disengaged. They were going to have to fly by hand. The gusts hit the plane on the left and shoved the tail to the right. Updrafts and downdrafts created sudden 300-foot surges and free-falls. The wings flexed, 4 feet up, 4 feet down, looking as if they might break. In their headphones the pilots and the three other members of the cockpit crew could hear the strapped-in dropmasters in the back vomiting onto the floor.

They couldn't see the *Bounty*.

They couldn't see anything.

They were still in Sandy's thick shroud, so they continued their descent, to 900, to 800, until they finally broke out of the clouds just under 700 feet above the Atlantic. The fierce rain pounded the windshield, dropping forward visibility to zero. They could see only out the smaller windows low on the sides of the cockpit. Here, under the cover of the clouds, there was hardly any light from the stars and the moon. On their NVGs, the lightest thing they could see, the brightest green on black, was the waves' wind-whipped white froth.

But no ship.

The C-130 turned around and settled into a D-shaped race track pattern.

We saw you, the *Bounty* radioed up.

The pilots asked them to shine a battery-powered spotlight from the deck. They banked the plane in the winds and flew back toward the *Bounty*. The beam of light shot into the dark. On the NVGs, which can pick up the tip of a cigarette from 5 miles away, the *Bounty's* spotlight looked like a torch. The plane flew to it. Over it.

What'd it look like? McIntosh asked.

Like a pirate ship, Myers answered, in the middle of a hurricane.

***

Prokosch lay still, squeezed hard against the wall that had stopped his fall, staring uphill to port. Christian sat beside him. On land, before the *Bounty*, she had cared for her diabetic father. She had taken to rescuing cats. Here, as Sunday turned to Monday and the situation on the leaning, sinking ship grew more dire, Prokosch thought Christian could tell it bothered him that he couldn't help. An able seaman. Disabled.

Are you comfortable? she asked him. What can I do?

Deckhand Josh Scornavacchi and others saw Christian with Prokosch. She's mothering him, they thought, leaving him only to race around the ship and return with updates.

In the engine room the floor had started to float, the water lifting up the sole boards. The pumps weren't pumping. Heavy work tables had pried loose from their bolts and banged around. Sloshing water had torn off the ladder to the tweens. The water was thigh-high, waist-high, chest-deep.

Around midnight Walbridge called the crew into the nav shack. He moved gingerly because of his back. His glasses remained on his face, held by the strings on the stems, but they were crooked and bent. He told the crew it probably would be first light before the Coast Guard could help. He said he still hoped for new pumps. Abandoning ship, he said, was a possibility. He told the members of his crew he felt good about their chances. The ship? He wasn't so sure. Svendsen asked the boatswain to get seasickness pills. Everybody took one except Walbridge.

The pilots considered the *Bounty*'s request for pumps. Too risky, they reasoned. The water in the ship was so high they weren't sure their 100-pound pumps ultimately even would help. And dropping them from 500 feet was perilous in such winds. Miscalculate and a pump could punch a hole in the deck. Go any lower, and one of those 300-foot free-falls would put them close to crashing into the water, or the masts. Come morning, they said, a helicopter might be able to deliver pumps from a safer, lower hover.

The *Bounty* asked if there were other ships any closer. No. Still no other ships that hadn't steered clear of Sandy.

At 2:03 a.m., an update on the ship's Facebook page: *THE CREW IS SAFE ... THE COAST GUARD IS ON THE SCENE.*

The pilots asked if there had been any change in the rate of the rise of the water. Yes, they were told, now it was 2 feet an hour. The flooded engine room was no longer safe. The water in the lower third of the ship had chased the crew up to the tweens.

McIntosh took the plane from 500 feet to 1,000, where the air was a little less soupy, and asked for a phone connection to land. He called the base in Elizabeth City. Helicopter co-pilot Jane Peña picked up.

This isn't going to be a helicopter dropping pumps, McIntosh told her. This is going to be helicopters hoisting people from the water. He told her he thought they should think about sending two helicopters, not one, as soon as possible.

He dropped back to 500 feet and radioed the *Bounty*.

If they hadn't put on their survival suits, he told them, they should do that.

Walbridge still thought they could hold on until the morning.

Around the ship, though, crew members had started filling dry bags and ditch kits with bottles of water, cans of food, flares, batteries for flashlights and headlamps, extra EPIRBs, money and passports — and their captain's licenses and training certificates, the paper evidence of their knowledge and experience. They futzed with the *Bounty*'s gas-powered fifth pump, the "trash pump," they called it, the backup to the backups, an afterthought bought cheaply in 2011 in Europe to assuage the British Coast Guard. They ran a long hose from the trash pump into the swamped engine room. The pump sucked weakly and intermittently. They laid out the blood-orange survival suits in the stern cabin.

On his computer near Chicago, Jim Salapatek saw a breaking news alert from a TV station in Virginia, saying the Coast Guard had a plane over the *Bounty* — 90 miles southeast of Hatteras, and 160 miles west of Sandy's center. At 2:53, he posted the update, adding a note of his own: *Your Prayers are needed.*

Svendsen asked Walbridge if it was time to abandon ship.

The captain said no.

Minutes later the first mate asked him again.

The captain said not yet.

Prokosch, still on his back, thought about his ex-girlfriend who had worked winter maintenance on the *Bounty*. She'd had a premonition that the ship would sink within seven months. He had told her to stop being so pessimistic. The crew wouldn't let that happen. He wouldn't let that happen. He thought about how he had told the captain and other members of the crew in the spring that he wished the *Bounty* had man-powered pumps, like the original ship, in addition to electric pumps, so they could dewater even if the generators broke.

He thought about how he wasn't sure he could move.

But he would have to.

Stay or go?

Move or die.

At 3:41, relying on battery power and the same program he had used to send the ship's owner an email not quite seven hours before, Walbridge emailed the Coast Guard.

We have lost all dewatering abilities, he wrote. *Estimate 6 to 10 hours left. When we lose all power we lose email — there should be an EPIRB going off — water taking on fast — we are in distress.*

Ship is fine, he added. *We can't dewater — need pumps.*

The ship's list increased to 45 degrees. Christian hurried to Prokosch.

Hey, it's time to get up, she said. She held his hand. She eased him to his feet. His back felt brittle, loose, as if it couldn't support his weight. Arm in arm, she guided him to a cabin on the port side, the high side, where she tucked him into a bunk. He should try to get some rest, she said. She said she would be with Sanders, her boyfriend, but she would come back to get him when it was time to go. She came back in less than 20 minutes.

***

The water in the tweens was shin-deep and rising. Walbridge gave the order. Don the survival suits. The captain sat to put his on because it hurt to stand. Some of the crew helped him. Barksdale, the engineer, put on his suit — the first time he had ever seen one. Faunt went to his flooding cabin and took off the T-shirt and shorts he had worn to work in the hot engine room and now put on his warmer, rough-weather foulies and ski bibs, into which he stuffed his ID and his waterproof phone sealed in a plastic bag. The rest of the crew put on their suits, and most of them also put on life jackets and climbing harnesses, so if necessary they could clip themselves to lines on the deck, sides of rafts, even each other.

Prokosch crawled from the bunk to the stern cabin where he got a suit and wiggled into it on his back and now he stood up. A deckhand used a Leatherman tool to help him tighten his harness. Prokosch grabbed a floating life jacket. He braced himself against the wall with his bulky gloved hands and moved through the nav shack and toward the deck.

As the crew filed up the steps, a few of the mates tried to do a head count, but it was hard to hear because of the swishing of the neoprene suits and the torrent of sea spray. Adam Prokosch coming on deck! he hollered. I'm injured and I can't help anyone but I'm here! In the dark, with the hoods of their suits tight around their heads, they all looked the same. They stayed low because of the heavy rocking in the waves, moving across the deck mostly on their hands and knees.

Svendsen stayed in the nav shack to talk to the Coast Guard.

Some other mates had their suits on up to their waists so they could keep their hands free to ready the lines to the life rafts at the stern.

Prokosch and Christian and others — and Salapatek and Hewitt, with their climbing harnesses roped together with a 3-foot lanyard — clustered by the back of the *Bounty*, by the mizzenmast and the helm, by the capstan, where four days before they had been given a choice, and where they all had decided to go. Now they wedged themselves against fixed objects on the deck, planting their feet against rails, flat on their backs but at times practically standing up straight, the *Bounty* tipping more and more.

Christian scurried to Scornavacchi's side and squeezed next to him. She smiled at him, flashing playfully what he considered her "determined face," furrowing her eyebrows and tightening her lips. He smiled back. She hustled to Sanders again.

Exhausted, pinned under the low, sinister sky, encroaching clouds and wind-blown rain, stuck in what felt like a fishbowl surrounded by steep black walls of waves, some of the crew closed their eyes and dozed, even as Sandy raged around them, even as their ship heaved in the waves, wave after wave after wave, and now another.

Svendsen called to Walbridge. The bow was going under.

She's going, Faunt heard somebody say.

We've got to go, Salapatek told Hewitt.

Prokosch's back throbbed. He gripped the helm.

Some of them jumped. Some of them slid.

What do I do? What do I do? Christian asked Sanders. Swim, he told her. Swim away from the ship. Swim to the rear of the ship. Swim.

In the sky, 1,000 feet high, the crew in the C-130 heard Svendsen say the same tense sentence, twice, in rapid succession.

We're abandoning ship. We're abandoning ship.

McIntosh, startled by the announcement, radioed down.

Roger, he said. What's your plan?

Silence.

Bounty, he said again. What is your plan?

Silence.

This was the worst-case scenario. People in the water. In a hurricane. In the dark. No helicopters in the air. Now the C-130 had to go lower than 500 feet. They had to drop life rafts. In the front of the plane, the pilots started the descent, fast, from 1,000 feet, down to 700, shuddering and rattling, to 500, to 300.

In the back, the dropmasters, weary from five hours of airsickness, unstrapped from their seats, stood in their vomit and prepared to push out the rafts filled with water and food, whistles and flares. They fastened their gunner's belts, heavy leather straps anchored to the floor with thick metal rings, and they hit the switch to open the back of the plane. The ramp lowered. The waves with the white tops looked like mountains in the low glow from the lights on the bottoms of the wings. The rush of the air and Sandy's wind and rain was so loud they had trouble hearing the countdown from the cockpit.

Thirty seconds.

The C-130 descended to 200 feet.

Fifteen seconds.

The C-130 raced to the *Bounty* at 150 mph. A downdraft pushed the plane to only 170 feet above the Atlantic.

Dropmasters are trained to push the rafts the instant they hear the first D of the command — Drop, drop, drop! — and now they heard in their headphones the signal over Sandy's roar. Drop, drop, drop! The plane screamed over the *Bounty*. The bright-red rafts tumbled toward the suits in the water.

DAY 3: FACING IT

The ship groaned and heaved in the dark in Hurricane Sandy's rain and wind. Able seaman Adam Prokosch let go of the helm on the sinking ship, slipping into the white tops of towering waves. He kicked and paddled through the grinding pain of his separated shoulder and the broken bones in his back. He strained in his bulky blood-orange survival suit to get away from this rolling ship, fleeing the miles of rigging, dodging her heavy masts and sharp spars rising and slamming down. A heavy wooden grating fell from the ship and struck his head with a crack. He choked on ocean and gasped for breath.

Not four full days before, the well-known replica of the old HMS *Bounty* had been tied to a dock in New London, Conn., her schedule calling for a trip to St. Petersburg for tours at the Pier. Veteran captain Robin Walbridge, who lived in St. Petersburg, and whose wife was waiting, wanted to go despite the threat of the massive storm. He gave the 15 members of his crew the unusual option to get off. None did.

That was a Thursday evening, late last October, and Prokosch chose to go for the same reasons he had gotten on the ship in the first place. Because he was an aspiring captain. Because he wanted to learn from those he respected. Because he yearned for authentic experiences, lessons learned from decisions made. Now it was before dawn on Monday, Oct. 29, and they were 90 miles off the North Carolina coast, each of the tight-knit crew thrust into individual struggles, fighting for their lives.

Josh Scornavacchi, a deckhand and Prokosch's good friend, had called his mother leaving New London and attempted to ease her worries by promising her he wouldn't die. Now in the water he could feel the suction of the ship, pulling him closer, holding him under, until he had to breathe, and so he inhaled salt water laced with diesel fuel. He fought his way to the surface. His heart hammered. He had a rock-climbing harness over his suit, to which he had clipped a small, rubber bag with water, food and a flashlight. He felt something from the rigging wrap around the bag, and it wrenched him under until his body fell slack. He thought about his little brother. He thought about his mother. He was so, so sorry.

Drew Salapatek and Jessica Hewitt, boyfriend and girlfriend, with their harnesses roped together by a 3-foot lanyard—if the ship goes down, don't lose me, she had told him—had started swimming clear of the ship on their backs. Something crashed between them, and dragged them down. They were stuck underwater because they were stuck to each other. Hewitt broke a molar trying to bite off her harness. Salapatek wiggled out of his, pushing it from his waist to his feet, slipping loose and shooting up.

John Svendsen, the earnest first mate, who had convinced Prokosch to come aboard in March, who had questioned the captain's decision but not in front of the crew, who had just made a hasty radio call to the Coast Guard's plane—We're abandoning ship—scrambled off the slick, slanted deck, onto a mast lying almost horizontal on the turbulent water. He looked back at the ship, a spectral silhouette against the dark gray sky, and saw Walbridge, wearing a survival suit and a life jacket, walking toward the rear of the deck. Svendsen, who had been a deep sea diver in Hawaii, leapt from the mast and swam toward a raft. A spar from above slashed at the surface. He yelled and threw up his hands, trying to protect his face, and disappeared under. The *Bounty* reared up, the spar breaching the surface, Svendsen now straddling it, and then the ship rolled, pulling him back under, gone.

Prokosch was alone. He saw the man-overboard barrel, a plastic trash can filled with canned food, bottled water, flares and a beacon with a strobe. Fearing it might still be attached to the ship he let it slosh past. He floated on his back, away from the ship but surrounded by the storm, for all he knew the only one alive, focusing on his breathing. One wave at a time.

***

In Elizabeth City, N.C., the phone rang at the Coast Guard's airbase. They're in the water, Wes McIntosh, the pilot of the C-130 flying over the *Bounty*, said to Jane Peña, a helicopter co-pilot. The plan had been to wait for daylight. That's what Walbridge had wanted. It was better, too, for the Coast Guard. Darkness is dangerous, and the deteriorating weather conditions meant that sending a helicopter—stout, but less sturdy than a C-130—would stretch the limits of what the agency considered acceptable risk. But life and death is the ultimate variable.

The plan now?

Go.

A second C-130, headed to relieve the first plane now low on fuel, raced down the runway.

Peña, pilot Steve Cerveny and two other crew members ran to their helicopter on the tarmac. A second helicopter crew hurried to the base.

Forging into Sandy's heavy bands of clouds and winds, Cerveny wore night vision goggles, or NVGs, turning what he saw into shades of green and black. He listened to the assault of the rain on his windshield. He saw blackness. Only the instruments told him where he was. He turned on the spotlight. It flashed back the thick haze of the inside of a cloud. When the screens in the helicopter told him they were "feet wet," meaning they were over open ocean, he started his descent. He asked the flight mechanic to tell him when he saw water. The mechanic slid open the side door. Cerveny lowered the helicopter, to 1,000 feet, to 700, out of the clouds, to 500, 400, 300 ...

I see the water, the mechanic said.

The waves bounded big and fast, surging in all directions. Violent gusts of wind lopped off their tops, lending the scene on NVGs a ghostly green vapor. The helicopter flew toward the *Bounty*, pushed by a ferocious tail wind, but it was still 20 minutes away.

***

Scornavacchi burst above the surface, coughing up salt water. He was dead, and then he wasn't—a divine reprieve, he believed. His boots had been sucked off and knocked around loose and heavy in the bottom of his waterlogged suit. It made swimming even harder in the giant, relentless waves. He grabbed at pieces of debris, wood, scattered emergency supplies and extra survival suits, the current ripping them away. He swam toward a cluster of life jackets some of the crew had tied together. He saw the cook on the other side of the life jackets, but then the hefty mizzenmast smacked the water between them and Scornavacchi couldn't see the cook anymore. He looked for something to hold onto to keep his face above the waves. He grabbed the mast and breathed, but now it bucked up again, hauling him high into the air. He jumped.

Doug Faunt, the oldest member of the crew, found the canister of an unopened raft. He yanked on the cord to inflate it. Not enough strength. He became afraid it still was attached to the ship and let go. He found a life ring. Maybe this, too, he thought, was still attached. He let go. He found another raft. He had swallowed so much salt water he started to vomit. He looked up near the clouds and saw the lights of the Coast Guard's C-130. They'll find me, he thought, if I just hold on.

Six more crew members, somehow, found their way to the raft, orange and covered with a canopy. They tried to use the flimsy rope ladder to the zippered doorway but couldn't do it. Waves crashed over them. They teamed up to give each other boosts from the water and inside. In this raft equipped for 25, there were seven of them—Faunt; Matt Sanders, the second mate; Jessica Black, the cook; Scornavacchi and fellow deckhands Mark Warner, Anna Sprague and John Daniel Jones – and they spread out, attempting to distribute their weight, lying flat on their backs.

Jones unzipped his suit long enough to check his watch. It was 5 a.m.

Sanders had brought an emergency position indicating radio beacon, or EPIRB, which meant the Coast Guard would find them, eventually.

Do you think everybody made it? somebody asked.

Yes, Sanders said. Everybody's alive.

They knew there was no way he could know that and was trying to bolster their spirits. Waves jostled the raft, tossing them from side to side.

Scornavacchi started singing softly, a Gaelic sea shanty, the *Mingulay Boat Song*. Two others joined in. The next four followed. They sang about windy weather and heading home.

Sprague thought about the woman's voice she had heard near the ship as she swam away. Help! Help! I'm caught! Sprague couldn't have gone back. Nobody could have gone back. The waves. The spars and the rigging. The reaching and the yanking.

Was it Laura Groves, the boatswain?

Was it Jessica Hewitt, the deckhand with Salapatek?

Or was it deckhand Claudene Christian?

Sprague couldn't help but wonder.

Over by a second raft, not far from the first but obscured by so many waves, six more crew members held onto each other. They boosted and pushed, too, one by one, until five were in —all except Prokosch. His shoulder made it painful for him to reach above his head. His back throbbed. He clipped his harness to the rope ringing the raft. He rested like that for a bit. He watched the C-130. He also saw the waves ripping the rope off the raft, stitch by stitch. He decided he had to get inside no matter how badly it hurt. Hands pulled him up. The pain was close to unbearable, but now he was with the others. Dan Cleveland, the third mate. Chris Barksdale, the engineer. Salapatek, who had slid out of his harness.

And Groves.

And Hewitt. Still attached to her harness was the 3-foot lanyard with which she had tied herself to her boyfriend. Still attached to the lanyard was Salapatek's harness. She got free because he got free.

But Christian wasn't in the raft.

The six who had gotten in passed around the survival provisions. Water. Food. Flares. Waves splashed through the seams of the door, water pooling a foot deep. They couldn't find a bailer, so they drained Groves' water bottle. They all took sips, water from the *Bounty*, they said, a small way of saying goodbye. Cleveland held an EPIRB out the door when he could see the C-130. For a while, he could see another raft, too. He called to it, but the storm was too loud, and he watched the raft drift away.

Maybe the other 10 members of the crew were in that raft, Prokosch hoped, but he couldn't imagine how all 16 of them could have made it away from the *Bounty* alive. He kept the thought to himself.

***

The Coast Guard's second C-130 relieved the first, battling the same violent updrafts and downdrafts, the plane's automatic sensors sending out sing-song warnings—Altitude! Altitude!—even occasionally alerting them that it was time to engage their landing gear. Peyton Russell, the pilot, flew over the *Bounty*, looking down through his NVGs.

Telephone poles in the middle of the ocean, he thought, eyeing the masts.

The crew of the first plane had painted a picture of what else he would see. The two Coast Guard rafts had solid lights. The ship's two rafts had blinking lights. But there was a third blinking light, too, separated from the others. The crew of the first plane couldn't tell what it was. Now Russell saw it, already three-quarters of a mile away from the ship. He flew to it and radioed the pilot of the helicopter nearing the scene.

I think this is where you need to come first, Russell said.

Cerveny plugged the position into his helicopter's computer and flew straight there. Blink. Blink. Blink. The helicopter's altimeter read 80 feet, 60, 70, 50, evidence of the undulations of the water below. Cerveny, his helicopter's nose pointed into the wind, hovered lower. Sixty. Fifty. Mike Lufkin, the flight mechanic, slid open the door. He and Randy Haba, the rescue swimmer, looked down at the blinking. Cerveny turned on the spotlight. A survival suit. The person in it waved.

Haba, dressed in his orange full-body suit, strapped on his fins, gloves, helmet, snorkel and mask, and Lufkin quickly cabled him down. The spotlight created a bright, 10-foot circle on the surface, and Haba swam as hard as he could. He reached the person in the suit. A wave wrenched him away. He swam back and reached again. Another wave. Reaching for him a third time, he grabbed the man and held on.

Svendsen.

Who had been bashed by the spar.

Who had found the man-overboard barrel that Prokosch had passed up. Who had taken its beacon with a strobe.

Are you alone? Haba asked him.

He was alone.

Are you hurt?

Svendsen said he felt sick from swallowing salt water. He said he might have broken his hand.

Haba side-stroked back to the cable, carrying Svendsen alongside. He used a large, padded sling to attach them chest to chest. Svendsen's face was pale except for reddening bruises and abrasions. Lufkin lugged them into the helicopter, Svendsen weighed down by the water that had seeped into his suit. Peña, the co-pilot, who was keeping the count of the survivors, noted the rescue of Svendsen.

One.

Cerveny, still looking through his NVGs, saw the *Bounty* not far ahead, and flew to the ship. Waves swept over her deck, the whitecaps looking like green smudges, her three stout masts breaking the surface and now again standing up straight. Cerveny circled the ship, checking the rigging for anybody stuck. Nobody.

Around 6 a.m., slivers of light poked through the clouds, turning the air a murky mix of white and gray. Cerveny flipped up his NVGs. He could see the fan of debris, planks, boxes and bags, a small rubber boat flipping in the waves, empty survival suits and loose life jackets with reflective patches, all floating southeast, the violence of Sandy's counterclockwise winds overwhelming the Gulf Stream's northerly current. He flew to a raft dropped by the first C-130, already a few miles from the ship. Nobody. He flew to the second raft. Same.

Russell, the pilot of the C-130, monitoring the rescue from 700 feet, radioed a reminder to the helicopter. The massive tailwind that had sped rescuers to the scene would make the return flight twice as long. The helicopter had to hurry.

Cerveny followed the debris field until he got to the first raft from the ship. The *Bounty* crew heard him coming and unzipped the door and looked out. They saw the helicopter. They saw a man swimming toward them. They watched as Haba kicked his way into the raft, propping his mask on top of his helmet.

Anybody injured? he asked.

Nobody was, they said.

Haba radioed to the helicopter. Seven P-O-B, he said. People on board. He asked for basket hoists, thinking that would be the quickest method.

In the raft, Haba looked at Faunt, easily the oldest person in it. He had curled up in a corner, nauseated by the salt water he had swallowed, his bowels having fouled the inside of his suit.

You first, Haba said.

He guided Faunt into the water, chasing the moving metal basket, assisting him in. The helicopter's rotor wash—the noise, the spray—was enormous, but the winds blew most of it behind them. A wave rocked the basket, knocking Faunt out. That happened a second time. A third. Lufkin tweaked his timing and attempted another hoist, successfully winching Faunt out of the waves. Haba swam back to the raft. He did the same with three more crew members.

Russell radioed from the C-130. Bingo, the Coast Guard calls it, and Cerveny and Peña knew it, too. Their gas. They had to go now if they were going to make it back. Peña updated the survivor count.

Two, three, four, five.

In the raft, Jones, Sanders and Scornavacchi couldn't hear the thwuck thwuck thwuck anymore. They would have to be picked up later.

***

Rescue swimmer Dan Todd surfed down the face of a 30-foot wave, his fins above his head, practically somersaulting through the second raft's door. He sat with his back to the flap and his fins stretched out in front of him.

Hi, I'm Dan, he said. I heard you guys need a ride.

They shouted their approval. Dan, that was awesome! You rock!

Todd was surprised by the response, but heartened, too, because nobody in the raft was panicking.

Is everybody okay? he asked. Anybody injured?

Rescue swimmers ask this almost immediately because they have to know who needs the biggest share of their finite energy. Prokosch spoke up.

My back hurts a little, he told Todd. I have some shortness of breath.

Can you get out of the raft?

I got in, Prokosch said. I can get out. I'll do anything you ask me to do.

In the second helicopter, flying at nearly 60 miles an hour just to stay still, the crew watched a 30-foot wave build and finally crash on top of the raft. The raft folded in two before snapping back, catapulting Todd across the inside where he landed on several of the survivors. He pulled himself off them.

We need to go, he said, radioing to the helicopter. "Zero-six P-O-B."

The flight mechanic directed the pilot to move the helicopter depending on where the winds were taking the basket. "Left 10. Left 10. Hold. Hold. Basket's going in the water."

"Altitude! Altitude!" sang the warning system.

Prokosch crawled out the raft door, flopping limply into the water. Todd swam him through the whitecaps to the waiting basket. At the cabin door of the helicopter, Prokosch braced himself with his left palm on the floor, rolling out of the basket. He scooted on his butt toward the cockpit, wincing as the pain shot through his back. He felt a tap on the hood of his suit. Jenny Fields, the co-pilot, handed him a wintergreen breath mint. A Life Saver.

Prokosch watched them hoist Hewitt. The pilot saw another wave heading toward the raft. "That's easily a 30-footer right there," he said. "Oh, there's a roller—that's going to be a bad one ..."

"Oh, yeah," the mechanic said. "Here we go."

"Ah," the pilot said. "The raft flipped over."

Down in the water, Todd sprinted back to the upended raft. The helicopter crew looked for the remaining four survivors to pop above the surface.

"Okay, we got one," the pilot said.

"Two."

"Three."

He waited.

"Four."

The flipped raft hastened the process. Now the crew were in the water. Prokosch, seated in the corner closest to the cockpit, watched them get hoisted in. Groves, the boatswain, had her hood off, her hair matted. She lifted the waterlogged legs of her suit out of the basket and exhaled deeply, then sat against the wall opposite the open door. Engineer Barksdale was next, squeezing in near Hewitt by the cockpit. Salapatek, without his contacts, lost in the frantic swirl after the ship tipped, was close to blind. He climbed out of the basket and leaned toward Hewitt and blinked. Finally, Cleveland, the leader in the raft due to his position as third mate, who had insisted on being the last to get hoisted, entered the cabin. With his wet hair and scraggly beard, he turned to Prokosch and the others and flashed "hang loose" signs, pinkies and thumbs extended, jubilant.

"Whoo!"

Fields, the co-pilot taking over the survivor count, logged the update.

Six. Seven. Eight, nine, 10, 11.

There were three still left in the first raft. The pilot asked Todd if he was too tired to go after them.

No, he said. I'll go.

"It's 2 1/2 hours to splash," Fields radioed the C-130, meaning when they would run out of gas and crash, "and we've got about half an hour on scene."

***

When Todd hit the waves for the second time, he could tell he was running out of gas, too. His strokes were lumbering, less race-pace. Be efficient, he thought. With the first six rescues, he had used the drag line that runs some 50 feet from the bottom of the raft to pull himself closer. Now he dove down, again looking for the rope, stroking toward it. Maybe he was tired, but he felt like he was floating. Down here he couldn't hear the helicopter. Down here there was no hurricane. The currents on the flip side of the monstrous waves rocked him gently. The warm water in the Gulf Stream was clear blue. He watched tiny fish dart about. An opaque, pink-purple jellyfish pulsed past.

He swam to the surface, back to the whitecaps, the rotor wash, the noise.

Three more people. Hoist, hoist, hoist.

Prokosch and the others in the helicopter watched as they arrived. Scornavacchi. Jones. Sanders. They squeezed into the cabin, forming the rough shape of a horseshoe, leaning against walls, against each other. Todd came up last. The flight mechanic slid shut the door.

"Exactly one hour on the scene," Fields radioed the C-130.

Bingo.

Fields updated the count.

Twelve. Thirteen. Fourteen.

Second mate Matt Sanders, on the floor by the door, looked around the cabin. There were three people he couldn't account for. One of them was his first mate, who had been rescued first. The other two?

Robin Walbridge. His captain.

Claudene Christian. His girlfriend.

Claudia McCann, Walbridge's wife, had stayed up all night in St. Pete. At 5:32, she sent a Facebook message to Tracie Simonin, the assistant of the owner of the *Bounty*. *Have they abandoned ship? I read the crew is safe but what does that mean? Off the boat or still on the boat?*

No response.

On the ship's Facebook page and website, Simonin and Jim Salapatek, the father of deckhand Drew Salapatek, had posted updates that were incomplete, misleading or wrong. Maybe it was stress. Maybe it was wishful thinking.

The crew is safe and accounted for, Salapatek wrote at 6:26.

There are 17 crew on board and at this moment all crew are accounted for and are in life rafts, Simonin wrote at 7:11.

At 7:51, Salapatek acknowledged the previous post had been premature, saying that *as of 10 minutes ago 14 of the 17 crew has been hoisted to safety!!!*

Now, though, around 9:30, Simonin and the Coast Guard posted conflicting messages.

This is a sad day, Simonin posted on the *Bounty*'s website. *The storm hit the ship pretty bad. One of the generators failed and the ship was taking on more water than it wanted. Distress call was sent out and the Coast Guard rescued ALL 17 crew. We are very thankful for that. Bounty was left at sea to fend for herself with the prayers of many. May God protect the ship from sinking!*

DON'T GIVE UP! KEEP THE PRAYERS COMING. NOTHING IS IMPOSSIBLE.

We will let you know how things are progressing with the ship. Thank you for your prayers.

To our wonderful Captain Robin: You did a great job and the very best that you could. Thank you for your efforts and keeping the crew safe. God bless you sir.

The Coast Guard issued its news release. The crew size: 16. The number rescued: 14. Those 14 were in helicopters headed for land. Two remained missing. The search continued.

Please bear with us, Salapatek posted at 9:39. *There are so many conflicting stories going on now. We are waiting for some confirmation.*

The crew got that confirmation in Elizabeth City. When the helicopters landed at the base, Svendsen and Prokosch were taken to the hospital. Svendsen was treated for trauma to his head, neck, chest and stomach, an inflamed esophagus due to ingestion of salt water, and a broken right hand, and Prokosch for his separated shoulder, the two fractured vertebrae in his lower back and the three broken ribs. The Coast Guard got the rest of them clothes, food, drinks and coffee, and gathered them in a conference room.

Now they all knew for sure who was still missing.

Walbridge.

Christian.

On the woodenboat.com message board, the posters who for days had tracked the ship and second-guessed the decision to sail exploded.

He was at the ultimate worst location under the worst set of circumstances.

I can hardly imagine a worse place to be than in the Gulf Stream off Hatteras in a hard northeast blow.

When the spot stopped moving before I went to bed I feared the worst.

The captain's wife, in St. Pete, learned two were still missing from a reporter. She knew one of them was her husband—just knew—even before the Coast Guard called to say so. More calls came. *Good Morning*

America. The *Today* show. CNN. She said Walbridge had "been in many storms" and "lots of hairy situations" and always had made it through. "He was just trying to avoid it, skirt it. Skirt through it, skirt around it. I'm sure he's devastated. Absolutely devastated. But the crew comes first and you have to save the crew." She added: "That's the image I have in my head. I'm sure he made sure his crew were all tucked in their lifeboats before he got off the ship."

Robert Hansen, the owner, was in Denver, where he talked to a local TV reporter. "She's been through worse," he said, "and she's always come through unscathed."

And in Oklahoma, Dina Christian, Claudene Christian's mother, spoke on the phone to a reporter about the last time she talked to her daughter. "She says, 'We're heading out and I just want to tell you and dad that I love you,' " she said. "And I said, 'What are you saying that for?' And she said, 'Just in case something happens.' "

In Elizabeth City, before the Red Cross gave the survivors stipends for food, clothes and rooms at a hotel, the Coast Guard interviewed them individually.

The most pressing questions:

Where had they last seen Walbridge?

Where had they last seen Christian?

They last saw Walbridge in the water, on the deck, on the deck by the mizzenmast, on the deck by the nav shack, in the nav shack with his survival suit zipped to his waist, in the tweens trying to make sure everybody else was okay, walking on the deck after everybody else was in the water, and going into his cabin, looking tired, moving slowly, lying down on his bed and picking up a picture of his wife.

They last saw Christian in the tweens putting on her suit, walking through the nav shack up to the deck, on the deck by the rail around the mizzenmast, on the deck smiling with her blond hair tucked into her hood, on the deck running to Sanders, and then with him in the water, asking, What do I do? What do I do?

***

The C-130 settled into search patterns based on wind strength and water currents sent by the Coast Guard's state headquarters in Wilmington. The pilot opened the back of the plane, and the two drop masters, their belts secured to the metal rings on the floor, scanned from 500 feet the growing field of debris. The arms of empty survival suits flapped in the gusts.

The third helicopter returned to Elizabeth City.

A fourth helicopter left Elizabeth City. Came back.

Now a fifth helicopter launched and flew to the debris. It was Monday afternoon.

Sitting at the edge of the open door, flight mechanic Casey Hanchette and rescue swimmer Ryan Parker looked down, straining to detect signs of life. It was no longer raining. The wind was blowing, but not as hard. The low clouds on the backside of the storm gave the sky an overcast pall. The helicopter flew long straight legs of 5 miles. Nothing. The helicopter was a little more than 8 nautical miles from the site of the ship, which had started to sink for good. It was just after 4:30.

Parker saw a single orange suit coming up on the helicopter's right side, and he watched as the helicopter flew toward it, over it and past it, this suit, all alone, face down.

Sir, he said.

The helicopter circled around, hovering down to 50 feet, to 40 feet, to 30 feet. The rotor wash flipped open the hood.

Blond hair spilled into the blue water.

Months before on Chesapeake Bay, shortly after she boarded the *Bounty*, Claudene Christian had put on a life jacket to go up on deck, because she was afraid, until she saw others laughing. In Boothbay Harbor, not quite half a year later, she had told a fellow member of the crew: It's really important for me to finish this. Her fake nails were gone by then. A summer of sun had turned that hair a brighter, lighter blond. The ship's watches had offered hard, empowering work, set within an easy ordering of her days, the uncertainty of the future ceding to the plainer beauty of the present. She could have called her parents from Boothbay Harbor. Please come get me. She could have called her parents from New London. Please come pick me up. On the day sail, though, the afternoon before the evening they all decided to leave from New London, she talked about how much she loved being on the *Bounty*, and how beautiful the sky was at night, no light but natural light, surrounded by so much of the sea.

Parker quickly cabled Hanchette to within 10 feet of Christian. He swam to her. He rolled her over and touched her neck to check her pulse. Nothing. He called for the sling. Parker hoisted them up, face to face.

They laid her on her back, and Hanchette knifed open the sides of her suit, down to her feet, peeling it away from her body. Water rushed onto the floor as the helicopter raced for shore. She was wearing a T-shirt, green sweatpants and Converse Chuck Taylor sneakers. A small chunk of the tip of her nose was missing. Hanchette checked her pulse, her neck, her wrist, again. Nothing, still. They wrapped her in a blanket. She was cold, but not so cold, and her lips were blue, but not so blue, and so they pressed on her chest and breathed into her mouth, alternating when they grew weary, and they did that the entire flight to Elizabeth City, which took almost two hours, until they got to the hospital, where Claudene Christian, 42 years old, was pronounced dead.

***

As Sandy did what the storm was predicted to do and worse, splintering boardwalks on the New Jersey shore, flooding New York City's subways, shutting down airports and knocking out power from the mid-Atlantic to New England, the Coast Guard searched for the missing captain. They sent planes, helicopters and ships from Elizabeth City, Atlantic Beach, N.C., Charleston, S.C., Miami and Clearwater, 100 miles off the coast, 125 miles off the coast, 145 miles off the coast.

They searched the rest of Monday.

They searched all day Tuesday. That night, the last strobe lights of the survival suits stopped blinking.

They searched all day Wednesday.

And every day the Coast Guard called Walbridge's wife in St. Pete, usually late in the afternoon, telling her it was still a search, not yet a recovery, because of the warmth of the Gulf Stream water, because he was wearing his suit. They searched for more than 90 hours, covering 12,000 square miles.

Thursday's call was different. There would be no search Friday. McCann thanked them for looking for her husband for so long. She thanked them for saving so many members of his crew. She pictured him going back to his cabin at the end.

His obituary would say his love for the ocean started with his mother, who encouraged him to pick up shells, touch slippery seaweed and smell the salt in the air. It would say he believed the sea was a teacher, a place where those who searched for meaning would find it. It would say he was a gentle soul, a quiet man, who would have but one request: *a tall ship, and a star to steer her by.* It would say he charted his own course.

***

Wet snow fell in Fall River, Mass., the first day of December. Tom Murray, one of the leaders of the business group that had brought the *Bounty* to the city in the early '90s, and later hired Walbridge, organized a memorial for the ship at the local marine museum. He expected maybe 50 people. Three hundred showed up, including 13 of the 14 survivors. Prokosch remained bedridden at home in Washington state, drowsy from Vicodin.

A picture of a pigtailed Christian smiled from inside a frame on a table, next to a picture of Walbridge, the portraits surrounded by red roses.

A ship and her crew, said the Rev. Robert Lawrence, "have filled our lives with purpose and meaning."

L. Jaye Bell, a freelance writer from Maine who sailed on the *Bounty* for a story over the summer, told those gathered at the museum about Christian.

"Once," Bell said, "when I asked her how to do something on the ship, she winked and said, 'Fake it 'til you make it.' Claudene spent a lifetime putting that motto into practice. ..."

She volunteered for the grubbiest jobs on the ship, Bell said. "She was most happy with streaks of tar on her face and a grin ... sweating and flushed, covered in mud, blond hair flying."

Shelly McCann, Walbridge's stepdaughter, observed that he had "a certain quirky style of communication," which elicited knowing, affectionate laughter from the former crew members.

"Robinisms," she called them, because that's what they called them, too.

"Wakey wakey, little snakey." "Okay here's my plan ..." "I truly believe ..."

But her mother's favorite? Walbridge's wife?

"Think about what you want," he would say, "not what you don't want."

Walbridge's stepdaughter said, "Personally, I felt loved by Robin. ... Robin did not have children of his own, but he called me his daughter, and he called my daughter his granddaughter. He wanted things for us, like we were his children."

What she didn't tell them was how, right before Mother's Day one year, Walbridge called to remind her to please call her mother, first thing, because that would mean a lot. She didn't tell them about the rough patch in her 30s when Walbridge called her and talked to her for two hours. Don't worry, he said. It gets better, he said. Keep going. She didn't tell them about the end tables and the jewelry boxes he built for her with wood from the *Bounty*. She didn't tell them about the notes he wrote to his wife and hid around their home, saying I love you, saying I miss you, and how maybe her mother hadn't found them all. She didn't tell them about the last time she was on the ship, the previous summer, in Newport, R.I., with her boyfriend and her daughter. Her boyfriend said to Walbridge, It must take a lot to take care of this old girl, to which Walbridge responded, It does, it does, but I want you to take care of these two girls.

***

In February, in a hotel on the water in Portsmouth, Va., the Coast Guard held eight days of hearings about the sinking of the *Bounty*.

The Coast Guard can't determine civil or criminal responsibilities or penalties. But it can call people to testify in an effort to determine the cause of a catastrophe. This was not a trial—though it could provide fodder for one. That's why Christian's parents' attorneys were present, along with the attorneys for the company that ran the *Bounty*, and it's why Svendsen, as the first mate, participated as a "party of interest," representing the rest of the crew. And it's why Hansen, the owner, declined to testify, invoking his Fifth Amendment right. But the 14 survivors testified. So did employees from the Boothbay Harbor shipyard. So did several of Walbridge's tall ship captain colleagues. Investigators had two key questions.

How did this happen?

Why did this happen?

Few of the 14 survivors saw the same things the same ways. Sometimes what they didn't say revealed as much as what they did. But all of it was enough.

How?

The *Bounty* sank because of the wood on the outside and the machines on the inside. Because the pumps weren't pumping enough. Because the backup to the backups was a facade. The *Bounty* sank because her captain sailed into a hurricane. Because he didn't call for help as soon as he should have. Because water works toward weaknesses, in ships and in the people who make them move. In the end, the sea finds the flaws.

The Coast Guard called Todd Kosakowski from the shipyard. He had passed along to investigators the pieces of the rotted wood he had put in a box and slid under his desk. He said he told Walbridge he was "more than worried about what we found."

The Coast Guard called Walbridge's colleagues to discuss the decision to sail.

"I still can't believe the choice was made," said Dan Moreland, the captain of the *Picton Castle*, based in Nova Scotia. He was supposed to sail south last October, too, but he stayed in Canada until the storm passed. "I can't begin to imagine what he was thinking." And to sail without hardy pumps? "Unconscionable on a good day."

"I still search for an explanation," said Richard Bailey, the former captain of the *Rose*, who hired Walbridge as a mate before he became the captain of the *Bounty*, and who considered him a "mechanical genius."

Next was Jan Miles, the captain of the *Pride of Baltimore II*, who had written on Facebook on Dec. 1 an open letter to Walbridge.

Robin, he wrote, *for all the experience you have, it was recklessly poor judgment to have done anything but find a heavy weather berth for your ship, rather than instead intentionally navigate directly toward Sandy with no thought given to deviate if the original plan of yours was not panning out. During the 17 years you were master of the Bounty you were the single reason she remained active. Under your command she went from being an aging wooden vessel with all the typical problems age brings to a reviving vessel as a result of several significant re-buildings over the last several years. You were a hero in everyone's eyes. Deservedly so I will freely add!!!*

I so respected your even, steady persistence to celebrate what the Bounty could be and as a result was becoming.

He continued. *Reckless in the extreme!*

So amateur as to be off the scale.

One of the Christians' attorneys, Ralph Mellusi from New York, asked Miles if he still believed what he'd written. Reckless. Incomprehensibly amateurish.

"Yes," Miles said.

"Yes."

Walbridge went when he shouldn't have gone. He went where he shouldn't have been. That was the how.

So why did he go? And why did the rest of his crew go with him?

The reasons were evident in the way they answered questions about their captain. Here there was consistency.

"He was never much of a yeller or screamer," Cleveland said. "I never saw him nervous or scared. It made you feel like you could handle things."

"He was someone I could learn from," Sanders said.

"He was highly involved," Groves said.

"I knew the captain had been on board for many years," Black said.

"He had a lot of experience," Scornavacchi said.

"I thought a great deal of him," Barksdale said.

"I thought it was pretty amazing I got to work with him," Prokosch said.

"My thoughts about Robin?" Salapatek said, slipping into the present tense. "He's a pretty quiet-spoken, kind of an introverted, thinking person."

"He thought rationally," Faunt said. "He had reasons for what he did.

"I loved that man," he said.

One of the investigators had a question for Svendsen. What if he, the first mate, whom the crew respected as much as they did Walbridge, had taken the captain's offer and opted to stay in New London?

"I believe he would have sailed," Svendsen said.

What if the second mate had stayed?

"I believe he would have sailed."

The third mate?

"I know I wouldn't leave," Svendsen said, "without any of my officers.

"For me," he explained, "the choice for Robin to sail into the hurricane was something based on his experience."

During a break, out in the hall, Mellusi, the Christians' attorney, shook his head. "There's no defense," he said.

Two months later, he filed the expected lawsuit against the company that ran the *Bounty*, accusing Walbridge of negligence and recklessness, asking for damages of $90 million.

***

In the golden age of sail, in the era of the original HMS *Bounty*, these stories almost always ended the same. All hands lost.

In the early 21st century, though, the men and women of the Coast Guard, and their modern machines, altered the script. This *Bounty*'s survivors were left to adjust.

In Oakland, Calif., in March, Faunt sat in his chilly, cluttered house, unopened mail stacked by the door, dusty books of maritime history lining the wall-to-wall shelves, his blood-orange survival suit laid out on a tabletop, and paused. "Just accepting the fact that I was alive," he said, "was nearly as hard as accepting the fact that Claudene and Robin are dead."

In Nellysford, Va., in April, Barksdale sat in his house in the country drinking coffee, wishing he hadn't gotten seasick, wishing he hadn't gotten hurt, wishing he had been able to do more. "I have regrets," he said.

Hewitt said she wanted to talk. Then she said she didn't. Couldn't.

I am having a hard time, she wrote in a Facebook message. *I'm just not ready to leave the house currently. But please don't give up on me.*

Throughout the spring she posted what felt like pleas to herself as much as promises to others. She posted a piece of a poem by Henry Wadsworth Longfellow. *The moistened eye, the trembling lip, Are not the signs of doubt or fear. Sail forth into the sea of life!* She posted a quote from Joseph Conrad's *Typhoon. Facing it—always facing it—that's the way to get through it. Face it.*

She got back on a tall ship—like Svendsen did, and Faunt, and Cleveland and Groves, and Jones and Salapatek and Black. She had to put on a survival suit for safety orientation. She cried. But she did it. And all summer when she jumped into water, especially off the ship, the sensation triggered panicky memories of trying to breathe under the *Bounty.* Of biting her harness. Breaking her tooth. But she did it.

Prokosch, after months of stretching and yoga and physical therapy three times a week, returned to Boothbay Harbor. Pain lingers in his ribs. He lives with his girlfriend, a former cook on the *Bounty,* in a small cabin at Linekin Bay Resort, where they teach sailing. He's also building his own boat. A wooden dinghy. He works, too, at the shipyard, the same shipyard where he worked on the *Bounty.*

One Sunday evening six months after the disaster, he sat at the bar at Pier 1 Pizza, drank Shipyard IPAs and a shot of tequila and talked.

He misses Walbridge.

"Robin had a very accurate and really true way of people development," Prokosch said. "He would put you somewhere you're not comfortable and then watch you grow to the position."

He misses Christian.

"I loved Claudene a lot," Prokosch said.

Pier 1 is where she had her raucous 42nd birthday party, where she racked up points on the Big Buck Hunter arcade game, where she played Grateful Dead on the jukebox and danced.

"Claudene took me arm-in-arm to keep me on my feet," he said. "We were going to get through it, and I, uh—lost track of her."

He was desperate and afraid. He got hit in the head with the grating. Hit with the spar like a dart. "The boat, I swear," he said, "tried to drown me a couple times." He struggled and thrashed, and the adrenaline coursed more powerfully, is all he can figure, than the pain from his shoulder and the broken bones in his back. "I wasn't sure I was going to make it."

And then he was away from the ship, and then he was alone in the ocean, the young man from the Pacific Northwest who had taught kids at camps to sit and stick their fingers in the dirt, to become more alert to what was around them, and to the moment, and to their presence in it. Out in the water, he said now at the bar, his mentality shifted. "I was positive and happy." He loved to swim, and there he was, swimming. He tried to fill his lungs with air and not water. He couldn't always breathe when he wanted. When he could, though, they were his best breaths ever.

Alone on the Hill

The Arizona Republic Online

By Shaun McKinnon

The firefighter paced on the broken pavement, where the road turned to dirt at the edge of Yarnell. A rusty haze swallowed the landscape. Trees shuddered in the wind.

He turned back toward two other firefighters, waiting by their trucks. On the radio, they could hear a crew in a plane overhead, talking about the smoke.

"It's kinda tough on us, but we'll, we'll give it a shot ..."

In a rush of static, another voice broke through, distorted.

"Breaking in on Arizona 16, Granite Mountain Hotshots, we are in front of the flaming front."

On the road, a firefighter spotted flames through a tree. "We've got fire right over here now," he said.

The fire crews had been sent there to prepare for the Yarnell Hill Fire. It had grown from a flicker on Friday night to a monster by Sunday afternoon. Now it was getting even closer, as trees near the road popped into flames.

The same distorted voice emerged from their radio again.

"Air to ground 16, Granite Mountain, Air Attack, how do you read?"

Granite Mountain. The hotshot team from Prescott. The crew had hiked up the ridge earlier in the day, before wind whipped the fire back toward Yarnell.

Outside their truck, the firefighters focused on the radio and talked, voices low.

"Is Granite Mountain still there?"

"Well, they're in a safety zone."

"The black." The black — already-burned area that should be safe.

On the radio, an operations chief tried to raise the hotshots.

"Granite Mountain, Operations on air to ground."

"Granite Mountain 7. How do you copy me?"

The radio squawked. In the background was a whining sound so familiar to wildland firefighters.

The firefighters at the truck tried to make sense of what they heard.

"Is that Eric?"

"I heard Granite Mountain 7."

"I hear saws running. That's not good."

"Not when they are in a safety ..."

The wind gusted. The orange glow through the trees pulsed. The air crewman's voice emerged from the radio again.

"We'll do the best we can. We got the type 1 helicopters ordered back in. Uh, we'll see what we can do."

Near the trucks, one of the firefighters watched the sky and listened: "Holy ..."

"Air Attack, Granite Mountain 7!"

The transmissions were confused, with the hotshots, the operations chief and the air crew trying to connect. Finally, a voice emerged, winded but clear. It was Eric Marsh, leader of the hotshots:

"Yeah, I'm here with Granite Mountain Hotshots. Our escape route has been cut off. We are preparing a deployment site and we are burning out around ourselves in the brush. I'll give you a call when we are under the she— the shelters."

***

Eight hours earlier, the Granite Mountain Hotshots had piled out of their crew buggies alongside a dirt road outside Yarnell and geared up to fight another fire. Together, 20 men hiked up the ridge, toward the flames.

One was 43, a fire veteran. Others were rookies earning a spot on the team.

They were jokers, gym rats, ex-Marines and ex-missionaries.

Seven were fathers. Three were fathers-to-be.

Some dreamed of permanent jobs on an engine crew. One dreamed of the ocean.

They went to sleep at night and dreamed the smell of smoke.

By the end of that Sunday, June 30, near the bottom of the hill, near the edge of town, 19 of them would confront a force too powerful to stop.

As they did, the elements of a tragedy converged:

A cluster of wooden homes amid the brambles, there for so long that no one felt at risk.

A wall of flame riding the winds of a storm, the heat of the summer and the tide of a changing climate.

A legacy of heroism amid the smoke. A century-old faith in the power of firefighting. And a daring team of young men ready for the fight.

Those elements came face to face in the course of a single weekend. But the forces that put them there were at work long before the fire began.

FRIDAY

Orange embers glowed as dusk eased into night, tracing broken lines on the slope like spattered paint. The 19 hotshots used the embers as a guide, cutting brush and scraping dirt as they tried to corral the fire before the sun and heat could speed its growth.

Lightning ignited the West Spruce Fire that Friday afternoon, June 28, in a storm-fueled fit through the Bradshaw Mountains and the Sierra Prieta. Of eight new fires, this one jangled nerves the most. It was burning in the Prescott National Forest below Highland Pines, a subdivision outside Prescott. It was too close for a city that had watched another fire threaten neighborhoods for the past two weeks.

The U.S. Forest Service had summoned two hotshot crews, a lot of highly trained manpower for a fire still smoldering on less than 10 acres. The crews, the feds' own Prescott Hotshots and the city's Granite Mountain Hotshots, would pull an all-nighter building firelines. If the lines held, the fire would never reach the subdivision.

The Granite Mountain crew was on its fourth fire of the month.

On the Doce Fire, which had licked at Prescott for two weeks, the guys had worked in the wilderness around the mountain that gave the crew its name. They had even saved a juniper tree famous as one of the oldest and largest specimens of its type.

With the fire under control, they had returned to the tree and formed a human pyramid to pose for a photo.

Friday night brought another fire and more line to cut.

Cutting line was a familiar routine for a hotshot, clearing brush in a line wide enough to keep flames from crossing it.

The cutters, a "sawyer" with a chain saw and a "swamper" to clear the debris, chewed through the dry vegetation. Behind them, crewmen with hand tools hacked away at the ground, trying to scrape it down to bare, fireproof dirt.

They had hauled their equipment up the hill, along with 45-pound backpacks. They carried water, plenty of it, because they could be out for days. They had food in case they didn't make it back to camp. And at the bottom of their packs, in pouches that were easy to reach, they carried fire shelters.

The tightly folded shelter was for use only in dire circumstances, and was sometimes the subject of grim humor among firefighters. Shaped like a sleeping bag, its outer shell is thin aluminum laminated to a silica cloth. An inner shell is made of thin aluminum laminated to fiberglass. The aluminum reflects heat; the silica is fireproof. But the fabric is hardly thicker than heavy paper.

Firefighters learn to deploy the shelters in 20 seconds: Crawl inside, face to the ground cloth, hands and feet into the hold-down straps to keep the shelter in place. It's a move every firefighter learns and hopes never to use.

The crew moved along the slope into the night, a snaking line of yellow shirts and heavy boots. Nineteen men had loaded up at Station 7 back in Prescott after the call came in. The twentieth member, Brendan

McDonough had been sick and would wait a day or two before returning
to work.

***

Working through the night was nothing new for the hotshots. A
regular schedule would have been novel.

Hotshot fire crews train and work as self-contained teams and conform
to their own standards. They pride themselves on their physical fitness,
spending long hours in the gym or hauling loaded packs up and down
a hillside. They learn how to do everything on the line, whether given
a shovel or a chain saw or a pumper truck.

They travel anywhere in the nation on request from incident commanders and can remain on a fire for days or weeks, sleeping on the line
if needed. Their name reflects their original role, when they fought the
hottest spots of a fire, but they often work away from the most active
flames, building firebreaks.

The Granite Mountain Hotshots were unlike even their brothers in
the hotshot fraternity. They worked for a city fire department rather
than a federal or state firefighting agency or an Indian tribe, the typical
sponsors for a hotshot crew.

Eric Marsh was working on a fuels-management crew for Prescott
when the Fire Department decided it would build a wildland crew. Marsh,
who grew up in North Carolina, had spent a summer in Arizona working
fires with a friend and, after he finished college, the lure of the fireline
drew him to Prescott. He was eager to get back in the wilds and signed
up for the new unit.

With a crew up and running as a "Type 2" team on local fires, Marsh
and Darrell Willis, a deputy chief, turned their attention to certifying
the crew as "Type 1" hotshot team.

The training, testing and paperwork took nearly four years, but in 2008, the Granite Mountain Hotshots joined the elite, becoming one of about 100 hotshot crews.

That first year, the crew worked 13 assignments over 95 days. They logged more than 15,000 miles across Arizona, New Mexico, California and Oregon. The next year, they flew east, pulling jobs at the Great Smoky Mountains National Park in Tennessee and the Pisgah National Forest in Marsh's home state of North Carolina. They also played "the big show," as they called it, the devastating Station Fire outside Los Angeles, where two California firefighters died.

***

That year, after a busy season, the "rookie of the year" award was bestowed on a 28-year-old Prescott native named Travis Carter. But Carter was no rookie on the firelines or even on a hotshot crew.

Carter had intended to play football at the University of Arizona, where he won a spot on the team as a walk-on. That dream ended in injury, and Carter decided college wasn't what he wanted just then. So, he headed home and worked on the family ranch south of Prescott.

Carter's sister described him as a bit of a nerd as a boy, a kid who wore Coke-bottle glasses and spent hours building things with Lego bricks and Erector sets.

"By the time he was in eighth grade, him and another buddy were building remote-control airplanes out of spare Erector set parts and Styrofoam," Melissa Lange said. "They'd build the engines and put all the little components together and go out and fly it until it crashed. And then it would all bust apart. And they'd take it all down and build another one."

In 2001, Carter joined the Prescott Hotshots, a team attached to the Prescott National Forest. He found an outlet for his mechanical interests among hotshots, who relied on chain saws and other equipment that took heavy abuse.

He roomed with another Prescott Hotshot, a guy about five years his senior named Jesse Steed, a Marine who found his calling on the firelines after his last tour of duty. By 2009, they had both joined the Granite Mountain Hotshots.

Both men became fathers and adored their kids, and both were fanatics about staying fit. After his injury in Tucson, Carter doubled down on his workouts, determined not to let any weakness stop him again. Steed had broken his leg a few years before and went on a tear in the gym.

His sister, Taunya Steed, described him as a beast. He would run 20 or more miles as often as twice a week. He competed in the P.F. Chang's Rock 'n' Roll Arizona Marathon in Phoenix in 2011.

"He was unbelievable in what that man could do," Taunya said. "He was a health nut. A big-time health nut. No junk food."

At Station 7, the hotshots' home base in Prescott, Steed helped assemble a gym. He scouted Craigslist for equipment, and he devised grueling workouts for the crew, eager to show up other gym beasts. A hand-painted sign sitting atop one of the weight machines designated the area "Steed's Dojo."

***

In the Prescott forest, wildland crews would work on the other fires Friday night after the storm moved through. Two of the lightning strikes had ignited snags, or old trees. Those fires would spread no further.

Two fires had started on Mingus Mountain, northeast of Prescott. Both would be held to about an acre. The Woodchute Fire, in a wilderness area west of Jerome, would burn across 33 acres but slow when it reached firelines built during the night.

A crew of six firefighters would respond to a strike near the Cross U. Ranch, outside Williamson Valley. A Bureau of Land Management hand crew would join them and work until about 9 p.m., staying overnight to make sure the fire stayed quiet.

The storm that sparked them all moved past Prescott down into the Weaver Mountains, still lighting up the skies. One bolt hit the ground amid boulders and chaparral on a ridge not far from Arizona 89.

Witnesses reported smoke at the site at about 5:30 p.m. At 5:36 p.m., the smoke and the flames got a name: the Yarnell Hill Fire.

Eighteen hours would pass before firefighters reached it.

BELIEF

Forty-four firefighters crouched in a narrow mine shaft, their faces covered in soot and fear.

Outside, fire ripped across the Idaho mountainside with the roar of a freight train.

The crew leader, Edward Pulaski, shouted instructions. The men draped blankets over the shaft's opening and splashed them with water. Timbers inside the mine caught fire as they worked. Pulaski used his hat as a bucket to douse flames.

Soon, the blankets caught fire. Pulaski helped replace them but smoke crept into the shaft, a thickening cloud closing in on the crew like a collapsing ceiling. Pulaski ordered the men to lie facedown on the ground, where the fresh air would be.

They were trapped, like rats in a hole.

One man rose to his feet—better to take his chances outside than to lie down here and die. He made a run for the opening.

Pulaski drew his revolver.

"The first man who tries to leave this tunnel," he said, "I will shoot."

Fire consumed the air around them, and the men began to lose consciousness. Finally, Pulaski, too, felt the choking grip of the heat and smoke.

As his eyelids closed, the biggest fire ever witnessed in the modern-day West faded from his sight.

***

Fires had started burning in the high country of Idaho, Montana and Washington in early August of that year, 1910, fed by grass and brush desiccated after a rainless spring. The 5-year-old U.S. Forest Service, lacking money and manpower to fight a big fire, rallied civilians and, later, U.S. Army troops.

On Aug. 20, just as crew commanders thought they had gained the edge, hell burst across the landscape. Walls of flame carried by hurricane-force winds chewed through forests, obliterating towns and logging camps. The skies darkened; the air filled with chunks of burning wood, each a bomb pushing the fire farther across the mountains.

Edward Pulaski and his men had been working on the fire lines above the mining town of Wallace. When the firestorm erupted, they had no way to get below the rising flames.

Pulaski rounded up as many members of the crew as he could and headed for the mine. A falling tree killed one man on the way.

By that afternoon, the rest were lying unconscious on the rock floor of the mine shaft.

Early the next morning, the men began to awaken. All but five had survived the night.

They would find no water to ease their pain—the creek outside was filled with ash and too warm to drink. But the men stumbled back to Wallace.

Pulaski's story became legend and he a hero.

By summer's end, 1,736 fires had blackened more than 3 million acres in the region and killed at least 85 people, 78 of them firefighters.

The combined blazes earned a new name, one that would stick for a century: "the Big Blowup."

The men had gone into a forest but come home from a battle.

It would be the first against the new enemy of the land: wildfire.

***

Before the Big Blowup, the role of fire in the wilderness had stoked rowdy debate among modern-day pioneers.

Railroads and even timber companies, which depended on clear access to the mountains, believed in "light burning"—using fire as a tool to control the forest, a practice used by Indian tribes long before European exploration.

In federal forests, still a new concept in the early 1900s, officials wanted no part of fire. They derided light burning as "Paiute forestry" and insisted fires must be fought.

The Big Blowup and Pulaski's heroism didn't settle the debate immediately.

The new National Park Service saw the 1910 disaster as proof the idea of fighting wildfire was a failure.

But the Forest Service's chief had faced the great fire firsthand. So had the next three men to hold the post. For the next 30 years, the growing agency built an apparatus to put out fires at all costs, a mission that seemed to some an attempt to refight the battle they had lost.

In 1935, with the last of the Big Blowup veterans in charge, the Forest Service imposed what became known as the "10 a.m. Rule." As a matter of national policy, fire crews would attempt to extinguish any new fire by 10 the next morning.

In 1944, Forest Service officials introduced the cartoonish Smokey Bear. Their beliefs had a face and an enduring message. Everyone could prevent forest fires—and fires that started had to be put out.

***

The day after he graduated from Brophy College Preparatory school in Phoenix in 1967, 18-year-old Stephen Pyne reported for work as a laborer at the South Rim of the Grand Canyon. That same day, a position opened up on the fire crew based on the North Rim. Pyne accepted.

He returned every season for 15 years, between studies at Stanford University, the University of Texas and a series of fellowships. On the fire crew, he saw firsthand much of what he would come to understand as a scholar, about fire and the militant approach fire agencies take toward stopping it.

"After the 1910 fires, the emotions took over," Pyne said. "It became 'How do we honor the dead?' That whole generation was never going to allow that again. They kept saying, 'We just didn't do enough.' They were going to refight 1910 and win this time."

Pyne began chronicling the history of firefighting in this country, amassing a library of books and documents that took over an addition to his Glendale home. He now sees fire history in short eras, starting with the post-Big Blowup years.

In the 1960s, as the old generation of forest chiefs retired or died, their replacements began rethinking the old policies. By 1968, the Forest Service moved to abolish the 10 a.m. Rule, although it lingered through most of the 1970s.

Slowly, the agency began setting fires, so-called prescribed burns, and finding opportunities to introduce fire to forests and ranges where nothing had burned in decades.

In 1988, a huge fire in Yellowstone National Park renewed debate, but reforms didn't come.

Then, in 1994, the South Canyon Fire in Colorado killed 14 wildland firefighters. Interior Secretary and former Arizona Gov. Bruce Babbitt led an effort to examine policies, walking the lines with a hotshot crew to learn firsthand how the system worked.

Land-management agencies moved to control the landscape themselves.

They devised plans for controlled burns to clear overgrown ranges and forests where fire had been too long absent. When lightning struck, they tried waiting rather than extinguishing, "managing" the fires for ecological purposes. And they proposed huge thinning projects that would combine fire with logging and brush-clearing, returning the wild to the state it had been in before generations of firefighters arrived.

What they found, Pyne concluded, was that the federal agencies didn't own the West. Fire did.

***

In 2000, crews touched their torches to the brush above the North Rim, clearing out the landscape in hopes of preventing a blowup. Instead, the weather changed, and the fire exploded out of control. By the time firefighters gained the upper hand, the blaze had blackened more than 14,000 acres.

Within days, another crew lost control of a similar prescribed burn in New Mexico. That burn menaced the Los Alamos nuclear lab on its way to burning 48,000 acres.

And in 2006, after fire agencies began managing a lightning-caused fire on the North Rim, the weather changed unexpectedly. What was dubbed the Warm Fire burned nearly 60,000 acres—one of the dozen largest on record in Arizona.

The forest-thinning was slow and costly, and it couldn't be done in lower ranges, where there were no trees, just fire-prone scrub.

By the end of the decade, the Forest Service and National Park Service could barely pay for basic fire-suppression needs. Understaffed fire crews faced ever-growing blazes, much as they had a century earlier.

Then, in 2012, the Forest Service issued a new set of instructions that turned policies back nearly that far.

In a directive to fire managers, it instructed that fires were too risky to leave to chance, and managing them until they burned out naturally required money and manpower the agency didn't have. Every fire should be fought when it started.

At the end of June 2013, as the Granite Mountain Hotshots climbed into the mountains outside Prescott, fire agencies at almost every level were still at war with wildfire—at war, in some ways, with the enemy that had struck in 1910.

Every fire had to be fought, not necessarily because it was the right thing to do, but because there was no other way.

And as they climbed the hillside, they carried wood-handled tools with a two-ended steel head. One end is sharpened as an ax blade, the other is a flattened pickax to dig into the soil.

The tool—named for its inventor, a firefighter himself—is standard-issue for all wildland crews. It is called a Pulaski.

SATURDAY

A helicopter from the Bureau of Land Management descended toward the side of Yarnell Hill. A crew in yellow shirts and hard hats toted their tools and stepped out into the dust.

The fire assignment would be gritty, but for many of the crew members, it was a kind of freedom. They were prisoners, from down the road in Buckeye.

The prison crew and its supervisors had responded to the call Saturday morning, setting out for the fire.

Because the smoldering brush was on a patch of property held by the State Land Department, Russ Shumate from the Arizona Division of Forestry had been watching it and calling in help.

There was federal land nearby, and Dean Fernandez, a firefighter from the BLM, had flown over the fire earlier that morning, sizing it up at about 8 acres. Shumate had called for the prison crew, a helicopter attack crew member and two small air tankers.

The prison crew dropped in about 11 a.m. Shortly after noon, the tankers reported their slurry drop had secured the north and west sides, and that a ridge and a Jeep road would hold the other two sides.

The day grew hotter. In Phoenix, the temperature reached 119 degrees. The chaparral on the ridge in Yarnell was at its driest, still awaiting the first monsoon rain. Afternoons often brought winds in advance of a storm.

With the fire seeming steady and a forecast of more lightning by afternoon, Shumate wanted to pull the fire crew off the ridge by 3:30.

Two weeks earlier, the National Interagency Fire Center had issued a special advisory about fuels and fire behavior in Arizona and New Mexico. Trees and brush were dangerously dry after years of drought. A small to moderate fire could blow up rapidly, especially if the weather turned hot and windy, and fires could continue to burn into the night.

It read: "Firefighters should acknowledge that fire growth and fire behavior they encounter this year may exceed anything they have experienced before."

***

The Granite Mountain crew finished up at the West Spruce Fire and checked on another lightning strike in an area called Mount Josh. If the hotshots could wrap up their work there by the end of the day, and that seemed likely, they could look forward to a Sunday off. Their last real break had been for two days in the middle of the month, after a 12-day assignment in New Mexico and just before the Doce Fire back home.

Some of the crew planned to spend time with family. Three men were waiting on babies at home, all to be fathers for the first time. A few hoped to get out of town on a day trip, maybe fishing.

Garret Zuppiger was always restless when he was in one place too long, but his favorite destination, the Oregon coast, was too far for a quick escape.

Zuppiger joined the Granite Mountain Hotshots at the start of the 2012 fire season, but fighting fire on land was as far from his first dream job as Prescott was from the ocean.

As a kid, Zuppiger wanted to sail boats, wanted to live on the water. He pestered his dad and finally earned his certificate to pilot a sailing dinghy around Long Beach Harbor in Southern California, where his father lived.

He earned a degree in business economics at the University of Arizona and then set his sights on the Coast Guard. He took the military vocational-aptitude test and scored so high, he started getting offers from the Army, the Marines, the Air Force.

"Everybody wanted him, and they offered him all these jobs," said J.E. Crockett, Zuppiger's friend and sometimes employer.

"No, I told you guys, I wanted to be a coxswain" —the operations chief — "in the Coast Guard," he would say.

The recruiters told him he would have to work seven or eight years to reach that level and that frustrated him, Crockett said.

"Well, I'm not waiting seven or eight years to drive a boat," Crockett remembered him saying. "I'm just going to go and do something else."

Crockett's brother-in-law, Andrew Ashcraft, was a hotshot in Prescott and had won rookie of the year on the Granite Mountain crew in 2011. Zuppiger decided he would apply, and he made it for the 2012 season.

He started on hand tools, but won a promotion to the saw crew almost immediately. He told people he loved the work, but he couldn't get the saltwater out of his system. Someday, he would move to Oregon.

***

In Yarnell, the wind started to pick up about 4 p.m. and with it, growing signs of trouble.

The air crews had predicted a Jeep road would hem in the fire. Instead, late that afternoon, flames jumped the road, finding a path into the open brush. The crew on the ground couldn't catch the fire.

Shumate called for air support. After 5:30, with flames still moving through the chaparral, he began requesting a full incident-command team, warning that the fire could move toward Peeples Valley in the next 24 to 48 hours.

About the same time, word came from the prison crew that had been on the ridge, cutting brush for a fire break. They were out of chain-saw fuel.

Fernandez, the BLM firefighter, took Shumate aside.

"Do you want me to take over the fire?" That would put the federal land agency in charge.

"Am I doing something wrong?" Shumate replied.

"No," Fernandez said. "I just wanted to make sure."

By early evening, the fire had grown to 100 acres. Shumate told the Yavapai County Sheriff's Office to prepare the reverse 911 system in case the fire forced nearby residents to evacuate. He ordered more fire crews and equipment, including structure crews who could defend homes.

Then he asked for three hotshot crews, which are typically dispatched from the regional coordination center in Albuquerque. The center put out a call to the Blue Ridge Hotshots, run by the Coconino National Forest, and the Arroyo Grande Hotshots, based on the central California coast but working on another fire in Arizona.

The third crew, the center advised, local officials could fill with the Granite Mountain Hotshots.

***

The hotshots finally finished mopping up at Mount Josh late in the day and were left to salvage as much of the evening as they could.

On a slower weekend, the guys might get together and grill steaks or maybe head up to Watson Lake outside Prescott and play disc golf.

Dustin DeFord and Billy Warneke would man the grill. Jesse Steed, the team captain, was popular with the kids. Juliann Ashcraft, the wife of hotshot Andrew, liked those times because it gave the families a chance to get closer to each other.

"I would always take cookies to the barbecues on Saturday, and they would tell me what their favorites were," she said. Then, she'd make the favorites to take to the station during the week.

Steed couldn't eat ice cream, so he liked Juliann's orange-dreamsicle cookie. It was the closest he could get to real ice cream, so Juliann made sure he was well-stocked during the Doce Fire.

During the Doce, the crew slept at the station, in case the fire took a bad turn in the night. The hotshots would report to Prescott High School at 5:30 a.m. for their daily orders, so Juliann would wake up the kids and trundle down to the school at 5:15, just to get a few minutes with Andrew.

Travis Carter missed his kids enough that he had decided this would be his last summer with the hotshots. He told his mother, Glenna Eckel, that in the spring, he was going to apply to work on the structural-fire team, an assignment that would give him a more predictable schedule.

He needed to finish an eight-week training course to make the switch, and Eckel offered to come from her home in Nevada to help with the kids. He told her he couldn't take the class now. That would be time he'd miss with the hotshot crew.

"They're counting on me, and I'm already committed to that," he told her. "I'll do it next year."

***

As the hotshots scattered Saturday night, the fire 30 miles south of them started to spread. It pushed to within a mile of homes in Peeples Valley, after a day when winds gusted to 20 mph and the temperature hit 101 degrees. The fire would burn through the night, a time when flames should shrink to embers as temperatures fall and humidity rises. The national advisory two weeks before had been right.

Shumate and his small team watched the fire take control. They were calling for more help—air tankers, bulldozers, fire crews. And hotshots. One of the supervisors called Eric Marsh, the Granite Mountain superintendent.

At 8 p.m., Marsh got an e-mail with the formal order. He put the team's phone tree into motion. First to Steed, the second in command, and then the crew bosses, then the rest: More work Sunday. Report by 5:30 a.m.

BRAVERY

The hotshot crew clambered up the brush-covered Southern California slope, slowly clearing a path. In the distance, flame spread its hot fingers through the oak and chamise.

Bob Sipchen, a rookie on the Del Rosa Hotshots, swung his Pulaski tool, feeling the sharp edge cut into the woody trunks. He had signed on with the hotshots from his hometown, San Bernardino, in 1972, looking for adventure and inspired by childhood memories of another band of firefighters that once saved his neighborhood.

The squad boss yelled, and Sipchen stopped and looked. The fire was blowing up. Time to bug out.

The boss ordered the men to retreat uphill along the designated escape route below San Jacinto Peak. Sipchen knew the crew leaders had scouted the route, but from his position, he thought he saw an easier way to safety. He sprinted downhill, then skidded to a stop. Buckthorn and scrub oak had snagged his gear belt. He pulled back against the brush, but he couldn't move. He was snared.

Sipchen watched embers drift into the unburned brush below him and then ignite. He was now on the wrong side of the fire—uphill from it and directly in its path, trapped.

He struggled again. Finally, his gear belt broke free from the thicket. He scrambled uphill, toward the safety zone. Over his shoulder, the patch of oak that had snared him exploded into flame.

Decades later, on a bike ride in the foothills above San Bernardino, he ran into that season's Del Rosa crew. He chatted with the men and recounted the story. Some of the other hotshots related their own close calls, the shared experiences of the men who fight the hot heart of wildfires, who take the riskiest jobs and never show fear.

"I think the hotshots do nurture that romantic, 'We're the best, aren't we tough' thinking," Sipchen said. "The actual work you do is often just brute, mule-like manual labor. For the most part, it's just having the gumption and bad judgment to be willing to work 40 hours straight in the heat and cold and eat a lot of dirt and breathe a lot of smoke."

Sipchen believes close calls on the fireline are rare. But when hotshots talk, the stories of their near-misses become universal.

***

The first hotshots didn't begin as hotshots at all. They were fire crews organized by the Civilian Conservation Corps, a public-works program that emerged from President Franklin Roosevelt's New Deal.

CCC crews worked mostly on building trails or erosion-control projects on public lands. They fought fires when crews needed manpower.

In 1946, a fire-suppression team from a CCC camp in the San Bernardino National Forest was organized as the Del Rosa Hot Shots, a name adopted because the crew worked the hottest spots of a wildfire.

Soon, two more crews were created, near San Diego and Santa Barbara.

The early crews worked their home territory for the most part, but as their reputation spread, they would accept assignments in other locations. In the early 1960s, the federal government established an interagency hotshot program and started dispatching crews to major fires.

The hotshots underwent special training and physical conditioning, but there was another difference: They worked alone. They went in with their own vehicles, their own tools. They often camped on the fireline, away from the rest of the firefighters. They supplied their own food and fuel.

Because the work was unpredictable, dirty and demanding, photos of crews from years past show mostly the fresh faces of youth. A hotshot team was a starting place for a young worker —usually a man, though today many crews include women—without the confines of a Monday-to-Friday schedule, for someone with a strong back and endless energy.

Because they could be sent to nearly any task, they earned the respect of fire commanders.

By 2001, when Prescott started its own wildland-fire division, hotshot crews had long since earned their reputation as firefighting's elite. And the more than 100 crews in the country had become stitched into the fabric of fighting wildfires. If a fire was big, hotshots went.

***

Sipchen grew up on the edge of the San Bernardino National Forest and he saw the hillsides burn, over and over.

One summer, when he was 9 or 10 years old, he watched flames tear down the mountain toward his neighborhood, fanned by Santa Ana winds. He and his buddy spotted a crew of firefighters, clearing brush, creating a line the fire would not cross.

The next day, Sipchen and his pal picked up shovels and hiked up the smoldering hill. Huffing and sweating, they worked their own fireline, a pair of young hotshots trying on the boots of the men who saved their street.

From then on, Sipchen saw himself as a firefighter—one who climbed foothills and canyons rather than ladders.

"As a kid, it was a personal affront to me when those fires burned," Sipchen said. "Fire was a force that had to be fought."

As a young man, Sipchen knew about the reputation of hotshot crews when a friend suggested he join Del Rosa. He had traveled in India and he was broke, but he wasn't ready to settle down. The hotshot job seemed like the perfect match of income and adventure.

"My friend had painted a romantic picture of it to sell me," Sipchen said. "By the time I got on, he had painted a more realistic picture. You really can't be prepared for just how hard and dirty the work is."

This was the 1970s and workplace-style rules were still years away. Crews worked without limits on their time out in the fires. "I think we worked a 50-hour shift once, with catnaps along the way," Sipchen said. "It was pretty intense."

He had yet to finish his training when Del Rosa was sent out on a fire in the high desert. Darkness had fallen before they rolled in. The men rode crew buses up a dirt road to the edge of the fire. Sipchen had to wait in the bus because he wasn't certified.

"To me it looked like they were marching into a 30-foot wall of flames," he said. "I thought, 'Well, there went my crew. What's going to happen to me now?' But they knew what they were doing and they came back."

***

It's the close calls that worry some fire experts. Wildfires have grown in size over the past decade, while hotshot crews still field 20 firefighters. And, the experts fear, hotshots are increasingly shouldering more of the work as firefighting agencies struggle to fill the growing demand for help with fire suppression.

Stephen Pyne worked the firelines on the Grand Canyon's North Rim starting in 1967 and has chronicled the history of wildfire at Arizona State University. He believes hotshot crews are being asked to do more because they're ready when no one else is.

"It's becoming like a professional army," he said. "They're on the line longer."

Sipchen said he isn't sure whether hotshot crews understand the risks of their job anymore. Fires don't behave the way they used to. They blow up faster and bigger. No one can predict how hotter weather and deeper droughts will further change fires.

"The risks that we could reasonably be expected to take back in the '70s," he said, "they may not be the same risks that firefighters are being asked to take now."

Yet he knows the attraction remains.

"I think one of the reasons I was drawn to firefighting, part of the romantic appeal, was that it got you out to beautiful places," said Sipchen, who now works for the Sierra Club in its national office. "It's not always under the best circumstances, but it was a chance to see the natural world. I saw rivers, streams, mountainsides that no one else ever sees."

***

Since the Del Rosa crew reported for duty the first time in 1946, hotshot crews have been attached mostly to federal agencies: the U.S. Forest Service, the Bureau of Land Management and the Bureau of Indian Affairs.

No city had undertaken the expense and effort of creating a municipal team until Prescott's Fire Department proposed the idea.

Prescott sits a mile high on the edge of a national forest and on the lower slopes of the Bradshaw, Sierra Prieta and Santa Maria mountain ranges. The city has steadily grown into the woods and the high desert scrub, areas that fire experts call the wildland-urban interface.

By 2001, the city had established a wildland-fire division, an eight-person crew assigned mostly to help clear brush and create "defensible space," buffers that could help halt a wildfire before it reached homes.

Three years later, the city created a 20-person fire crew and named it the Granite Mountain Hotshots.

In 2008, the hotshots were certified Type 1 and joined the ranks of the interagency crews.

Prescott would later struggle to maintain the team. Eric Marsh, the superintendent, complained of equipment shortages, shabby accommodations and too few full-time crewmen. But the Granite Mountain team returned each year, acquiring heavy-duty transport trucks called crew buggies, a new station and the sought-after reputation as one of the elite.

And in 2013, in the midst of another busy fire season, they continued to operate in the paradox of a city-run hotshot crew: They often spent as much time working outside their home state as in it.

But among hotshots, they were also the paradigm. In a world filled with close calls, they worked hard and went home safe.

So, on the last weekend of June 2013, fire managers called them again.

SUNDAY MORNING

On an industrial stretch of Sixth Street in Prescott, near the corner of East Z Street (and its truncated sign: "EZ ST"), the first vehicles pulled into a gravel parking lot in front of a blue corrugated metal building. A sign hung above the front door, lettered in Old English style: Granite Mountain Interagency Hot Shot Crew.

Eric Marsh, the crew's superintendent, tried to avoid calling the men in before 6 a.m. He liked them to get a full night's sleep before starting a job. But the state forestry commander wanted to meet with crew chiefs by 7 a.m. and try to get a line around the Yarnell Hill Fire.

The hotshots had moved into Station 7 in 2010. They found themselves with a real fixer-upper and not much money for the fixing. The previous tenant was a gas company, not another company of firefighters. There were no living quarters, no gleaming garage floors.

But it was a real home. The hotshots had been working out of a drafty space in a sketchy side of town. They took the city's small contribution and added time and effort.

In the front hallway, beige tiles surrounded black ones that spelled out GMIHC. In the center of the station, the guys worked out in a gym assembled on the cheap with weights, benches, barbells, a stationary bike and shelves of medicine balls.

Though Jesse Steed and Travis Carter emerged as the gym beasts, the whole crew lived and breathed fitness. Their workouts were competitive, but they tried to motivate each other, in the station gym, on cross-country runs or at Captain Crossfit, a commercial gym a short walk from the station.

A garage door opened up on a workroom. Toolboxes sat against one wall, a workbench in the middle. A set of hooks on the side held spare chain-saw chains. The sawyers, who hefted the saws on a fire, often set the pace as the crew built a fireline. If the saw team could cut brush at a good clip, the other guys could move in and get the line cleared in a hurry.

Scott Norris worked as a sawyer for the Payson Hotshots for four years and then joined the Granite Mountain crew in 2013, partly so he could live closer to his family and his girlfriend, Heather Kennedy. The sawyers had to repair their own saws, sharpening the chains, checking every part.

Norris would tell his mother, Karen, that he liked working the saw. "He said they really could see changes so quickly in the landscape," she would remember later. "You're sawing through brush and you're pushing it aside. ... They make a difference."

The saws themselves, with their orange Stihl motor housings, were kept on shelves in a supply room, along with the other things that kept a crew running for weeks on end. Field rations. Hand sanitizer. Foot powder. A bottle of Pepto-Bismol. Shovels, axes and Pulaski tools lay horizontally wedged in slots between equipment shelves. Pants, shirts, ponchos, gloves and other clothing sat on shelves in the center of the room.

A refrigerator, a coffeemaker, a stove and an ice machine formed a makeshift corner kitchen. The crew rarely ate or slept at the station. If someone did spend the night, he might get stuck on the cramped brown and gold sofa in an office.

The men added other personal touches over time: a height chart on an exposed wooden support beam. A "dreamcatcher" made of paper clips and pens. And the whiteboard in the briefing room, maybe one place where the hotshots let down their guard.

Typically, Marsh would gather the crew in the briefing room. On the far wall, the names of every hotshot were written in marker, and under the heading "Granite Mountain Physical Percentage" were numbers, scrawled during roll call.

The ritual started one day when Travis Turbyfill, a Marine who started fighting fires in 2005, answered with a number when asked how he was doing.

"I'm about 80 percent," he might say from then on, the number ebbing and flowing depending on how he felt. Soon, all the guys were doing it, and it turned into both a running joke and a sometimes unexpected glimpse of the real hotshot.

When the firefighters left the station Sunday morning, they left behind the measure of 20 men.

Eric Marsh, 43, was one of the founders of the Granite Mountain Hotshots and its superintendent.

"Eric 68%"

Jesse Steed, 36, was the captain who had run the crew for a few weeks earlier in the year when Marsh was out with an injury.

"Steed 76%"

Clayton Whitted, 28, started with the Prescott Hotshots out of high school, left for a while to become a youth pastor, then joined the Granite Mountain crew.

"Clay 69%"

Robert Caldwell, 23, married in November 2012. He was a cousin of another crew member, Grant McKee.

"Bob Moderate Duty"

Christopher MacKenzie, 30, the son of a former firefighter, had a fondness for movies and Facebook.

"Chris 77% & ↑"

Travis Turbyfill, 27, a family man and a Marine, had a reputation for his jokes.

"Turby Fro-tastic"

Andrew Ashcraft, 29, was a father of four whose mustache earned him the nickname Stachecraft. He had recently shaved it.

"Ashcraft Stache-less"

Brendan McDonough, 21, was known around the station as "Donut," a play on his name, and had been studying fire science.

"Donut Hell ya"

Joe Thurston, 32, the father of two and a native of Utah, had long wanted to work as a firefighter.

"Joe 90%"

Anthony Rose, 23, started volunteering with the Crown King Fire Department as a teenager. His girlfriend was expecting their first baby in October.

"Tony 62%"

Wade Parker, 22, was the son of a Chino Valley firefighter and had been the hotshots' rookie of the year in 2012. He was getting married in October.

"Wade 70.12%"

Garret Zuppiger, 27, earned a degree in economics, took the test to join the Coast Guard and then decided to be a hotshot.

"Zupp Yeah buddy!"

Scott Norris, 28, a Prescott native, had worked on the Payson hotshot team before joining Granite Mountain.

"Scott 74.2%"

Dustin DeFord, 24, came from a Montana family history of firefighting. He had studied to be a pastor.

"DeFord 37.6 and dropping"

William Warneke, 25, a Marine, had wanted to be a firefighter since he was 6. His first baby was due in December.

"War-neke 35 or so %"

Kevin Woyjeck, 21, was the son of a Los Angeles County fire captain and had started training as a firefighter directly after high school.

"Woy-jack 87%"

Grant McKee, 21, had studied fire science and earned his EMT certificate at Yavapai College. He was engaged to be married, too.

"Grant 10^2 percent"

Sean Misner, 26, came from a firefighting family and aspired to carry on the tradition. His first baby was coming soon, in September.

"Misner 55.01%"

Travis Carter, 31, was a father of two and a native of Prescott who liked making model rockets and working out at the gym.

"Honey Badger 88.88 repeating"

John Percin Jr., 24, was a high-school baseball player from Oregon who had just finished training at the Arizona Wildfire Academy.

"John 100 percent"

***

As the fire crept closer to Peeples Valley and Yarnell, Russ Shumate, the incident commander, had called in two men from Prescott to oversee protection of the homes in the two communities.

Gary Cordes was a career firefighter and the training chief for the Central Yavapai Fire District. He also worked on the district's wildland fire program.

Darrell Willis headed Prescott's wildland fire division and was a driving force in the department behind the Granite Mountain Hotshots.

Shumate assigned Cordes to Yarnell and sent Willis to Peeples Valley. Deep in the predawn hours, Cordes had driven through Yarnell. The scene wasn't promising: yards thick with tree branches, hulking boulders and everywhere brush.

If the fire got there, the houses probably couldn't be saved. He scouted the town for safety zones, areas where firefighters could find protection from advancing flames. One promising location sat on a knoll outside of town, a cluster of buildings on a bare patch of ground called Boulder Springs Ranch.

Willis met Bruce Olsen, a fuels specialist for the BLM, at a ranch outside Peeples Valley. There, too, most of the structures were at risk if the fire moved in. Willis and Olsen talked about using roads as firelines and trying to protect specific locations even if they couldn't defend a full line. As they scouted outlying ranches, they looked up to see an orange glow atop the hill.

Willis returned to Shumate to talk tactics for the crews that would be arriving soon. And he brought back discouraging news. At night, a fire should "lie down," active flames succumbing to cooler, damper air. But the flames on the hill had been kicking up all night.

***

Outside Station 7, the hotshots loaded up their two white buggies, Ford F-750 passenger trucks painted with the team logo.

As they got ready to head south, Zuppiger pulled out his cellphone and called J.E. Crockett, his boss when he worked construction, brother-in-law of hotshot Ashcraft.

Zuppiger was moving and had to clean everything out of the apartment by month's end. It was June 30, and his two motorcycles were still in the garage.

"Hey, I've got to get those out of the garage today," Crockett remembered him saying. "Would you mind going today when you get a chance?"

He had bought one of the bikes from Crockett's brother, Joseph. The other had been a gift from his granddad a few years ago. His granddad lived in Peeples Valley and, it would turn out, was on alert to evacuate by then.

"Just leave it at your place until I can get back," Zuppiger told Crockett. "I'll take care of it."

***

After dawn, crews began to arrive.

Willis would oversee two engines and 31 firefighters and would start at the vulnerable Double Bar A Ranch.

Cordes' Yarnell group would include four engines, two water tankers and 12 to 20 firefighters. Cordes said it wasn't enough to protect the town.

Before the briefing, Shumate and Cordes met with two operations chiefs to outline a plan.

Division A—"Division Alpha," on the radio—would start near the south end of the fire, the heel where it had begun. That crew would build an anchor point, a stretch of fireproof bare earth, that would eventually connect to other lines to ring the fire and stop it.

Below them, crews would cut a dirt line with a bulldozer. Connect the two lines, and the crew would put a roadblock between the fire and Yarnell.

BUILDING

Long before there was a highway climbing Yarnell Hill, prospectors brought back gold from the Weaver Mountains. And they brought stories. A man could pick gold nuggets off the ground as he scrambled up through the boulders.

Virgil Earp lived on a ranch over the hill in Kirkland and when he heard the stories, he sent word to his brothers Wyatt and Jim. With Wyatt's friend Doc Holliday, they made their way to Arizona to join the rush.

As the miners prospered, so did the mining towns.

The winding road from Wickenburg through Yarnell became the main route to the territorial capital of Prescott. Miners settled in among the granite rocks and thorny scrub until houses seemed to meld with the hills. Historians say the miners worked such long hours that the bars in Yarnell never closed.

By the turn of the century, the mines produced less and less ore, but Yarnell did not fade away like other communities. Ranchers moved in and the area started attracting people from Phoenix looking for an escape from the summer heat.

Over time, Yarnell spread as far as it could. Boundaries of state trust land formed its edges, and beyond a certain point, locals say, Yarnell was "boulder locked."

In the late 1940s, a developer named Porter Womack bought property south of Yarnell, a ranch once owned by Elzy Pike.

Womack had made a name for himself in Phoenix, building central city neighborhoods like Bel Air and Melrose Manor. He began plotting a new neighborhood in ranch country. There, below Yarnell, there were fewer boulders in the way, so the streets would follow gentler curves.

The Yavapai County supervisors signed off on the plan Nov. 24, 1947.

The original plat maps of Womack's subdivision carry the official stamps and rigid lettering of engineers. They also carried a personal touch.

Womack had a daughter, Ilah Womack, who would have been a teenager when the first plans were put to paper. When the drawings went into the record books, they bore a set of capital letters in elegant Roman typeface that spelled out the name of that new place: Glen Ilah.

Within 18 months, the first houses were occupied. Womack would expand the subdivision three times by 1954 and home sites were sold for years afterward. With the miners gone, vacationers and commuters settled in among the same towering boulders, the same carpet of thorny scrub.

In the 1970s, there was a small grocery store. There was a restaurant called the Wrangler, where neighbors would bump into one another over breakfast or lunch, where the chamber of commerce met. There was bingo on Thursday nights.

In the mid-1970s, there were four bars, all on the eastern side of Arizona 89. Mining days were over, so there was never much action at Betty's Gold Nugget or the Twin Oaks bar. Most people were home by 9 p.m.

There was a shootout on Broadway, the main street through town, in 1976. There was a bank robbery in 1977 so big that the newspapers and wire services held their deadlines to get photographs back to Phoenix.

Apart from occasional outbursts, it was a place that seemed content, where the subdivision from 1947 was "the new side of town." It was a place that seemed quiet and safe.

***

East of Glen Ilah, 150 miles as the crow flies, Ed Collins wheeled his truck off Arizona 260 and into a subdivision in Lakeside, in the heart of the White Mountains.

Collins, district ranger for the Apache-Sitgreaves National Forests, idled through the neighborhood past tidy houses with pine trees towering over them. Pine boughs jutted out of patios, gathered in clusters around a garage, scraped walls and roofs.

Collins rolled through the neighborhood and stopped at the edge. Across a fence, the forest was sparse, trees farther apart.

"We finished a thinning contract over there last year," he said. "And as homeowners arrived back for the season, they called us to complain."

It was 2012, 10 long years after the Rodeo-Chediski Fire burned nearly to the doorstep of Lakeside and its pine-shaded cabins. The fire, at its time the largest on record in Arizona, destroyed 481 structures. It led forest managers to vow that they would thin out the decades worth of undergrowth that fueled such monster fires.

But it hadn't changed the way homeowners built and maintained their houses. The town of Pinetop-Lakeside adopted a thinning ordinance after the fire but enforced it only on new construction. Cities and towns were wary of citing residents. Voluntary compliance was spotty, and Collins' tour was proof.

At the same time, Arizonans surged into the backcountry like a brush fire.

Over the past 2 ½ decades, builders put more than 200,000 properties in, or up against, the flammable wild.

Though state and federal agencies bear most of the cost of fighting wildfires in forests—the forests that attract homeowners—local authorities OK the building, and any rules on brush-clearing are up to them.

The result: firefighting costs that have gone up year after year, and tens of thousands of new wooden structures amid what remains of the thick, shady forests.

But neighborhoods like the one in Collins' ranger district are hardly the only places at risk.

The houses spill like a patchwork across the state, into areas nobody would think of as new, in country where nobody would imagine a forest fire.

***

Thomas Swetnam worked as a hotshot in New Mexico and has fought fires in chaparral. He now studies the wild landscapes as director of the Laboratory of Tree-Ring Research at the University of Arizona.

In dense chaparral, like the thickets of the Weaver Mountains surrounding Yarnell and Peeples Valley, there may be no way to remove enough trees and brush to prevent a fire or even slow its spread. Winds can carry embers across miles and if there is vegetation where the embers land, the result will be more fire.

"People have tried," he said. "They've tried to build mile-wide fire breaks in chaparral, but it may not be enough."

If a town does try to fireproof its landscape, the work can't ever stop. The trees and shrubs grow back. Areas scorched by the Rodeo-Chediski Fire already need thinning, just 11 years later. Chaparral can be even more persistent.

Brush clearing is no foreign concept in Yavapai County. Prescott's Fire Department created a wildland division to help thin brush and trees from neighborhoods. The original team assigned to such projects evolved into the Granite Mountain Hotshots.

That thinning gives firefighters a chance to slow or stop a fire before it gets into a neighborhood.

Once fire reaches houses, the game changes.

Stephen Pyne, the ASU fire historian, has studied photographs of towns and neighborhoods that burn.

"Fires go house to house, with the houses burning the trees next to them rather then the other way around," he said. Along many streets he looked at, trees still stood next to houses that had burned to the ground. Embers from the wildfire had blown into the neighborhood and ignited the house.

"It only takes one ember," he said.

A county project helped thin about 375 acres in Yarnell and 40 acres near Peeples Valley between 2005 and 2011.

But a study in 2013 found a different situation in Yarnell itself. Of more than 500 houses in town, only 63 had cleared enough brush to prepare for wildfire.

On the last morning in June, the ones that had not became quickly apparent.

Fire supervisors pulled their trucks off the highway and into the neighborhoods. They saw oak boughs jutting over patios, crowding garages, scraping walls and roofs.

It was a firefight they couldn't win.

MIDDAY SUNDAY

Joy Collura and Sonny "Tex" Gilligan set out from Congress before 4 on Sunday morning, hoping to scout out the fire. Joy and her neighbors below the mountain wanted to know if they were at risk. As they climbed the hill above Glen Ilah, they pressed through manzanita and catclaw, trying to keep the sharp branches from shredding their skin.

Joy and Sonny hiked the Weaver Mountains almost daily, sometimes covering 20 or 25 miles with no particular goal. They were an unlikely pairing: Sonny was an old prospector, a bourbon hound who sometimes lived in a tent or a cave. He spat contempt for what he called the cookie-cutter lives of townspeople. Joy had moved to Congress 10 years before and bought a house with her husband. She was known for her long hikes and, in recent years, had come to rely on Sonny for his survival skills.

As the light grew, the two hikers could see smoke from the fire to the north. But as they tried to get a closer look, the chaparral above Yarnell blocked their path at nearly every turn.

***

Juliann Ashcraft listened to the voice mail from Andrew when she awoke for the second time. She had been half-asleep when her husband left the house at 5 a.m.

"We're headed to Yarnell," he said in the message. "There's a fire in Peeples Valley. I'll let you know."

Fire season took Andrew away more days than not, so Juliann shifted into her one-parent routine. Sunday morning meant church, and Dad's absence wouldn't change that. She dressed the four kids—Ryder, Shiloh, Tate and Choice—and loaded them into the car.

The three-hour block of church meetings started at 8 a.m. at the Willow Creek Ward chapel on the edge of town. Six-year-old Ryder had prepared a short talk about keeping Jesus in his life and in his heart, a moment his dad had hoped to see.

Andrew converted to the Church of Jesus Christ of Latter-day Saints when he married Juliann. In the off-season, he visited other members of the congregation and shared religious messages with them. He wore a white silicone wristband with the words "Be Better," a reminder of a lesson he had taught his family during a weekly church activity at home.

But his devotion to church wasn't unusual on a team infused with faith.

Dustin DeFord had studied for the ministry at the Cornerstone Bible Institute in South Dakota and had preached as a missionary. Clayton Whitted worked as a youth pastor in Prescott as he cared for his ailing mother and joined the Granite Mountain Hotshots intent on spreading the word. Travis Carter confided that he found solace in church when his life took him on a rough path. The men prayed together on firelines and would engage in theological discussions in the middle of cutting brush. During the night they spent on the West Spruce Fire, Andrew later told his wife, the guys talked about God for hours.

She didn't think it was coincidental.

***

As fire crews pulled in from the north and the south, some of them gathered at the Yarnell fire station, a tan metal building on Looka Way down the street from the Presbyterian church.

Russ Shumate, the forestry division officer who had been in charge of the operation since late Friday, gave a 7 a.m. briefing. Eric Marsh, the Granite Mountain Hotshots superintendent, joined it.

The group opened up Google maps on an iPad. Shumate oriented the arriving crew chiefs and he pointed out Boulder Springs Ranch, a cluster of mostly industrial buildings at the base of a hill southwest of where the fire was burning. He did not distribute paper maps for the crews to take with them.

Since the 1990 Dude Fire near Payson, where six firefighters died when fire swept over them, crews have trained using a core set of basic principles known as LCES, for lookout, communication, escape route and safety zone. At any point in the day, a crew needs to know the most direct escape route to a safe location.

The ranch property sat on a rocky knoll west of the Glen Ilah community. The owners had cleared wide areas around three large buildings, creating a near-perfect example of what fire experts call defensible space. With that much bare dirt between the buildings and the scrub brush, even flames dozens of feet high wouldn't reach across.

The crew chiefs talked strategy, although few of them had seen the fire up close. They needed an anchor point where the hotshots could start.

Crews usually establish an anchor near the coolest part of the fire. They cut, burn or scrape away brush down to bare dirt that forms the beginning of a fireline. The hotshots would start near the heel of the fire, the south end, for now a safe distance from the front.

Marsh was assigned to supervise what would be called Division A, working that southern anchor with his own hotshot crew.

A second division, Division Z, would be run by Rance Marquez from the federal Bureau of Land Management. Marquez hadn't arrived yet, but Granite Mountain was ready to go.

With Marsh assuming more responsibilities, Jesse Steed, the hotshots' captain, would take over as crew superintendent. But Marsh and the other 19 men would climb the same path together, toward the fire.

***

After Marsh left the briefing, the hotshots got a tour from Gary Cordes, the Yavapai wildlands chief supervising structural protection in Yarnell.

Narrow roads wound through boulders and over hills, turning sharply at times as the ground rose and fell. The crew saw homes surrounded by brush and trees or at the foot of a rocky incline that could offer fire a clear path down toward them.

The caravan parked above a house on a dirt track known as Sesame Street. Cordes pointed toward the southwest and again described Boulder Creek Ranch. He called it a "bomb-proof" safety zone, then reminded them, "Of course, you also have the black."

"The black" is what firefighters call a patch of ground that already has burned. With the brush charred, it offers a safe zone if flames turn or advance.

Marsh scouted farther down Sesame, until the the road ended. The crew met him at the truck for a briefing. Marsh told the crew the weather would be hot and windy. Fire threatened an increasing number of houses and other structures. With the changing weather, he said, the only escape routes were into the black or back to the vehicles.

Finally, Marsh outlined their first task: Secure the anchor on the fire's southern flank. They would clear brush with hand tools and burn out more difficult patches of ground until they connected their line with a bulldozer line closer to town.

A few of the men stashed cellphones in their packs, hoping to text notes or photos back home. Scott Norris, a veteran of the Payson hotshot team in his first season with the Granite Mountain crew, would send updates to his mother, who would pray for him when he was on a fire.

Norris knew she worried about the danger, but he liked the adventure, the physical challenges of the firelines. Still, after years in the wild, his goal was to earn a position on a city fire engine, which was one reason he left the Payson crew. He wanted to be closer to home and his girlfriend.

Earlier in the week, before the hotshots reported to West Spruce, Norris took a walk through Mountain Valley Park with his girlfriend, Heather Kennedy. They ran into his mother, Karen; his sister, Joanna; and his nephew, Eli.

"That never happens," Karen would later say. "What are the chances of that happening? It was beautiful and the sun was setting."

On Sesame Street, the hotshots unloaded their packs and stepped into the heat of the day.

Before the team got too busy, Ashcraft texted his wife: "How did Ryder do in his talk?"

"He did really good," Juliann replied.

"Please tell him I'm so proud of him," Ashcraft texted back. He was wearing his white "Be Better" band as he fell in with the rest of the crew.

***

Fire commanders had established a makeshift incident command post at the Ranch House Restaurant, a landmark eatery on the highway in Yarnell. By 9 a.m., chiefs had moved north to the Model Creek School in Peeples Valley, closer to the fire's most active edges.

On a large wildfire, while firefighters set up pumper trucks or cut brush, fire managers establish a business operation indoors, at the command post. They need communication, planning, even people to handle the budget.

Inside the school, crew chiefs hung maps on the wall and set up easels to view photos. They brought in laptop computers and printers. Radios squawked with chatter from crews in the field and dispatch centers in Phoenix and Albuquerque.

Representatives from the state Forestry Division, the Bureau of Land Management and the Yavapai County Sheriff's Office set up work spaces. Weather updates were posted as they came in from the Flagstaff office of the National Weather Service.

Supervisors met at 9:30 for another briefing. Among them was Roy Hall, a retired U.S. Forest Service firefighter with nearly 40 years of wildland experience, who, inside the hour, would take over as incident commander. Hall would oversee operations as the organization grew into a Type 2 team, for a fire big enough and dangerous enough to warrant more manpower and more equipment.

Hall arrived in Yarnell early, hoping to get aircraft over the fire.

Shumate wanted to hand over control as soon as possible. He told Hall he had been up for 30 hours. He was tired.

At his first briefing inside the school, Hall laid out his strategy.

"Be aware," he said, "we have just experienced four of the hottest days this summer." Heat dries out the plants fast, makes them more combustible.

He referred to weather updates predicting thunderstorms and wind. And he warned the crews on the line: "Any position you get into with the fire below you is a compromising position. The fire will come up and get you."

The new command team was still incomplete. Hall had no planning chief and no safety officers. A safety officer can evaluate hazards as firefighters work on a line, suggest safety zones and escape routes and listen in on radio transmissions to make sure crews are communicating properly. Shumate had filed a request for two safety officers late the night before, but no one had yet reported to the scene.

After the briefing, the Blue Ridge Hotshots were assigned to Yarnell. The crew was based in Happy Jack and was familiar with Arizona.

Regional managers had dispatched a third crew, the Arroyo Grande Hotshots from coastal California. The crew was already in Arizona, finishing up on a fire on the San Carlos Reservation. But as members prepared to move, their superintendent's truck stalled out with a fuel-line problem. The crew, stuck waiting for repairs, would never make it to Yarnell.

The fire continued to move northeast. Flames burned 40 to 50 feet high at 10:30, unusual for so early in the day. By 10:45, parts of Peeples Valley started evacuating.

***

Joy and Sonny picked their way across the hillside, a meandering path in search of the fire.

The brush had grown dense and dry, the scrub oak and juniper choked with dead and dying limbs. Manzanita reached up 6, 8, sometimes 10 feet. Without an ax, the hikers sometimes had to retrace their steps.

They were surprised when they spotted a lone man nearby. He wore a bright-yellow shirt, heavy pants and boots, good protection from the ragged branches, but hot on a day like this.

He was tying ribbons to trees as he walked.

"What are you doing up here today?" the man asked.

Joy studied him. He seemed pleasant enough, even though he seemed to be wearing some sort of official insignia.

"I'm a hiker," she said. "I wanted to see the fire for myself."

The man nodded. "So you know the area pretty well?"

The three talked about different routes, paths up the mountain, before parting ways.

The hikers continued to circle the ridge and encountered the man again, then again. The third time, he wasn't alone anymore. A full crew of other men in yellow shirts headed up another trail—firefighters, lugging their gear.

The man they had first met took Joy and Sonny aside.

"It's better if I tell you this instead of someone with more authority," he said. "You're not geared up and you don't have uniforms on. We can't do retardant drops as long as you're here. You need to get back to town."

Joy snapped a few photos before turning back. She watched the men as they headed up. To her, they looked tired, worn out.

It would be more than a day later that Joy would learn she and Sonny had met Eric Marsh and the Granite Mountain Hotshots.

The pair headed back toward a ridge above Glen Ilah. They argued as they considered their next move. Sonny wanted to go straight up the mountain. Joy wanted to take a more indirect path through a pile of granite rocks.

To make headway, they would crawl under the manzanita, against the dirt, and then reach a dead end and have to retrace their steps. They saw evidence of a bear and a mountain lion, which could move easily through the thicket.

But for them, the brush was like a maze.

BURNING

From a scrubby knob at the top of a steep canyon, Engine 57 Capt. Mark Loutzenhiser could see smoke and flames on the ridges around him.

Far below him, outside Palm Springs, Calif., the Esperanza Fire was working its way up into the San Jacinto Mountains that morning, Oct. 26, 2006.

Spreading out on both sides of him was a panorama of chaparral.

The slopes rose above the desert, high and cool enough for plants to flourish. The ripples of brush—manzanita, mountain mahogany and sage —yielded to unbroken vistas.

Engine 57 was one of five U.S. Forest Service crews dispatched. The fire, started by an arsonist, was still small and their assignment was to protect homes in the communities scattered along the mountainside.

Loutzenhiser and his four crewmates had found their vantage point outside a vacant house, an octagon-shaped structure with a pool out back. They were devising a plan for burnouts, torching off the brush around the house to keep flames from advancing. The pool would supply their gas-powered water pump.

Loutzenhiser outlined his intentions to the other captains over the radio.

Other engine crews that had been helping to direct evacuations took up similar positions at houses nearby.

Sometime after 6 a.m., Battalion Chief Bob Toups found Engine 57 at its position, where the hillside cleaved into a dry creekbed, dropping off steeply below. He would later report how he had advised Loutzenhiser to move back, down the road and away from the edge.

Southern California's Santa Ana winds were blowing that week. As in almost every autumn, a heavy column of cold air was sinking onto the high desert to the northeast. As the constant pressure of air reached the ground, it rushed outward, becoming a kiln-dry blast of wind on a race toward the ocean.

Those gusts from the northeast, measured at 31 mph at a nearby weather station, had already pushed the fire into the chaparral. It jumped roads as it went, forcing one engine company into retreat.

If the fire made a run up the dry canyon, the battalion chief warned, it could trap Engine 57.

Loutzenhiser insisted he was in a good spot for the fight. After Toups left, the crew stretched 100 feet of hose from its pump to the swimming pool. He updated the other captains on the radio.

Sometime after 6:45 a.m., the fire began roiling at the bottom of the drainage. Loutzenhiser radioed Engine 51, stationed at another house down-slope, to begin the burnouts.

Then his crew turned the water pump to wide-open throttle.

The fire reached them at the top of the canyon and didn't stop.

It raced across the overlook, gutting the octagonal house. It rushed over the engine, so hot it deformed the heavy-duty metal leaf springs in the truck's suspension and burned all six tires down to their cords. The window glass shattered and melted into the floor of the truck cab.

Three of the firefighters died instantly. The other two, including Loutzenhiser, died in a hospital. Investigators found two emergency fire shelters, only partially deployed.

The Esperanza Fire burned uncontained for four more days, ultimately charring 41,000 acres.

An auto mechanic convicted of starting the fire was later sentenced to death.

But fire investigators who studied the event would outline the factors that turned the fire from malicious to deadly.

Crews misjudged the risks, they said. The wind drove the flames. And as the flames moved, they burned into what may be the most dangerous territory of all: chaparral.

***

Chaparral fills Arizona's middle elevations, between desert and pine forest, in a swath from Kingman southeast toward Safford.

The habitat, with its small, woody bushes, seasonal grasses and scarce rain, has inspired both fear and controversy over the role that fire plays in its nature.

Some land managers have called it "built to burn," and some fire agencies have advocated for regular burn-offs in hopes of reducing the amount of fuel.

Others, like scientists at the California Chaparral Institute, argue that chaparral, unlike pine forests, doesn't need frequent blazes to stay healthy. Old-growth shrubs can be a natural, healthy habitat, and planned burn-offs can harm more than they help.

But everyone agrees on a few things.

Chaparral has always survived in a delicate balance of summer heat with little rain. Climate change, which has created hotter, drier conditions, threatens to tip such fragile landscapes out of balance, leaving them more vulnerable to fire.

And burning chaparral is nothing like a burning forest, where a natural or "good" fire moves slowly through the undergrowth.

When fire does burn in chaparral—whether it's frequent or rare, natural or prescribed—it burns hot and fast. The small bushes dry quickly with the heat, making them easier to ignite. As they do, they become airborne embers that can ride a wind gust for miles, past any firebreak.

With the wind behind it, a chaparral fire is nearly impossible to stop.

***

When Thomas Swetnam signed up with the Gila Hotshots in New Mexico, he was following his father's lead. His dad had worked the forests as a ranger. The younger Swetnam cut trails and burned lines in the same ranges, hiking into the mountains or rappelling from a helicopter with fire tools in tow.

What he learned on the lines, starting in 1978, helped him in his studies of dendrochronology, the science of reconstructing ecological history through tree rings. He now heads the University of Arizona's Laboratory of Tree-Ring Research and has built a career on understanding wildland fire.

"Chaparral is inherently dangerous to fight fire in," Swetnam said. "Even the most experienced people out on a line can be taken by surprise."

But other factors are as important as what grows on a landscape: Location. Weather conditions. Climate. Maybe more than anything now, climate.

Drought struck much of the West in the late 1990s. In Arizona, 2002 was the driest year in a millennium of records and tree-ring evidence. That same year, the Rodeo-Chediski Fire burned 468,638 acres and, in 2011, the Wallow Fire burned even more.

Fire and forestry experts have noted that the monster fires charred forests that had grown too dense after a century of fire suppression. But Swetnam argues that the forests had already grown dense by the 1950s. It took record-drought conditions and rising temperatures to trigger the fires.

"It's apparent this is primarily a climate-driven thing," Swetnam said. Hot weather can overstress plants already feeling the effects of drought.

Add a string of hot days to a landscape weakened by a string of dry years and the result is evident in a flash of lightning.

On a shelf in a gleaming new lab building on the UA campus, Swetnam keeps a slice from a ponderosa pine, carefully preserved and labeled. The tree grew about 46 miles south of Flagstaff, from roughly 1793 to about 1979.

Looking at each ring, Swetnam can trace what he sees as the history of firefighting and land use. From the tree's earliest years, a fire scar is evident on a regular cycle: 26 fires, about every four years. Then, after 1898, the fires stop. There's not another scar until the tree died. People had taken fire out of the forests.

On another wall, Swetnam pointed to another display, this one a record of fires in the West. At the end of the 20th century, the fires grew in number and size once more. The attempt to control fire was failing in the face of extreme drought and rising temperatures.

"The scale of these fires should get our attention," he said. "They are 10 times larger than they ever were before. Fires are burning in ways we've never seen. It's all just blowing up."

The changing climate drives chaparral fire in much the same way, but there's a key difference. Swetnam's lab contains no tree rings, no cross-sections of plants from the scrubby ranges below the pine forest.

When fire burns in chaparral, it leaves nothing behind.

***

In August 2009, an arsonist set a fire in the chaparral north of Los Angeles. By the time fire crews brought it under control more than three weeks later, it burned 161,000 acres, destroyed 89 homes and killed two firefighters.

The weather was hot and dry and crews battled through 50-year-old scrub, some of it up to 8 feet high. The slopes crackled with dead oak and juniper.

Fire crews struggled to stay on the line. A recently certified Type I hotshot crew was called in from out of state. During one harrowing episode, a boulder fell off a cliff, slammed a crew member in the ribs and drove him into a chain-link fence. Down a man, that crew—the Granite Mountain Hotshots—went back to work.

Early on, fire experts and elected officials seized on the idea that the Station Fire had exploded because the hills were overgrown and Los Angeles County had failed to clear underbrush. Ecologists argued otherwise.

"The main reason this fire spread as quickly as it did," wrote Richard Halsey, director of the California Chaparral Institute, in a response to other reports, "had more to do with current long-term drought conditions and the steep terrain than the age of the vegetation. When conditions are this dry, anything will burn."

The drought that began in the late 1990s has persisted. And there have been other shifts: Today, climate experts say, summer starts earlier and ends later across the West.

In late June 2013, Arizona sweltered in record heat. Prescott reached a record-high 104 degrees on June 28—15 degrees above average. Moisture levels in plants on the hills plunged.

As the Granite Mountain Hotshots climbed into the shifting sunlight of the morning, they picked their way through chaparral. The woody stalks were dense and combustible by nature, heated by the day, and cluttered with deadwood ready to burn.

SUNDAY AFTERNOON

The Granite Mountain Hotshots watched the fire crackle in the dense brush, branches so dry and thin they acted as their own kindling. Flames spread along the two-track road that led down the ridge. This fire was theirs.

Since their morning briefing down in Yarnell, the crew had planned to build a line to keep the fire from spreading south into Glen Ilah. They would dig from the top of the ridge down toward a bulldozer track, creating an anchor for the other firefighters.

The chaparral grew thick and clearing it was slow work.

As the sun bore down, crew superintendent Eric Marsh decided to switch tactics. He would try burning out some of the brush.

The strategy is called indirect attack. Crews clear the ground away from the fire's edge. Then, if conditions are right, they can burn the brush back toward the flames. A wildfire stops its advance when it reaches the black area. Firefighters say, "The best line is a black line."

Around 11:30, with the beginnings of a line cleared, the hotshots started a test fire on the ridge. They always carried fusees, ignition sticks that look like road flares, and drip torches, a more rugged version of a household blowtorch, to burn out lines.

About 10 minutes later, a small air tanker made a pass over the hill, engine whirring. Its fuselage doors opened and a stream of red fire-retardant slurry spilled onto the ground—directly onto the crew's backfire.

Marsh grabbed his radio, frustrated. He told the air crew he wanted to continue the burnout.

Negative, the air commander said. Return to a direct attack.

The small tanker flew another pass and dropped more slurry on the crew's fire. The flames flickered out.

***

About 10:30, the Blue Ridge Hotshots parked their crew carriers next to Granite Mountain's buggies on the dirt track called Sesame Street. Gary Cordes, the Yarnell structure supervisor, asked the crew to start clearing out the road with a bulldozer.

Brian Frisby, the Blue Ridge crew superintendent, called Marsh for a rundown on the fire activity. Frisby complained about having gotten a poor briefing that morning. Marsh warned Frisby about bad radio communications. And that was just part of it.

Rogers Trueheart "True" Brown, the Blue Ridge team captain, had met other firefighters who had been on the fire since Saturday. They were confused about tactics. The prison crew thought they had buttoned down the fire, but it made a new run overnight. A crewman from *Globe* said he had not been briefed, had no maps and had trouble with communications.

Speaking by radio, Frisby and Marsh tried to figure out who was in charge on the ridge. Marsh had been designated Alpha Division leader. The Zulu Division leader had yet to report. Frisby didn't know if his team was part of Alpha or Zulu, and he didn't have jobs for most of his crew.

Finally, Brown put one of the team's squad leaders, Cory Ball, aboard the dozer. Ball would start a line pointing toward the hill. Higher up, the Granite Mountain Hotshots would work their way down. For the plan to work, someone would have to figure out how to connect the two lines.

The rest of the Blue Ridge crew headed back to Shrine Road, one of the staging areas. They had no clear assignment.

A little while later, the air tanker snuffed out Granite Mountain's test back-fire.

Frisby and Brown rode the ATV up the ridge to meet with Marsh. They talked strategy again. Granite Mountain would continue to work. Frisby would start on the connecting line.

They needed a lookout. Marsh said his team had a regular lookout, but he would send Brendan McDonough this time. McDonough climbed aboard Frisby's vehicle and rode down the hill, then hiked north.

McDonough set up on a rocky rise. He could see the fire, test weather conditions, and keep notes in his log. He looked toward the blaze and picked a "trigger point" —if the fire reached that spot, he'd have to move back.

**

Rance Marquez arrived at Model Creek School in Peeples Valley about 10:30 a.m. A fire-management specialist for the Bureau of Land Management, he had been asked to lead a division of fire crews in Yarnell.

To him, the school, which had been designated the incident command post, seemed in chaos. He would later recount how chiefs there scribbled assignments on slips of paper and thrust the paper at crew members.

Finally, Marquez was sent with instructions to find Marsh and divvy up the work on the fire's rear flank. He wandered among Yarnell's meandering streets and had to stop once for directions. He finally found the crew buggies and a Blue Ridge crewman working the bulldozer. Marquez scanned the ridge and the fire. He spotted Granite Mountain working nearby, in a blackened area.

A little after 1 p.m., Marquez tried to radio Marsh directly, but couldn't raise him. He borrowed a Blue Ridge radio. Marquez told Marsh he was taking over Zulu Division and needed to work out boundaries.

Everything else was unclear. Marsh wanted both hotshot teams and the bulldozer in his division. Marquez thought he should take over Blue Ridge. Marsh cut in.

"Hey, listen, we need to decide and go with it." His frustration was clear. "If you want, I'll take the whole west side."

Marquez backed off. He suggested using the corner of the dozer line to create a second anchor point. They still couldn't agree on how to divide the ridge. Finally, Marquez returned to the command post. There, he told chiefs the vegetation was too thick, the terrain too meandering. He couldn't see a way to make things work. He wanted to request more support, more hotshot crews, three to five of them.

**

The Blue Ridge crew headed back to their buggies, still without any clear duties. They looked up at the thrum of the air tankers and saw a heavy tanker and a helicopter nearly collide.

Travis Fueller, one of the Blue Ridge crew members, said the air-attack fleet sounded overwhelmed. The choppers seemed to be freelancing, dropping slurry wherever they wanted. From the ground, the tactics were hard to follow. Hit and miss. Water drops that hit black areas.

"It's like the Swiss cheese effect," one crew member said. Mistakes occur in different parts of an organization until gaps line up, like the holes in slices of Swiss cheese. Disaster follows.

"We need a piece of cheese," Brown replied. "This is just one big hole."

***

Up on the mountain, Marsh had been scouting ahead.

He knew the crew was tired. The men had worked 28 days in June. They had fought two big fires, the Thompson Ridge Fire in New Mexico and the Doce Fire outside Prescott. In between, they took two days off, as required by federal rules.

During fire season, days can stretch to 16 hours. Sometimes hotshot crews can work 32 hours straight over consecutive days. The pace is grueling, even for a team with an intense workout schedule.

The men hit a boulder-strewn rise and broke for lunch.

They carried the packaged, military-style "meals, ready to eat" on the line, though they always hoped they would be spared from eating the stuff. Marsh liked to carry cans of Spam just in case. He'd sometimes heat it with an ignition fusee and slice off hunks to share. This time, there would be no chow line.

Ashcraft and Christopher MacKenzie snapped photos. Their faces were gritty from the soot.

The men had talked a few days earlier about how they would wake up sometimes smelling smoke after a day on the line. Smoke dreams, they called it. Fires in their sleep.

***

As the sun traced its arc through the afternoon sky, a line of storms began to build. High on the lip of the Mogollon Rim, the broken bits of vapor boiled up, riding the summer heat.

The ragged strand stretched from Flagstaff 75 miles to Forest Lakes. The clock turned and the storms edged down off the Rim toward Prescott.

Recent days had brought a series of these same storm lines, the kind of dry, unstable systems that kick up wind and lightning to herald the coming of the monsoon.

Lightning, especially, had put on a show over the past few days. It sparked fires in the Bradshaw Mountains, the Sierra Prieta near Prescott —and the ridge above Yarnell.

In Albuquerque, at the center that coordinated wildfires across the Southwest, meteorologist Chuck Maxwell watched the storms build on radar. He could tell early they would play havoc with winds in Yarnell. He sent word to the incident commanders. They responded that they saw what was coming.

***

Juliann Ashcraft had taken the kids swimming and had just returned home when the storm hit.

They took a better look out the open windows.

As the storm kicked in, the wind shifted, blasting in through the windows.

"This is nuts," Juliann thought.

She rushed to close the windows on one side of the house and sent the kids to the other side.

***

At 3:26, fire commanders in Peeples Valley got a new forecast. Thunderstorms moving in. Wind speeds 40-50 mph. Strong downdrafts likely.

By 3:30, the wind had turned 90 degrees. It was pushing toward the southwest, along with the storm.

***

Just before 4 p.m., McDonough turned his eyes toward the fire.

He had been watching the flames push north all afternoon. Now they were coming toward him.

They passed his trigger point. Time to leave.

McDonough keyed up his radio and called Jesse Steed, the crew captain. He was moving back, to the open area where the Blue Ridge team had bulldozed in.

"OK, cool," Steed replied.

McDonough hiked toward the grader, scanning as he walked for other lookout spots. But the fire was moving fast. If it caught up to him, he would have to shake open his foil fire shelter.

He radioed Steed again, who was watching him from above. He looked around for an open space.

As he did, Frisby roared up—a ride out, just in time. The two wheeled around and headed back toward the crew trucks.

A few minutes later, McDonough looked back at the hill he had just left. It was burning.

***

Cordes had set up trigger points of his own.

From Yarnell, the structure-protection chief had laid out three lines to gauge the fire's movement. The first was a ridge a mile north of town —it meant prepare for evacuation.

The second trigger point, closer, marked the time for firefighters to pack up.

The third point meant everybody out.

As the wind turned, the fire crested the ridge, the first trigger point. Evacuation orders started. Commanders had believed they would have an hour until flames reached the second trigger.

Instead, it took 10 minutes.

**

Engine crews had been working outside a youth camp on Shrine Road.

After Frisby dropped McDonough off at the buggies, he turned toward the road.

Wind launched bits of flaming brush from a half-mile out, turning manzanita and oak into torches.

There, Frisby saw engine crews still in place. The fire was moving fast, and the crews weren't. Load up, he told them, and get out.

A Blue Ridge crew member shot video from his truck as they headed up the highway, black smoke building a dome over the town.

"We're just pulling out," he said. "Yarnell's blowin' up."

**

Overhead, a new crew had taken over air attack. The transmission from the departing crew: "You have the fire, I'm leaving."

The three men in the plane listened to the chaotic radio traffic. They felt the wind shift and saw the fire turn. Flames blew through the mottled red line where tankers had been dropping slurry.

Smoke stretched across the ridge, an angry filter over the late afternoon sun.

**

On the ground, trucks headed toward the Ranch House Restaurant at the crest of the highway. Its parking lot would offer a safe space.

As the last of the fire engines and chiefs' pickups pulled back from the edges, embers fell like fiery snow, igniting spot fires that spread out and converged.

Smoke turned the bright afternoon to an eerie darkness. At Boulder Springs Ranch in Glen Ilah, a security camera switched from day mode to night.

At the Ranch House parking lot, some of the chiefs gathered and looked back. Propane tanks vented off columns of flame. Yarnell and Glen Ilah were burning.

One crew was not with them.

***

Just before 4 p.m., Steed's radio crackled—McDonough had reached his trigger point and was pulling back.

"OK, cool," Steed had replied.

He could see McDonough moving away. Steed radioed: "I've got eyes on you and the fire and it's making a good push."

Wade Parker, a second-year hotshot from Chino Valley, took a picture with his phone and texted a message home: "This thing is runnin straight for yarnel jus starting evac..."

Scott Norris sent his mother a message: "This fire is running at Yarnell!!!"

The Granite Mountain Hotshots could see the fire moving.

But on the other side of the fire, the storm that had dropped down from Prescott was pushing out a solid line of wind.

On their radios, crew members talked about their plans.

Below them, fire crews were pulling back. Above them, airplanes focused on a last-ditch tanker drop to save the town.

No one was watching the 19 men on the ridge.

Sometime after 4 p.m., the time came for them to move, too.

The Granite Mountain Hotshots, alone on the hill, set off together for the last time.

BROTHERHOOD

The hotshot superintendent gathered his crew at their camp on an island in the Boundary Waters wilderness area in northern Minnesota. The men were tired and wet after two weeks of fighting a fire in a setting unlike any previous assignment.

Lightning sparked the Pagami Creek Fire on Aug. 16, 2011, in a remote area near the U.S.-Canadian border. Now, midway through September, flames had burned across more than 100,000 acres. About 500 firefighters were on the scene, including crews from across the country.

With the onset of cooler weather, fire commanders believed they had slowed the spread of the fire, but they still needed help.

They had summoned the crew superintendent to ask if his team would work another seven days, even though they were due for a break. The superintendent returned to his team to see what they thought.

His name was Eric Marsh. The team was the Granite Mountain Hotshots.

Ted Ralston, a hotshot on the team that year, remembers listening with his crewmates as Marsh laid out the situation.

The past two weeks had been tough on the men. Before they began work, they underwent training at a Boy Scout camp to learn how to paddle canoes and portage them over land, along with diesel-powered water pumps.

Supplies arrived on a helicopter, which dropped them into Moose Lake. A crew member would paddle out to retrieve the packs. The terrain was difficult to maneuver in, the dry land laced with creeks and inlets from lakes. They sometimes had to split up at night to maintain smaller campsites in the wilderness.

"He asked us what we wanted to do," Ralston recalled. "One of his great qualities was how he asked everyone for their opinions. He wasn't a dictator at all. He wanted to know how everyone else felt."

Marsh explained the request, went back over the team's options, noted that under the rules, they were due for a break. Then he waited.

"Most of the time we didn't have to say a word," Ralston said. "He could tell by our faces what we were thinking."

Marsh looked at their faces and found his answer.

He declined the fire bosses' request. The crew packed up and headed home to Arizona.

***

Each year at the start of the fire season, the hotshots would gather for a family barbecue. They would hear about the new guys who had hired on, and they would explain the significance of the team logo.

A new guy couldn't wear a shirt with the official logo, just a plain black shirt with the motto: "Esse Quam Videri" —to be, rather than to seem. The newbies had a year to prove they lived that way.

When they reported at the station each day, Marsh would talk to them about being good citizens, starting with the little stuff: You carry groceries. You hold doors open. You help someone with a flat tire or with yard work.

"You're a good man, Number 1," he would say.

Then he would talk about safety and work and the risks of the fireline, and he and the others would watch the rookies. At the end of the season, the team held another barbecue. And Marsh would present a patch with the logo to each rookie who had earned it.

Juliann Ashcraft remembers the year her husband, Andrew, earned his.

"It was like Christmas morning," she said. "He was presented rookie-of-the-year because he was always an overachiever. Then his logo. ... It was not work for them. It was like a fraternity, like this society. You had to prove yourself and you got your place in it."

***

Marsh had led the hotshots since the team became a nationwide firefighting crew in April 2008. He was one of the few constants on a roster that changed from one season to the next.

Among the firefighters, friendships grew. They barbecued together, shared house rentals during the fire season, challenged each other in the gym, prayed together.

In August 2012, the crew took an assignment on the Holloway Fire in the remote wilds along the Nevada-Oregon border. Lightning sparked the fire, which grew rapidly in the sagebrush.

About 30 miles down Nevada 292 from the turnoff to the firefighters' staging area, Denio is a small patch of irrigated green cropland. Glenna Eckel lived there with her husband.

Eckel had heard from her son, Travis Carter, that he and his hotshot crew were working the Holloway Fire. She drove over to visit him a couple of times, meeting up for 15 minutes or so when he came down for supplies.

Eckel had worked for the U.S. Forest Service in Prescott for years and knew life on the line could get lonely. Carter had celebrated his birthday just before reporting to Nevada, so she decided she would mix up a small batch of her homemade ice cream and take it to him, with a side of chocolate syrup.

She met him about 9 one night during a supply run. He was happy to see her and the ice cream. But he could see there was barely enough for him, much less his crew.

"Could you make enough for the whole team?" he asked.

Eckel told him she couldn't, but she promised to return home and bake enough chocolate-chip cookies for everyone. Carter smiled.

And when he took the ice cream back to the tents that night, he shared it with Andrew Ashcraft.

***

After his four-year tour with the Marines ended in 2001, Jesse Steed wanted to find another job that would challenge him and still offer the camaraderie and the brotherhood he felt in the Corps.

He found what he wanted as a firefighter for the Prescott National Forest. He joined the Prescott Hotshots and spent time with the eight-person helicopter crew. In 2009, he signed on with the Granite Mountain Hotshots as a crew boss.

His sister, Taunya Steed, watched Jesse grow into his job as a firefighter and she could see he loved the work. He found what he was looking for on the crew.

"It's kind of crazy to say because he was my brother," she would say later, "but those boys were even closer to him than I was, on a different level. Not necessarily by blood but ..."

Jesse Steed would tell guys on the crew he loved them.

Not everyone was comfortable with that. One former Granite Mountain hotshot, Phillip Maldonado, would reply, "Yeah, OK," or just "thanks."

Then one day, Maldonado spotted a tree falling toward Steed. Maldonado yelled a warning and Steed pushed the tree away with one hand. Maldonado stared wide-eyed, and as the men realized how close they'd come to disaster, Steed said again, "I love you."

And for the first time, Maldonado said it back.

***

There's a story that made the rounds of Station 7 occasionally, Juliann Ashcraft said, usually when someone wanted to needle the bosses, Marsh and Steed.

The crew had been on a fire, sometime back, when two parts of the team got separated. A line of fire had crept between them and, as the story went, Marsh started to panic. He grabbed his radio.

"Are you guys OK?" he said.

"I'm fine," Steed replied, the radio crackling.

Marsh froze. Tears filled his eyes.

"Oh, my gosh!" he cried. "Steed's blind!"

Steed jumped back on the radio. "No, I'm fine! I'm fine!"

"Steed's blind!" Marsh cried again.

Finally, other crew members jumped in to calm him down. He had just heard wrong, they told him. Steed was fine. Fine.

From then on, around the firehouse, Marsh was "Papa," the old man who worried about his boys, whether they needed it or not.

***

Glenna Eckel tells another story, about the conversation she had with her son every time she saw him since he joined the hotshot crew. Eckel wanted to know that Carter understood what it meant to follow, that the measure of a good team member was knowing which way a path led before falling in line.

Glenna Eckel knew that the men had decades of wildland fire experience among them. She knew safety was foremost and that they were family men who wanted to go home. But she also knew her son.

"Trav," she would tell him every time he'd leave, "just remember, there's a lot of people running fires nowadays that don't have a lot of ground experience. And they might ask you to do something. So just be damn careful and make sure you communicate."

Speak up, she would tell him. If something doesn't look right, she would say, say so. If you have a bad feeling, she would say, tell somebody.

After the fire, she said, she didn't blame anyone for what happened. But she wondered if he would have taken her advice to heart.

"I have a feeling my son just isn't that type," she said. "He's so much of a team member, he would have trusted his leaders, whoever they were. And he would have done whatever it was, even if he'd had a feeling that it maybe wasn't quite right."

***

Before the start of the 2013 fire season, Marsh wrote an essay that circulated within the firehouse and attempted to explain what kept this crew together. He described the physically demanding work, the often miserable conditions, the long hours. He called it "the most fulfilling thing any of us have ever done."

He reveled in the way family and friends and the community supported the crew. But ultimately, he was an insider in a world outsiders couldn't know: "It's just difficult for anyone to grasp the magnitude of suffering and joy that we experience during a given fire season, unless you have been there yourself."

Marsh did not address the essay to anyone by name, but he wrote it during a troubled time in his tenure with the team. Prescott had rebuffed pleas to hire more full-time firefighters or provide better equipment. In his annual job review, Marsh had talked about his frustrations and his hopes that the situation would improve.

Darrell Willis, the deputy chief who oversaw the hotshot crew, acknowledged Marsh's concerns, but urged him to "let the system work ... and make the best of the situation."

By June 2013, the team had worked eight other fires. On the last day of that month, the team would report for work at the Yarnell Hill Fire, and test themselves against Marsh's standards one more time:

"We are not nameless or faceless," Marsh had written. "We are not expendable, we are not satisfied with mediocrity, we are not willing to accept being average, we are not quitters."

SUNDAY EVENING

At 10 minutes past 6, the crew of Ranger 58, a Department of Public Safety helicopter, spotted a ragged cluster of fabric below the hill.

The spot was in a charred, rocky basin west of Boulder Springs Ranch. The fabric looked like emergency fire shelters.

The helicopter landed and Eric Tarr, a medic, hiked about a quarter-mile to the site.

The ground was black and crusted, the surface broken by charred branches. He saw the metallic parts of a chain saw. An ax head without its wooden handle. Fuel bottles.

As he neared the shelters, Tarr heard voices. He yelled. Once, then again. No one responded. He walked through the site.

There were no survivors.

The voices were coming from handheld radios lying on the ground, still working.

Investigators would arrive to study the scene, gather notes, collect photographs. They would find the burned equipment. A charred page from a pocket guide for firefighters. A crew patch — the one awarded after the end of the rookie season — smudged with ash, singed on one edge, mostly unburned.

Ultimately, officials would craft a simple diagram, a final measure of 19 men.

Eric Marsh, the Granite Mountain superintendent, was not covered by his shelter. Most of the foil material lay to his right.

Jesse Steed, the crew captain, was fully covered by his shelter.

Clayton Whitted, a squad boss, was partly exposed.

Robert Caldwell, another squad boss, was fully covered by his shelter.

Travis Carter, the third squad boss, was mostly covered by his shelter.

Christopher MacKenzie was found near Whitted, mostly covered by his shelter.

Travis Turbyfill was found near MacKenzie. His fire shelter was underneath him.

Andrew Ashcraft lay next to Carter. He was mostly covered by his shelter.

Joe Thurston was found near Steed, mostly covered by his shelter.

Anthony Rose was found near Marsh. The shelter was beneath him.

Wade Parker was found near Turbyfill on the far corner of the site. Most of his shelter lay next to him.

Garret Zuppiger lay near Caldwell. He was mostly inside his shelter.

Scott Norris was found next to Zuppiger and Caldwell. He was mostly inside his shelter.

Dustin DeFord was found near MacKenzie. He was inside his shelter.

William Warneke lay between Marsh and Whitted. Most of the material was beneath him.

Kevin Woyjeck was found near Whitted and MacKenzie. He was fully inside his shelter.

Grant McKee lay near Steed. Most of the material was underneath him.

Sean Misner was found along the edge of the site, near Parker and DeFord. Most of the material was on the ground behind him.

John Percin Jr. was found next to Ashcraft. Most of the material was spread out on the ground next to him.

Only the first few on the scene saw the aftermath. Soon the men's remains would be draped in flags and carried away.

The site where 19 men unfurled their paper-thin fire shelters was small, less than half the size of a tennis court. Every one of them was within arm's reach of another.

***

Pieces of the hotshots' final minutes can be known from the radio calls they made.

The Blue Ridge Hotshots kept logs that capture part of the afternoon.

"I copy fire is progressed to the buggies." — Eric Marsh. He was talking about the crew carriers parked on Sesame Street, a dirt road on the edge of Yarnell. "Also going to make our way through out escape route."

"Are you in good black?" —Brian Frisby, the superintendent of the Blue Ridge crew. He used a firefighting term that describes an area burned enough to give a crew a safe working space.

"Picking our way through the black to the rd in the bottom out towards the ranch." — Marsh. The hotshots had been told that Boulder Springs Ranch, a cluster of buildings on a knoll above Glen Ilah, would provide a safe shelter.

"The rd we came on w/the ranger." — Frisby. He would later say he thought Marsh meant a two-track road on the ridge.

Around 4:30, the air-support plane flew a path for a heavy tanker carrying a load of retardant. The air crew would remember Marsh calling them, calm, after they passed: "That is exactly what we are looking for, that is exactly right."

Other calls can be heard in real time.

The firefighter standing outside his truck, near Shrine Road where the pavement turned to dirt, was wearing a helmet camera as he listened to his radio. He was perhaps a mile away from the hotshot team when his camera began recording transmissions just before 4:40 p.m.

Over about three minutes, he captured calls among a commander on a plane called Bravo 33, an operations chief on the ground and at least two of the hotshots:

Hotshots: *"Breaking in on Arizona 16, Granite Mountain Hotshots, we are in front of the flaming front."*

Operations: *"Bravo 33, Operations, you copying that on air to ground?"*

Hotshots: *"Air to ground 16, Granite Mountain, Air Attack, how do you read?"*

Operations: *"Granite Mountain, Operations on air to ground."*

Hotshots: *"Air Attack, Granite Mountain 7, how do you copy me?"*

Bravo 33: *"OK, I was copying a little bit of that, uh conversation uh, on air to ground. We're, we'll do the best we can. We got the type 1 helicopters ordered back in. Uh, we'll see what we can do."*

Hotshots: *"Air Attack, Granite Mountain 7!"*

Bravo 33: *"OK, uh, unit that's hollerin' in the radio, I need you to quit. And, uh, break, Operations, Bravo 33."*

Operations: *"OK Granite Mountain 7 sounds like they got some trouble, uh, go ahead and get that, he's trying to get you on the radio, let's go ahead and see what we've got going on."*

Bravo 33: *"OK copy that, uh, I'll get with Granite Mountain 7 then."*

Hotshots: *"Bravo 33, Division Alpha with Granite Mountain."*

Bravo 33: *"OK, uh Division Alpha, Bravo 33."*

Hotshots: *"Yeah, I'm here with Granite Mountain Hotshots, our escape route has been cut off. We are preparing a deployment site and we are burning out around ourselves in the brush and I'll give you a call when we are under the sh — the shelters."*

Bravo 33: *"OK copy that. So you're on the south side of the fire then?"*

Hotshots: *"Affirm!"*

Bravo 33: *"K, we're gonna bring you the VLAT OK."*

The very large air tanker. It carried a belly full of wet slurry, ready to slow the path of the fire. If it could find the crew.

The air chief ordered it to circle. A helicopter launched from nearby. The smoke was thick.

Bravo 33: *"OK, uh, we're workin' our way around there. We've got uh several aircraft comin' to ya. We'll see if we can't take care of business for you."*

He listened for a response.

Bravo 33: *"Division Alpha, Bravo 33, I need you to pay attention and tell me when you hear the aircraft, OK? 'Cause it's gonna be a little tough for us to see ya."*

The radio squawked. No voice broke through.

Bravo 33: *"Division Alpha, Bravo 33. Do you hear a helicopter?"*

Static again.

Bravo 33: *"Granite Mountain 7, Bravo 33 air to ground."*

Bravo 33: *"Granite Mountain 7, Bravo 33 air to ground."*

***

In the space of two minutes, 19 trained men with chain saws, Pulaski tools and ignition sticks can clear a patch of brush to bare ground, maybe a patch large enough to deploy 19 emergency shelters.

Investigators would conclude the Granite Mountain crew had little more time than that.

In two minutes, they would have seen few good locations. A patch of rocks sat uphill, too far to reach. They needed a place where they could remain together.

In the fire training classes Eric Marsh taught, he always stressed the importance of deploying together.

In ideal conditions, deploying a shelter would take about 20 seconds. High winds could slow the process.

Marsh would teach his students to crawl into the foil and lie facedown on the ground cloth, using the hold-down straps to keep the shelter in place.

And he talked about what made a bad deployment site: "Flashy" fuels. A narrow creek or streambed. A saddle, the low point on a ridge, where wind was more apt to funnel fire.

When they deploy their shelters, crews are taught, they should ditch their gasoline and flares, and keep tools clear of the shelter. The sharp edges can cut through the material, exposing the firefighter.

At the bottom of the hill, the burned remnants of tools were found scattered around the site. Ignition sticks and fuel containers were found away from packs.

Investigators found stumps where the sawyers had cut some of the brush away. In two minutes, the men would have had to clear a stretch of bare earth longer than the wind-driven flames, at least 70 feet of it. The rule for surer survival is a space four times that long.

In two minutes, they would have run out of time.

***

For a hotshot, the long hours digging, the taste of dirt and smoke come with rewards. Every working day is a day outdoors, even if the work is clearing brush around houses. Hotshots see places most others never will.

And hotshots earn a degree of autonomy. They answer to chiefs, to an incident commander. But in the wild, the crew is often on its own, left alone to finish the job.

The last photos of the Granite Mountain Hotshots show them at the rocky slope where they had eaten lunch. The crew stands amid partly burned brush, "in the black," as firefighters say.

There, around 4 p.m., they would have assessed their next move.

They decided on their own, by all indications. Brendan McDonough had left his lookout point. The crew was watching the fire without another lookout. At some point, they would have decided to move.

They would leave the anchor point, the bare ground they had cut into the hill.

They would have shouldered their packs, hefted their saws and turned south.

About that time, they would have felt the wind change, roiling around them. It could have seemed like the kind of change the last weather update had predicted.

They would not have seen what meteorologists would soon track on their radar screens: a downdraft from the thunderstorm that hit the ground and pushed outward, kicking up a clear wind line.

For the crew, that line of wind was still hidden behind a column of smoke in the distance. It would rush out of the north like a jet, 43 mph, carrying the fire south.

The crew would have worked its way south too, probably along the old jeep road on the ridge. Marsh radioed to commanders the crew's intent to reach their safety zone, "picking our way through the black."

There were 19 of them, able to accomplish almost anything together. No one else was watching them. They were on their own.

As they hiked, they reached a saddle, a dip in the ridgeline.

To their right, the heel of the fire crept through the brush, blackening the earth behind it.

In front of them, the jeep road wound southwest, down the hill but away from town.

To their left was Glen Ilah, and three hulking buildings on the ranch, its bare yard seemingly fireproof.

The hotshots would have seen all of this.

To their right, they might have found safety where the fire had passed, a patch of black. But that path would cut them off from everyone else.

In front of them, the road went "down and out," the firefighter's key words for safety. Heat rises. Staying below flames can mean staying out of trouble. But the road dropped off toward the endless desert.

To their left, the saddle dropped into a bowl-shaped canyon, where rainstorms had carved out a dry creek bed. The bowl went down and out too, toward the ranch's safety zone.

Locals say the brush in that canyon was thick, a head-high maze. Sometimes, the only way through it was to crawl. Sometimes there was no way through.

The hotshots would have seen all of this.

Above them, an air-command plane circled. Its crew was trying to guide a tanker plane ready to drop retardant on the fire.

By then, the hotshots' decision was theirs alone.

Together, they turned left.

As they descended into the basin, the fire in the distance disappeared from their sight. Smaller ridges to the north, near McDonough's lookout point, would have blocked their view.

The climb down would have been slow, through the same brush that had stymied two hikers that morning. Finally, they neared the bottom of the hill.

As they did, the wall of flames emerged from behind the ridge. The fire and the fire crew came face to face.

THE HOTSHOTS

Eric Marsh, 43, was the founding superintendent of the Granite Mountain Hotshots. He served with the team since its inception and taught firefighting classes. The crew called him "Papa."

Travis Carter, 31, grew up in a ranching family near Kirkland, not far from Yarnell. He fought fires with the Prescott Hotshots, then became a squad boss with Granite Mountain. He was passionate about the outdoors, firefighting and his two children.

Jesse Steed, 36, was the captain of the team, the second in command and the leader in Marsh's absence. A former Marine, he was a devoted father of two. And he was a workout leader — the firehouse gym was dubbed "Steed's Dojo."

Travis Turbyfill, 27, a former Marine and Forest Service firefighter, beamed in every picture. When he was away overnight, he read "Goodnight Moon" over the phone to his two daughters.

Garret Zuppiger, 27, went to high school in Phoenix and graduated from business school at the University of Arizona, but preferred a life outdoors. He traveled the West Coast, worked in construction and then found firefighting.

Dustin DeFord, 24, was the fifth of 10 children from a town in Montana so small it had only one paved road in. He studied for pastoral ministry and worked as a missionary before joining the hotshot crew.

Billy Warneke, 25, grew up in Southern California, then joined the Marine Corps. He and a high-school sweetheart reconnected and married, moving to a country home outside Tucson where they could raise a family. They were expecting their first child, a daughter.

Kevin Woyjeck, 21, pursued his dream of becoming a firefighter, like his father, with a laser focus. Friends said his smile could light up any room, or any dance floor.

Scott Norris, 28, worked on a Payson fire crew before returning to Prescott. Friends remember that he loved to study travel, languages and weather, noticing every shift in the clouds.

Joe Thurston, 32, played guitar and drums, married his high-school sweetheart, studied chemistry and zoology and loved his two sons. Making the hotshot team was one of the highlights of his life.

Robert Caldwell, 23, seemed like the older brother growing up, though he was the younger. Seven months before the fire, he married his fiancee and became a stepfather to her 5-year-old son.

Grant McKee, 21, loved adventure, trying every sport. He left Southern California for Prescott, where his cousin Robert Caldwell worked on the hotshot team. McKee joined the team in April.

Andrew Ashcraft, 29, worked on the fire crew in summer and the snowplow crew in winter. He went home to his wife and four children. The youngest, a boy, arrived in 2012, eight weeks early, on his father's birthday.

Clayton Whitted, 28, studied the ministry before returning to fire-fighting, where he kept his sense of humor and faith. One of his Bibles, fraying and dog-eared, had a prayer list written inside. The list included his family and the hotshots.

Sean Misner, 26, came from a firefighting family. He moved to Prescott from California with his new wife. On New Year's Day 2013, he learned he would become a father. On April 8, he started work with the hotshots.

Wade Parker, 22, grew up in Chino Valley schools, where he played shortstop and helped other students in metal shop. He followed his father into the fire service, and planned to marry his girlfriend in October, just before his 23rd birthday.

Christopher MacKenzie, 30, was always in motion, as a snowboarder and ski-area worker, a BLM crew member and a hotshot in Southern California. A former captain there invited him to apply to join Granite Mountain.

John Percin Jr., 24, left Oregon for Prescott, where he graduated from wildfire training in 2012. He posted his last Facebook update on the morning of June30: "Lord, watch over us as we go into battle."

Anthony Rose, 23, grew up in Illinois before moving to Crown King to live with an uncle, who was a firefighter. A fire there sealed his desire to join a hotshot crew. His girlfriend was expecting their first child, a girl, in October.

Brendan McDonough was the only member of the crew not trapped by the fire. After that day, he said he hoped to remain strong for his own daughter and for the families the other hotshots left behind.

ABOUT THIS REPORT

The final hours of the Granite Mountain Hotshots have been the subject of numerous inquiries and two official reports: one from a Serious Accident Investigation Team commissioned by the Arizona State Forestry Division, another from the Arizona Division of Occupational Safety and Health. Though the two reports drew different conclusions about any failures or culpability, they largely agreed on the basic facts of events on that final Saturday and Sunday in June. The Forestry Division subsequently released investigative documents including photos, videos and hundreds of pages of interview notes and staffing logs.

The *Arizona Republic* also obtained thousands of pages of e-mails and other documents about the hotshot team from the city of Prescott, in response to requests under Arizona's open-records law.

This material provided the basis for much of "Alone on the hill."

Other elements of the story come from extensive interviews with people who were in the area at the time, fire officials, former members of the hotshot team, and friends and relatives of the firefighters. Reporters and photographers visited the fire station, the ridge above Yarnell and other sites key to the story. Lead writer Shaun McKinnon also researched public records from forestry and firefighting agencies related to five previous fatal wildfires.

Dialogue in the story comes only from interviews with people who heard the words directly, or from documentation of those words in the official investigative material.

The project was edited by Republic associate director Josh Susong.

ALMOST JUSTICE: THE BEAU ZABEL MURDER

THE PHILADELPHIA INQUIRER

JUNE 16, 17, 18, 19, 20, 2013

By Mike Newall

CHAPTER 1

A murder that tore at the city's soul. Few clues to go on. A break in the case at the cost of another life.

Monday, she had written.

A date. His first in Philadelphia.

Uff-da!

That's what Beau Zabel said when he was excited.

And Beau Zabel was beyond excited. He had been in Philadelphia 42 days and he was swooning in the newness. Like big-boy summer camp.

None of it felt real yet.

The Italian Market rowhouse with his roommate, Meg Guerreiro, and Kismet, her Maltese Yorkie. His soon-to-start student teaching program.

His daily explorations with his Not for Tourists Guide to Philadelphia. Sometimes 50 blocks through Center City. Sometimes with Kismet. Always with his iPod, comedy podcasts loaded.

He was far from Austin.

Austin, Minn. Population: 24,000. Spam Town USA! Birthplace of that wonderful luncheon meat and home to the Spam Museum, where he had worked in high school, juggling and making balloon animals.

But Austin was Austin.

A year out of college, he'd been working the late shift at Mrs. Gerry's Kitchen, a salad dressing factory 20 miles from Austin. The pressure washers made his hands sore, and the dreary hours allowed his mind to dwell on unrequited loves.

He thrilled in the randomness of Philadelphia.

Like his new summer job at Starbucks on South Street.

"Rocking the espresso machine and blending some fraps!" he boasted on Facebook.

And now, this date, and with it, the possibility of a new friend. Her name was Jess. They met on Craigslist.

He tried not to get ahead of himself. He could be impatient with friendships and want to jump levels quickly. Not in a romantic way, but in a long-lasting way.

Of course, he loved his family, friends, his cats back home, Cleo and Mac. And there was his devotion to Stephen King, who was sooo much more than a horror writer.

But what did he know about love? Amour? Only what he'd seen on the screen and read on the page. He paid homage to it in his poetry.

"Life is love," he had written in his spiral notebook. "To love is to live. "

And life was beginning now.

He untied his apron. The watch dangling from the belt loop of his cargo shorts read a few minutes past 1 a.m., the end of a Saturday-night shift, June 15, 2008.

It was one of his last training sessions. Tomorrow, he'd be able to work the drink machines.

He stuffed his work cap into his backpack. Put on his black fedora. He had $17 in his wallet and 50 cents for a Mountain Dew at the vending machine on Washington Avenue—his nightly sugar buzz. He slung his bag over his shoulder and switched on his white iPod classic. He was on a Stephen Colbert kick.

He was 23 years old.

Twelve blocks straight up Passyunk. His regular walk home.

"Be careful," a coworker once warned him. "It gets sketchy. "

Meg had brought up safety, too. Beau was tall but soft, like a teddy bear. She didn't think he understood how dangerous Philadelphia could be. Maybe some Mace or a Taser for the apartment, she suggested. He made a joke of it, said he'd just carry a baseball bat wherever he went.

He crossed Bainbridge. A woman had been robbed at gunpoint outside the gym there a few weeks earlier. Beau didn't know about that robbery. And he didn't know about the two men police believe were cruising in a tinted-out Monte Carlo. The quiet older one in the passenger seat with a 9mm handgun. The younger, heavyset one behind the wheel.

"On route," they called it. Looking for someone to rob.

***

Beau spent a lot of time thinking about a soul mate. He and Jess exchanged e-mails during the week.

"We can grab a bite to eat, drinks, walk around, get ice cream," she wrote. "Whatever, I'm actually pretty easygoing. "

He asked her favorite coffee flavor so he could bring a gift.

"We have like a thousand flavors, so maybe I'll just close my eyes and pick randomly," he wrote.

He didn't want to come on too strong, but he'd barely have time for anything else once his teaching training began.

He was the middle child. An older sister, Brook. A younger brother, Brice. His mother, Lana Hollerud, and father, Douglas Kammeier, separated before he was born. He had a stepsister in Iowa City. When he was a toddler, his mother married Terry Zabel.

He grew up in a tidy, white-shingled house with red shutters and an American flag over the daisy garden. A wood-paneled bedroom with Grandpa's dusty hunting rifle encased on the wall. Through the window, the choking sweet smell of the Hormel plant, where the Spam was made.

Boy Scouts with Terry. Troop 109. Cuyuna Scout Camp, near the northern lakes.

"All God's critters got a place in the choir, some sing low, some sing higher," they'd sing.

By 17, Order of the Arrow and the highest honor, Eagle Rank. A photo in the Rochester Post-Bulletin, his face still plump with baby fat.

Math league, debate, viola, first bass and then baritone in the choir. Bouncing always between cliques, but never feeling a member of one. He called his mother Momma. She called him Sunny Bunny.

Listening to his iPod, he passed the bars near Christian Street.

***

College was at Augustana in Rock Island, Ill., along the Mississippi. Urgent years spent thirsting for connection.

Even if he doubled the hours in a day, he wouldn't have had enough time for the things he wanted to do: school, work, choir, guitar, weightlifting, running, international club, Spanish club, friends, sleep, reading for pleasure, biking, and poetry.

Plus, he wanted to teach himself French, swim three times a week, write short stories, shoot pool, watch some sunsets, and learn photography.

He made friends, mostly with girls.

Alice Parker, the choral composer, led a campus hymn festival. He went with three girls. Afterward, they went to one of the girls' parents' house and baked cookies and sang show tunes at the piano. It was one of the best random nights of his life.

As a child, he was told if he believed in Jesus, he would go to heaven. In college, he doubted, then decided: He would follow the words of Christ, but also the teachings of Buddha and Confucius. They were all great men he could spend a lifetime pondering.

He neared Washington Avenue with its gated tire shops and cellphone stores. Ahead, the neon of Geno's Steaks lit the sky orange.

***

A summer semester in Ecuador solidified his desire to live a life for others. He slept on a schoolhouse floor in the jungle, jogged a dirt road with barking dogs at his heels, and stood on a cliff overlooking the continental divide. Somehow the clouds seemed more majestic.

He bought a Panama hat and red rosary beads. In San Pedro, he ate six fish eyeballs on a dare. He tried a mai tai, but was more comfortable being the responsible one who made sure his friends got home safe.

He started to think in Spanish. The natives gave him tips. Don't say adios casually, because adios literally means "to God."

Once he mistakenly said *estoy exitado* to his house sister, which does mean "I am excited," but in a wedding-night sort of way.

In Ecuador, he fell for an American girl named Ann Marie. They read each other's poetry. He made her host family Spam and cheesy eggs. She fell asleep on his shoulder at *Star Wars Chapter III.* Afterward, she insisted she was fine taking a cab. He wrote the license plate and cab company on his hand just to be sure.

He slept near an active volcano.

The vending machine on Washington Avenue was next to a razor-wire fence. Two young people walked near, laughing in conversation. Beau was still listening to his iPod.

***

After graduation, he moved back to Austin. Went to work in the salad dressing factory. Grew lonely.

"I was at a movie theater the other day, and there was a girl sitting behind me that sounded just like you," he wrote a school friend.

In his childhood bedroom, he typed out the applications for student teaching programs. Miami. Chicago. Philadelphia. Places he would be needed. The Philadelphia Teaching Fellows was math-centric.

"Mathematics is one of my dearest passions," he wrote in one application essay. "Some mathematicians would describe their field as a soap opera that they love to watch unfold. We love to see how the characters interact. I hope to someday instill at least part of that passion into my students."

In Philadelphia, he'd teach his own class and take teaching certification classes at Drexel University, tuition-free if he stayed in the city five years.

"See you in the funny pages," he e-mailed his family.

But he worried, too.

"Some days, I feel uber-excited about becoming a teacher," he wrote a friend. "Occasionally, I have cursed days where I fear that teaching won't be all I hope it will be."

He found the Ellsworth rowhouse on roommates.com and flew in to see it over Easter. Meg was an education major at Temple University, preparing to be a student teacher, too. Beau arrived with a bouquet of white flowers.

As a thank-you for agreeing to be his roommate, he bought Meg the astronomy software Starry Night. Mailed a note:

"I don't know if I believe in astrology, but the placemat at a local Chinese restaurant describes me freakishly well: You are ambitious yet honest. Prone to spend freely. Seldom make lasting friendships.

"Freaky-deaky." he wrote. "I'm looking forward to living with you and hopefully starting a long-lasting friendship, in spite of my zodiac."

He arrived on a Monday in a van with his mother. Six states, 18 hours. He unpacked his childhood comforter, adorned with a red dinosaur wearing blue tennis shoes. Many of his things were in shoe boxes. His passport. His teaching supplies. A pocket Constitution.

Lana said goodbye on the sidewalk, and hugged Meg. "Take care of my son," she said.

That first night, Meg took Beau to Rita's Water Ice. We don't have water ice in Minnesota, he told the counter girl. Meg watched the counter girl grow impatient.

Many mornings, Meg would come downstairs to find Beau out exploring with Kismet.

He let his sandy blond hair go long and grew a beard.

He liked sticking out. He wore his Spam tie-dye. Played up his accent: "Doncha know? "

Meg landed him the Starbucks interview. He listed his mother as his first reference.

He couldn't get this one coworker to like him. Whatever Beau said, the kid snapped at him. The harder Beau tried, the harsher the kid got.

"I'm just going to keep being nice," Beau told Meg.

He sipped his soda and crossed toward Ellsworth.

***

He had already gone on his first teaching interview. A high school in North Philadelphia. Meg helped him pick an outfit. "Oh, my God, you need a solid-colored tie," she said, exasperated with all his patterned ones. He looked so out of place in his leather jacket and fedora. Meg made him promise to call when he got there. He thought it went well.

He turned on to Ellsworth Street.

Earlier in the week, he had adopted a mangy orange Tabby and named it Jake, after Jake Chambers, a character in King's Dark Tower series. Kismet didn't sleep the whole time Jake was in the house. The two animals just stared at each other. Jake wouldn't eat or drink and was doing this weird thing with his mouth.

He was eight houses from home. Some low-hanging branches, a red rowhouse door, a blue truck parked at the curb, a streetlight ahead.

Just the night before, Beau did a neighborhood tour for his cousin Lauren Chaby, who was taking summer courses at the University of Pennsylvania. He showed Lauren the Italian Market, took her to a cafe where they melted Hershey bars into hot chocolate. He shared his excitement about his upcoming date.

Lauren felt timid in the city but confident around Beau. She didn't want to leave him that night. She idolized him. He was brave and honest and principled. A thinker. A dreamer. He was beautiful.

Police do not believe there was a struggle between Beau and his killer. He was shot from behind. Maybe, lost in his comedy, laughing at punch lines only he could hear, he didn't realize a thing. Or perhaps he had turned to face his killer before turning to run.

Maybe, in an awful instant, he knew.

The bullet entered below his left ear. He died instantly.

The police officers stood over him. The neighbors crowded. His backpack was still on his shoulder, but the pocket where he kept his iPod had been turned out and the iPod was missing. The blood on his face made his eyes look so blue.

An officer took the wallet from the backpack. Opened it.

"Beau from Minnesota," he said.

Chapter 2: The Hunt for a Killer

> Clues were few, but police savvy and a little luck landed a crucial lead.

The story so far:Beau Zabel, a 23-year-old aspiring teacher from Minnesota, was thrilling in his new life in Philadelphia. But that life was cut short 42 days after it began.

A body in the shadows.

A killing, no witnesses.

A bump in the night.

Detective George Fetters sat in a cramped cubicle watching Beau Zabel's final moments—studying the snowy frames, looking for something, anything, in a case of nothings.

Like every aspect of the investigation, the grainy surveillance footage was more frustrating than fruitful. Parts were blurry beyond recognition. The killing was offscreen. The killer strolled by, head down, his face just eluding the camera. Like a taunt.

After two dead-end weeks, the footage, retrieved from a seafood stand and an auto garage, was the sole lead in the high-profile murder investigation.

Zabel had moved from his native Minnesota to South Philadelphia to teach math in the public schools six weeks before he was shot in the neck on June 15, 2008, near the Italian Market. He was walking back from his summer job at a Starbucks. He died steps from his new home.

For a brief time at least, the murder of the trusting and idealistic 23-year-old jolted a city grown callous to violence. There were headlines, anger, even introspection at the killing of a young person who came here to help.

"What Zabel slaying robs us of—his dreams gone, ours tested," lamented one editorial.

The detectives who worked the case painstakingly pieced together a narrative of the crime. With investigative savvy, inspired hunches, and the aid of a skillful jailhouse informant, they would unravel the tale of a manipulative killer and his clueless confederate—and of Philadelphia streets where naivete can get you killed.

As the case unfolded, another young man would die. Two anguished mothers from different worlds would embrace, brought together by violence.

This story of two murders is told here in depth for the first time on the fifth anniversary of Beau Zabel's death. It reveals the imperfect but practical workings of a criminal justice system that managed to provide a patchwork form of closure for Zabel's family, but not without collateral damage and compromise.

The investigation continues, and a city grinds on.

Almost justice.

***

The case fell to Three Squad, the dozen or so investigators, including Fetters, tasked with solving homicides during the busy overnight killing hours.

City Hall and the bosses wanted the job done, they knew. It was a black eye for a city reeling from some of the highest homicide totals in a decade. The new mayor, Michael Nutter, had promised to cut homicides in half. Now there was a dead teacher in the Italian Market area.

When Zabel's mother, Lana Hollerud, arrived on Ellsworth Street Monday morning, children played basketball feet from where Beau had died. News crews swarmed. Beau's blood was still in the cracks of the pavement.

"I'm sorry," lead Detective Levi Morton told her. "Philadelphia is sorry. "

But the investigators' initial sprint turned up little. No one had seen the actual attack. There were no suspects, little evidence. Just the blurry video and—the most common residue of an urban killing—a 9mm bullet casing.

The murder took place after midnight on a residential street. Those who glimpsed the fleeing killer from a doorway or window had only vague descriptions. Black. Medium build. Short hair. One neighbor saw a man walking from Zabel's body, his left hand holding his T-shirt to his eyes to cover his face. Another neighbor figured the boom was a blown transformer.

No gun was recovered. Lab tests on the pocket where Zabel kept his iPod—in the chance the killer left behind a hair or fiber—found nothing. Apple couldn't trace the iPod, even if the killer had plugged it into an iTunes account.

In the hardened idiom of homicide, Zabel's killing was a bump in the night.

All of Three Squad ran on the case in the first crucial days.

Starbucks and others staked a $35,000 reward. America's Most Wanted came to town.

Detectives chased a tide of bad tips:

Two guys from a halfway house on Bainbridge Street did it . . .

Three dudes in an alley on Lawrence Street were bragging about doing the teacher . . .

The boy who does robberies around Fifth and Washington . . .

Calvie from above the barbershop.

***

Fetters knew that when string ran out on a job, you went back to the beginning.

A stocky, round-shouldered man nearing 50 with glasses and light brown hair, Fetters was a third-generation cop. Homicide was a family business.

His father, Sgt. George "Pop" Fetters, had retired in 1978 after a heart attack. Pop had envisioned his oldest son wearing the blue and gold of the Naval Academy, not the blue and the badge.

Fetters was accepted to Annapolis, but after his father fell ill, he no longer saw himself attending college. He felt he had to earn.

He took the police test, and while awaiting the result, shipped off to Texas for a construction job. Nine months later, he was home, working at Frankford-Torresdale Hospital—running the halls with the crash cart used to revive dying patients—when the department called.

Then, old-timers had no time for rookies. One shift early on, Fetters walked up to a crowd on Thompson Street and saw a guy going wild with a bat, breaking car windows. Other cops looked on.

"What, are we waiting for him to tire out?" Fetters said, then tackled the guy. The veterans were fine with Fetters.

When Fetters got to East Detectives in 1996, a veteran told him that if he handled every case like it were family, he'd be ahead of the curve. Impossible, but Fetters got the point. He had three teenage children.

After hours of watching, he could narrate the Zabel video from memory.

Zabel buys his Mountain Dew at the vending machine against a razor-wire fence near the intersection of Eighth and Passyunk.

Zabel had walked into a trap. Pause it. Look at the intersection. It's shaped like an X, with jutting side streets. Plenty of targets and escape routes. Two blocks from Pat's and Geno's, but dark, with a steady trickle of people heading home or for a cheesesteak. The shooter was perched off Eighth, hanging back near a dead-end. He could see everyone coming and going.

Zabel crosses out of camera view, heading south toward his apartment on Ellsworth. The killer hurries after. Two minutes pass. Two taxis speed by.

Beau's dead now, in the shadows.

The killer comes hustling back into sight. His face isn't clear, but he's got a peculiar gait. He seems to take a little hop like every fourth step. Back on the dead-end street, he bends down, pulls something from his waistband—his gun, Fetters thinks—and puts it in a flowerpot. He peeps in a window, probably checking to see if someone saw him. He paces, trying to get a glimpse of the crime scene a block away.

He heads out of view again. Two minutes pass. Fourteen cars speed by, including a police cruiser racing to some other scene. A girl in a pink top. Finally, the shooter strolls back, stuffs whatever he hid in the pot under his shirt, and calmly takes earphones out of his pocket—Zabel's earphones, the detectives believe from the start. He places them in his ears and saunters toward Washington Avenue.

Pause it again. Look at the back of his head when he puts in the earphones. The beginnings of a bald spot. A monk's spot, Fetters called it. A peculiar gait. Male-pattern baldness.

Somethings in a case of nothings.

***

Lt. Mark Deegan knew how to work cases that had hit a wall.

Before taking over Three Squad, Deegan commanded the Special Investigation Unit, which handled cold-case murders. Thick-shouldered and bald, Deegan's imposing presence was offset by his quiet demeanor.

The 32-year veteran had a reputation for calmly steering investigations while he absorbed the pressure from above.

The cruel arithmetic of murder in Philadelphia was working against the squad. In the two weeks since Zabel's death, Three Squad had caught seven fresh jobs. No more manpower was coming.

The brass had already sent over two plainclothes officers from South Division to work robbery details near the Italian Market, hoping to catch the killer in the act. Ten nights after Zabel's murder, those cops interrupted a robbery at Eighth and Fitzwater. Chasing one of the attackers, Officer Mark Uffelman, the son of a slain police officer, was shot through an elbow. Those attackers, though, were ruled out in Zabel's killing.

Deegan also requested the help of Chris Lai, a 17th District plainclothes officer. Only 30, Lai owned a reputation as one of South Philly's most skilled street cops. Assistant district attorneys and detectives knew to call Lai when they needed something done: A reluctant witness rounded up. An address to go with a nickname. An explanation of why certain blocks were warring. Call Lai.

The 17th spanned Point Breeze and Grays Ferry. West of Broad. That was Lai's turf. Zabel was killed on the other side of Broad, but Deegan knew it was just as likely that the killer came east looking for easy prey.

The initial investigative steps covered, Deegan saw an opportunity to refocus. He ordered a review of the previous two months of South Philadelphia gunpoint holdups, looking for robbery patterns. To solve Zabel's killing, Deegan knew his detectives might have to solve other crimes first.

Fetters typed in the districts, dates and code for gunpoint robberies and about three dozen cases popped up. They rejected some cases outright: white and female suspects, domestic incidents.

In others, similarities emerged: Weaker victims. Especially violent attacks. The perp managing to slip away despite quick police responses, which pointed toward a getaway driver.

A case caught Fetters' eye. A woman named Cuie Lu was robbed near Federal Street, two weeks before Zabel's murder and only two blocks away. The suspect descriptions matched.

Lai and Homicide Detective Joe McDermott arrived at Lu's Seventh Street walk-up. It was late and she was putting her children to sleep. A tiny woman, Lu, 35, spoke little English. When she had called 911 after the robbery, she waited five minutes before someone who spoke Chinese came to the phone.

She had tried telling her story to the policeman who responded, but he didn't understand.

Lai, born and raised in Chinatown, spoke Mandarin and Cantonese.

She had missed her morning bus, she said, and saw a stocky man—he was about 30—across the street in a black jacket. He pulled a gun from his waistband and yelled, "Give me the bag. " The man waved the gun at her stomach, pulling hard on her purse strap until it snapped and she fell down. The attacker ran toward Washington. He got her phone, a cracked white Samsung. When the next month's bill arrived, Lu noticed calls made in the hours after the robbery.

Detectives zeroed in on four calls to a South Philadelphia dialysis center, including one just 17 minutes after the robbery.

Two days later, Fetters and Lai picked up Loni Gay, a 29-year-old medical technician at the center, in front of her Point Breeze rowhouse. Who had called her at work from a stolen phone?

Tyrek Taylor, her sometimes boyfriend, she said.

***

He called her from all different phone numbers, Loni Gay told them, because of his lifestyle. Dealing, selling—"trapping," like the Young Jeezy song.

But she didn't know him to carry a gun.

And that fit with what Lai knew about Taylor. On the streets around 17th and Wharton, they called him "Reek" and "Rick Ross" after the oversize rapper, because of his beard and heavy frame. He sold drugs over his phone, but he wasn't a shooter, he was a jokester, a clown. He was way too big for the guy in the video or Lu's robbery. But maybe the getaway driver?

Within an hour, Lai and Homicide Detective John Keen pulled up to 17th Street in an unmarked car.

"Wassup?" the 19-year-old Tyrek said through the driver's window of his Monte Carlo.

On the seat next to him, the cracked white Samsung.

***

Tyrek squeezed behind the metal table in homicide interview Room B, a bland, claustrophobic space with a two-way mirror. Fetters reviewed his paperwork. Tyrek was a licensed driver with valid registration and insurance—solid makings of a getaway driver.

Fetters put the phone on the table and told Tyrek he was being questioned as part of the investigation into the murder of Beau Zabel.

"I don't know what you're talking about," Tyrek told them.

The beginning of a dance.

"You sit here until the walls get tighter and tighter," Fetters told him, "and you think. "

"I bought the phone from a smoker that rides around selling things," Tyrek finally declared. "His name is Ant. "

"If I knew that it was taken in a robbery I wouldn't have bought it. "

He bought phones from Ant around 17th and Wharton, he said. The morning he bought the Samsung, he had been coming from Center City and had run into Ant on his bike around 12th and Catharine. That's why he was able to make the calls so quickly after Lu was robbed, he claimed.

Fetters could feel Tyrek weakening.

"You tell us who he is, and we'll get this knucklehead out of the way," Fetters said.

"They call him Ant, but I don't know his name," Tyrek said. "I can guess his name is Anthony. . . . If I could see a picture of him, I would show him to you."

He gave them something. Ant was 30 or 40, about 5-foot-8, on the slender side, "no hair right here in front . . . "

Tyrek told detectives he didn't know anything about the Zabel killing.

"Only what I saw on the news," he said. "I heard people saying you better stay off the streets at night, cause the police are looking for who did this. "

Detectives thought Tyrek was lying, but he had been at homicide for 24 hours and they had little to hold him on. They could charge him with receiving stolen property, a misdemeanor, but that would just shut down communication with Tyrek.

By now, 17th Street would know Tyrek had been picked up. After being tossed back, perhaps Tyrek would realize cooperating with police was his best move. If nothing else, his release might stir up information somewhere else. Like shaking a snow globe.

They had to find Ant. If he existed, he was now the prime suspect in the murder of Beau Zabel.

"Tyrek, just because we're letting you go doesn't mean we won't be back," Fetters said.

Taylor left, upset to be caught up in the mess. Ant was crazy. He'd have to call him.

Let him know he didn't tell police a thing.

CHAPTER 3: THE WHEEL MAN

Tyrek Taylor had returned to Philadelphia to make his name. That's how he met Ant.

The story so far: The murder of 23-year-old aspiring teacher Beau Zabel sets investigators to work on a scant trail. Street work and good hunches lead them to Tyrek Taylor. They believe he knows more than he's saying.

Tyrek Taylor pulled his black Bonneville on to Bouvier Street on a gray September morning that threatened rain. It had been three months since the teacher was killed, and police were still hitting corners, asking: Who's Ant North?

Tyrek had given the cops Ant's name when they brought him in for questioning. He gave them that much.

They had grabbed Tyrek after tracking him to a phone stolen in a robbery. Near where the teacher, Beau Zabel, was killed.

Tyrek told them Ant sold him the phone. They suspected he was Ant's getaway driver, said his best move was to give up Ant. Before releasing Tyrek, they told him they would be talking to him again.

Tyrek told Ant North he didn't tell police a thing.

Tyrek parked on the curb a few doors from his mother's house. Bouvier is a narrow one-way of mostly bruised rowhouses and vacant lots near 17th and Wharton.

He lifted his heavy frame from the car, the Center City skyline behind him. He wore Timberlands, khakis, a Polo shirt, and, as always, a matching Polo baseball hat.

Across the street, in an abandoned rowhouse, a balding man with a gun tucked beneath his tight black shirt sat on a milk crate, peering through a cracked door. He smoked a Newport.

He had been in the crumbling house, waiting. Watching.

Tyrek's neighbor, Kimberly, was walking her dog.

"Where you going, girl? " Tyrek asked.

"Work and school. "

"You better be good," he said as she fed her pet.

"Don't get too close," Tyrek teased. "I don't like you smelling like dog before you go to school."

Tyrek leaned in to get some things from the front seat.

The man with the gun burst from the house.

***

Tyrek wasn't built for Philly.

That's how the older bulls saw it.

That's why he got in over his head and started hanging with Ant North in the first place, why he got all caught up in a high-profile murder case.

The case was the 2008 murder of 23-year-old Zabel, who came to town from Minnesota to teach and ended up killed on a South Philadelphia street for his iPod.

Now the neighborhood was hot, the cops hassling everyone.

Tyrek was born in Philly, but not bred there. He grew up in Chester with his father, a disciplinarian who wouldn't let him run the streets. He had only recently come back to 17th Street to live with his mother.

You have to find your place in South Philly, your lane and speed. Tyrek, 19, had nothing to define him. He wasn't a shooter. He had a car, that's it. Hanging with Ant, 29, was a way to define himself.

Tyrek's older cousin Harun Byrd had warned Tyrek about Philly.

Tyrek had a good heart, Byrd thought. He was funny, silly. Tyrek was such a good dude, you'd want to cling to him and chill with him. He wasn't stupid. But as tough as Chester was, Philly was a totally different cup of coffee. Faster. Deadlier. You stick out when you're not from here, Byrd told him. People know.

He understood Tyrek's wanting to come to Philly. He saw his older cousins making money, and he wanted the girls and fancy watches, too. But Byrd wished Tyrek had stayed in Chester.

"You're into some grown-man shit now," Byrd told him.

On 17th Street, Tyrek hung with a couple of guys his age, driving to the clubs. He bought a diamond watch. Posed with it in cellphone photos.

Tone it down, Byrd would tell him.

Tyrek's first arrest came a year after he moved back. Bundled in a blue hoodie, Tyrek sold $20 of crack to a police informant. When the cops swarmed, he ran into his grandparent's old house on 17th Street.

Byrd was upstairs, chilling with a girl. With police chasing him, Tyrek tried to stash five packets of crack in the piano in the living room. He got them both arrested.

Tyrek spent the first years of his life in that house with the piano, living with his grandparents, mother, and cousins. He was the middle child. An older brother, Mike Wynn; a younger sister, Cinquita.

Both his parents worked: Monteil Bennett now as a customer service representative at a Sam's Club in Northeast Philadelphia. His father, Andre Taylor, was with Cintas, the uniform company.

When Tyrek was 6, he and Cinquita went to live with their father. Andre Taylor had a nice twin in Chester. A small lawn. A basketball hoop.

Tyrek was big for his age. A warm, soft kid with a playful smile. Cinquita called him "Reek. " He called her "Quita" and "Li'l Sis. " They were best friends. She was the quiet one, but he could make her laugh. His father married and Tyrek had three more siblings. He walked Quita and their sister, Adrienne, to school. One morning, rapping aloud to his headphones, he slipped on ice, to his sister's delight.

"We could hear the ground shake," they teased him.

It was a strict household in Chester. Be a leader, not a follower, his father told him. He cut lawns and worked a maintenance job. He had a front-porch curfew and would sit out nights talking girls and Philly with his friends Mingo and Mark. He got a B in math and wore a pressed purple shirt to the prom.

One summer, he visited his father's family in Alabama. Another summer, he worked on a Lancaster farm as part of church program. Most summers, he and Cinquita went to South Philly.

During one Philly trip, Tyrek was shot in an arm. A flesh wound. He wasn't the target. He was coming out of a Chinese restaurant. There was a crowd, gunshots, people running.

Monteil heard the shot and came running.

"I just got shot," Tyrek kept telling his hysterical mother.

He wasn't himself for a few months. His parents have trouble remembering exactly how old he was when he was shot outside the restaurant. About 16, they think.

Cars were his thing. He got his license at 17. Andre Taylor let him drive his white Oldsmobile Intrigue. Then his step-grandmother gave him her royal-blue Grand Marquis. He sold that for a blue Caprice, like the one from that movie All About the Benjamins. With some help from his parents, he bought a Monte Carlo. Black on black. Tinted. He drove it to Philly.

His father was raised in South Philly. He was against the move—"You know what happened the last time you were down there? "

But Tyrek couldn't get there fast enough. The summer before his senior year, Tyrek moved into the middle bedroom on Bouvier Street and finished school at South Philadelphia High. Cinquita followed him.

Monteil worried about Tyrek's coming to Philly, too. She grew up on 17th Street. She knew what it was like to be around certain people. She knew who they were in her neighborhood, and how to spot them. She worried Tyrek didn't.

She warned Tyrek about the corners, said she couldn't watch him 24/7 with work.

"I'm all right," he'd say. "I'm all right. "

In February, someone stole the stereo from the Monte Carlo. That's how he met Loni Gay. She was at the auto-body shop on Federal Street. She was 10 years older, a medical assistant with a pretty face. She was getting a CD player. He boasted about buying a louder stereo than before.

"They gonna be surprised when they hear me coming up the block," he said.

She had a man. He had a girl. It was casual. He was a kid. He was funny.

They'd sit on her front steps or in the Monte Carlo. He'd tell her about Chester. How he wanted to do right by his mom, she worked so much. How he wanted to get her off Bouvier. Or at least fix up the house with a new front door and windows. He didn't want Cinquita in the streets.

Loni knew Tyrek was dealing, but he wasn't a gangster. That was obvious when her boyfriend confronted Tyrek about their relationship. Tyrek tried to calm the situation, not wanting trouble.

He liked to call himself a "Trap Star. " Like the Young Jeezy song.

"I'm a T-R-A-P S-T-AR

"Got the city on lock

"Big shoes on the car. "

Tyrek sold crack over his phone, delivery style.

Trapping. Dealing. Making money.

He'd spent his money on designer labels at Torre Big & Tall Menswear on South Broad. Monteil chided him about all that Polo.

"Mom, I got to look cute, I'm a big dude," he'd say.

Tyrek was with Loni in her car the second time he got busted. He'd taken a call and asked her to drive to Dunkin' Donuts. He had a bad feeling but went anyway. A handshake deal. A $20 bag. Another police informant.

"I knew I shouldn't have gone," Tyrek said, handcuffed in the back of the police cruiser.

"I thought your fat behind was going to get doughnuts! " Loni said, cuffed at his side.

Soon, word went around 17th Street that some guys were planning to rob Tyrek. That he was an easy target. Tyrek sought help from Ahmad Crawford, who was older and hung with Byrd.

Crawford told Tyrek he shouldn't be in the street, period, that he wasn't cut out for it.

"You want all the good," Crawford said, "without any of the bad."

***

Ant North had been gone for a while, but now he was back.

North. Like North Philly. That's where he was from, but as a child, he stayed with his aunt on Colorado Street, around the corner from Bouvier. Growing up, he ran from block to block with Tyrek's older brother, Mike.

He was a loner, distant. Short, stocky, with a balding head. Robberies were his thing. Corner stores, women. He shot a woman on Reed Street during a drug robbery a few weeks before the teacher was killed.

Byrd didn't know Tyrek was hanging with Ant. He would have told him not to.

Ant North could sense weakness. He was manipulative. On the hunt. Tyrek wouldn't know what he was getting into, hanging with Ant North.

Tyrek never introduced Ant North to Loni Gay, but he talked about him. Ant would call when they were together—that's my homie, Tyrek would say. Tyrek would hang up and say he had to pick up Ant somewhere.

Ant North did robberies, he told Loni. He'd say, "This nigga just did a robbery. He's crazy. "

He would laugh to Loni about how crazy Ant was. Then he would leave to go pick him up.

Loni began to notice things in Tyrek's backseat, items he said he got from Ant North. Like a digital camera. He wanted that for a "White Party," when everyone goes to a club party dressed all in white. Tyrek wanted to take pictures.

Another time, he got a cellphone from Ant North, a cracked white Samsung.

He never said anything about a dead teacher.

But he complained to her after the homicide detectives brought him in for questioning

"They had me in there all that time, trying to say I helped him rob the guy," he told Loni.

He told her he had called Ant North to straighten it out, that he told him he didn't say anything.

He had his own problems anyway. The Monte Carlo had been stolen. To replace it, his godfather's brother sold him the Bonneville on a payment plan.

A Bonneville SS, he bragged to Loni, with the emphasis on SS. She guessed that meant it was better than a regular one.

For Monteil, watching Tyrek leave the house each day became nerve-racking, and discouraging. He'd tell her he was job-hunting, but she knew better, and that hurt. She thought her son could find, and do, any job.

Mobile again, he drove back to Chester and told his friend Mark he planned to go to school to study computers.

At a Labor Day BBQ, he told his father he wanted to get into real estate, fixing and flipping houses. The police interrogation was no big deal, he said. It was all over a stolen phone.

Just one day before he got out of his car on Bouvier Street, Tyrek and Loni went to court for a hearing on their drug arrest. Tyrek told Loni not to worry—that he'd make it all right.

They stepped into a crowded elevator, and an older guy from South Philly recognized Tyrek.

"What are you doing here?" he asked, surprised. "Ain't like you to be in trouble. "

"Doing what I do best," Tyrek said. "I'm a Trap Star. "

The next day on Bouvier Street, Sept. 6, 2008, Tyrek was oblivious to any danger as he chatted up the girl walking her dog.

"You better be good," he had said as the man with the gun burst from the abandoned house.

Like Beau Zabel, Tyrek never saw his killer coming. The bullet struck him in the back of the neck, almost precisely the spot where Zabel had been shot. The girl walking her dog ran.

The killer rifled through Tyrek's pockets and car. He put on Tyrek's hat and jogged away.

Quita was asleep on the couch when the shot jolted her awake. She was first to reach her brother; then came Monteil. Neighbors tried pulling them away from the body. Blood ran slowly into the gutter from a hole beneath Tyrek's right ear.

When the police arrived, Monteil Bennett was cradling her son. Now, the rain was falling.

CHAPTER 4: TWO KILLINGS, ONE SUSPECT

With Ant North in custody, police look for help to charge him in the murder of Beau Zabel.

The story so far: Tyrek Taylor was detectives' best hope for solving the murder of Beau Zabel, the aspiring teacher from Minnesota killed in a robbery for his iPod. Now Taylor was dead, shot in cold blood just like Zabel.

Ant North sat slumped in Homicide Interview Room B, the same cramped space where Tyrek Taylor was questioned months before in the murder of Beau Zabel.

Now, Ant was charged with murdering Taylor, shooting him down in the street from behind.

Ant wasn't talking about it.

He wasn't talking about Zabel, either.

He sat at the small metal table, staring at the wall behind Detective George Fetters. He picked at his beard. The detective could have been speaking French.

If the Zabel case had been a race, the cops had lost.

Months earlier, as part of the investigation, Fetters had tracked a stolen phone to Taylor—a Samsung taken at gunpoint from a South Philadelphia woman. That crime, police thought, was a crucial link to the high-profile

2008 killing of Zabel, the 23-year-old Midwesterner who had come to Philadelphia to teach, only to die six weeks later in a robbery for his iPod.

Taylor said he had nothing to do with any murder, but Ant had sold him the phone.

Investigators suspected Taylor was the getaway driver in both crimes. But without hard evidence, they released him and concentrated on finding Ant.

Now it looked as though Ant had gotten to Taylor first, silencing him with a bullet.

The media didn't know about the suspected tie between the two killings. Taylor's murder received three lines of newsprint, his name spelled wrong.

Supplied with only a nickname, police had searched hard for Ant.

Homicide wasn't the only squad hunting for him.

South Division Detective Edward Tolliver and his partner, Stephen Caputo, were after him in the shooting of a woman in a Reed Street drug robbery 13 days before Zabel's killing. The woman survived a bullet to her stomach. All Tolliver had to go on was that vexing nickname: Ant North.

Tolliver was raised in South Philadelphia and had worked South Division for 15 years. His street sources were telling him they wanted Ant North off the corner. He brought too much trouble.

Robberies were his thing. He was reckless. Bad for business. He came and went. He'd do his dirt and disappear. All anybody knew him as was Ant North.

"You know him, you know him," they told Tolliver.

He robbed Chinese restaurants. He robbed women.

"He's cool with us, but we're not into what he's into," they said.

Tolliver searched the department's photo suspect database for every variation of Ant: Anthony, Antonio, Antoine, Antwan, Antwon.

He must have pulled in a dozen people to look at mug shots. He interviewed one woman, supposedly Ant North's aunt, but she claimed to know him only as Ant North, too. It got to where he was just stopping guys in the street.

On slow shifts, he searched arrest reports for people picked up around 17th Street, where Ant was said to hang.

Finally, Tolliver's diligence paid off. Six months after Zabel was killed and three months after Taylor was gunned down, he asked a patrol officer to bring up a suspect arrested near Wharton Street on a gun charge. Tolliver laid his mug shots across the table. The suspect pointed at a photo.

That's Ant North's cousin, he said. He lives on Colorado Street. Ant stays with him sometimes.

Tolliver took the tip to Homicide. A database search of the cousin's address listed a Marcellus Anthony Jones.

No one had checked middle names.

Now the case unfolded quickly. Another search showed Jones was already in custody; he'd been locked up for violating parole. Police arrested him in North Philly for stealing a bicycle from a teenage girl.

***

Fetters believed it was him the instant he saw the mug shot.

"It's the same dude," he said.

The same man he had seen countless times in the grainy surveillance footage from Zabel's killing. The blurry figure that emerges from the side street moments after Zabel was shot to death.

The same body size. Same general appearance. Same-shape head.

And his criminal history fit.

Ten arrests. Three convictions. Four aliases. Nine addresses. Drugs, robberies, violent attacks.

At 17, he was charged with sticking up a Tasker Street deli, but the owner never showed in court.

At 19, Jones burst into a South Philadelphia rowhouse and beat a 19-year-old woman in front of three young children. Days later, he pedaled up to the woman's front door, chased her inside, threatened to kill her, and fled only when the family's dogs attacked him. He pleaded guilty to assault and intimidating a witness and was sentenced to two years.

At 21, he and an accomplice robbed three laborers at Broad Street and Washington Avenue. Jones smashed one victim in the face with a handgun before the men chased him into the subway and held him for police.

In 2005, he was paroled to a halfway house on Broad Street, which he walked out of and didn't return. Before long, he was imprisoned again, for selling crack and robbing a man of jewelry and a wallet. He was paroled again in March 2008 and, a month later, once more walked away from the Broad Street halfway house.

That's when police say he went on a five-month crime spree, which they believe included the gunpoint robbery of Cuie Lu in South Philadelphia, Tolliver's Reed Street shooting, and the slayings of Beau Zabel and Tyrek Taylor.

The case against Jones in Taylor's killing was strong. Three witnesses had picked his mug shot out as Taylor's killer.

Then there was the Newport cigarette butt left in the abandoned house where the killer had hid before shooting Taylor. A DNA swab would tie Jones to the cigarette.

The Zabel case was different. Investigators believed Jones killed Zabel, but their only potential witness, Taylor, was dead.

Walking into Interview Room B, Fetters had little leverage.

He'd try to break the ice. Open up a line of communication before working his way to his only bargaining ploy:

Look, we got you on Tyrek. We know all about that. And we know you killed Beau Zabel. We'll eventually get you on that. Give it up now. Give the Zabel family that much. Tell us where the gun is. Plead guilty to both and maybe we can get the death penalty off the table.

Fetters talked at Jones for two hours. Jones never said a word.

Standing up, Fetters noticed the beginnings of a bald spot on the crown of Jones' head. The same one from the Zabel video. A "monk's spot," Fetters had called it. Fetters got a camera. He wanted a photo—something that could help tie Jones to the video.

Jones sprang to life. He put his hands up and shouted.

"What you doing this for? No. No."

"Damn! You are there!" Fetters said.

Fetters said he was going to take the picture either way.

"You want to be restrained?" Fetters asked. "I can have people come in and restrain you."

Fetters stood on a chair behind Jones and snapped the photo.

***

With Jones' silence, the Zabel case had hit another wall. There was a $35,000 reward, but no one was stepping forward. Police needed someone —maybe a girlfriend or a family member—who Taylor or Jones might have confided in.

In his 8-by-6-foot state prison cell, 100 miles from Philadelphia, Devonne Brinson was deciding whether to give them what they needed.

He was the confidant police were looking for. But for Devonne, talking would mean defying a code.

He had grown up near 17th and Wharton Streets—War-Town, as he called it. A few houses down from where Ant North stayed on Colorado and around the corner from Bouvier Street, where Tyrek Taylor lived and died.

In 2009, Devonne was 27, a father of three, and early into a 10-year sentence for violating probation, after a conviction for gun possession in a 2003 shooting. He beat the attempted murder charge.

He had argued hard for leniency—that he didn't realize he was on probation and that he was heavily sedated for a psychological issue on the day of the hearing. The handgun in the console of the car wasn't his, he said.

The judge called him a liar and a thug.

Devonne felt abandoned.

He had given too much. Had helped make 17th Street what it was, a brand to be respected.

But no one was looking out for him. No one had come up with bail money or a decent attorney.

The hood wasn't paying homage. The message had to be sent: Turn your back on me, spit on my shoes, and I will do everything in my power to make you respect someone of my caliber—a franchise player.

His family came first, and no one was protecting his family. One of his brothers had already been killed on the streets.

His daughter was born only days before his arrest. He needed the reward money.

All his life, Devonne rolled with punches until he saw a clear path to a straight jab, then he'd pounce. Life was presenting him a path.

He would put his story down on paper:

The night of Beau Zabel's killing, Devonne was sleeping in his cell on D Block at Philly's Curran-Fromhold Correctional Facility. About 2 a.m., he was awakened by the illegal cellphone he'd bought inside the jail with a $300 Father's Day gift.

It was Tyrek Taylor.

The neighborhood knew that if you wanted to reach someone in prison, Devonne was the man with the phone. Tyrek sounded panicky. He was asking for his older brother, Mike Wynn, locked up a few cells down.

Tyrek told him he had been out with Ant North on a robbery and some "dumb-ass shit happened. "

In the morning, Tyrek called again. This time, Devonne pressed for information.

He and Ant had been "on route" —on the prowl, looking for a victim to rob, Tyrek said, when they jammed some boy who didn't really have anything.

So Ant "rocked him. "

Devonne knew that Tyrek and Ant North were a robbery team. Everyone on 17th knew that. Tyrek drove and stayed with the car. Ant did the robbing.

The next day, Devonne saw an article in the *Philadelphia Daily News* about Zabel.

"Aspiring young teacher from another state was killed on a robbery, yadda yadda, extra stuff, still looking for the culprits," as he would recall it.

The newspapers hammered away at the story day after day. Devonne was a faithful reader. He folded the first story away among photos of his children.

Three months after Zabel died, word reached his cell that Tyrek was dead—and that Ant North had killed him.

With nothing but time, Devonne turned the murders over in his mind. Killing the teacher was senseless, Devonne thought. He wasn't some caped crusader, but on principle, it wasn't called for. Rob a fool driving a BMW, not some Joe Schmo white boy walking in a South Philadelphia neighborhood. Devonne would have stolen copper pipes from an abandoned house before doing something like that.

As for the murder of Tyrek, Devonne hated to say it, but he understood it. By Ant North's thinking, it was kill Tyrek or do life.

Besides, it was detectives who got that man murdered, Devonne thought. When they picked up Tyrek, they struck too soon with too little, and Ant panicked.

You couldn't help but notice that Tyrek didn't fit on 17th Street. It was like a version of that Sesame Street song, he thought—"One of these kids is doing his own thing, one of these kids don't belong. "

Tyrek was out of his league with Ant North. Devonne could see how it all went down. Tyrek had a car, he wanted status, Ant North could control him. "Come on, let's take a ride," Ant would have said, and that would be about it.

Within a few months, Devonne would have the opportunity to go over it with Ant North himself.

They met up inside Graterford Prison in Montgomery County. Ant North was sent there to await his trial in Taylor's murder.

When Devonne saw him on E Block, Ant North smiled at a familiar face.

The two men talked a few days later at "noon yard." Devonne didn't bring up the murders. They caught up on South Philly as other inmates exercised.

The next time they talked was in chow hall, where Ant worked serving water from table to table.

Devonne was sitting by himself at a table by the window. Ant took a break to sit on a radiator.

Devonne started the conversation with a joke. He thanked Ant for putting down Tyrek before he did, because he had heard Tyrek had been fooling around with the mother of his child. Ant laughed.

Devonne pressed him about Tyrek.

"Why you really kill him?" he asked.

The way Devonne remembered it, Ant North's answer was simple:

Tyrek kept bitching about the teacher. Kept asking why he had to kill the teacher.

He was weak, Ant North said. He might fold. Snitch.

That's what Devonne needed.

He wrote it all down in a letter to Homicide.

It hurt. But he was not being respected.

CHAPTER 5: ONE TRIAL, TWO MOTHERS

Families of Beau Zabel and Tyrek Taylor united in case against Ant North.

The story so far: Beau Zabel and Tyrek Taylor are dead, and police think Marcellus "Ant North" Jones murdered them both. A witness gives them the link to both killings.

Beau Zabel's mother sat in the lonely pews of a Philadelphia courtroom. She had prayed for strength and grace for what lay ahead. Another woman walked in, wearing a strained smile. It held back waves of sorrow.

"This is Tyrek's mother," the prosecutor said.

The women shook hands.

"I am sorry for your loss," said Beau's mother, Lana Hollerud.

Lana seemed like a sweet woman, thought Tyrek's mother, Monteil Bennett. She felt sorry for her.

The mothers' uncommon bond was forged in prosecutors' belief that the same man killed their sons. The trial offered a chance at a clear verdict for one and some form of justice for the other.

With DNA and eyewitnesses, authorities were trying Marcellus Anthony Jones, known as Ant North, for the murder of 19-year-old Tyrek Taylor in September 2008. They believed he executed Tyrek to silence him about the killing of Beau Zabel, the 23-year-old teaching student from a small town in Minnesota shot for his iPod three months earlier near the Italian Market.

But they had a problem. As Jones' suspected getaway driver, Tyrek represented the only potential witness in Beau's murder.

Though they lacked enough evidence to charge Jones directly in Beau's death, they faced a lower burden of proof in establishing his motive for killing Tyrek. Pennsylvania allows evidence of "Prior Bad Acts" —even uncharged crimes—if they explain another crime.

Beau's death completed the picture of Tyrek's killing, they said.

Statements to police by Devonne Brinson, who would play a central role at the trial, provided prosecutors a link between the killings. Jones killed Tyrek because he thought Tyrek would snitch about the teacher —Brinson said Jones told him that in jail.

But without physical evidence in Beau's killing—the gun or his stolen iPod—prosecutors still needed more than Brinson's testimony for a conviction.

At Jones' trial, Assistant District Attorney Deborah Cooper Nixon would tell the story of two murders, with a shot at justice for only one.

Nixon was anxious about notifying Beau's mother about the trial. No arrest had been made in his killing. She worried over the pain she would bring to bear.

But as she prepared for the trial's opening on May 30, Nixon was saying Beau's name as often as Tyrek's—she was giving life to his case, too.

She picked up the phone.

When Lana thought of her son's final moments, she imagined he met up with evil. In the family's hometown of Austin, she worked as an advocate for domestic violence and rape victims, a job she held before his death. Beau's stepfather, Terry Zabel, would have been grateful for a few minutes in a room with Beau's killer, but anger did not consume the couple.

Lana needed to see Jones—to confront evil. Doing so, she hoped, could tell her whether Jones was the one who hurt her son.

Getting off the expressway, Lana, 54, and Terry, 51, passed Drexel University, where Beau was to have earned his teaching degree. Had he lived, Beau would have graduated already.

Monteil Bennett and Tyrek's younger sister, Cinquita, took the Route 17 bus to the courthouse. Monteil, 43, had arranged time away from her job at a Sam's Club at Franklin Mills mall.

When she saw Lana, she realized whom she must be.

Lana held no anger toward Monteil. Tyrek had paid the stiffest penalty for whatever role he played in Beau's death. It was just sad that someone else died because of what happened to Beau.

The trial did not attract spectators. A sheriff's deputy instructed the two families to stay to one side in case Jones' relatives showed. They never did.

Nixon directed Monteil to the first pew. Lana and Terry sat behind her.

Jones, 33, was led in through a side door. He wore his orange prison clothes. He scanned the courtroom. Terry glared; Jones turned away.

Monteil wanted to scream. Take his head off. Jones had played with her older son when they were children. There was something wrong with him even then. He was always mean. Tyrek had trusted him. To take his life like that—.

Monteil fought back tears.

Lana thought she would have a physical reaction to seeing Jones. But he was just a person. A little man. That's all he was.

When Nixon introduced Homicide Detective George Fetters to Monteil, he recognized her from her job at Sam's Club. He shopped there with his family. They had exchanged pleasantries countless times, with Fetters never knowing she was Tyrek Taylor's mother.

It was Fetters who interrogated Tyrek after linking him to Beau Zabel's murder through another robbery. He had told Tyrek he would talk to him again.

Fetters felt a flash of guilt. "I am sorry for what happened to your son," he told Monteil.

Each morning, Fetters would bring water to Cinquita, 22. Try to make small talk. Make her at ease. She seemed so angry.

"Why is he not getting the death penalty for killing my brother," she snapped one day, "but he would for killing the white boy? "

Monteil and Lana began to talk during breaks.

Monteil said she had to keep a smile on at work. That was hard. She had gone to a meeting once for mothers who lost children to violence and talked to a counselor there, but never went back. Her neighbors didn't bring up what happened. She was handling it on her own.

Lana shared something she often told the victims she works with: No matter the outcome of the trial, it won't restore you to whom you were before.

"You have to be prepared for that," Lana said.

Sometimes Lana found herself comparing her experience to Monteil's. Monteil had been there to hold Tyrek; she had not been for Beau. That scared her the most—that Beau had been alone.

Then she would think of Monteil. She had been there. Had seen Tyrek so hurt and been unable to help.

It was an impossible choice.

A medical examiner described how the bullet tore through Tyrek's neck, killing him instantly—a wound nearly identical to Beau's. Monteil broke down. Lana hugged her.

A forensics expert testified that DNA on a Newport—the cigarette found in the abandoned house where the killer waited for Tyrek—matched Jones'. The likelihood of the pairing was one in 3.4 sextillion.

Carl Boyce, a neighbor of Monteil's on Bouvier Street, said he had been talking with his nieces when he saw Jones burst from the house and rush up behind Taylor.

Wanted for a probation violation, Boyce, 46, had initially given police his brother's name. Jones' attorney, David Rudenstein, attacked Boyce as a liar.

"I don't do cops," Boyce said. "But I went in anyway, because what I saw wasn't right. "

James Claiborne, 60, said he heard the shot and looked through his bedroom window to see a man who matched Jones' description rifling through Tyrek's pockets.

The Army vet decided to testify because "you got to stand up for something."

***

A guard banged on Devonne Brinson's cell at 3 a.m., told him to get ready.

On the ride to court, Brinson, 30, said, he felt like Caesar crossing the Rubicon. No turning back.

He wasn't promised anything for his testimony.

The District Attorney's Office wasn't offering any time off his sentence. The Zabel case was still open, so there was no reward money yet. Just the chance down the road, he hoped, that a parole board, or a judge, or somebody would look favorably upon his cooperation.

As he saw it, the city wanted justice for Beau Zabel's killing—for some sort of civic pride. He just wanted his life back.

He gave Jones a hard stare as a deputy escorted him to the stand. He always looked a man in the eyes before putting him down.

Nixon approached the witness box. Moved the microphone to the side.

Brinson glanced at the room. Monteil and Cinquita were the only ones from 17th Street there. Some of Tyrek's own friends knew who had killed him, yet it was him up on the stand. Cowards.

"Is that them? " Brinson asked Nixon, looking out toward the Zabels.

"They didn't sign up for this," he said.

Brinson told his story.

Tyrek had called him on his prison cellphone the night of Beau's murder, looking for his older brother. Ant North had "rocked" a dude when they were out on a robbery, he said. Months later, at chow, Jones told Brinson he killed Tyrek because he feared he'd snitch about the dead teacher.

Stepping off the stand, Brinson felt a sense of accomplishment.

When Jones took the stand, he wore a suit jacket over his prison jumpsuit.

He did fine with his lawyer. He didn't know Tyrek. Didn't kill him or Beau.

When Nixon rose, Jones leaned back in his chair.

His DNA was on the cigarette, she told him. Two witnesses put him on the street. Before long, she accused him of the crime.

Jones flashed rage. He shouted. "No, no, I didn't! "

Nixon attacked.

"You were worried that Tyrek was going to flip on you, he was going to flip because he wasn't built for this, and he was the weak one, did that happen? "

"I mean, possibly with somebody else," Jones said. "Not with me, though."

***

The night before closing arguments, Nixon had sat on a sofa watching a dance show with her 11-year-old daughter. She thought of Monteil and Cinquita and their blank stares. Of Lana, so stoic and gracious. Of the blemishes of her witnesses. That her words would be inadequate. She began to cry.

"What's wrong, Mommy?" her daughter had asked.

To the hushed courtroom, she began with a childhood story about her father, a meticulous preacher who prepared his sermons equally as hard when he ministered at the jail as in church, she said.

"When I start making distinctions amongst who I serve, I want that to be the last day I preach," he would say.

In the same way, jurors had to overlook any flaws of Boyce and Brinson. "If you cannot see the truth and beauty in what they say, then I hope this is the last homicide I try," Nixon said.

Not wanting to face justice for killing Beau Zabel, she said, Marcellus Jones had decided to be Tyrek Taylor's judge, jury and executioner.

Nixon pointed at Jones.

"He knew that if Fetters got an opportunity to get a photo and come back and talk to Tyrek Taylor, you might get the full story," she said. "You might really find out what happened to Beau Zabel when he was walking with his earplugs in his ears, when he was probably listening to his music, oblivious. "

She paused before adding:

"But we will never know, and now Monteil Bennett doesn't have a son. "

The mothers wept.

"And that's why we are here," Nixon said, "to give justice to one mother for justice one mother may never know."

***

Lana and Terry went home to Minnesota. They did not wait for a verdict. Lana now knew who had hurt her son.

The prosecutors and police working Beau's case had always talked to Lana about closure.

Before leaving, she hugged Monteil goodbye.

"I hope the verdict gives you some of the closure everyone is always telling us about," Lana said.

The jury took less than an hour to reach a verdict. The foreman said "guilty," then scanned the courtroom for the Zabels.

***

Nothing can restore you to the way you were before, Lana had said.

And what has been restored?

The murder of Beau Zabel remains open. There is a $55,000 reward. Fetters works it between new cases, convinced he's got some live leads. He wants to be able to tell Lana they have charged the man who killed her son.

Sometimes he sees Monteil while shopping. They still exchange pleasantries.

Devonne Brinson continues his appeals. Some nights, he lies awake to the clanging of inmates banging their metal tables.

"In the end," he says, "you get left all on your own without no help, and only a smile that says thanks."

He still reads the newspapers. He is up for parole in 2017.

Marcellus Jones will spend the rest of his life in prison for the murder of Tyrek Taylor.

Since his arrest, he has stacked up 170 behavioral infractions, which include attacking guards and throwing urine on staff.

He is kept in lockdown 23 hours a day, with no books, magazines, or television. He receives meals through a slot. In the recreation yard, he is confined to a small caged-in area.

He is allowed a box of personal papers and a "safe pen."

"Hi, how're u?" he answered a letter recently. "I'm better than some worse than others."

He maintains his innocence.

Monteil felt something close to joy the day of the verdict. She and Cinquita walked home instead of taking the bus. Monteil couldn't bear to be around all those people who didn't know.

But life back on Bouvier Street swallowed that feeling.

Monteil still smiles at work. Still struggles to keep it all at bay, to think of the good, not the bad.

She collected the stuffed animals from Tyrek's sidewalk memorial and kept them in a living-room corner. She kept his car, too. The Bonneville.

She used to drive it, feeling close to him when inside it. But the transmission is going. It's parked on the curb. Where Tyrek always parked it. Where he parked it that day. Weeds grow around it.

The abandoned house where Jones waited still sits shuttered. There is talk a neighbor might fix it up.

And every day there is that reminder—that spot of ground where she held him.

"It's like a picture," Monteil said in her soft voice on a recent afternoon, sitting on her front step. "And I can't get that picture out of mind. "

She wiped at tears.

"The hurt," she said, "just stays hurt."

Tyrek is buried in a patchy rise of earth on the outskirts of a Delaware County cemetery. He has no headstone.

"Most of the business we get are from gunshot victims from Philadelphia," said a woman working at the cemetery office.

Some remember Beau in small ways.

His housemate, Meg Guerreiro, went on to work as a teacher in Philadelphia and always shared Beau's story with her students. They seemed to connect to the loss. She kept Beau's teaching supplies. His pocket Constitution.

Beau's old Boy Scout troop at Camp Cuyuna in Minnesota laid a stepping-stone by the lake and built a tree house in his honor.

"All God's critters got a place in the choir, some sing low, some sing higher," the troop sung at the dedication.

Lana Hollerud will come back to Philadelphia if there is ever a trial in Beau's killing. And she will stay for a verdict.

But a mother's closure cannot be found in a courtroom.

She has faith, and believes someday she and Beau will be together again. That will be her closure.

For now, she misses him always. She wishes Beau had found a soul mate before he died—that he knew what that felt like.

In the warm months, Lana visits Beau's grave daily. It sits in the full sun, and the flowers wilt quickly without water.

Sometimes, the deer come up from the tree line and eat the tops of the flowers. Lana likes to think of the deer coming to visit Beau.

About This Series

Reporter Mike Newall's reconstruction of Beau Zabel's death and its aftermath took him to Austin, Minn., where the Zabel family made available letters, e-mails, journal entries, poetry, and other material.

The suspects in the case were profiled through family and friends in Philadelphia and Chester, as well as neighborhood residents.

Newall interviewed a half-dozen police investigators and top prosecutors, and consulted police crime scene photos, homicide logs, surveillance video, interrogation transcripts, and arrest reports. He exchanged letters with two prisoners involved in the case, interviewed prison officials and prosecutors involved in their various other cases, and reviewed psychological and social worker evaluations. He also reviewed court files and transcripts.

THE BOSTON GLOBE

OCTOBER 13, 2013

By Sarah Schweitzer

Together despite all, glimpsing the distant finish.

Three days had passed since the bombs went off.

Doctors had done what they could and left him to recover in a coma. She was sitting by his side when he opened his eyes. There was panic in them.

She asked him: Who's the most beautiful girl in the world? It was a question he had posed rhetorically and answered a thousand times.

Jenny May, he whispered.

He remembered.

18 DAYS AFTER

The thousands who thrum through Massachusetts General Hospital, crowding corridors, searching for answers, have gone home. Marc Fucarile's room in the Sumner Redstone Burn Center smells of the day's comings and goings: Purell-rubbed hands and cookies sent by strangers who, not knowing what else to do, had packed offerings of solace into lidded tins.

In the bed, Marc is surrounded by a press of family. They came after hearing the day's news: His remaining leg could be too damaged to save. They had amputated his right leg above the knee in the immediate aftermath. Now, there was talk of the left.

In the operating room earlier, doctors had peeled away bloodied gauze and found dead tissue around the ankle. They removed the blackened mass. Then they rewrapped all his injuries with new gauze—his singed back, his burned hand, the infected stump of his amputated leg, his broken knee, his shattered foot—and waited for Marc to wake so they could tell him that the foot was a bigger problem than they'd thought.

If the tissue didn't stop dying, they would have to consider another amputation.

His family hugged and shed tears out of Marc's sight. Then they entered the room and began urgently, frantically chatting. Anything to avoid the topic of the foot.

A social worker comes to Marc's bed. She holds a thick folder and starts to talk with him and Jen Regan, his fiancée, about their 5-year-old son, Gavin. I can't hear, Marc interrupts, pointing to his ears. His blown-out eardrums make everything sound like a watery underground tunnel.

Jen and the social worker step aside to talk. Marc can do only what he can do. But in moments like this especially in a moment like this—Jen can't help wanting more. She wants the old Marc who shared the load with her. Now she can't imagine burdening him: She hasn't told him that after Gavin smiled through his first visit to the hospital room a few days earlier, he had collapsed at the elevators, into her arms, sobbing.

Jen takes the social worker's card, promises to follow up, and says goodbye. She makes her way to the foot of Marc's bed. She hunches over and chews her thumbnail. There is a half-moon of skin where her nail used to be.

Marc's floor nurse flits into the room and above the hubbub calls out: Your ICU nurses want to pop in and say hi. Marc is straightening, pushing his torso as upright as it can go without disturbing his foot dangling off two pillows. "I'm dying to see them, and I need to see them. Eddie? Eddie, do you want to let them know?" he says, dispatching his older brother down the hall to retrieve the nurses.

Jen stares in disbelief. Suddenly, for nurses, the old Marc is back? The charmer, the guy who has time for everyone and hates to disappoint anyone? She yanks her hair into a tight ponytail. Her eyes fix on him. He's a flirt. She knows that. He can flirt with any nurse he likes. But if he has energy for them, why couldn't he talk to the social worker about Gavin?

"What?" Marc asks her.

"You were extremely rude to the social worker. She doesn't think so, but I do."

"I can't hear. I couldn't hear the conversation."

"I understand that, but everybody else can wait when it has to do with our son."

"I haven't been with my kid in two weeks! What do you mean? She was asking me questions about how he's acting. I don't know. I haven't seen him," he says. "Jenny, I'm useless to that situation."

"It's over. It's fine. It's done," she says sharply.

There is quiet, and then Marc, his voice deflating, says, "Sorry, everybody."

"It's all right," the gathered family murmurs iu unison. They tilt heads downward, prayer-like, as if willing Marc and Jen to step away from this moment of discord that makes the stakes so painfully clear.

Yes, Marc had lived. Yes, he'd woken from the coma. But the bomb on Boylston Street that maimed him also shattered their calibrated divisions of labor and love, the daily minuet of a life lived together. He was like so many of the Marathon day victims, transformed in an instant from a face in the crowd to the face of the tragedy. Outside the hospital the talk was of heroes and strength and resilience. Inside, it felt like something else. The pain and uncertainty almost unbearable; patience tested to its absolute limit; love the final reserve. Would he make it? Would they?

"Kiss! Kiss each other right now," Marc's sister Stephanie says urgently.

"She's cranky pants," Marc says.

"She's not cranky pants," Stephanie says. "She's amazingly strong."

Jen offers a half-smile, but makes no move except to chew what remains of her ragged thumbnail.

***

For as long as they can remember, they've known each other. They come from Irish-Italian families well-known in Stoneham. Jen's father a captain in the fire department, Marc's brother is on the police force. His mom waitressed at the Ninety-Nine over the line in Woburn.

The links between the Regans and the Fucariles interlace like a giant map of six-degree connections. Jen's grandmother often took her along to the other side of town to visit Marc's mother, whose daughter was best friends with Jen's aunt.

Marc was older by four years. When she still had middle school bangs, he was a wide receiver for Stoneham High. He'd be around sometimes when she visited with her grandmother, but rarely for long. "Hey Jen," he'd shout as he rushed out to meet buddies. Her eyes followed him out the door. Her crush was barely contained.

"I'm going to marry Marc someday," she confided to Marc's mother.

A decade later, on a summer night in 2006, Marc, then 28, went with a buddy to Hugh O'Neill's in Malden. Across the bar, he noticed a girl with porcelain skin and crystal blue eyes. "Who's that?" he asked his buddy. "That's Jen Regan," his buddy answered.

"Do you know who I am?" was his opening line.

Jen refused him her number. He got it from his friend. They went to a movie. She wore jeans and a sweatshirt, hoping not to look overly interested. She added heels at the last minute.

By nature, he was playful, on to the next thing before the first was finished; she was deliberate and focused. She was often burrowed in thought while Marc managed a crowd with wisecracks. She didn't answer her phone when an unfamiliar number flashed. He always picked up.

Naturally, it turned serious.

They spent New Year's together. A photo from the night shows their faces pressed together, his lips smudged with her pink lipstick.

Then unexpected news: She was pregnant. Marc wanted to get married. She worried that he felt obligated. Besides, it was too soon. She wanted to do it right: Meet, date, go on an island vacation, at the end of which, a ring would be proffered on bended knee. Her friends joked that she needed to wean herself from the romance movies she loved. Perhaps, Jen would say. Privately, she told herself she was allowed to have expectations.

Gavin was born Sept. 19, 2007. Two weeks later, they moved into the second floor of the duplex in Stoneham that had been her great-grandparents'. Her father lived on the first floor. Marc mounted ceiling fans and built a foldout table in the breakfast nook. She hung a print of sunflowers dancing against a mountain backdrop that reminded her of her grandmother's house in Vermont.

Weeks were helter-skelter, juggling Gavin and two jobs, she as a cardiac nurse at Melrose-Wakefield Hospital and he at a Peabody roofing company, in charge of delivering rolls of sealant and five-gallon drums of glue to construction sites. Come weekends, they would climb into their car. They had no destination, just driving until they found something that struck their fancy. Life together wasn't without challenges. But they loved each other, and that, they said, was what mattered.

TIME TO MOVE

IN LATE MAY, an ambulance ferries Marc to Spaulding Rehabilitation Hospital. The building is days old. Months earlier, Marc had delivered the roofing for it. Now the building smells of paint and polyurethane and fresh starts. Marc's room is spacious and light-filled. It looks out on boats bobbing on the water.

"I'm nervous," Jen confides to Eddie that afternoon when they duck down to the cafeteria. The transfer to the new building should feel like progress. But it doesn't. It feels like another unknown. Maybe because she doesn't know the nurses here. "Don't be nervous," Eddie says.

Days blend into weeks, and by July, brown paper bags sit in the room's corners bulging with gifts from strangers, hand-sewn quilts and woolen hats with tags that read "Knit with Love, Compassion, and Heart." The bulletin board is covered with snapshots of Jen and Marc and Gavin, happy smiling moments from before the bombing, and perky cards written in the blocky print of his nieces and nephews.

Most nights, Jen sleeps in the guest bed, which no one bothers converting to a couch anymore. A rotation of friends and family take her place when she heads to her mother's house to be with Gavin. He desperately misses his father. He is bewildered by his absence. "When will Daddy come home?" he asks over and over again. One night, he rips a Boston Strong poster from a door.

On the nights she's with Gavin, she calls to check on Marc. Often she's crying. "I'm worried about you," she tells him.

"I don't want you to worry, baby girl," he says. "I'm fine."

He isn't. At night, the pain in his fractured knee is unbearable. But worse is his foot. The tissue around his ankle had stopped dying, but not before leaving exposed bone. He lies in bed restlessly drumming his stump, up and down. It lands on the sheets with a soft thud, like a tossed baseball glove. Often, panic attacks swallow him. Walls shrink, the world caves. Without the day's distractions—friends to be entertained, a brave face for Gavin, physical therapists to be razzed—he is alone with his amputated leg and mangled foot, an endless parade of nurses poking and prodding him, and all this pain.

"It's killing me," he yells to Jen one night as midnight approaches. "I'm telling you. If the pain doesn't stop, I'm going to tell them to take it off."

Later, he awakes screaming from a dream. He was a guinea pig in an experimental trial.

The screams don't wake her, but only because she hasn't slept since she went to the federal courthouse four days earlier for Dzhokhar Tsarnaev's arraignment. She keeps thinking back to the image of the accused bomber's attorney patting his back to soothe him.

By day, the photos of their happiest moments before the bombing pegged to the bulletin board taunt.

"Look at that," Jen says to Marc's sister, pointing to one where her arm is around Marc and her fingernails can be seen. They are smoothly filed, with glossy bases and tips painted pearly white.

"He'll be home soon," Marc's sister Stephanie says.

It's what everyone has been telling them. Doctors, friends, family. Focus on getting home and the rest will come.

It makes all the sense in the world.

WHAT'S LEFT BEHIND

Morning sunlight is pressing urgently into their apartment in Stoneham. The July day is going to be a scorcher. Jen takes a long, hard sip from a Dunkin' Donuts iced coffee.

The center of the living room is jammed with half-filled moving boxes. There is no staying in the second floor apartment. Jen's dad had offered his first-floor apartment. But the doorways are too narrow for Marc's wheelchair. On Craigslist, she and Marc had found an apartment in Reading with low-to-the ground light switches, shower hand grips, and wide doors. So she is packing. Any minute, Marc's friends will be here to haul stuff into trucks.

Beneath the topsy-turvy, the apartment has a time-stopped quality, like Miss Havisham's mansion. Jen and Gavin haven't slept in the apartment since the night before the bombing. A new Spiderman shower curtain that Marc bought for Gavin hangs from a towel rod, still in its plastic packaging. A bin of folded laundry sits in the living room. Her ironed hospital scrubs lay flat against the back of the couch. In the apartment a few days earlier, she lay down on his side of the bed. It smelled like him.

She shrugs off the memory, standing straight as if to reposition herself in the present. "It's not like he's dead," she says. "It's just different. I get nervous that it won't be him. You have to think: What will it be like?"

She stuffs a Halloween costume into a box, then yanks it out. Should she get rid of it? She stuffs it in again.

She hates moving. This is Marc's job. He's the one who tapes boxes, sweeps dust bunnies, sifts clutter.

Most of the stuff is his anyway. He can't throw anything away. He stores it all in blue-topped plastic bins. She calls him "bin-boy."

A knock at the door. It's Marc's friends. They heave boxes into arms and march out the kitchen's back door and down stairs.

A pair of boots peak out from behind the kitchen door. Marc had kicked them off there after his last shift that Friday night before the bombing. Their leather is strafed and pocked. He worked 60-hour weeks in these boots.

She picks them up. She pivots, as if to head back to the living room and the boxes, and then stops. The boots dangle in her hands at her waist, and she stands still, uncertain of what to do next.

THE HUNDREDTH DAY

"Are you mad at the bombers, Marc?" a reporter asks.

Cameras fan across the width of Spaulding Hospital's atrium. Microphones are rigged to a stand, and behind them Marc stands with crutches. He is wearing a New Balance shoe with an electric white sole that makes his shrunken leg look that much more fragile. On this day, the 100th since the bombing, Marc is going home, the last victim to leave the hospital.

Marc pauses. He's nervous, but he's a natural in front of the cameras. "I'm more mad at what they did to the families that they took their children from. I'm more mad at that than what happened to me. I'm here." Reporters nod appreciatively. They make way for him and Jen and Gavin to pass through the sliding glass doors and into the late July humidity, then trail him as his car heads north to Reading.

A buzz. The apartment complex doors unlock. The camera crews follow Marc onto the elevator, down the hallway. As he enters the new apartment, waiting friends and family applaud. Cold cuts are loaded into sandwiches and chocolate sheetcake is cut. Are you nervous to be home? one reporter asks. "Jen's nervous. She's going to have two kids to take care of. I'm not going to be able to help out as much as I want."

As the afternoon sun peaks, camera tripods are folded, and soon only a clutch of family and friends remain.

Marc sinks into the couch next to his grandmother, Mabel. "I'm finally home, Grammy," Marc says. She pats his arm.

He leans back and surveys his new home: the high white walls, the track lighting, the echoing bathroom. Jordan's had given them a voucher and just about all the furniture is new. The biggest pieces had been delivered that morning: a mahogany dining room set, an L-shaped sectional with an electric recliner that he needs for elevating his leg, and an entertainment unit, for now equipped only with a flat screen TV.

Marc's phone is ringing. It's the property manager returning his call. She understands his concerns, but no, the handicap accessible apartment does not include a space in the garage, only parking space outside. From the bedroom a toy is emitting a sound like the whine of a balloon being emptied. Marc holds the phone away from his ear. "Take that toy away! Whatever it is, take it away! ... OK, well, get back to me please."

"It's like 100 degrees in here," he says, laying his phone down. Fans are fetched. Blinds are drawn. "Is anyone else hot?" He massages his fractured knee. It's time for his meds. He takes 49 pills a day. His mother is just back from CVS with a new batch. Two of the medicines cost $300 out of pocket.

"So much stress," he says. It's all too much.

"Turn on the TV!" Marc says. Someone finds the remote. "Can you turn it up?" he asks. A voiceover blares and the screen shows Aaron Hernandez being led into court. "He's a gangsta," Marc says. "The worst gangsta," says his friend, Dave, sitting next to him. The two laugh, like kids watching cartoons.

"For you, honey," his mother says, handing Marc a package that came in the mail. It's the Zombie Slayer, a gag knife he ordered off late-night TV at Spaulding. It has neon trim and a comically menacing blade.

Jen sits kitty corner on the sectional. She's reading the bill for his prescriptions, trying to figure out why insurance didn't cover them. Her face is screwed into a frown.

To no one in particular, she says "I hate knives. I can't even stand to wash them."

Marc reaches for his crutches. "I'm going to CVS with Dave," he announces. His mother offers to go for him. No, he says. She missed the point entirely. "I need to go with Dave." Jen stands. "I'm leaving," she tells him, hoisting her purse onto her shoulder. She has a 5:30 appointment for a spray tan; they're going to a fund-raiser the next night for bombing victims and she wants to mask her paleness after a summer spent in hospital rooms.

The front door clicks. Jen is gone. Moments later, Marc flees their home as well.

Edge of the world

Three weeks into being home, they are rarely there.

The refrigerator-mounted white board on Aug. 6 is typical: Monday: 11:30 a.m. Dr. Kwon @ MGH; Tuesday: 10 a.m. PT@ Peabody Spaulding, 2:15p.m. Dr. Goverman @ MGH; Wednesday 10:15 a.m. Dr. Crandell, 11:15 a.m. Speech therapy, 3 p.m. Dr. Schneider@ Spaulding; Thursday: 9:30a.m. visiting nurse; Friday: PT 10:30 a.m., OT 11:30 a.m.

Jen pads out of the bedroom shortly before 9 a.m. Her hair is combed into wet pleats and her skin is scrubbed to a taut sheen. Eyeliner seems to hold her eyes open.

She was up until3 a.m. watching "Real Housewives" but not really watching. She was thinking: About how they are going to live, about the things she has to do. Like getting Gavin into therapy. He has been talking about the bombers. He had a dream and they looked like perfectly normal people. Only with backpacks. She thought about how Marc and she got into a fight. About stupid stuff. He feels like he can't do anything. He's frustrated. He's swearing a lot and Gavin hears him.

At 4 a.m., Marc awoke screaming. His leg was shooting pain. They lay in bed willing sleep to come until the sun rose.

She wishes she could go to work, leave all this behind for the day. But she quit her nursing job. She wonders if writing in a journal would help.

Or maybe there's a book with advice that she could buy. "Like one for people who come home from the war—for their spouses."

For now, Gavin's lunch for preschool must be made. "Strawberry milk!" Gavin says. Jen pours the milk, and Gavin spills it on his shirt. "I got it," Marc says. He wheels his chair to the bathroom with Gavin in tow. Moments later, he calls, "Jenny, the toilet is leaking!" Jen sighs and makes her way to the bathroom.

Marc wheels back to the kitchen. Before the bombing, he never would have asked Jen to fix a toilet. He was the guy who took care of things: fixed friends' cars, cleared snow from his mother-in-law's driveway, gutted his mother's house.

Jen called him a man's man.

Now, he's the guy who has to be chauffeured.

He chafes in the passenger seat. Turn here! Get in the left lane! he orders Jen or Dave or whoever is driving. He yells unheard at other drivers. Everyone driving slower is an idiot; anyone driving faster is a maniac. Like George Carlin. Only, he's not really joking. He fumes about handicap spaces taken by the able-bodied. "Guy with one leg here!" he yells out the window.

Crowds bother him. People bump up against him. Kids stare at the space where his leg was. Worse, their parents let them. Well-wishers corner him and tell him to keep up his spirits, don't let the terrorists win. And then there are those who astound. At Olympia Roast Beef and Pizza, a place he used to go regularly on lunch breaks, a counter worker asks where he's been. "I was in the bombing," he shouts over the din of the midday crowd. "Oh," she says.

He's begun talking about moving to New Hampshire, away from the congestion. But maybe it's the pain meds that make the congestion bother him. He will ask his doctors to reduce the meds. Jen doesn't want him to. She says the nights are bad enough.

"I'm going to the porch," Jen announces as she returns to the kitchen. It's her cue to Marc to tend to Gavin.

"Whatcha doin'?" he asks Gavin, peering over at the pocket-size Minecraft video game that Gavin holds in his hands. The game is frustrating Gavin. He's having trouble building his virtual world.

"Daddy, can you help me find my house? I need to destroy it," Gavin says, handing over the game. Marc fiddles with the keys. Gavin fidgets. "I don't even know what part of the world you're in," Gavin says impatiently.

"The edge of the world," Marc says. "Where I usually am."

***

When The One Fund's $1.1 million arrives, the sum seems staggering. Then Marc reads in the paper that for a guy about his age, the lifetime cost of an above-the-knee prosthetic, which must be replaced every three to five years, will be, minimum, $1.5 million.

"So I need to come up with another half-million just to cover my legs," Marc says.

Other expenses are piling up. Parking for his medical appointments is hundreds each week.

"I gotta get back to work, I gotta get going," he says. But he can't. Not yet. "I've got too much pain, too much medication."

***

Traffic is backed up in Longwood Medical area. A visit to get a second opinion from an orthopedist lasted longer than expected. The doctor told them that a gel insert for his shoe might relieve some of the painful pressure on the heel. A surgery could shave the bone and do the same. Neither was a sure thing, and down the line, he might find himself, once again, considering amputation.

And no, the doctor tells him, it would not be wise to curtail the pain meds.

Jen and Marc stare out windows. For the second time, a top doctor has told them what they didn't want to hear: His foot, quite possibly, is permanently mangled and unfixable.

Jen's phone rings. She lets it go to voicemail but immediately listens: There are free tickets for bombing victims to see Zac Brown, the country singer, at the Comcast Center. If they're interested, she or Marc needs to call back and relay which day they prefer, Thursday or Friday.

Zac Brown sings one of Jen's favorite songs. "Knee Deep." They will go. But they can't agree on the day. Voices rise. Tempers flare. By the time they reach the interstate, the day's disappointment has been swallowed in a volley of words.

***

They keep doing it. Funneling their anger and frustration onto one another. People tell them they're mad at the situation, not at each other. They know that. They know it in the way that everyone knows it. But in those moments, those cold, terrible moments when they feel alone with the disaster, the smallest things trigger.

One day, they join other bombing victims in Boston to meet veterans from across the country. Some are missing legs, some arms. Some have no limbs. The veterans share stories. They offer advice.

Marc and Jen listen closely. But they find themselves fixated on the veterans' spouses. Marc thinks about how hard it must be for them. Jen imagines the plans they once had for how life, marriage, children would unfold. In a second, their plans were gone, too.

Yet, here they are, a year out, sometimes more, from their disasters. They are hanging on and making it work.

SIX MONTHS GONE

One weekend they head north. Just the three of them. In the White Mountains, they stop at Santa's Village. They ride the Yule Log Flume.

The next day, on a whim, they motor to nearby Six Gun City. Jen rides the go-karts with Gavin.

A few days later, Marc's prosthetic leg is ready for fitting. He hopes to wear it in a few weeks for his brother's wedding, where he'll be best man. Slipping his stump into the prosthetic, he stands. It's painful, and he can take only uncertain steps. But for the first time since the bombing, he's taller than Jen. He leans down and kisses her.

For Gavin's sixth birthday in September they book the Stoneham Elks Lodge. On a clear-skied afternoon, the club's wood paneling is garlanded in balloons and crepe paper and banners. A Teenage Mutant Ninja Turtle hulks among the crowd. Kool-Aid Jammers and Ninja Turtle party favor bags overflow on a foldout table.

At the front of the room, Marc is DJing. Bill Withers, Stevie Wonder, and Marvin Gaye play.

He could have brought an iPod. But he insisted on having his old DJ equipment, which means he must man it. Which means once again Jen must assume a domain that had been all his before the bombing: making sure the party runs smoothly.

"Aggravated," she whispers to a friend, motioning toward Marc.

The friend is an old friend. She knows Jen. She knows Marc. "That's what he needs to be doing right now," she says gently.

From the speakers, Motown is replaced by Zac Brown:

Gonna put the world away for a minute;

Pretend I don't live in it;

Sunshine gonna wash my blues away.

Marc is playing the song for her.

She stands still, tilts her head back, and hums.

CPSIA information can be obtained at www.ICGtesting.com
Printed in the USA
LVOW11s1209260515

439902LV00003B/3/P